MANAGEMENT SERVICES HANDBOOK

Also by B H Walley

HOW TO APPLY STRATEGY IN PROFIT PLANNING

HOW TO MAKE AND CONTROL A PROFIT PLAN

MANUAL OF OFFICE ADMINISTRATION

B H Walley

Management Services
Handbook

 *LONDON*

A BUSINESS BOOKS HANDBOOK

First published in Britain in 1973
Second impression 1975

ISBN 0 220 66226 6

FOR GILLIAN, SHEILA AND BARBARA

Set in 10 on 12 point Times
Photoset and printed in Malta by St Paul's Press Ltd
for the publisher, Business Books Limited
24 Highbury Crescent, London N5 1RX

CONTENTS

The following chapters, except the last, are subdivided as chapter 5

Illustrations

Acknowledgements

I am indebted to the following for permission to reproduce copyright material:

1   ICL: the Careers Progression Chart, from their "Planned Careers," which is shown in the text as Figure 2.1; the three diagrams associated with the chapter describing PERT and Critical Path Planning which is Chapter 14; Two diagrams associated with the Distribution Networks Chapter 24.
2   The National Computing Centre: the systems analysis documentation associated with Chapter 20.
3   The Editor of *Work Study and Management Services*, also the Midlands Electricity Board, the British Oxygen Co and British Insulated Calendars Cables for permission to publish charts in association with the organisation of Management Services departments in section 1:3.
4   IBM for the RPG II programming documentation shown in Chapter 20 on Systems Analysis.

Though many of the concepts and techniques discussed are in use in the Turner and Newall organisation, this book in no way reflects official policy.

I am aware of the debt I owe to the writers of the many books quoted in the sections on Further Reading. I regret if at times some ideas have been discussed for which I have not given full and appropriate reference in the text.

B H Walley

Part 1

ROLE OF
MANAGEMENT SERVICES

Management services concept

─────────────────────────────────

1:1 Introduction

As a by-product of computer usage, many hybrid departments linking organisation and methods, clerical systems study, systems analysis, computer programming and data processing operations, and even in some cases work study, were created under the title of "management services."

This is a curious name. All sorts of specialist departments such as "personnel" or "economists" also give a service to management, but have never received a sobriquet such as "management services."

Throughout the 1960s the strength of management services departments waxed considerably. There was an acute shortage of appropriate personnel and salary scales rocketed. But by the end of the decade there was increasing scepticism about the value of the work being performed by MS personnel. The staff in such departments appeared to lack humility, they often failed to communicate appropriately and solutions they produced were often unworkable in practice.

At the same time the older work study techniques were ceasing to have their initial impact. For example productivity bargaining was utilised as an alternative to time study.

Most computers, though seemingly indispensable, were certainly not paying their way and the people in computer departments were speaking a language no one else understood.

If there have been failings in MS personnel, equally line managers have not used MS techniques to full advantage. The techniques have remained misunderstood or their importance unrecognised or even not known at all.

The result has been an inadequate rise in productivity, reduction in costs or use of resources.

It is hoped that this book will help to propagate knowledge of the MS techniques which are available and in fairly constant use. It should also help to improve a situation where MS personnel can play their full role in helping to achieve higher profitability and a more ready adaptation to a changing environment.

1:2   Role of the MS specialist, responsibilities, authority and relationships

A specialist by definition is a person who devotes himself to a particular branch of a profession or science etc.

It may be inferred, therefore, that management services personnel are specialists in management. This is not often the case. By training, aptitude and career a member of a management services department will usually be a specialist in a series of management techniques (perhaps computer orientated) with enhanced analytical ability. They will not be generalists, as most line managers have to be and many will not have the basic knowledge about business which is essential for senior line managers.

Their role should mostly be advisory but it is possible, perhaps on some occasions vitally necessary, that MS personnel will take executive authority for some activity.

There is a good case to be made for MS departments to provide auxiliary line management ready to step into a line manager's position when a crisis occurs only to relinquish it when it is over. But normally the role of a specialist is advising and the followng table gives an actual situation where roles have been well defined, in a profit improvement program.

PROFIT IMPROVEMENT PROGRAM

Introduction
The introduction of changes which appear to be acceptable to the company requires detailed design and control. It is suggested that a method of implementation should be agreed between local management and management services department which will ensure that everyone concerned with the assignment is aware of their appropriate roles. The method must provide:

1   A clear indication of all the anticipated changes on which agreement between local management and MSD has been established. Before any implementation starts, line management must be aware of the changes in detail, the long-term implications of them and the effort which local management must make if implementation is to be successful
2   An analysis whereby the total assignment can be broken down into phases which can be controlled by timetabled action plans. These will list the activities to be carried out, the timescale for their introduction and the personnel responsible for the activity. Each phase will be

listed in detail highlighting all the key activities which must be undertaken

3 A plan for introducing each phase. It is possible that this may differ in each case, as the implementation of each phase may demand more or less MSD time, written operating details etc

The phases

1 Phase I should cover the measurement, implementation of appropriate systems and the exploitation of the results in the following fields:
a Labour control
b Material utilisation
c Production planning and control
d Maintenance control for each production line
2 Phase II should cover the application of standard costing and budgetary control
3 Phase III should cover the application of new EDP equipment
4 Phase IV should cover the extension of phases I and II into a fully integrated profit improvement programming activity

Executive command—the role of local management

It is strongly recommended that local managers are allocated the responsibility for the formulation, agreement, implementation and exploitation of each phase.

Their role will be to ensure that MSD personnel supply appropriately detailed systems outlines for discussion. They will ensure that discussion takes place and agreement is reached. They should then arrange for implementation to be carried out to an agreed timetable, reporting on the progress of the implementation to the senior assignment manager and chief executive as required.

It is recommended that Mr Smith has executive authority for the total assignment; Mr Jones is given executive authority for the implementation of Phase I; Mr Brown is given command of the implementation of phases III and IV. Mr Smith's overall role should be:

1 To provide a link with the chief executive, reporting when necessary on the progress being made
2 To plan and control the total assignment, particularly the use of line management and MSD personnel's time allocating such time so as to maximise profit improvement opportunities. To agree on an investigation and implementation methodology with MSD personnel and ensure that it is carried out
3 To undertake the control of each phase in co-operation with the phase managers, ensuring that:
a Appropriate directives are given, particularly in the implementation of agreed proposals

b   Timetables and action programs are designed so as to ensure that everyone concerned with the assignment is aware of his role and the timetables associated with it

c   There is smooth running of the assignment—calling meetings, discussions and issuing memoranda, etc, which will promote the willing involvement of local management

4   The phase managers should have the following functions:

a   Agree basic constituents of the phase and ensure that these are known and agreed in the company

b   Ensure that MSD provides the initial system's design when required

c   Obtain agreement with all participating managers in the company for the systems changes which are contemplated

d   Help to carry out education in new system's applications as and when required

e   Help to draw up an implementation timetable and action programs for their phase, allocating agreed responsibilities for each segment

f   Hold regular meetings, discussions, inspections, etc, which ensure that the timetable is being achieved and report accordingly

g   Ensure that modifications new systems design, etc, are carried out when necessary so as to achieve the results required

Advisory services—the role of MSD

It will be the responsibility of the management services department to provide the technical system's expertise required by the company to enable local management to carry through the assignment. MSD will:

1   Provide outlines of proposed systems changes and all associated documentation as a basis for discussion when required by the company

2   Provide on site expertise in the techniques and systems being introduced which will help local management to introduce the agreed changes

3   As far as time permits carry out on site investigations and help with implementation, to ensure that the assignment is successful

4   Help local line management in any education or training which becomes desirable

5   Once implementation has been successful, write an operating manual for use in the company covering all the systems areas where changes have been introduced

MSD personnel should be skilled in the full use of management service techniques, but not in basic engineering or product chemistry. Such areas of the investigations should be avoided by MS personnel in favour of local line management. This, however, should not exclude the suggestion by MS of methods of investigation in technical areas, for use by line management.

Copies of all investigational techniques or systems will be made available to local management as part of the assignment.

THE INTERFACE WITH OTHER FUNCTIONS. The techniques which can be covered by MS personnel are generally those which are later described in this book plus any which are listed in the skills audit, from which it is possible to ascertain the competence levels of MS personnel.

By their nature, all staff personnel have a consultancy role. It is only MS personnel, however, who have a fully advisory and usually non-executive function. The consultancy element may impinge on other functions mainly because it is taking place in a consultancy situation.

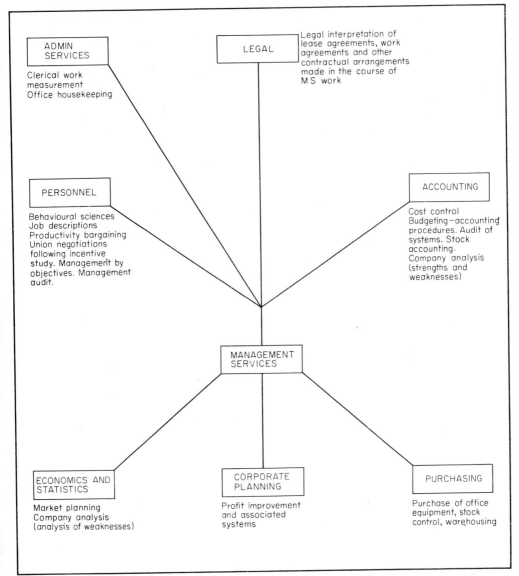

Figure I.I INTERFACE WITH OTHER FUNCTIONS

MS, therefore, may have considerable interface problems with other functions, mainly in the areas listed in Figure 1.1.

1:3   Organisation of MS departments

It might be useful to list the various factors which help to determine organisation structure:

1   The company and company style
2   The scope given to the department. What it includes: organisation and methods, work study, operational research, EDP, business systems study, training of various kinds, job analysis, monitoring of company performance, etc
3   The importance given to each function. For example, is EDP paramount? Has O & M been abandoned in favour of OR? Is OR considered to be so important that it is established as a separate function divorced from other productivity services?
4   The client interrelationship. Is the department to operate as an entity on its own, perhaps on a consultancy basis where all services have to be paid for? If so, an appropriate structure will be one which is basically a "consultancy organisation" established so as to sell its services

       Conversely it is possible that the department will be used to provide productivity technique knowledge and experience within a project team situation. Therefore the department should be organised to provide this service
5   Status awarded to the department. This will largely determine the number and calibre of the members of the department. This in time will help to formulate departmental relationships, numbers of senior and junior members etc.
6   The job description given to members of the department. In one company the definition of systems analyst will differ totally from another organisation. This may have little to do with the overall function of the department but everything to do with how the department is organised internally

These are some of the major factors which influence companies in the way they set up their MS departments. But there are other, probably more important, functional factors. For example, the problem of centralisation *v* decentralisation is greater than most companies realise. The benefits of a centralised unit are as follows:

1   It is more likely that a greater breadth of vision, the interplay of ideas and the generation of new thinking will take place if the members of the department encourage brain storming and creative thinking. Several one- or two-man units operating on the periphery of the company may establish good client–MS personnel relationships, but have no opportunity to generate new ideas by intellectual combat with fellow practitioners

2   Pay off usually goes with scale. The optimum use of resources will often be enchanced when a match can be made between the demand for MS personnel and total personnel available

3   A large unit should have the disciplines which can foster the project team idea which makes use of all the MS talent available, not just the techniques that one or two personnel can provide

4   A large unit will also provide the basis for a career structure, which small peripheral units are unable to give. This should lead to greater stability, decreased tension and improved morale

5   Training, especially gaining on-the-job skills should be enhanced by the interdisciplinary facilities available in the department. This in turn should promote more highly trained personnel

A centralised organisation, therefore, has considerable advantages over small peripheral units. They in turn, however, may be able to establish client–specialist relationships which help to ensure that good assignments regularly come their way and that they have a large chance of successfully implementing what they propose, to the satisfaction of their clients and themselves.

The importance of the behavioural aspect has already been stressed. Certainly it has been proved that it is often far more important than knowledge of one or more techniques. If peripheral location can help achieve good working relationships between line and staff, then this is a potent reason for having such an organisation.

Yet problems of logistic support, training, choice of assignment (as opposed to accepting every assignment that comes along) may tip the scales the other way. Certainly the political pressures on local units are often great. Centralised units can usually shrug off political situations at local level. This must be a great help in achieving impartiality.

Another factor often ignored is that MS organisation ought to provide the climate for creativity. This aspect is covered by an article written by Professor Knut Holt. ["Creativity and Organisational Climate," Professor Knut Holt, *Work Study and Management Services Journal*, September 1971.] He states that creativity is something we know little about, but innovation (a synonym he suggests for creativity) is essential if competitive power is to be improved. An organisation is essential, therefore, which allows innovative people to be innovative. R & D into management is obviously closely related to innovation and MS organisations should be organised to provide the basis of such an R & D program. [See Chapter 13 in my book *How to Apply Strategy in Profit Planning*, Business Books 1971. This sets out an R & D in management program.]

Efficiency and effectiveness are the key to judging the worth and value of an MSD and it may be interesting to first consider the efficiency yardsticks listed on page 54 and then assess whether the department's organisation is to blame.

TYPES OF ORGANISATION.   Figure 1.2 suggests what has now come to be accepted as the standard MS organisation. It is assumed that there are three distinct areas of activity in the department: computer or EDP, operations

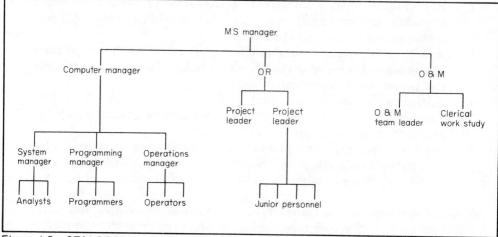

Figure I.2   STANDARD MANAGEMENT SERVICES ORGANISATION

research and organisation and methods. As this has been tried (and still exists) in many companies it must have some validity. The division between systems analysts, OR and O & M personnel is obvious. Does this gulf really exist, however, when many of the functions or scope of these individuals are similar?

BUSINESS CONSULTANT ROLE.   A much more realistic approach is taken in Figure 1.3. There are still three divisions, but they are now divided between business systems, computer operations and work study. The significant difference is that O & M, OR and systems analysts have now been combined into a "business systems unit"—something that is growing progressively more common.

It follows an assumption that the most important element in designing success-

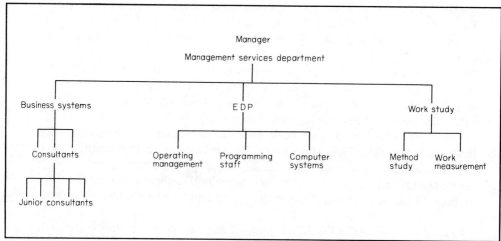

Figure I.3   MORE REALISTIC MANAGEMENT SERVICES ORGANISATION

ful computer systems is to divide the specialism between understanding business and what systems it needs to measure, plan, control, motivate, etc, and how these systems can be translated so they can be run by a computer.

Figure 1.3 also assumes that fundamentally there is no difference between OR, O & M and consultancy. They are all problem solving functions. All should use maths during the course of an assignment. Some personnel may be better at this than others.

MS IN THE MIDLANDS ELECTRICITY BOARD. Figure 1.4 shows an example of management or productivity services in the Midlands Electricity Board. [Taken from an article in *Work Study and Management Services* July 1971, written by D J Foster.] Originally it was not the intention to split the department in functional groupings, or even into personnel who apply a series of related techniques, but to try to consider the department from the point of view of the demands likely to be made upon it.

The extension of work study activities into management controls is a factor which other organisations are taking up. After applying incentives, it seems desirable that work study personnel should continue to check on their efficiency after they have been implemented. Work study personnel provide an unbiased, well trained staff capable of assessing labour performance.

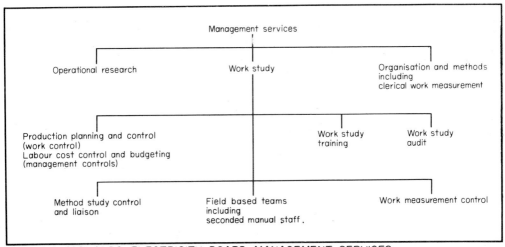

Figure I.4 MIDLANDS ELECTRICITY BOARD MANAGEMENT SERVICES

BRITISH OXYGEN COMPANY. The management services division of BOC covers a much wider range of functions. The division's activities are shown in Figure 1.5. [Described in an article by J M Williams, "The application of the concept of productivity services in BOC", *Work Study and Management Services*, January 1971.] The link between audit and productivity services is a logical one. In stock control, for example, internal auditors should be able to use criteria suggested by systems personnel, to check on line management performance.

MANAGEMENT SERVICES DIVISION				PERSONNEL DIVISION	PR DIVISION
Accounting services	Computers and systems	Productivity services			
Investment approval	Systems analysis	Problem analysis PIP		Employee motivation	Public/press relations
Internal audit	Systems design	Target setting		Management training	Market research
Budgetary control	Programming	Payroll job evaluation			Marketing services
Distribution costs	O & M	Productivity bargaining		Environment/ medical/safety	Advertising
Standard costs	O R				Internal communications
Purchasing systems	Training telecommunications	Value analysis training			

Figure I.5   B O C CORPORATE MANAGEMENT SERVICES DIVISION

BOC, however, have arrived at a conceptual situation where they have linked management services with all the functions in the company which are involved with the measurement of productivity and of change.

Does this mean in effect that we are moving towards the management services division idea shown in Figure 1.6?

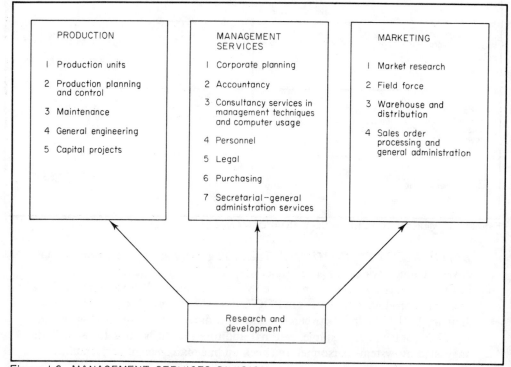

Figure I.6   MANAGEMENT SERVICES DIVISION

A manufacturing company has two basic functions: to make and to sell. It may or may not have a research and development department. All the remaining activities (outside those required by the Companies Acts) are necessarily joined in providing information and general assistance in order that the two main functions can be carried on more efficiently. In this role they are providing a management service.

PRODUCTIVITY SERVICES IN BICC. The use of productivity services in BICC, a large company with numerous geographically spread operating units, is also worthy of note. [Described in an article in *Work Study and Management Services* by P M Burman, June 1971. Involving MS personnel in budgeting will make obvious savings. This article is also interesting in its review of the relationship between central and local productivity services staff.]

BICC operate a method, which I have long advocated, which allows productivity services personnel to take part in the setting of technical standards. The function (known as technical cost measurement) helps line management to know the proven least cost operation of their unit. Anyone who has been involved with budgetary control knows that the basic weakness of the system lies in establishing the initial budgets. The use of MS personnel to help to establish these with line managers is a potent way of using the available expertise. Line managers will not always know of the techniques and methods which will help them to reduce and contain cost.

THE FUTURE. Organisations must adapt to meet changing environments and undoubtedly the organisation types listed in this section will prove inadequate in due course. Several factors are certain:

1   Techniques which were used ten years ago are now fairly commonplace and most line managers can use them. Hence MS personnel must constantly discard old and learn new techniques. This will have an effect on the function of MS departments and so on their organisation

2   The involvement of MS personnel in wider spheres of activity, notably budgeting (i.e. establishment of budgets) and training, etc, will also motivate a changed functional emphasis. This too will affect MS departments' organisation

3   The computer may become an operating unit separate from MS activity. It is a machine which should be treated as an operational unit perhaps not much concerned with innovation and change. This activity belongs to the business systems designer who should be capable of translating "business requirements" into a form which can be easily fed into the computer

**1:4   How assignments normally arise and
how more appropriate ones might be gained**

Assignments for MS personnel largely arise from three distinct sources:

1   Problems which arise suddenly in the company

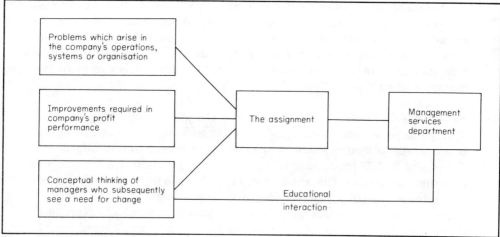

Figure I.7 HOW ASSIGNMENTS ARISE

2   A desire to improve company profit performance
3   Conceptual thinking of managers who subsequently see a need for pro-
     fitable change

PROBLEM OR "FIRE BRIGADE" ASSIGNMENTS.   This is the worst type
of assignment which a management services department can be offered.
   A crisis can blow up at any time, even in the best planned organisations.
People die or leave, environments change rapidly, and so on, but for every
assignment to be of a crisis nature is to impose fundamental constraints on the
efficiency of an MSD. Consider the situation where every assignment comes
unheralded out of the blue:

1   Practitioners will be forced to suffer a feast and famine in work load. A
     planned utilisation of scarce technical resources is impossible
2   A match between MS resources and requirements will be impossible.
     Expertise and planned opportunities to use it will be non-existent
3   Inevitably skilled personnel will have to carry out unskilled activities.
     Talent of the highest quality will often have to be squandered on fairly
     profitless ventures
4   Consequently recruitment and retention of personnel will be difficult.
     Frustration and overwork will ensure a ready turnover of personnel

Yet many MSDs have long accepted this role, content to sit quietly for considerable periods in exchange for brief moments of intense activity. The reasons
for this operational method are easy to understand:

1   Senior management feel this is how an MSD should be run. An "always
     on call" situation is implicit in the department's establishment

2   Equally there is a general understanding that because of its "service nature" it is impossible to plan MS activities

It is accepted, of course, that fire brigade activities will always form some part of an MSD's role. A rapid redeployment of available skills is clearly a constant possibility and should be considered in a contingency plan. The department's manager must be as adept at forecasting future company environmental changes as the corporate planner, economist or the marketing research specialist.

"If the inventory control assignment breaks because of a worsening cash flow situation, who will best be able to do it; who at least will be available?" is the kind of self-questioning which should be carried out.

ATTEMPTS TO IMPROVE COMPANY PROFIT PERFORMANCE.   These assignments often result from the organisation coming under pressure to improve profits or reduce costs. Occasionally a "fire brigade" philosophy will ensue with all the shortcomings listed in the previous section, but more often a planned approach will be made and thinking should be more contemplative than crisis dominated.

The most desirable situation will be motivated by the use of profit planning or corporate strategy techniques. It is hoped that such management methods will ensure that key results will be recognised and MS personnel utilised first on the major areas of profit improvement.

This would be an obvious advance on fire brigade operations and it should be possible to plan MS activities to try and match expertise against requirements in the company.

Yet a line manager harassed to make a cost-reduction plan may not know how MS personnel could help him. He may not be aware of the full range of techniques which he could usefully have deployed on his behalf. He may be under such pressure that his judgement of the aid required will be warped. His timescale may be inadequate; he may underrate how long term the required improvement may have to be.

Even though profit planning or other planning techniques may be in operation, line managers may still not wish to have help from MS personnel.

CONCEPTUAL THINKING.   The line manager who actively asks for the co-operation of MS personnel to help him in some aspect of conceptual thinking is rare. When such an opportunity does occur it is usually in line with a desire by MS personnel to have a research and development role. It helps such personnel to practice unique skills; techniques and systems thinking can be advanced.

In an environment which is normally sceptical if not vaguely hostile, MS personnel can be forgiven for welcoming such opportunities to work with dedicated line managers. The trouble is that they may become too dedicated, absorbing MS personnel's time out of proportion to the importance of the assignment.

At the same time, MS personnel have often been accused of finding comfortable niches where the storms of company controversy and profit activity fail to reach them. Some critics rightly complain of techniques being used just to prove how clever the user is and not necessarily to improve company profit performance.

Assignments resulting from "conceptual thinking" may therefore have considerable snags. Not least is the possibility that work will be done for a line manager because it is known that he is enthusiastic and that the application will succeed. Yet the activity may not be a "key result"; it may not be crucial in helping to improve company profitability and other more important assignments may not be carried out in consequence.

ACHIEVING APPROPRIATE ASSIGNMENTS.   Where MSDs are judged by the achievement of profitable change they engender, the department's assignments have to be viewed critically. Are the assignments which the department is asked to carry out appropriate to the objectives which the department has been set? Opportunities to help to carry out potentially profitable assignments must exist.

There are obvious situations where MS personnel just cannot succeed. Company style and psychology, line management competence, departmental rivalries and jealousies, the history of co-operation or non-co-operation, will all have some effect on both the assignments on offer and the probability of success which is likely to be achieved.

These factors ought to be recognised by senior management in the company and the objectives of the MSD established accordingly. As in all good MBO applications, constraints must be recognised and where possible quantified.

However, it is in the self-interest of the department to foster the kind of assignments which help it to achieve a recognisable degree of profitable change, perhaps as follows:

1   Whilst not eschewing "fire brigade" assignments, the department should actively propagate the use of cost-reduction planning techniques. A suitable chart listing symptoms, diagnosis and treatment in the form of techniques and controls should be part of the department's educational role. It is hoped that the cost-reduction plan approach will help the following activities:

a -   In propagating coherent, logical and analytical views on cost reduction, especially in the analysis of potential trouble spots which could produce "fire brigade" assignments at a later date

b   In suggesting techniques which might help line managers to reduce their costs or improve productivity. The techniques may have been unknown to them before a plan was mentioned

c   In identifying the need for MS resources, specialist skills and techniques; recruiting and deploying such resources in an optimum way. MS personnel, therefore, ought as a priority to propagate planning techniques to help to ensure the better use of the MSD

2   MS personnel must learn to market their skills and experience. They have a product to sell to often highly sceptical individuals and their approach should be exactly the same as a skilled marketing manager's who sells his product in a highly competitive field. The steps in such an approach are as follows:

a   Identify the need for skills and techniques in the organisation, not only for immediate use but for (say) five years into the future. A certain amount of market research will be necessary beginning by assessing company weaknesses and the non-use of profitable techniques and control systems

b   Ensure that the specialist skills are such that the techniques and control systems can be applied when necessary. A price will have to be paid for skills but this will be secondary in importance when compared with the potential gain of a successful application

c   Make certain that line managers are aware of the techniques which might help them and that personnel competent in their use are available. (To gain acceptance that competent personnel are available is extremely important)

d   Identify and then promote identical self-interests between line managers and MS personnel, which will help to ensure that requests are made for the use of the department's services

e   Promote the product. This can be done in many ways, some of which are listed below:

i   Ensure that line managers are aware of successful applications. The use of information sheets is recommended. Word of mouth, though extremely important, could distort the achievements made

ii   Make sure that line personnel are aware of the skills available in the department. An information schedule of staff qualifications and skills is useful if senior line managers can be persuaded to read it

iii   Speed up the educational and receptivity situation by taking part in or totally organising training courses for line management which set out techniques, etc, which are available. Also discuss successful applications of these in other organisations

iv   Successful applications are the best means of promoting future assignments. Nothing should be spared to achieve success in key areas. At the same time, the department should not purposefully seek credit for the success achieved. "We worked with Mr X (the line manager) to achieve this success" is the appropriate line to take

v   Public relations are important. Any means which suggests a good image for the department should be used. Articles in business magazines which are known to be read in the company are useful. Mention of the department in any field which brings credit should be placed in the local newspaper for example or in the company house journal if one exists

f   Control the use of products very carefully, by checking their acceptability once they have been bought. After purchase maintenance must be guaranteed

These are some of the ways to obtain the kind of assignments which will bring credit to the department. The important aspects to constantly consider are:

1   Know which assignments are really key results for the department and the company
2   Know that the department can handle them if they are offered
3   Do not refuse "fire brigade" assignments, but ensure that as far as possible they are few in number
4   "Sell" the department
5   Carry out any exercise which will enhance the department's ability to pick and choose assignments in the future

MANAGEMENT SERVICES PLANS.   Why make a management services plan? To any member of an MS department suffering from a feast and famine in work load, the answer if obvious.

When organisation and methods was first formulated and then developed as a management technique, textbook theory propounded that O & M practitioners should sit and wait until someone demanded their services. How else, it was argued, could co-operation, that vital element in achieving success, be gained?

It was not long before this approach to gaining assignments was under heavy criticism. Its success was conditional on line managers being aware of the need for help. Line managers had (and still have) differing standards of efficiency and attitudes towards the use of specialists. O & M personnel were called in to help in departments which were already comparatively efficient, while others, far less efficient, were shut off by unknowing and ineffective managers.

The co-operation, so keenly sought after, very often evaporated as soon as controversial proposals were made.

Any plan which sets out to optimise the use of departmental resources must start with the question of what resources are needed. What comes first, the tools to carry out a job or the job itself? This is a difficult problem not easily answered. It depends to a large extent upon the organisation for which the plan is being made. For example:

1   Company *A* has many obvious weaknesses, line managers are reasonably co-operative with staff functions and the likelihood of many future profitable assignments is great. In these circumstances it seems justifiable to recruit specialists in anticipation of an enhanced work load for the department
2   Organisation *B* has few obvious weaknesses even though line managers are co-operative and inclined to utilise service personnel to help them. Here, the department should be built up slowly so that there is a gradual expansion of work load. It will be inevitable that initially departmental recruits will be under utilised, even when recruited slowly
3   Company *C* has many weaknesses, but line managers are uncooperative and not inclined to use specialists. Recruitment to the department should

be extremely slow. Potential assignments might be in excess of available personnel to carry them out

4   Company *D*, despite a need for help, has an aggressively independent line management which does not anticipate using staff functions at all.

Until attitudes change, it seems undesirable to recruit in these circumstances. It is valueless recognising potential assignments if they can never be carried out. Company analysis of the type previously outlined will help to identify how quickly a management services department should be built and to what potential levels. Determination of total departmental strength will largely be conditioned by identifying potential assignments which have a large probability of coming to fruition

A new recruit should have approximately one year's firm (perhaps negotiated)

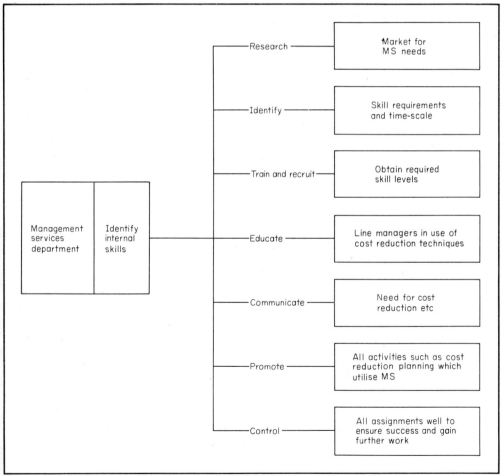

Figure I.8   GAINING APPROPRIATE ASSIGNMENTS FOR MANAGEMENT SERVICES DEPARTMENTS

Date

Assignment	Aims	Jan	Feb	Mar	Apr	May	June	July	Aug	Sept	Oct	Nov	Dec	Personnel	Comment
Installation of system 3 with profit improvement program	Major savings of £50 000 pa Management information systems improvement													R Copper 1/c, Taylor SA, S Young SA, I A Tooth from SY Stapely --	Major assignment for department this year
Clerical work measurement	Reduction of 10% in clerical work force													D B James, C Bellingham	Departments and savings identified appropriate sub-programs worked out
Stock control	Reduce inventories in X division by 15%								H O L					G Simpson, M Glover	Training required in statistical control techniques
Help in management development program									I D A Y					R Copper, G Taylor	Preparation work required installation of systems 3 delayed in consequence
Work simplification	General improvement in clerical systems				AS AND WHEN ARE AVAILABLE					STAFF					
Work study	Time study in X, Y and Z divisions													G Proctor, P Whitemore, L Vaughan, T L Forsyth	Continuing activity
Budget establishment	Appropriate budgets set													P Godfrey, M Monks	Activity linked with budget validation

Figure 1.9 MANAGEMENT SERVICES DEPARTMENT PLAN – ASSIGNMENTS ACCEPTED

Figure 1.10 MANAGEMENT SERVICES DEPARTMENT PLAN – RESOURCE UTILISATION

Practitioner	Skills	Allocated assignment	Jan	Feb	Mar	Apr	May	June	July	Aug	Sept	Oct	Nov	Dec	Comment
1) R Capper	Major business skills	1) Profit improvement program and I/c systems 3 installation 2) Management development program													Working on key result area. Appropriate assignments
2) G Taylor	Systems analyst major business skills	1) Profit improvement program and systems 3 installation 2) Management development program													Key result area
3) G Simpson	OR specialist	1) Stock control													Further assignment/s required
4) M Glover	OR specialist	1) Stock control													Further assignment/s required
6) G Proctor	Time study method study	1) Time study													The method study element missing

Utilisation — "NO JOB" (Aug–Oct)

Date

assignments in front of him, with another two years' potential work which could well mature. This amount seems to be about the minimum to form the basis for recruitment.

Identification of the company environment will help to recruit the kind of personnel the organisation and department need. In company A, for example, the recruits should obviously be technique orientated. In organisation B, the specialisms needed should be extremely well defined and personnel recruited accordingly.

In the other two organisations, behavioural relations will dominate the MS function and consequently MS staff should be strongly orientated in that direction, even if this means a comparative weakness in the deployment of techniques.

A situation audit and evaluation of company style will not only help to determine the type of personnel required (especially the behavioural attributes) but also the potential numbers. This latter point, of course, needs to be viewed not against the potential use of the department but from an opportunity viewpoint (with the foreseeable co-operation of line management).

A situation audit can obviously be a long, hard and difficult analysis to carry out. If a corporate planner is employed by the organisation such a review may already be in hand and an appropriate appreciation of company style and management attitudes be forthcoming. If such an audit does not exist one will have to be built up from scratch.

Job analysis of MS personnel

2:1 Introduction

Some of the more common forms of organisation which have been and are being adopted by management services departments have been briefly described. This chapter lists some of the more important members likely to belong to such a department. The division between business systems and computer orientated personnel is recognised. The business systems staff are assumed to act in the capacity of internal consultants.

2:2 Writing job descriptions

Writing a job description is a formal method of informing the reader about the essential features of a job. The description should show what there is to do, how it is done and why the job exists.

A typical approach to writing job descriptions is to consider job activities under five headings:

1   *Purpose.* What is to be achieved by doing the job, why does it exist, what is paid for?
2   *Dimensions.* Under this heading the magnitude of the job should be quoted. This can be recorded as money or men or any other resources or measurement which will help to determine the job's dimensions
3   *Nature and scope of the position.* This will be the most important part of the job description. It should deal with the following aspects:
a   Organisation. Where does the job fit into the organisation? To whom does the job holder report? How many people of what category report to the

job holder? These should be listed in detail, showing functions covered and dimensions in each case.

b Knowledge. What knowledge, qualifications, experience is it likely that the job holder should have? What technical knowledge is required, as well as experience of handling complex human-relations problems?

c Key problems inherent in the job: What in effect is the greatest challenge in the job? What is the most satisfying and the least satisfying element?

4 *Constraints and Authority.* This heading should cover all the freedoms and controls which the job has. For example authority to: hire and fire, raise salaries, discipline staff, agree capital expenditure, change company methods, etc. What can be done without reference to a superior? What can be done by reference to a superior? What are the main rules and regulations covering the job?

5 *Key accountabilities.* What are the main objectives or key results which the job holder must pursue? Against what performance criteria is the job holder judged? How must the job holder motivate people? How will objectives be established. How will results be measured? What criteria of effectiveness will be used? The degree of freedom to act must be stated as well as the job holder's potential impact on results. The magnitude of the key results ought to be stated if possible.

DEPARTMENTAL FUNCTION AND JOB DESCRIPTION. Job definitions will largely be determined by the job duties which a management services department is allowed to perform. It is interesting therefore to consider briefly what such duties might cover. A hypothetical example follows:

Structure of the department. The department will be commanded by a senior manager, designated "manager of the management services department." He will report direct to the managing director. The department will have three sections:

1 A business systems section, with personnel acting largely as internal consultants to the company. This section will contain personnel skilled in:

a Operations research

b Profit planning

c Business systems analysis

d Organisation and methods

e Work study

f General business problem solving

2 A programming or computer systems section, which will be responsible for converting line management's and the business systems section's requirements into computer applications. This section will contain personnel skilled in:

a Hardware evaluation

b Software evaluation and writing

c Programming in commercial and machine orientated languages
d Program specification writing
3 The computer operating section, which will be devoted to the operating of the data preparation and computer operating function. This section will be skilled in:
a Data preparation and control
b Machine control

Assignment and projects. Assignments will stem from the involvement of the department in on-going situations such as efficiency auditing and budget validation but also from requests by line management. Normally all the department's activities should be paid for by the line manager requesting them, though this payment can be waived at the discretion of the manager of the department.

Projects will be closely controlled and at all times a project file or diary will be kept which can be inspected by senior management. Assignments will always be covered by a timetable which has been agreed between the line manager and the manager of the department.

It is anticipated that the savings which the department will make will be equal to at least three times its current annual cost.

The brief outline of an MSD's function might dictate the use of all or some of the jobs listed below:

POSSIBLE GENERAL DUTIES OF MS MANAGER. To recruit and train management individuals of mixed disciplines in order to perform the following functions:

1 To carry out at the request of the board and line management specific assignments to improve profit and reduce costs, as far as possible choosing those assignments which will have most reward for least effort
2 To translate business systems into computer language in order to optimise the use of the computer
3 To operate the computer to provide a least cost service to all line managers who require a computing service
4 To take part in all on-going operations designated by the board
5 To keep the board and line managers advised on the latest developments in management techniques and control systems and computing technology, and in so doing advance company profitability
6 To advise line managers of the manning of their departments through the use of work measurement techniques
7 To collaborate with other departmental managers in providing team members, general expertise and guidance for profit improvement teams
8 To help the personnel and training staff in education in management techniques, information systems and computer appreciation

9   To compile and maintain records of management techniques, office equipment and methods of company analysis which can be referred to by line management at any time

10   To have an appropriate liaison with professional bodies and outside consultants who could provide support or knowledge to the department which will increase its effectiveness

11   To vet all terms of reference for assignments and activities within his department so that only appropriate assignments are carried out to a strict timetable which will ensure the best use of his departmental staff

12   To submit a quarterly review of his department's activities to the board of directors, listing assignments which have been and are being carried out and the savings gained

A job description written in the style set out in on page 23 for the leader of the business systems section might produce the following:

JOB DESCRIPTION

Job: Section leader in charge of business systems section
Job holder: A K Smith
Reports to: Manager, MSD
Date: ....

Purpose.   Research, develop and apply appropriate management techniques and methods which could make major contributions to company profitability.

Dimensions.   This job can impact at any time on major areas of profitability within the company. For example, a project on "company inventories" may bring about savings of £½M a year.

Staff: 2 senior assistants
          3 junior assistants

Nature and scope.   The activities of the section consists in providing a research and development and a general consultancy service for directors and line managers in the company. Within the department the holder liaises and works in close co-operation with his manager and the other two section leaders. This is especially important in the case of the programming section when systems analysis has progressed to the point where it could be applied to the computer. In addition the holder works closely in a consultancy role with management at all levels in the company in all stages of his work. He must play a major part in promoting and exploiting the techniques and general skills available both in his section and the department. The work if necessary falls into two main areas:

1   *Research and development.*   Research is carried out by the holder and his staff into all management methods and techniques which are considered to have a potential within the company

2   *Assignments.* These stem from requests by directors and line managers as well as taking part in on-going situations such as budget validation

To operate effectively the holder needs to give a significant proportion of his time to his own personal development. In addition to desk research, knowledge must be increasingly acquired from seminars and courses on recent developments in management techniques. Considerable time must be spent on developing his subordinates by closely directing and leading them on assignments, editing their work and ensuring that their knowledge and experience is developed through a variety of assignments and courses.

The challenges of this job focus mainly on promoting and gaining acceptance in the company of improved management techniques and methods. Related to this are the problems of installing systems and the changes needed in organisation and methods for their operation. In addition to persuading personnel at all levels to accept changes, training must also be put in hand and this must be planned for by the holder.

The job is operated and assessed first on the achievement of agreed plans and assignments where methods and techniques have been applied with a measurable improvement in profit or performance; second, the ready availability (for eventual use) of all management methods and techniques which will aid substantially company profitability.

Key Accountabilities

1   Keep abreast of all management techniques and methods
2   Research into those management techniques and methods thought to have profitable application within the company and develop those which are appropriate to the stage where they can be applied
3   Provide the company with a source of sound advice, knowledge and expertise on all management techniques and methods
4   Identify aspects of the company's activities where better management techniques would result in improved profitability, and initiate proposals for their application
5   Carry out agreed individual or joint assignments where the application of management techniques contribute to the improvement of management performance and profitability
6   Maintain effective communication, consultation and co-operation with the manager, colleagues and the company in the development, application and promotion of the section's resources
7   Ensure that the section is staffed by high calibre, well trained and motivated personnel

Assistants to the section leader may concentrate on one or all of the techniques or areas of activity of the section. For example:

JOB SPECIFICATION FOR AN O & M
OFFICER IN THE BUSINESS SYSTEMS SECTION

1   *Responsibilities.* The O & M officer is responsible to the section leader, and he may be assisted from time to time by staff as directed by the section leader.

2   *Job summary.* The job requires him:

a   To compile and maintain, in convenient form, an *aide-mémoire* of management techniques, office services, machinery and equipment, etc, and to act as a focal point for the collection and subsequent dissemination of information on these subjects to other interested parties

b   To maintain the necessary liaison with equipment suppliers, outside parties and individuals with similar interests in other companies and organisations

c   To keep the section leader and the manager of the department advised in general terms on the latest development in the subjects mentioned in 2a above

d   To draft and keep up-to-date departmental administrative instructions, to keep the departmental project visual control board up-to-date, and to do other departmental administrative work as requested by the manager of the section

e   To carry out special surveys and assignments, including applications work as requested by the section leader of the business systems section

3   *Job results.* The results expected from the successful work of the O & M officer are the prompt and accurate dissemination of information and response to information demands, which will improve the effectiveness of the work of the management services department.

Graduate assistants may form part of the section:

JOB SPECIFICATION FOR GRADUATE ASSISTANT

1   *Responsibilities.* Graduate assistants will be responsible to the section leader of the business systems section, although from time to time they may be seconded to work under other section leaders or in profit improvement teams. As part of their training they may occasionally be required to be responsible for the work of trainees or other assistants

2   *Job summary.* The job consists of:

a   Assisting the section leader or any other nominated project leader in consultancy assignments. (Training covering the development and application of management techniques—for example, method study, O & M, systems analysis, development of production control, stock control and management information systems, EDP applications—will be given.)

b   Carrying out special investigations and surveys at the request of the team leader, or manager, MSD

3 Graduate assistants will normally spend up to four years receiving experience and training in the MSD. During this period they can expect to develop from assisting project leaders with detailed supervision to the completion of significant individual assignments on their own initiative

4 *Job results.* The results expected from the work of a graduate assistant are an increasing evidence of ability to complete work successfully, according to program. His contribution to direct cost reduction and/or intangible benefits, must be obvious

COMPUTER OPERATING SECTION. This section covers data preparation and the running of the computer. The main job duties of the personnel in the section might be as follows:

Operation manager (section leader). [Some of these duties have been adapted from ICL's booklet *Planned Careers.*] The operations manager will:

1 Be responsible for the planning, organisation and operation of the data preparation and computer activities of the company

2 Establish an operations budget and ensure that appropriate cost control and the charging of computer facilities to users is carried out. He will ensure that a timetable for data preparation and computer activities is prepared and that it is completed as laid down

3 Select appropriate staff with the aid of the MS manager and ensure that they are properly trained. He will write job descriptions for all personnel under his control. He will supervise all operations and be prepared to give merit ratings for his staff

4 Liaise with section leaders of the business systems, computer systems and the management services manager in planning the future work load of his section. He will help to plan each new project in detail ensuring that a timescale is agreed and adhered to

5 Lay down standard operating procedures for the computer and the data preparation parts of his section. He will co-operate with the computer section in establishing programming standards

6 Calculate running standards for each job at all data processing operations and keep log sheets to prove that those standards are maintained. He will also keep a log sheet of machine down-time and maintenance activities

7 Keep abreast of current developments in computer hardware so that at any time he will be able to offer advice on the purchase, lease or rental of new equipment

Shift leader/operations supervisor. He will:

1 Be responsible to the operations manager for the effective operating of the data preparation section, the computer and its peripherals during one shift

2   Supervise computer operatives to ensure that the timetable for computer operations is maintained in accordance with the established code of practice

3   Liaise with user departments to ensure that the data input is appropriate and that output is delivered on time

4   Assess any faults which occur in the equipment and call in maintenance engineers when necessary in order to minimise machine down-time. When necessary he will arrange for stand-by facilities to be used when these are proved to be necessary

5   Be responsible for completing the shift log sheet and making a shift report to the operations manager

6   Give on the job training to operating staff and suggest improved methods of operating practice

Chief systems analyst.   His main duties will be to:

1   Maintain a close working relationship with all levels of management, staff and employees affected by DP systems. He must therefore:

a   Be personally acceptable

b   Have understanding of management thinking

c   Appreciate the business and its problems

2   Manage complex systems and the work of the high-calibre staff involved. This will require a good appreciation of systems and data processing. He will operate by budgetary control. He will select and train his staff to the standards required

Project analyst.   He will review each systems project in detail. He will also:
1   Review existing systems and flow of work
2   Help to review present and future needs of management
3   Specify new systems objectives and tie in related systems
4   Evaluate new systems

Systems planning analyst.   He will:

1   Specify inputs and outputs
2   Sketch the contents of files
3   Define controls on accuracy and quality of systems
4   Plan clerical procedures associated with input and output
5   Help to design codes for products, accounts, part numbers etc

Systems conversion analyst.   He will help to:

1   Plan training of the clerical personnel affected
2   Establish procedures for cleaning up and transference of records
3   Establish procedures for systems test, parallel runs, full change-over
4   Document new systems

Systems maintenance and improvement analyst.   He will:

Review procedures, systems objectives, usefulness of results, effectiveness of controls

Software consultant.   He must have:

1   An appreciation of management information requirements, objectives and techniques
2   Knowledge of systems design: data-base; on-line; real-time response; multi-programming
3   He must be able to evaluate hardware: peripherals, ancillary equipment, data collection and transmission equipment.
4   He must be able to evaluate manufacturer's and proprietary software:
a   Executive and operating systems
b   Languages
c   Utilities
d   File organisation
e   File handler
f   Application packages
g   Systems measurement—i.e. measurement of program performance and use of configuration
5   He must be capable of developing the use of common routines and sub-routines—i.e. design modules for widespread application
6   He must be capable of developing the use of systems and programming techniques, for example:
a   Decision tables
b   Modular and segmented programming
c   Data processing standards
d   Training modules for specialist staff and general management
7   From day to day he should plan, control and supervise the high-level design of computer systems, especially:
a   File organisation and structure
b   Segmentation of programs
c   Use of standard packages, sub-routines and modules
d   Use of hardware and software to optimal throughput
e   Programming languages
8   He should be responsible for the setting of objectives and progressing for the projects for which he is responsible; supplying technical advice on other projects
9   He must ensure that there is adherence to standards
10   He should be responsible for the testing of modules, programs, systems:
a   Sequencing, desk checking, standards for scrutiny and error correction
b   The recruiting and training of computer specialist staff
c   The maintenance of programs

Senior programmer.   He will:

1   Be responsible for converting program specifications into coded program schedules. He will define the files and programs needed and their interrelationship
2   Assess program writing and testing time and set up an appropriate control mechanism
3   Control the use of a programming project team and will allocate programming responsibilities in accordance with the agreed timetable and his assessment of the competence of programmers and junior programmers under his command
4   Provide all information which could be needed to assess the value of running the program specification on the computer and to confirm that the programs which have been written meet the requirements of the systems analysts
5   Arrange for the appropriate testing, correction and linking of programs his team has written; maintain responsibility for them until successful parallel running has been completed
6   Keep program costs under review at all times and report when costs are exceeding those budgeted
7   Ensure that appropriate procedures and documentation is maintained at all times
8   Ensure that his programming staff are appropriately trained and are aware of all the limitations in current hardware and software

Junior programmer.   A junior programmer will:

1   Form part of a programming team normally responsible to the senior programmer.
2   Be responsible for the planning, writing and testing of small programs or the maintenance of programs which have already been established
3   Expand systems specifications in sufficient detail in order to ensure that programs can be written from them
4   Write programs (under supervision) from program specifications. He will assemble programs and, with the senior programmer's guidance, carry out program testing
5   Assist in programming documentation

2:3   Career structure and grading of personnel

With the establishment of management services as a career in its own right, it is obvious that some formal career structure is necessary if a satisfactory morale/operational situation is to be assured.

Formal career structures are likely to have some of the following effects, each of which might substantially aid departmental efficiency:

1   Lesson the turnover rate. To train a chief systems analyst from scratch is likely to cost in the region of £2000. To recruit one may cost the same amount. Anything, therefore, which reduces the departmental turnover rate is desirable

2   Relate effort and reward. A career structure, if related to a job evaluation scheme will tend to relate effort to reward. Hopefully it will help to facilitate the use of job evaluation and merit rating schemes

3   Relate internal and external salaries. It is likely that a career structure will help to relate salaries paid internally with those paid externally

4   People will know where they stand. Departmental morale should be improved by a knowledge of current and future job responsibilities and salary prospects which a career structure should give

ICL in July 1971 issued *Planned Careers* a suggested career outline for computer personnel—largely to sell their training courses. It has an intrinsic value, however, in suggesting various categories of computer personnel and the likely training courses which will be of benefit to them in their job progress.

Whether or not there is agreement concerning the career paths shown in Figure 2.1 some principles seem important.

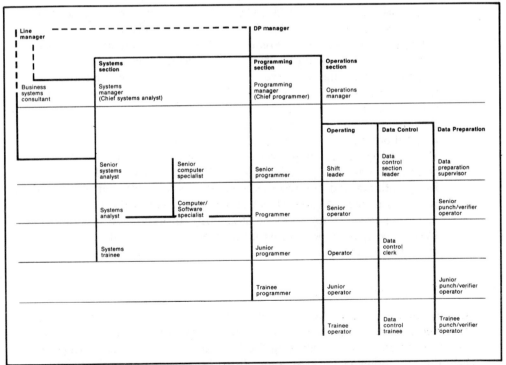

Figure 2.1   ORGANISATION OF MANAGEMENT SERVICES DEPARTMENT SHOWING LINES OF CAREER PROGRESSION (transfers between departments are not shown)

1   There have to be definite career stages, each with a job responsibility and job description

2   Each job has a salary band which is related to the job description and also to outside jobs with an equal responsibility

3   Once a formal career structure has been accepted a program of training for each grade should be drawn up

4   Before promotion from one grade to another, suitable checks on proficiency, experience and training can be made

5   Newcomers should be slotted into an appropriate grade and trained and paid according to that grade. Equally it should be possible for personnel to leave a grade for a line career or change from a programming path to a systems path etc

While there are valid reasons why a career structure should be introduced, there are various factors which have to be taken into account:

1   It is difficult to assume that there will be automatic progression through all grades. Departmental establishment may prohibit this or individual calibre may militate against such a move. It would be wrong for anyone to assume that a career structure is equivalent to an escalator

2   As a corollary of (1) it is difficult to lay down the time individuals should spend in each grade. Calibre and opportunity should really decide

3   Salary bands for jobs of apparently equal status in different carreer paths, can never be the same if outside influences dictate supply and demand

4   Calibre and training may have to differ according to the applications (in the case of computers) being performed. For example, the likely progression of applications on a computer might be as follows:

a   Routine recording, stock recording, sales ledger etc

b   Control procedures—material and labour control

c   Forecasting and planning—production planning and control

d   Integration and simulation. It is likely that individual knowledge, experience, training and competence requirements will differ at each stage, within each grade. A career structure will have to cope with such situations

5   Career planning is not a precise mechanistic operation. At any time it is likely to be up to 50 per cent wrong in forecasts. For the sake of the 50 per cent correct situations' however, a career structure is worth while

2:4   Technical information service

If management services have been established to aid line management in making profitable change then one aspect of their activities should be to provide a technical information service concerning the techniques and equipment which will help this aim. Some of the suggestions listed below might cross the functional boundaries of purchasing departments or production engineering, but the service should be established somewhere in the organisation.

The outline should also serve to indicate the information/knowledge which ought to reside in an MSD.

BUSINESS EQUIPMENT
1   Adding and calculating machines
2   Accounting and accounting systems machines
3   Cash and cheque handling equipment
4   Communications (telephone, teleprinters etc)
5   Computers (software as well as hardware including all peripherals)
6   Dictating machines
7   Filing
8   Mailing
9   Micro filming
10   Paper handling
11   Punched card equipment
12   Reprographic equipment (addressing, duplicating, photocopying etc)
13   Typewriters

TECHNIQUES APPLICATIONS.   Largely those listed later in the skills audit.

MANAGEMENT INFORMATION SYSTEMS
1   Finance, including standard costing and budgetary control as well as financial control and general cost control, marginal costing
2   Production and production services—production planning and control, maintenance control, performance incentive calculations
3   Purchasing
4   Sales—marketing—market research, market data, sales order processing, stock control
5   Personnel control
6   Company control—profit planning, long-range planning etc

EDP STANDARDS
1   Installation planning and progress
2   Systems analysis standards and documentation
3   Programming languages and program testing procedures
4   Data preparation, operating and control practice

MATERIALS HANDLING
1   Conveyors
2   Cranes, hoists, gantries, including special retrieval systems and monorails
3   Use of pallets and containers
4   Special vehicles—fork-lift trucks, reach, side and straddle etc
5   Packaging
6   Warehousing and stores location
7   Modes of transport, advantages and disadvantages

PRODUCTION EQUIPMENT
1   Bulk storage equipment
2   Mixers, agitators
3   Extruders, impregnators
4   Ovens, driers
5   Spray units
6   Machine tools
7   Saws
8   Weighing, counting and measuring equipment
9   Numerically controlled production machines

OFFICE LAYOUT TECHNIQUES
1   Layout concepts—*Burolandschaft* etc
2   Heating
3   Lighting
4   Ventilation
5   General environmental conditions—housekeeping servicing etc

ORGANISATION'S METHODS
1   Cash handling
2   Wages payment
3   Bonus calculations
4   Canteen arrangements
5   Secretarial services
6   Car usage
7   Postal arrangement

RECORDS.   These should be kept and regularly updated showing:
1   Current equipment available, its advantages and disadvantages and cost
2   Details of current techniques and details of successful applications
3   Methods of applying techniques

2:5   Training aspects

To survive, MS personnel should be constantly going through an old technique rejection and a new technique acceptance. The practitioner who is not going through this cycle is intellectually moribund and will soon be obsolete in his job practices.

This attitude of mind should come easily to MS staff. Unfortunately the reverse seems true. A well-worn technique is often preferable to a new one. Adaptation to the changing use of techniques appears extremely difficult.

It is equally difficult for MS personnel to know what new skills to acquire. Certainly they should not rely on senior management to tell them. If MS personnel, who should be in the vanguard of management, do not know where the vanguard is going, then it is hard to expect senior management to know.

It seems useful to regard the skills audit as a means of indicating where training and new skills are required. A constantly updated skills audit on the lines suggested seems essential.

THREE

Carrying out assignments

3:1 Defining the problem

The odds that the terms of reference covering an assignment will adequately determine the problems involved are extremely small. Terms of reference are usually written by senior executives who are aware that a problem exists but often are unable to determine it precisely—otherwise they might have solved it themselves. Frequently a problem is wrongly stated. A transport problem can resolve itself into a sales and marketing failure. A poor stock control situation may really be caused by an inadequate production planning and control system.

What is really the problem can often only be seen after the assignment has begun. It is useful to have a preliminary investigation in the areas concerned, but this may not always be possible especially in an organisation where terms of reference tend to be handed down like mosaic tablets.

An open-ended situation is equally absurd and an assignment which goes on and on jumping from one problem area to another could end up by solving nothing.

The main problem to be solved, therefore, has to be determined and a timescale for its solution and the practical correction of the situation established. If the original terms of reference have to be amended in the process, then this should not be shirked.

3:2 Methods of investigation

A standard investigational method is obviously an advantage. Training of MS personnel is facilitated, as also is command of the investigations. Divergences from plan are soon spotted and irregularities in the situation quickly brought to light. It is possible to substitute investigation team members, if a largely standard approach is made. (However, detailed long-distance control which might reasonably follow is always dangerous.)

A recommended method is control through an assignment diary or file. The file is available for review at any time. It serves not only to control the assignment but also to protect those taking part in it. The following factors are determined and appropriately recorded.

METHOD OF WORKING. Who does what? Who controls which part of the assignment? Is a project team to be set up? If so, what is its constitution? How long will its members serve—a week, a month, the assignment in total? Who will report to whom and at what intervals? What form will the reports take—verbal, written, complicated or uncomplicated etc?

What general structure will the assignment follow? Will local personnel play a leading role? Can the assignment be structured to suit local conditions or is an overall standardised approach being followed?

ESTIMATION OF THE TIME SPAN OF THE PROJECT. Estimation of the work content of an assignment is often extremely difficult, particularly when an adventure into completely new territory is planned. A project often goes on and on never reaching a satisfactory conclusion because no one really knew at the beginning or tried to estimate during the project, how long it would take. Yet without some time estimate (based on logical assumptions) a project can become a morass into which more and more resources are pushed with no apparent result obtained.

The important factors on which a project's work content might be judged are given below:

1   *Past experience.* No matter how new or adventurous the assignment, past experience should be useful in determining what the likely work content will be. A broad "X man months" of activity can quickly be assumed. This broad assessment should then be carefully controlled

2   *Estimation of subassignment work content.* Once the time content of the main assignment has been estimated, a breakdown of the whole into subunits should be possible. An allocation of personnel should follow. Timescales will largely be determined by the individuals who will be delegated to work on the subassignments. Calibre will differ from individual to individual and so, therefore, will the time estimate

3   *Work sampling.* It will usually be possible to carry out some work sampling at the beginning of the assignment. This will help determine the whole and a "corrected" estimation may then be relevant

4   *Competence.* Estimating will grow with the constant monitoring of assignments. It is always useful (though often resented) to have log or work sheets completed each day by the assignment team. It tends to concentrate the mind if team actions are to be subsequently monitored. Intuition will

still play a large part in time estimate. If there is a recognition, however, that an assignment should be carefully controlled right from the beginning, intuition can often work

3:3   Situation audit

It is unfortunate that in most assignments a valid situation audit will not be possible until a few weeks after an assignment has started. It would be left to the senior consultant or project team leader to assess and as far as possible take account of the "situation" in the organisation both in carrying out the assignment and in presenting proposals. The following aspects should be considered.

THE SEARCH FOR ALLIES.   A consultant brings threats of change, maybe redundancy. Inevitably if line managers have to co-operate with the assignment team, their total work load will be increased.

They will often resent the intrusion of so-called expert outsiders. They will certainly withhold information and co-operation if redundancy threatens. Their ego-motivation alone could prevent any co-operation at all.

The consultant therefore has to search for personnel with whom he can work, and who want to work with him. The cost accountant, a production manager or assistant engineer, may be all who will lend help and assistance. The assignment will then have to be orientated to rely on such individuals, with a major effort made on the part of the company which is co-operative etc.

The co-operation of even the managers quoted may have definite ulterior motives and the consultant should probably be aware of them.

STRENGTHS AND WEAKNESSES.   These ought to be assessed. They will include:

1   *Company style.*   Is it inimicable to change or even modern management thinking of any kind? Are there key managers who refuse to change?
2   *Chief executive.*   His role is vital. Will he:
a   Affect company style for the better
b   Set demanding objectives for his managers
c   Motivate personnel appropriately
d   Engender co-operation as far as this is possible
e   Encourage change
f   Reshape his organisation to meet objectives
g   Take his full part in the assignment and refuse to delegate key tasks to his subordinates
3   *Company environment.*   This covers both internal and external environment, particularly the competition the company is facing and the technical superiority or inferiority of the company's products. Such factors will help to determine the objectives of the assignment
4   *Competence of local line management.*   It is usually part of the arrogant

stock in trade of MS personnel to decry the professional ability of local line management. Unfortunately it is a fact of life that most line managers will be less knowledgeable of systems and management techniques than an internal consultant. The ability of local line management to accept and eventually take over and run new systems and methods should determine the sophistication of the proposals which will eventually be made, the speed at which they will be implemented and the total support which MS personnel will need to supply to ensure the assignment's success

Attitudes towards change will need to be identified and appropriately considered. Antagonism towards change may have little to do with competence but will certainly help or hinder in gaining profitable change of any kind.

The situation audit, therefore, is a considered value judgement on the socio–economic condition of the company and what its future is likely to be. Obviously a small assignment, involved (say) with the change of a minor system, will not need a detailed survey. A major one—production planning and control for example—certainly will and the assignment should be designed to cope with the audit details which are revealed. This is not an easy task, and ability to view companies in the way outlined is necessary. Once the situation audit has been carried out priorities and key results can be established. These ought to be agreed with local line management. In some companies the relationship will be one of doctor and patient, in others co-equals discussing an interesting problem and in some (luckily the minority) the MS personnel will be servants brought in to pull some of the master's chestnuts out of the fire.

Constraints and limitations on the assignment should definitely be established at an early stage.

3:4 Data gathering and analysis

Long experience suggests that insufficient data gathering is the rule in MS assignments rather than the exception. Quantification is often the key to quashing line management doubts about proposals for change. For example, a well-authenticated piece of data on stock obsolescence will often help the acceptance of a new stock control system. What needs to be decided is:

1 What data is needed?
2 How can it be obtained?
3 How long will it take to obtain it (man-days)?
4 What is to be gained by obtaining the data?
5 How is it to be presented?
6 What accuracy is required?
7 What accuracy will be accepted?
8 To whom will it be given?
9 Considering the situation will data presented in the way suggested be sufficient?

Use of statistical methods is essential. Correlation, mean average and absolute deviations, ranking by element, etc.

3:5   Setting up an exercise and its control

An example of how an overall assignment was set up was given in the table on page. 4. It showed how the division of functions between MS and line personnel was established. This example followed an appreciation of the company style, the competence of local management and the work to be done.

A marriage between these three factors produced the example quoted. Tight control necessitated that each phase had its own methodology and control. The following example shows how this was done.

PROFIT IMPROVEMENT PROGRAM

Phase I
This phase covers the following activities:

1   The establishment of current and future work standards
2   The implementation of control systems for:
a   Labour control
b   Material utilisation
c   Production planning and control
d   Maintenance control
3   The exploitation of the establishment of work standards and control systems

Work standards
Work standards should be established for labour and material usage, machine manning strengths and output speeds for each significant operation or cost centre for each production line. Two standards should be set:

1   The currently accepted standards
2   The standards which have to be met if the required company profit is to be achieved

Copies of the standards should be available for factory, cost and administrative personnel, but should have an extremely limited circulation with numbered copies. Once established, standards sheets should be regularly updated. They should be used in setting budgets and estimating future profit as well as in judging current production performance.

Control systems
Control systems should be established which will give information on labour, machine and material utilisation. The method and timing of pro-

ducing information must facilitate the close control of the factors mentioned and at the same time help to improve overall performance.

Exploitation
Once the gap between current and required standards has been established and control systems implemented, it will be necessary to raise action programs listing the activities works personnel consider will help to close the performance gap. An action program is a list of considered activities which will produce improved performance. The following main headings should be used:

1   Area of location for activity
2   Nature of fault or activity being eradicated or improved
3   Activity or action
4   Improvement anticipated (money should be quoted if possible)
5   Responsibility (manager responsible should be shown)
6   Timescale

Methodology
The following methodology seems appropriate in the company for introducing phase I.

   Following discussion with local management the MSD senior consultant will give a detailed outline of the method of:

1   Establishing work standards
2   Establishing control systems
3   Exploitation procedures (action programs)

These will be discussed with line management on site, amended where necessary and implemented. The senior consultant will then withdraw and revisit three to four weeks later to discuss success, redesign the systems in the light of implementation difficulties and reimplement if necessary. Once a successful implementation has been made (and agreed by line management that it is successful) the MSD senior consultant will write an appropriate manual to cover the activity.

Timetable
A timetable for the introduction of phase I has been drawn [shown as Figure 3.1]. It should be regularly updated, so that at any time the current state of the assignment can be seen.

Date _____
Updated _____
Updated _____

Department/ line or section	Manager(s) responsible	Operating standard			Documentation for system			Progress of control systems			Time for completion	Action programs to improve standards			
		Measurements for	Received	Not yet received	Initial yes/no	Final manual yes/no	Date due	Control system	Implemented yes/no	Date intro'd		Available yes/no	Program number	Date due	Person responsible
Line 1		Labour						Labour control							
		Material utilisation						Material control							
		Machine output						Production planning and control							
		Set-up time/ breakdown						Maintenance control							

Figure 3.1 PROFIT IMPROVEMENT PROGRAM PHASE I
Measurement control and exploitation lines 1, 2 and 3

Measuring
competence and performance

4:1 Skills audit

The most effective way in which to measure competence and performance in an MSD is to assess the skills which are extant among the personnel and how effectively they have been deployed. The initial evaluation might take the form of a skills audit as quoted in Figure 4.1.

The full range of MS personnel attributes and techniques needs to be listed. Then a weighting is given for each item shown.

IMPORTANCE.   A weighting from 1 to 10 is allocated as an indication of the importance of the technique or attribute in modern management.

1 = Must be aware of the technique but not the method or detailed applications
10 = Vital to have a detailed working knowledge of the technique and its applications

RELEVANCE.   Relevance refers to the relevance of the technique or attribute in the company. This may differ significantly from the importance factor rated above. What may be considered important in the broad field of management, may be unimportant within the company. It is of little use becoming skilled in an obviously important technique, which the company is unlikely ever to use.

9–10   High probability that the technique or attribute will be used in the company within the next six months
7–8   Important, probably will be used fairly soon

		Importance	Relevance	Required level of knowledge	ASW	SEP	FIP	VSS	SAT
I	Project control and implementation								
1.1	Problem identification								
1.2	Time-scale estimation								
1.3	Reporting								
1.4	Organisation of project								
1.5	Ability to: write								
	speak								
	listen								
1.6	Acceptability to: senior managers								
	assistant managers								
	white collar staff								
	plant operatives								
1.7	Proven record of success?								

Figure 4.1   MANAGEMENT SERVICES DEPARTMENT SKILLS AUDIT

46

	Importance	Relevance	Required level of knowledge	ASW	SEP	FIP	VSS	SAT
2 <u>Quantitative management techniques</u>								
2.1 Linear programming								
2.2 Dynamic programming								
2.3 Queueing theory								
2.4 Replacement theory								
2.5 Model formulation								
2.6 Statistics								
2.6.1 Regression methods								
2.6.2 Correlation								
2.6.3 Design of experiments								
2.6.4 Confidence limits								
2.6.5 Probability distributions etc								
2.6.6 Analysis of variance								
2.7 Modelling								
2.7.1 Regression and econometric								
2.7.2 Simple arithmetic								
2.7.3 Behavioural								
2.7.4 Simulation								
2.7.5 Markovian								
2.7.6 System dynamics								
2.8 Decision theory								
2.8.1 Risk analysis								
2.8.2 Decision trees								
2.8.3 Sensitivity analysis								
2.9 Game theory								
2.9.1 Two player zero sum								
2.9.2 Complex								
2.10 Network analysis								
2.11 Simulation methods								

Figure 4.1   (continued)

	Importance	Relevance	Required level of knowledge	ASW	SEP	FIP	VSS	SAT
3 <u>E D P and management information systems</u>								
3.1 Design of M I S								
3.1.1 Financial								
3.1.2 Marketing								
3.1.3 Production								
3.1.4 R & D								
3.1.5 Distribution								
3.1.6 Profit planning								
3.2 Programming and systems analysis								
3.2.1 Languages								
3.2.2 Modular programming								
3.2.3 Coding								
3.2.4 Flow charting								
3.2.5 Programming standards								
3.2.6 Systems standards								
3.2.7 Systems investigation								
3.2.8 Systems design								
3.2.9 Systems implementation								
3.2.10 Estimation of time for control								
3.3 Techniques and knowledge								
3.3.1 Multi-programming								
3.3.2 Multi-processing								
3.3.3 Time-sharing								
3.3.4 Real time systems								
3.3.5 Data requirements								
3.3.6 Data vetting								
3.3.7 Data bases								
3.3.8 File organisation								
3.3.9 File security								
3.3.10 Testing system								
3.3.11 Operating system								
3.3.12 File library handling								
3.4 Miscellaneous								
3.4.1 E D P training available								
3.4.2 E D P department organisation								
3.4.3 E D P post implementation audits								
(a) System								
(b) Installation								
3.4.4 Applications packages								
(a) I C L								
(b) Other								
3.4.5 Costing time for user departments								
3.4.6 Control of machine time								
3.4.7 Performance/cost standards for hardware								
(a) I C L								
(b) Other								

Figure 4.1   (continued)

			Importance	Relevance	Required level of knowledge	ASW	SEP	FIP	VSS	SAT
4	Human and personnel factors									
4.1	Organisation theory									
4.2	Objective assessment and MBO									
4.3	Ergonomics									
4.4	Management auditing									
4.5	Job evaluation									
4.6	Job descriptions									
4.7	Manpower planning									
4.8	Motivational theory									
4.9	Supervisory style									
4.10	Management development									
4.11	Incentive schemes									
4.12	Productivity agreements									
4.13	Industrial relations training									
4.14	Safety and health regulations									
4.15	Environmental factors									
4.16	Communication theory									

Figure 4.1 (continued)

		Importance	Relavance	Required level of knowledge	ASW	SEP	FIP	VSS	SAT
5	O & M								
5.1	Office layout								
5.2	Office environment								
5.3	Office equipment								
5.4	Printing methods								
5.5	Forms design								
5.6	Analysis and design of systems								
5.7	Work simplification								
5.8	Clerical methods analysis								
5.9	Activity sampling								
5.10	Flowcharting, procedure analysis								
5.11	Movement diagrams								
5.12	Clerical work measurement								
5.12.1	VFP								
5.12.2	CWIP								
5.12.3	GCA								
5.13	Job responsibilities								
5.14	Office organisations								
5.15	Other services								
5.15.1	Postal								
5.15.2	Telephones								
5.15.3	Cars etc								
5.16	Rent, lease or buy decisions								
5.17	Coding systems								
5.18	Metrication								

Figure 4.1 (continued)

		Importance	Relevance	Required level of knowledge	A S W	S E P	F I P	V S S	S A T
6	Financial and accounting factors								
6.1	Financial accounting								
6.1.1	Book-keeping (double entry)								
6.1.2	Taxation								
6.1.3	Investment grants								
6.1.4	Relief and development grants								
6.1.5	Capital fund raising								
6.1.6	Money market considerations								
6.1.7	Legal requirements								
6.1.8	Depreciation								
6.2	Management accounting								
6.2.1	Asset and stock valuations								
6.2.2	Management ratios								
6.2.3	Inter-firm comparisons								
6.2.4	Profit planning systems								
6.2.5	Total and marginal costing systems								
6.2.6	Cash flow calculations								
6.2.7	Credit control								
6.2.8	Contribution analysis								
6.2.9	Budget setting								
6.2.10	Budget validation								
6.2.11	Labour control								
6.2.12	Materials control								
6.2.13	Reporting procedures								
6.2.14	Methods of overhead recovery								
6.2.15	Lease, rent or buy decisions								
6.3	Capital investment appraisal								
6.3.1	Risk analysis								
6.3.2	Sensitivity analysis								
6.3.3	Present worth and IRR								
6.3.4	Decision trees								
6.4	Corporate strategy								
6.4.1	Formulation of objectives								
6.4.2	Environmental analysis								
6.4.3	Strengths and weaknesses analysis								
6.4.4	Budgets and plans								
6.4.5	Control systems								
6.4.6	Feedback and replanning systems								

Figure 4.1 (continued)

			Importance	Relevance	Required level of knowledge	ASW	SEP	FIP	VSS	SAT
7	**Marketing and distribution**									
7.1	**Marketing objectives**									
7.2	**Market planning**									
7.3	**Marketing mix**									
7.4	**Market research**									
7.5	Promotional aid evaluation									
7.5.1	Advertising									
7.5.2	Service levels									
7.5.3	Sales representation									
7.5.4	Displays and exhibits									
7.5.5	Others									
7.6	R & D evaluation									
7.7	New product pricing									
7.8	Standardisation and variety reduction									
7.9	Packaging									
7.10	Materials handling									
7.11	Storekeeping									
7.12	Methods of distribution									
7.12.1	Own vehicles									
7.12.2	Casual hire									
7.12.3	Contract services									
7.12.4	Export factors									
7.12.5	Air									
7.13	Depot location									
7.14	Routing and sequencing									
7.15	Marketing models (see 2.7)									
7.16	Stock control systems									
7.16.1	Periodic review									
7.16.2	EOQ and EBQ's									
7.16.3	Exponential smoothing									
7.16.4	Box–Jenkins									
7.16.5	EDP packages									

Figure 4.1 (continued)

			Importance	Relevance	Required level of knowledge	ASW	SEP	FIP	VSS	SAT
8	Production									
8.1	Production planning									
8.1.1	Job shop									
8.1.2	Process industry									
8.2	Plant maintenance									
8.3	Quality control									
8.4	Replacement theory									
8.5	Value analysis									
8.6	Purchasing techniques									
8.7	Stock control (see marketing)									
8.8	Standard costing (see finance)									
8.9	Productivity agreements (see personnel)									
8.10	Work study									
8.11	Quantitative techniques (see section 2)									
8.12	New plant investment (see finance)									

Figure 4.1   (continued)

5–6   Could be used in the next 9–12 months
3–4   Not very possible that any use will be made of the technique in the next year
1–2   Extremely unlikely that any use will be made of the technique during the next few years

REQUIRED LEVEL OF KNOWLEDGE.   The weighting will indicate the level of knowledge which is apparent in the department. For example:

10 = A leading expert in the field
 8 = Considerable knowledge and experience of successful use
 5 = Knowledge and some slight experience of use
 3 = Knowledge but no experience of use
 1 = No knowledge of the technique at all

DEPARTMENTAL EXPERTISE.   Against each technique and attribute, members of the department should be rated. It is inevitable that all weighting will be subjective to some degree.

It will perhaps be better for each departmental member to assess his own and then each of his colleague's apparent skills. This may produce a few psychological tremors, but should still produce a broad consensus of views, essential to the production of a reasonably accurate result.

Once the full weighting has been given comparisons should be made between the four figures quoted: importance, relevance, required level of knowledge and current expertise in the department. It should then be simple to see the areas where the department is strong and weak. Training needs can be assessed. Recruitment can also stem from the results of the audit, so that ultimately the department's skills should be matched against the company's requirements.

4:2   Performance evaluation of an MS department

There is a "congenital" difficulty in assessing the performance of any staff function. Despite the advent of management by objectives and other techniques which aid the evaluation of performance, the appraisal of staff departments especially an MS unit is exceedingly difficult.

Should monetary savings be paramount and if these are not achieved ought the department to be disbanded? Or should it be the general regard in which line managers hold MS personnel? Surely not. Or perhaps the department should put up its own evaluation of the work it performs and the rewards it achieves, and this should be used as an evaluating mechanism.

Questions of this kind need to be asked. Boards of directors should want to know if they are getting value for money from the use of MS personnel, who themselves like to know how they compare with other such personnel in other organisations.

The elements which might be used in a performance evaluation are complex, perhaps as complex as the objectives of the department—if these have been established appropriately. All the factors that go to make a successful department have to be taken into account. The following seem appropriate.

SAVINGS. In a function which exists primarily to reduce costs and increase profit, monetary savings are paramount. How these are computed and how aggressively they are followed depends upon the department, the calibre of its personnel and the company in which it operates. But savings there must be.

Savings, however, have to be related to opportunity. If no major assignments are ever given to this function, then why expect major savings?

INITIATION OF CHANGE. If adaptation to a changing environment is the only sure way an organisation will survive, then MS personnel must help in this process.

Monetary savings may not be important but change certainly will be. Does the department motivate change in attitudes, behaviour, organisations, management methods? If not it is failing.

PROFESSIONALISM. This is a dangerous word. When defined it perhaps means to be both learned and dedicated to one's job. Many MS personnel obviously are not either of these. An extremely high standard of education in MS techniques and ability to do the jobs asked of it ought to be in evidence in the department.

PLANNING AND ORGANISATION. Does the department show sound planning and organisation? Do the personnel chase around like fire brigades with all their efforts dissipated, their potential squandered on projects and areas which are probably not worth while? Like every other function in the company the MSD must be drawn into the overall profit plan.

DEPARTMENTAL OPERATIONS. As a corollary to the comments made above, MS personnel often get diverted from systems study—the cornerstone of an MSD's activities. They get bogged down with equipment appraisals, audit of minor systems or help with some unimportant training or educational activity. These are obviously blind alleys which should be avoided.

DEPARTMENTAL MANAGEMENT. Many MS managers degenerate into becoming a personal assistant for the chairman of the board or the director to whom the department reports. Consequently there could be a failing to lead and manage basic MS activities. Managers should initiate and control assignments. Their knowledge of basic techniques should be as good as that of their staff. They should act as co-ordinators in a project, carrying out crucial interviews with senior line staff who are involved.

TRAINING. Is the department well trained? Do all personnel get a fair chance to carry out all the important assignments? As well as courses, is on-the-job training given? Personnel who have specialist knowledge should be prepared to share it with their colleagues.

Brainstorming and project discussion generally are very useful in showing all members of the department the problems which are being faced in an assignment and how they are being overcome. This is an invaluable part of education in MS activities.

DETERMINATION AND ENTHUSIASM.   It is in the nature of MS activities to receive rebuffs if not abuse. The good MS man is one who fights his schemes through when there is intense opposition against them. Without a certain amount of sheer "guts" an MSD can wilt under the psychological pressures against which it has to work. Not only must there be a wish to succeed, there must be a strong positive effort to ensure success.

INITIATIVE AND CREATIVE ABILITY.   The occasions when sheer hard original thought is needed are rare. Many problems present a solution as soon as they are investigated and an experienced practitioner will know most of the answers to basic problems. But initiative and creative ability need to be shown. The department ought to be judged on this basis.

POTENTIAL FOR DEVELOPMENT.   The world of business is growing more complicated day by day. The MSD ought to have the potential to develop accordingly. The techniques of yesterday need to be dropped and new ones taken up which can be used today and tomorrow. Has the department this sort of potential?

These conglomerate factors relating to the activity of an MSD are a useful guide to discovering how effectively an MSD is operating. Of course they are not all of the same importance. Savings are obviously paramount, the remaining elements less so. It is possible to weight each factor, allocate points achieved and in this way determine the total effectiveness of the department. This still does not indicate what final standard of efficiency an MS department should achieve.

4:3   Further reading

1   P M Burman, "Productivity Services in BIC Co," *Work Study and Management Services,* June 1971

2   J Robert Gale, "Internal Management Consulting in Modern Business," *Financial Executive,* March 1970

3   J M Williams, The Application of the Concept of Productivity Services in BOC," *Work Study and Management Services,* January 1971

4   D J Foster, "Productivity Services in Electricity Distribution," *Work Study and Management Services,* July 1971

5   D B Candlin, "*O & M—a Management Service,* Pergamon, 1969

6   H P Cemach, *Work Study in the Office,* (4th edition) Maclaren, 1969

7   J A Larkin, *Work Study Theory and Practice*, McGraw Hill, 1969

8   I L O, *Introduction to Work Study*, I L O, 1969

9   C J Gardner, *The Administration of Organisation and Methods Services*, published UNO, 1969

10 Laura Tatham, *The Efficiency Expert*, Business Books, 1964

11 T B Ward, *Management Services—The Way Ahead*, ANBAR Publications, 1965

12 W Seney, *Effective use of Business Consultants*, Financial Executive of the Reserve Foundation Inc, New York, 1965

13 Dr S Hyman, *An Introduction to Management Consultancy*, Heinemann, 1962

14 G E Milward, *Lauching and Managing O & M*, Macmillan, 1965

15 R M Currie, *Work Study*, (2nd edition) Pitman, 1963

16 R Rushford, "Productivity Services Management in a Change Situation," *Work Study*, July 1971

17 H Higdon, *Business Healers*, Random House (Management Consultants), 1971

18 T P Sherman, *O & M in Local Government*, Pergamon, 1968

19 P E Randall, *Introduction to Work Study and Organisation and Methods*, Butterworth, 1969

20 J N Archer, "A New Look at CSD Management Services," *O & M Bulletin*, February 1971

Part 2

DIAGNOSIS AND
APPRAISAL TECHNIQUES

Attitude surveys

5:1 Introduction

Attitude surveys, theoretically, have always been a useful method of diagnosing company ills. Success has rarely been achieved, however, mainly because managers will only speak the truth if they know what they say will not be prejudicial to their future. To convince them that nothing detrimental will subsequently occur is difficult.

5:2 Description

Attitude surveys are a means of determining the psychological postures of management and staff which are common in the company. This is usually done by the completion of a questionnaire.

Surveys can be carried out to determine attitudes concerning the company, its management methods and general philosophy and to gain views on such factors as a new wages structure, a proposed office block or even a rescheduled car-parking scheme.

Various checklists have been drawn up to indicate company style or the dominance of a function [See B H Walley, *How to Apply Strategy in Profit Planning*, Business Books, 1971], which will show general attitude traits, but what is normally sought is extra information not easily obtainable by normal diagnostic analysis.

An attitude survey should utilise sampling techniques to carry out the analysis (with as little bias as possible).

5:3 Successful areas of application and examples

Attitude surveys can arouse strong emotions. Any senior management that asks: "What do you think of the company?" or "Are the management any good here?" is looking for trouble. The response to such questions will usually be totally negative.

Yet the key to a company's survival may be in appreciating and then changing the corporate attitudes which exist. Anyone who has tried to apply profit planning and control is usually conscious of the management attitudes which have to be changed before such an application can be successful.

A survey to try to assess such management attitudes is always useful, but dangerous. Cynicism may not be out of place, indeed it may be essential for sanity in many organisations, but to give it full rein could be disaster. Surveys, therefore, ought to have two main characteristics:

1   They should be specific as far as possible, pertaining to one element of the company's business
2   Failing this, they should be set out in such a way that they cannot be used as an all purpose vehicle for slanging everything in sight

It would be very brave of a chief executive who has held his job for a long time, to carry out a general attitude survey. Someone who has recently been appointed, however, should certainly want some information on management psychology and morale generally. An attitude survey could provide such information.

WHAT TO ASK.   The objectives of the excercise have first to be clarified. In a general attitude survey, prior, say, to changes in company style or management methodology, the following objectives may be set:

1   How bad are our communications?
2   Do our managers understand what they are doing and have faith in the company?
3   Is the company considered to be fair and to give rewards and promotion only to those who merit them?
4   Do the managers consider that we have any basic weakness in company style or management methods or major failings in one department or function in the company?
5   What is morale like?
6   What actions could improve it?

HOW TO ASK.   If the danger to avoid in an attitude survey is of management becoming overemotional about the questions they are asked, then the questionnaire ought to have the sanctity of numbers and laconic utterances imposed upon it. Questions should be capable of being answered "yes" or "no" or "agree" or "disagree," with a scale of agreement or disagreement.

If this method is used then respondents can answer appropriately but give an indication of the degree of feeling they have about the question. At the same time such a method will facilitate the collection and collation of total company feelings. It does not solve the problem of shades of opinion and the "Yes, but . . ." answers, but it helps. Anything more would encourage emotion in the survey.

Questions probably need to be asked at least twice in a different guise. Some correlation between answers can then be made to ensure that the questions are being answered truthfully.

Questions should be mixed together, so that the true objectives of the survey are at least partially hidden.

THE SURVEY. An appropriate survey is shown below. A scale of 0–100 agreement or disagreement is suggested and managers should be asked to mark both their agreement or disagreement with the questions asked and the degree to which they agree or disagree.

Anonymity is extremely important, as also is a lack of collusion among participants. The survey should take account of both these factors.

It is difficult to suggest how managers can be reassured that they will not suffer for their opinions. Only complete anonymity will improve their confidence.

100	0	100
Agree		Disagree

1 This is a great company
2 The company is well led
3 People always know what they are doing
4 We are always kept informed about what is happening
5 I feel secure here
6 My future and promotion are assured
7 The company is very conscious of the long-term effects of its policies
8 Training is taken very seriously
9 Key results recognition is a very important part of my job
10 I have complete flexibility and freedom to achieve my objectives
11 My performance is reviewed dispassionately and I know that I am rewarded according to my performance
12 All managers in the company are rewarded according to their performance
13 Delegation is an important part of company operating procedures
14 I think morale generally is very good
15 I know precisely what is expected of me
16 Good men seldom leave this company except to better themselves substantially
17 Outside recruitment is rare and only for specialists or fairly junior positions
18 Managers are required to improve their performances constantly, though fairly

19   I can always go to my senior and ask for and obtain guidance relevant to my job and the problems associated with it; it is always given quickly
20   I know what key company objectives we are all trying to achieve
21   I think the way priorities are established is logical and produces appropriate results
22   The company has sound policies and will achieve success in:
23   Production
24   Marketing
25   R & D
26   Diversification
27   Labour relations
28   Warehousing and distribution
29   Engineering
30   Administration
31   Control of our activities
32   We are better than most of our competitors in the use of techniques and expertise
33   We have no head office problem in our company
34   I am allowed to take part in strategy making
35   Managers always collaborate fully in achieving corporate objectives
36   We are not controlled too rigidly
37   Common sense and flexibility are always allowed, despite strategy and planning activities
38   I know that my company is good at management development
39   If a manager fails, he will be treated fairly but will be removed from his current responsibility
40   I am unsure of the company's long-term plans as well as its immediate problems
41   Competition if not welcome is always tackled vigorously
42   We are a marketing dominated company
43   We are a production dominated company
44   I am fully aware of the likely quantified results of the decisions I make
45   I am aware of the company's financial position and profits

5:4   Problems in the use of the techniques and conditions for success

1   There have been occasions when companies have desired attitude soundings on the lines described, and when the response has been totally unexpected. In one practical instance the clamour of complaint was so great that senior managers decided never to allow an opportunity for second-line management to express their opinions again
2   Attitude surveys are a little like Pandora's box—once open and all the troubles of the company and maybe life in general are let lose. A profit making company is not always best run by democratic means

3   Carrying out a general attitude survey will elicit responses which may not have much relevance to the good running of the company. There are obvious areas in policy making and company methodology where the interests of the company could clash with those of its managers. Managers are largely egocentric, often requiring job enrichment and facilities generally which it is not in the long-term interest of the company to give. The results of an attitude survey, taken too literally, will not always help company pro-fitability

4   The needs for anonymity and to avoid collusion have been strongly stressed already

5:5   Conclusion

Attitude surveys taken in moderation are a useful diagnostic tool, particularly for a new executive. Their dangers are obvious.

5:6   Further reading

1   W G Bennis and E H Schein, *Leadership and Motivation*, MIT Press, 1968
2   L Bernstein (editor), *Management Development*, Business Books, 1969
3   S W Gellerman, *Management by Motivation*, AMA, 1968
4   E C A Gibb, *Leadership, Selected Readings*, Penguin, 1968
5   L W Porter and E E Lawler, *Managerial Attitudes and Performance*, Irwin 1968
6   N A Rosen, *Leadership, Change and Work-Group Dynamics*, Staples, 1969
7   R E Schellenberger, *Managerial Analysis*, Irwin, 1969
8   Harold Koontz, *Appraising Managers as Managers*, McGraw Hill, 1970
9   G W Dalton and P R Lawrence, *Motivation and Control in Organisation*, Irwin-Dorsey, 1970
10   C Sofer, *Men in Mid-Career, A study of British Managers and Technical Specialists*, Cambridge, 1970
11   R W Revais, *Developing Effective Managers*, Longmans, 1968
12   Peter & Hull, *The Peter Principle: Why Things go Wrong*, Souvenir Press, 1970
13   R Likert, "Motivational Approach to Management Development," *Harvard Business Review*, July-August 1959
14   Douglas McGregor, "An Uneasy Look at Performance Appraisal," *Harvard Business Review*, May–June 1957
15   J C Robertson, "Some Hard Questions on Management Audits," *The New York Certified Accountant*, September 1971
16   B H Walley, "Efficiency Auditing," *Work Study*, February 1972

SIX

Symptoms and causes of inefficiency

6:1 Introduction

It is difficult to know where to use management services personnel and their techniques completely effectively if no appraisal is ever done to find which parts of the company are most inefficient or vulnerable to competitive challenge. An efficiency audit is an essential part of deciding where M S techniques application will achieve the greatest reward for least effort.

The need to recognise key results is stressed. The postal room may have a disproportionate number of staff to the machine shop, but is that important enough to warrant spending several man-weeks of the time of a skilled specialist there? The machine shop may yield far higher rewards for the same amount of effort.

6:2 Description

There are a variety of methods which can be used to determine the symptoms and ascertain the causes of inefficiency within an organisation.

GENERAL MEASUREMENTS. Measurement of all activities which spend or receive money is an essential first step in determining a company's efficiency. The company balance sheet is important in this respect, but scarcely gives all the detail which will pinpoint areas of inefficiency. For example, the following measurements seem the least that should be available:

1   *Total company*
     Profit
     Profit margins on all major products

Value of fixed assets
Marginal cost of production
Production capacity
Working capital
Cash flow
Debtors
Company objectives
2   *Sales*
Turnover
Market shares
Costs of selling (representatives)
Costs of advertising
Costs of administration
Profit margins on all products
Utilisation of salesmen
List of debtors and bad debts
Customer preferences
a   *Stocks*
Quantities, types held and value
Delivery/service levels
Age analysis
Costs of inventory holding
Cost of order placement
Number of orders handled
Costs of packaging, breakages, transport
and materials handling
b   *Costs of distribution*
Warehousing
Stocks
Transport
Materials handling
3   *Production*
Direct labour cost (at each production cost centre)
Indirect labour costs
Factory overhead (suitably broken down)
Labour efficiency
Factory administrative costs
Material costs
Material utilisation per cent
Material scrapped and salvaged (and causes)
Machine utilisation
Machine breakdowns
Machine change-over times
Order cycle times
Orders delivered on time/delayed

4   *Administration*
     Cost of administration
     Departmental costs
     Administrative personnel (numbers) by department
5   *Research and development*
     Cost of research and development by project
     Numbers of new products and profitable developments made
     Company profit gained from new products
     Company profit from new methods
6   *Capital expenditure*
     Assessment of return on recent investment
     Progress of projects

Measurements of this kind if they are available will help to identify areas or activities of inefficiency, potentially the most important or key results areas. Initially, therefore, it may be necessary to launch a measurement program.

Sufficient measurements should be on file, they must cover key results areas and they should be accurate enough (not too accurate) for fundamental policy decisions to be made from them. If the measurements quoted are available, it is likely that they will yield some indication of where things are going wrong in the company.

MANAGEMENT RATIOS.   By comparing two related measurements it is possible to pinpoint adverse trends. Straight measurements will not always give a satisfactory indication that some aspect of company affairs is rapidly going out of control. For example, the cost of one department or activity may be rising out of all proportion to that of another related department or activity. The use of management ratios over a period will indicate where this is happening.

GENERAL SYMPTOMS.   In each of the areas quoted there will be general symptoms which will indicate that a system, section of the company or function is failing. The symptoms would be known to local management, and fairly soon to any good consultant who investigated the company, but not necessarily to the senior management or the board of directors. Symptoms are warning signals that something is wrong which needs correction. They do not quantify what is wrong. Symptoms which might be sought are:

1   *Total company*
     Poor profit performance
     Falling sales
     Loss of competitive position
     Strikes and poor industrial relations
     Low management morale
     Declining return on investment
     Lack of objectives at all levels

2   *Sales*
Falling sales
Reducing market shares
High selling costs
Poor advertising with low response rate
Delays in order processing
Poor delivery performance
Many customer complaints

a   *Stock*
Wrong type of inventory held
Rising inventory, lowering service levels
Poor deliveries
High frequency of ordering

b   *Warehousing and distribution*
Slow handling of orders
High packaging costs
Long vehicle turn-round times

3   *Production*
Poor housekeeping
High accident rate
Poor workmanship
Inefficient material usage
Shop-floor cluttered with production
Lack of communication between sales and production
Poor deliveries
Lack of tools, raw material, labour when required
Lack of knowledge on deliveries, production rates, order position etc
Excessive overtime

4   *Administration*
High administration costs
Mistakes in all activities
Delays in processing data
Poor housekeeping
Lack of information concerning cost of company activities
Excessive overtime
Duplication of function
Dual reporting

5   *Research and development*
Failure to produce new products and methods
Personnel embroiled in intellectual arguments and barren activities

6   *Capital expenditure*
Indifference towards capital expenditure and its control
Major overruns on spending at all times

CHECKLISTS.   Checklists are one of the most effective methods of diagnosing company inefficiencies. Many experienced MS personnel consider them un-necessary. They treat each assignment as unique relying on their native genius to bring about a fitting solution to the problem being investigated. However, most people are not in the genius category and a theoretical standard of exellence will always be helpful.

METHODOLOGY. The first part of this chapter has listed the important analytic tools which can be used to indicate where the company is failing. Their use is an essential prerequisite in recognising where inefficiencies in the company are occuring. But mere recognition is insufficient, it is necessary to determine which are the important inefficiencies which have been uncovered. These must be the key results, the things which, if put right, will yield most profit for the company. It is not always easy to recognise these key factors. The following may help:

1*a*   List in order of importance the items making up the cost of sales. Determine which of these elements can be improved. Calculate the percentage improve-ment possible in each case, then list the total monetary savings.
 b   Choose the elements with the largest savings potential
 c   Decide the methods, techniques, management improvements generally, etc, which will make a substantial impact on the inefficient areas. Assess the man-weeks of effort plus the capital expenditure needed to carry out this improvement. Evaluate this effort, etc, monetarily
 d   Draw up action programs beginning with the items that appear to yield most reward for least effort. Timetable and allocate responsibilities
2*a*   List in order of importance the factors in the company, not covered in (1) that have most importance in providing current and future profit
 b   Suggest which can be improved and by what techniques—new methods, organisational change, management development etc
 c   Calculate (if possible) the profit reward likely. Determine the man-weeks of effort needed and choose the items for action programming which yield most reward for least effort

6:3   Successful areas of application and examples

Figure 6.1 suggests how the appraisal might be made.

Column 1 in the figure lists the areas which might serve as the major functional areas to be analysed.

Column 2 records the management ratios which might be used, once basic measurements are available. The ratios need to be viewed over four to five years if they are really to prove that an area, function or department is out of line with the rest of the organisation.

Column 3 suggests further analysis which may be required. The total company analysis which is listed will obviously be difficult to obtain in a hurry unless the company has already a well founded and efficient corporate planning method-ology.

Company area or cost centre	Management ratios which might be used (use last 5 years' figures)	Other analysis required	Possible failure	Remedies including the use of MS techniques	Planning and control systems required
1 Total company		Past/present company performance, past strategies. Profit outlook		Managements audit Job study – Manpower planning	Corporate strategy Profit planning
1.1 Return on investment	Gross profit/operating assets	Environmental analysis (economic, technical, product/market) (Product life cycle, vulnerability audit)	Company has not recognised environmental changes listed and not adapted accordingly	Organisation planning Use of computers	Standard costing and budgetary control
	Profit/direct and indirect personnel Fixed assets/total capital employed	Skills and competence audit Gap analysis Past and present company performance turnover, market shares, profit	Skills and competence not built up to meet competitive situation Failure to meet technological challenge	Optimisation techniques, including model making Budget validation Behavioural sciences/company style analysis Inter-firms comparisons	
1.2 Sales	Profit/sales	Cash flow analysis Organisation analysis	Company style not appropriate to company environment Aversion to change	Appropriate style and method must be determined	
1.3 Production costs	Production costs/sales Labour cost/sales		Management methodology incapable of providing framework for appropriate decisions	More capital, improved employer-employee relationships, adequate job training and management development	
1.4 Distribution and marketing costs	Distribution and marketing costs/net sales Distribution costs/net sales		Poor management Lack of good personnel policy		
1.5 Admin costs	Admin costs/net sales Admin costs/net profit	Skills audit in financial management, technology etc			
1.6 R & D	R & D costs/net sales R & D costs/net profit	Skills audit			

Figure 6.1 COMPANY APPRAISAL SHEET

Company area or cost centre	Management ratios which might be used (use last 5 years' figures)	Other analysis required	Possible failure	Remedies including the use of MS techniques	Planning and control systems required
2 Sales	Export and home sales Sales costs/net sales	Outline of current sales/marketing organisation for organisational analysis	Product mix analysis might lead to a reduction in product range	Standardisation and variety reduction	Marketing cost control
2.1 Sales and marketing	Home market sales/total market Export market sales/total market Debtors/net sales Sales promotion costs/total marketing costs/sales Area sales/total sales Area costs/area sales	Technological, product market, competitive, profit outlook analyses Analysis of competitors' strengths and weaknesses compared with own strengths and weaknesses: in pricing, production, sales promotion, distribution, product development, market knowledge, technical services, general management, current and forecast sales for next 3 years	Differential marketing (by market segment) not attempted Selling strategy failings	Management by objectives Market planning Forecasting - regression analysis Probability theory Marginal costing and contribution analysis Value analysis Profit volume analysis Market research	Sales control
2.2 Stock	Stock of finished goods/sales per day Stock-outs/calls	Age analysis of stock held Profit-stock margin analysis Service level analysis Stock-outs	Future of inventory control system Inadequate forecasting	Forecasting (exponential smoothing, Box - Jenkins etc) Computer analysis	Inventory control
2.3 Warehousing and distribution	Distribution cost/sales cost Vehicles miles/deliveries		No work measurement or incentive schemes. Lack of standard product, packages and material handling equipment	Vehicle routing, warehouse location, work measurement, materials handling surveys	Inventory control Transport control
3 Production	Total labour costs/total manufacturing costs Cost of scrap/total cost of material Weight of finished goods sent to warehouse/weight of material issued to the factory Direct labour costs/other labour costs Sales per direct operative Sales per indirect operative Standard hours of product made/clocked hours spent	Cost breakdown between product division, product groups, production organisation, product mix	Poor standards of supervision Quality control standards too high Excessive materials handling Production layout not optimised Poor machine maintenance Lack of liaison between marketing and production personnel Low output standards Lack of incentives and adequate work measurement Obsolete equipment	Methods analysis (method study) Work measurement Productivity bargaining/incentive schemes Productivity measurement Cost-reduction planning Production planning Materials handling Plant maintenance Value analysis Motion study, fatigue study Production study Operations research techniques: linear programming, queueing theory	Scrap control Quality control Production planning and control Quality control Labour control Material control

Figure 6.1 (continued)

Company area or cost centre	Management ratios which might be used (use last 5 years' figures)	Other analysis required	Possible failure	Remedies including the use of MS techniques	Planning and control systems required
4 Administration	Admin dept costs/total admin costs Admin personnel/total company personnel Actual cost/planned cost	Organisation study Personnel audit Attitude survey	Lack of clerical work measurement Poor data handling equipment Inadequate EDP expertise Systems inadequate and badly designed	Clerical work measurement Work simplification Clerical method study Standardisation of equipment Systems analysis	Credit control Budgetary control Cost control
4.1 Accounting	Trade debts/sales per day Working capital/sales	Book-keeping system investigation Cash flow analysis	Inadequate system of accounting	Standard costing and budgetary control	Cash control
4.2 Purchasing	Cost of order purchasing/value of orders placed Value of orders placed Orders received on time/orders delayed Departmental cost/cost of orders placed	Orders placed per month		Use of EBQ's Break-even points	Purchasing control
5 Research and development	R & D expenditure/sales gained or retained	Skills analysis	Inadequate control over use of R & D skills and finance Lack of ability to communicate ideas and techniques Lack of personnel of appropriate calibre	Brainstorming Risk analysis PERT Removal of all chores which prevent R & D personnel from carrying out their own function	R & D plan Budgeting control Company diversification plan
6 Capital expenditure				Forecasting techniques Decision theory, risk analysis Sensitivity analysis Probability theory	Discount cash flow

Figure 6.1 (continued)

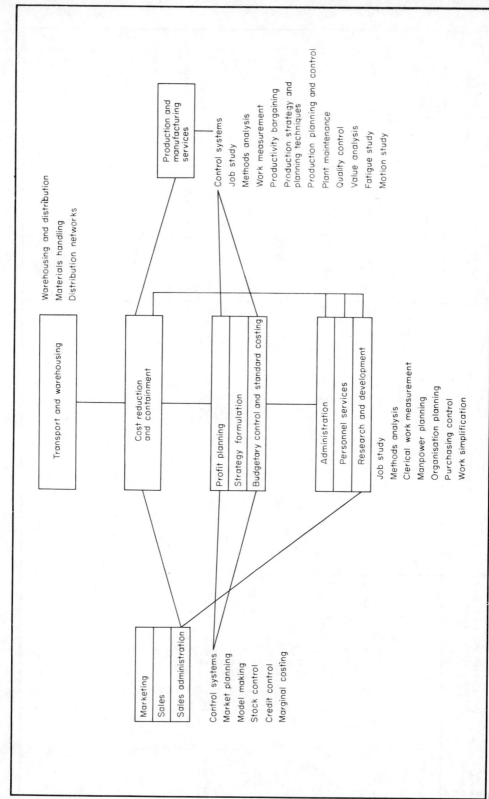

Figure 6.2 METHOD OF INVESTIGATION, APPRAISAL TECHNIQUES

Column 4 in the figure lists some of the possible failures which the analysis might show.

Column 5 shows some remedies which may be appropriate and also the management techniques which might help to eradicate the failures.

Column 6, the last, indicates various control systems which could be used to improve control over the operations and functions being analysed.

Combined with the measurements and symptoms of inefficiency previously quoted the data shown in the figure should certainly indicate where a company is inefficient and needs correction. The match between inefficiencies and corrective techniques will also be (in part) established. The approach, therefore, can be turned into an efficiency audit.

6:4 Problems in the use of the technique and conditions for success

1 The use of the approach outlined should lead to the discovery that one or more areas of the company are inefficient or are showing adverse trends. Unfortunately this could be due to management incompetence or competitive factors, which the use of management services skills will not help

2 Problem finding (which is what this section is about) may develop analytical skills of a high order. However, too much measurement and analysis can go on. The immediate correction of an outstandingly inefficient activity may, in the long run, serve the company better than to go on and on in search of problems to solve

3 As a corollary of (2) it is always possible to proceed myopically in detailed analysis, scorning the overall business environment. There is a sound reason that suggests that MS personnel should remain psychologically distant from a problem; once they become emotionally involved with it achieving an unbiased solution is practically impossible

4 Time may be of the essence and a lengthy laborious analysis is unnecessary when inefficiencies are blindingly obvious and solutions ready at hand

5 Occasionally perception and imagination and intuition will be superior to analysis, but only occasionally

6:5 Conclusion

Problem finding is as important as problem solving if one objective of MS personnel is to ensure the optimisation of resources. To achieve this aim, analysis of the order outlined in this chapter is essential.

6:6 Further reading

1 B H Walley, "A Symptoms, Diagnosis and Treatment Chart," *Work Study*, January 1965

2 S A Tucker, *Successful Managerial Control by Ratio Analysis*, McGraw Hill, 1961

3   *Efficiency Comparisons Within Large Organisations*, BIM and the Centre
     for Interfirm Comparisons, 1958
4   S R Goodman, *Techniques of Profitability Analysis*, Wiley, 1970
5   D Solomons, *Divisional Performance: Measurement and Control*, Irwin.
6   F M Eisener, *Accounting for Product Line Reporting*, Eisener.
7   K Seiler, *Introduction to Systems Cost Effectiveness*, Wiley 1968
8   H Johnson, "Company Appraisal," *The Cost Accountant*, June 1964

SEVEN

Job study

7:1 Introduction

Chapters 5 and 6 recorded how to carry out a management audit and how to search for causes of inefficiency.

To complement these two appraisal techniques, it is necessary to discuss job study. The writing of job descriptions was recorded in some detail in discussing management services personnel in Part 1, so it will be done again briefly in this chapter only to provide a rounded comment on job study.

7:2 Description

Job study is a conglomerate term given to all the factors which determine job descriptions and definitions, job evaluation (and, hence, wages payment) and job performance. This latter factor has been superseded somewhat by the various performance analyses introduced by "management by objectives," but it is still valid as an integral part of performance assessment.

JOB DESCRIPTIONS. Job descriptions are the cornerstone of any performance analysis, merit rating or more basically still, profit planning. Unless managers and other personnel are aware of their total responsibilities, their key results and major objectives, the constraints inherent in their job and the factors on which their performance will be appraised, it is unlikely that they will perform appropriately, and they will certainly suffer from frustration and lack of direction. Without adequate job descriptions, recruitment, salary/wages payment and promotion will be haphazard at best. If personnel are absent, or leave, job descriptions give some guidance to others of the work which is not being performed.

Name_____

Job title_____

Department_____

FOR PERSONNEL DEPARTMENT USE ONLY	
Job number	Job grade

Monthly / weekly staff_____

Regular day work / shift work_____

Normal hours (excluding overtime)_____

Approximate hours overtime to be worked per

week_____

Description of duties: (Describe each duty clearly, defining the tasks which make up each duty. Start with the most time-consuming duties and finish with the minor duties. State whether the holder of this job directs or supervises the work of other employees and for what duties. In the column at the left state the approximate percentage of time normally spent on each duty.)

N B   This description may be kept in the form of a diary for one working week with duties shown separately if they occur monthly, quarterly, etc.

Percentage of time

Figure 7.1   JOB INFORMATION FORM
This form should be completed by the person holding the position

The best way to obtain accurate job descriptions is to ask staff to complete forms designed for the purpose, as perhaps the example shown in Figure 7.1.

Once the initial job description has been recorded it needs to be rewritten as an acceptable record using the following principles.

The job description is a formal mechanism for translating the essential features of a job into a factual and concise format, so the key job areas can be recognised and objectives set for the job holder. The job description must show:

1   What is done—the key areas of the job

2   How it is done—what methods, skills, expertise are required

3   Why it is done—what the job is about

The record should then describe the job under the following main headings:

1   *Purpose.* Why does the job exist? For what is the job holder paid? What company objectives must the job holder help to achieve?

2   *Dimensions.* The pertinent ones of money, capital and manpower considerations should be listed

3   *Nature and scope.* The various headings which ought to be considered in this section are:

a   What organisational position has the man? To whom does he report? Which other job holders report to the same person? Does the job holder have a seat on a committee or a planning group?

b   What supporting staff respond to the job holder? Have they any grades? If so quote them. What experience have they generally?

c   What technical, managerial, behavioural and organisational skills are apparently needed to carry out the job successfully? What qualifications are needed? What experience (quote type and length of time) is desirable? How does this compare with other jobs of apparently equal status in the company?

d   What problem solving is carried out? Are intricate and intellectually demanding problems solved frequently? What creativity is necessary?

e   What is the greatest challenge in the job? What appears to be the most rewarding element?

f   What freedom of action is given to the job occupant? Is he, for example, responsible for:

i   Recruitment, selection, dismissal

ii   Capital expenditure

iii   Setting prices

iv   Changing production methods

v   Changing design and quality

vi   Changing salaries

g   What are the principal constraints in the job?

h   What are the inherent difficulties in carrying out the job?

4   *Key accountabilities.* What key accountabilities are inherent in the job, for example:

a   In setting objectives, planning, determining company policy

b   Directing the attainment of objectives—directing, organising, staffing, communicating, motivating

c   Measuring results

d   Promoting innovation

e   Developing people

JOB EVALUATION.   Job evaluation is the systematic comparison of the value of a range of jobs so that ultimately an equitable wages or salary payment scale is produced for them. In the past, job evaluation has largely been used for manual/shop-floor workers, but it is more and more being used for clerical and managerial staff.

Four different methods of job evaluation have been tried. In order of successful introduction these are as follows.

Points method.   This system has proved to be the most popular job evaluation method, particularly when shop-floor applications have been carried out.

A committee, representative of company management lists what it considers to be the job factors which can be used to evaluate any job. A points weighting is then given to each factor depending upon its relative importance.

The committee then reviews jobs which fall within the job evaluation scheme and makes recommendations about the points which should be given, for each job factor.

Usually a base wage rate for all jobs is set. Points are then allocated to individual jobs and the result added to the base rate. All jobs therefore have wages/salaries in proportion to the job evaluation points allocated to them, plus the base rate.

Current rates of pay are established by giving each point a monetary value. The wage rate = points gained × monetary value of each point plus base rate.

Grades often need to be established in order to make the points system usable. (It is usually too cumbersome to have everyone who has been evaluated on an individual pay scale.) The pay scales for the graded jobs should be compared with outside rates and an assessment made of the probability of attracting and keeping personnel with the pay evaluated for them. Grades and pay rates need to overlap so providing flexibility in making merit and long service rewards.

Factor comparison methods.   In this method main job factors are utilised to compare ten key jobs in the organisation, so that a company-wide basis for job evaluation is established. The usual main job factors taken are:

1   Education and training
2   Job skill
3   Effort
4   Responsibility
5   Working conditions

A committee is utilised to rank ten key jobs for each of the factors being considered (the jobs ought to be representative of the main work performed in the company). Individual committee members are asked to list the job which is most demanding of the factor concerned first—the job least demanding of the factor last, etc.

The committee chairman then has to reconcile the choices of individual committee members and effect a final ranking of the key jobs for the five factors listed. The total committee then allocates points to the jobs which have been ranked (and perhaps a value on each of the points given).

Once the original key jobs have been ranked all other company positions are ranked in the same way using the ten key jobs as markers or guidelines for the process.

Ranking methods (matched pairs). This is the simplest method of job evaluation commonly used. From job descriptions each member of a job evaluation committee takes the range of jobs which are done in one department and ranks them in order of importance. It is usual to rank pairs of jobs, matching and rematching pairs until the whole of the department has been ranked.

The jobs in different departments are then considered and integrated by "matching pairs."

This is a simple and useful way of establishing job grades or groups of jobs which appear to have the same importance. The allocation of pay is not as easy as with the points and job factor schemes and it is not, therefore, so valuable a method of job evaluation.

Time span of discretion. This is not strictly a job evaluation method but has some bearing on the pattern of establishing equitable wage rates. The method was first formulated by Dr Elliot Jacques in 1956 who suggested that the length of time during which a job holder could carry out his job and particularly make decisions without correction was the crucial factor in determining wage rates.

The longer the discretionary period, it was suggested, the higher the rate of pay for the job should be. Obviously this bald statement has to have many qualifications. Most senior accountants, for example, have a monthly check on their ability, etc, through monthly profit and loss accounts, yet a junior stock records clerk could go on from one stock taking operation to the next. But even so time span of discretion appears to be another useful way of looking at comparative wages payments.

JOB GRADING. Job grading can have very positive merits. It helps to define areas of responsibilities, provides a logical promotion ladder and if associated with job evaluation can be utilised to provide an equitable wages structure.

The essence of good job grading is that job descriptions have been written and a form of job evaluation carried out. If a points evaluation has been carried out it is comparatively easy to allocate a points range for each grade being considered.

MERIT RATING. Once job evaluation and perhaps job grading have been established some method of evaluating a job holder's performance is necessary.

Merit rating has largely concentrated on the unmeasurable aspects of a job holder's performance while management by objectives has added the dimension of "quantification." Objectives have to be quantified as far as possible in order for them to be evaluated in due course.

Even so merit rating still has considerable advantages and once key job factors have been chosen and an evaluation carried out, it is likely that merit rewards will be more fairly distributed than under an arbitrary scheme.

7:3   Successful areas of application and examples

JOB DESCRIPTIONS.   Job descriptions can be applied to any worker of any rank with great or small responsibilities. There are many formats which could be utilised for the purpose.

The following example shows an engineering manager's job description which details the basic functions, or objectives, to whom the job holder reports and the main duties and responsibilities of the job.

Not only must day-to-day jobs be appropriately defined, but non-routine situations need to be covered. For example, if a project is to be established to carry out an assignment then the functional members' tasks should be defined appropriately.

All the job descriptions should have one thing in common: they are attempting to lay down unambiguous responsibilities which should help to ensure that the tasks given to the job holders will be achieved.

JOB DESCRIPTION

Engineering manager
Position: Section head, development engineering
Department: Mechanical engineering department

Basic function: To direct and co-ordinate the design and development and engineering of a major part of a division's present and future product lines ensuring that the products are suitable to manufacture and competitive technically as well as in respect of quality and price.

Reports to: chief engineer

Duties and responsibilities: Supervises a large group or two or more smaller groups of engineering and related personnel in the design, development and engineering of a major part of a division's present and future product lines.

Initiates designs from specifications and general layouts agreed by the chief engineer. Guides and co-ordinates subordinates in detail design, development and engineering required to achieve the objectives, which may include the technical and cost improvement of existing products and the development of future products to meet known or estimated market requirements.

Discusses periodically design in progress with senior production engineers to enhance the product's suitability for manufacture.

Directs the preparation and issue of technical information concerning the products to manufacturers and customers as necessary.

Represents the division in committees set up for the exchange of technical information.

Contacts senior customer engineers to discuss specific technical problems, as necessary.

JOB EVALUATION. A fairly frequently used list of job factors and an appropriate points weighting is:

		POINTS ALLOCATION
Education and training		
1	Qualification needed for the job	30
2	Mental development and maturity	15
3	Experience in the job	20
4	Previous experience necessary	20
5	Training experience; time necessary	15
Job skill		
6	Job knowledge	15
7	Accuracy	12
8	Ingenuity	7
9	Imagination	12
10	Judgement	10
11	Intelligence	15
12	Resourcefulness	9
13	Ability to do detailed work	10
14	Social acceptability	10
Effort		
15	Mental effort	8
16	Mental application	8
17	Concentration	8
18	Visual application	8
19	Fatigue due to mental effort	12
20	Fatigue due to visual effort	12
21	Nervous strain	12
22	Monotony of work	12
Responsibility		
23	Responsibility for equipment	15
24	Responsibility for work of others	25
25	General supervision	15
26	Accuracy in counting or weighing	6

27	Spoilage of materials	15
28	Protection of materials	12
29	Co-operation with others	12

Working conditions

30	Hazards	7
31	Exposure to health hazards	8
32	Dirty working conditions	10
33	Disagreeable environment	10

The same list is often used in the job evaluation of administrative and managerial staff. Against each factor a brief description of the same factor in the job being evaluated would be given. A points rating would then be calculated.

MERIT RATING.   Figure 7.2 shows a typical staff approval or merit rating sheet of the kind which are recorded annually ready for a counselling session with the job holder.

7:4   Problems in the use of the techniques and conditions for success

1   Results of job grading and evaluation have not always been entirely favourable. Some unions, for example, have used such schemes to force all round increases in wages. Many companies have found that a job grading scheme has limited the amount of merit payment which can be given to a worker of above average ability. Thus management has lost much of its wage payment flexibility

2   Job evaluation is not concerned with the actual person or people employed. It takes no account of speed at which a job is performed or the overall efficiency with which it is being tackled. Job evaluation should take away all legitimate complaints that one job is being paid more than another even though the latter job intrinsically deserves more

3   The importance of using joint consultative machinery is stressed. A fair scheme must always be recognised as such, otherwise there will be constant carping from personnel being evaluated

4   Job evaluation is not an easy technique to implement. When first applied, it usually uncovers many anomalies in a company's wages and salary structure. Jobs which for decades have been thought to be important and consequently have been well paid are suddenly demoted in the pay scale. This will inevitably bring resentment. The introduction of job evaluation must be handled very carefully; usually no job should suffer or its pay decline until it changes hands

5   The job evaluation system ought to be tailored to meet the needs of the organisation. All companies differ, and to use the same weighting as that developed in another organisation without considerable investigation would be totally wrong

6   The danger that job evaluation committees tend to average up all job

Location	Date of birth	Date of starting	Name and initials	Grade
Department			Position	

JOB KNOWLEDGE

A	Exceptional range and depth of knowledge
B	Sound knowledge of function
C	Good knowledge. Needs occasional help
D	Fair knowledge. Still some gaps
E	Has a lot to learn about the job

EFFECTIVE OUTPUT

A	Outstanding in the amount of work he does
B	Gets through a great deal of work
C	Output satisfactory
D	Does rather less than expected
E	Output regularly insufficient

ACCEPTANCE OF RESPONSIBILITY

A	Seeks additional responsibility. No supervision required
B	Accepts obligations. Minimum supervision required
C	Requires only general supervision
D	Unsure of himself. Needs frequent supervision
E	Avoids responsibility. Needs constant supervision

ANALYTICAL ABILITY

A	Can solve original problems. Keeps to essentials
B	Picks out relevant details. Reaches correct solution
C	Generally sound. Sometimes led astray
D	Adequate analysis of simple problems only
E	Tends to make unwise decisions

CO-OPERATION

A	Goes out of his way to be helpful
B	Fits in well with group
C	Generally works well with group
D	Co-operates if given a lead. Sometimes awkward
E	Prefers to get through single handed

RELIABILITY AND ACCURACY

A	Very accurate and completely reliable
B	Makes few mistakes and seldom forgets
C	As accurate as most. Reliable on the whole
D	Makes a few mistakes. Requires supervision
E	Tends to be inaccurate. Needs frequent attention

INITIATIVE

A	Quick to seize opportunities and develop them
B	Resourceful in most situations
C	Generally decisive. Sometimes needs guidance
D	Slow to act without conformation
E	Routine minded. Will not act on own initiative

ORGANISING ABILITY

A	An extremely able organiser
B	Good organising ability. Can plan ahead well
C	Efficient in normal circumstances
D	Not a very good organiser on the whole
E	Sometimes gets in a muddle. Hold-ups occur

OVERALL RATING OF EFFECTIVENESS IN PRESENT JOB

To be completed by departmental manager

Barely adequate	Adequate	Average	Very good	Outstanding

Figure 7.2 STAFF APPRAISAL

PERSONNEL DEPARTMENT

FURTHER COMMENT—Please complete in all cases. Consider health, courses undertaken during year, new qualifications and anything of significance not mentioned overleaf. Highlight strength(s) and weakness(es)

Action taken

RECOMMENDED ACTION—What action is proposed in view of strength(s) and weakness(es) disclosed above? Consider training, transfer and promotion

POTENTIAL—How do you rate the employee's future potential?

POTENTIAL CODE

FP	Has now reached full potential
P1	Could do a job one grade higher than his present one
P2	Could do a job two grades higher than his present one
CP	Considerable potential. Should eventually reach senior management level
NP	Has not the capacity to do his present job adequately

First assessor	Second assessor	Interviewed by	Date of interview
Date	Date		

Figure 7.2 (continued)

points must certainly be considered and guarded against. Many committees try to avoid this natural tendency by producing a high, low and mean job for each job element and then comparing the job under discussion. This helps to avoid any serious over or under allocation of points

7 Pay scales need to be flexible and also comparable with outside wage rates. Because a job evaluation system suggests £X a week for a job, it should not be rigorously applied if £$X+5$ is the going outside rate. A rigid adherence to the rated pay scales could lead to disaster. In the long run, considerations of the outside pay scales are very necessary

8 Job grading suggests inflexibility, a firm edge round every job; the introduction of hard unbreakable lines of command. Obviously this should not be introduced except where the advantages will be considerable

9 Some companies have introduced job grading without stating upper and lower limits of payment for each grade. This seems a self-defeating operation if the mystery of who is paid for what remains

10 Flexibility can be ensured by limiting the number of grades. Technical grades can be introduced to accommodate specialist staff

11 The problems arising from merit rating are largely those which would be solved if greater quantification of objectives were introduced

The job factors quoted on the staff appraisal sheet are annually given the same points rating. There seems no good reason why this should be so

12 Managers will still tend to average out performance, giving ratings in the middle range

13 Any scheme, even though strictly formalised, will not prevent a superior from praising or penalising a job holder who does not deserve praise or blame

14 Managers may still assess too superficially staff they scarcely know and will perhaps tend to overrate their own staff. Much will depend upon the analytical and objective appreciation of merit which managers can muster

15 Various objections which can be made about management by objectives are stated in Chapter 39

7:5 Conclusion

Job study has been recorded in some detail because the elements—job description, job evaluation, etc—are still not fully appreciated in some organisations and only very badly applied in many others. Yet, appropriately, job study can have a very potent effect in improving morale and organisational efficiency generally.

7:6 Further reading

1 *Job Evaluation*, BIM Management Publications, 1969
2 C Berenson and H O Ruhnke, "*Job Descriptions—How to Write and Use Them*," *Personnel Journal*
3 T H Boydell, *A Guide to Job Analysis*, BACIE, 1969

4   H E Roff and T E Watson, *Job Analysis*, Institute of Personnel Managers, 1961

5   Elliot Jacques, *The Measurement of Responsibility*, Tavistock Publications, 1961

6   *Job Evaluation*, ILO, 1958

7   *Job Evaluation and Merit Rating*, The Trades Union Congress, 1956

8   *Merit Rating—a Practical Guide*, BIM, 1960

9   *Job Evaluation—a Practical Guide*, BIM, 1961

10   M T Akalin and M Z Hassan, *"How Successful is Job Evaluation?"* *Industrial Engineering*, March 1971

EIGHT

Methods analysis

8:1 Introduction

Methods study or methods analysis first originated in the work study field where the following definition was coined: "Methods study is a systematic process of recording and critically analysing a method of carrying out an operation with the object of devising and implementing a better method." Often other, more esoteric, terms have been used for the same function—procedure study, functional analysis, systems study. But in the main, methods analysis or methods study is the usual term used.

8:2 Description

The approaches to methods analysis and work simplification are largely similar. Work simplification is dealt with separately (Chapter 44) mainly because its application should be, largely, by non-managerial services personnel. But as will be explained in this chapter, methods analysis can also be applied by line managers and other non-MS personnel. If the discipline is learnt and applied appropriately a cornerstone for cost reduction and profit improvement will have been gained. The usual way methods analysis is described is by using the six words: choose, record, examine, develop, install and maintain. These are the canons of method study law, long used by most MS practitioners.

CHOOSE. This word is an indication that a choice is possible (for many MSDs it is not, of course). The necessity to recognise key results has been strongly stressed throughout the chapters devoted to analysing the role of MSDs. This is really what "choice" should be about.

RECORD. Appropriate recording techniques are an essential element in methods analysis. Some practitioners tend to record badly or not at all. This is a crucial mistake. Analysis is impossible without accurate initial data, appropriately recorded.

It is not sufficient to merely record; quantification is perhaps more important still. Recording in some or all of the following ways will be necessary:

Daily log sheets. Personnel being investigated are asked to fill in a log sheet, recording activities carried out, number of documents handled, time taken, interruptions etc.

Flow process charting. A pre-printed form similar to the one shown in Figure 8.1 is used to record operations by symbols. A brief description of the operations is also made.

The use of symbols for inspection, storage, delay, etc, have been in use for a long time. They enable a practitioner to see quickly anomalies and weaknesses.

It has been the practice to count the recorded symbols in an original system or method and then again in a revised version. If there is a significant decrease in operations, for example, the new system is considered to be superior to the old. This activity may certainly be misleading as an operational symbol could be of an indeterminate time. A reduction of 50 per cent in symbols could mean no reduction in total time spent on the system.

System or department	Procedure for Order receipt and entry
Sales dept	
Chart No 1	

Ⓒ Clerical operation	□ Inspecting for quantity operation	Elimination	What? — Is
Ⓣ Typing operation	◇ Inspecting for quality operation		
Ⓜ Machine operation	D Temporary storage operation	Combination	How? Who? — Could — Why?
⇨ Transport operation	▽ Permanent storage operation	Change of sequence	Where? When? — Should

Operation Number	Operation Symbol	Description of operation (or step)	Quantity	Time	Distance (metres)
1	O	Accept orders from the mail	41	–	–
2	O	Stamp order number on each order	41	0.05	–
3	O	Translate into company terminology using translation form	41	1.2	–
4	→	Orders/translation sent to typists	41	–	20

Figure 8.1 METHODS ANALYSIS—UNIT DOCUMENT

Flow diagrams, string diagrams, and work movement charts are all aimed at indicating work flow. A scaled drawing is made of the work area being invest-igated and work flows then charted. String is sometimes used as an indicator of work progress.

Such diagrams can be used for work flow on the shop-floor as well as in an office. The completed diagram will often indicate excess materials movement, bottlenecks, and key work stations which may need increased manning at certain times of day. (See Figure 8.2.)

Document flow charts are often used in systems study. Wall boards are utilised on which documents used on a system are pinned. Normally the docu-ments are completed as they would be during the operation of the system.

Work distribution charts can be utilised to ascertain which person or group carries out which activity in a total system.

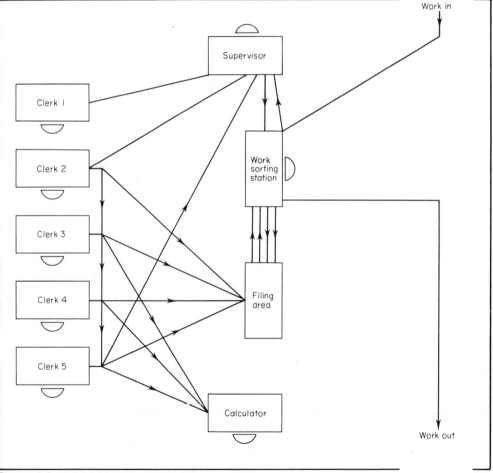

Figure 8.2 PROCEDURE ANALYSIS
Simple string diagram showing work flow

Multiple activity charts.   This type of recording chart is often used in machine activities where it appears necessary to record the activities performed by two or more operatives. The activities are timescaled and shown side by side.

Micromotion.   A film is made of the operation and is critically examined and a simultaneous motion chart is drawn. The chart makes use of therbligs or job element symbols, which were first suggested by Gilbreth, the work-study pioneer —"therblig" is his name spelt backwards (almost).

The object of the chart is to relate the therbligs to time standards and is particularly useful where fine analysis of motion patterns is required.

The therbligs cover the following operations: search, find, select, grasp, hold, transport, load, position, assemble, use, dissemble, inspect, pre-position, release load, transport empty, rest for overcoming fatigue, unavoidable delay, avoidable delay, plan, etc.

Chronocyclograph.   In this technique lights are attached to an operator's hand and switched on, while a plate camera is used to record an operational cycle. In this way the motion patterns of an operative can be traced and motion improvements carried out.

Functional breakdown.   The weakness of most recording systems is that like functions are not shown together. In consequence systems and methods are often tidied up but rarely improved radically. If similar functions are shown together and their logical connection emphasised, it is likely that a much better method or system will emerge.

EXAMINE.   This part of method analysis is often referred to as critical analysis. "Critical" refers to the detailed questioning which takes place. The use of checklists (examples of which are quoted throughout the book) seem mandatory.

As many improvement ideas as possible should be generated and brainstorming is a useful technique by which this can be done.

The essential factor in "examine" is that a disciplined approach is crucial, otherwise vital parts of the recorded method will be glossed over. A critical examination sheet similar to the one shown in Figure 8.3 is necessary. Purpose, place, sequence, people performing tasks and resources provided need to be discussed under the headings shown. Alternatives ought to be recorded and those which need to be developed should be stated.

DEVELOP.   This, the fourth stage, is usually quoted in the methods analysis procedure. It could equally be called "finding the best solution" or "devising a new method."

There are no set rules or patterns which can be utilised in carrying out the inductive leap between examine and develop. The "solution" is often dependent upon the calibre, experience, and knowledge of the investigator.

The use of techniques quoted in this book is often beneficial but some other guidance may be necessary as follows:

1   Was the problem solved? The original problem should have been solved. If not, why was this impossible? If a partial solution only has been devised,

Job _____

Department _____

Description of element _____

Reference number _____ Page _____ of _____ Date ___/___/19___

	The present facts	Alternatives	Selected alternative for development
Purpose – WHAT is achieved?	IS IT NECESSARY? Yes No If YES – why?	What ELSE could be done?	What SHOULD be done?
Place – WHERE is it done?	WHY THERE? Advantages Disadvantages	Where ELSE could it be done? A D	Where SHOULD it be done?
Sequence – WHEN is it done?	WHY THEN? A D	When ELSE could it be done? A D	When SHOULD it be done?
Person – WHO does it?	WHY THAT PERSON? A D	Who ELSE could do it? A D	Who SHOULD do it?
Means – HOW is it done?	WHY THAT WAY? A D	How ELSE could it be done? A D	How SHOULD it be done?
NOTES			

Figure 8.3 METHODS ANALYSIS – CRITICAL EXAMINATION SHEET

the practitioner should explain what conditions and constraints have prevented a total solution

2   Full co-operation by line management is necessary in devising any new solution. They will need to help install it, so should have had a large say in its development

3   Time, cost, accuracy and control. These four factors are the kernel of any method or system

a   *Time.*   Time is often the key element. Is there any way in which the time taken to do the job can be reduced? How much time has been cut from the original method?

b   *Cost.*   How much cost reduction has there been? Could more have been done, if so how? Has a time/cost table been made? (In systems study this could be established under the following headings: day, the time taken to process documentation, the system, labour cost weekly, machine cost weekly)

c   *Accuracy.*   A predetermined accuracy level should be established. Often systems accuracy, quality control standards, grading tolerances, etc, are set at levels which are far too high for the function being performed. Accuracy can be bought at too high a price

d   *Control.*   Is control over the new method effective? Will the proposed savings really be made? Will installation go as planned?

e   *Environmental and job duty factors.*   Have all environmental and job duty factors been taken into account? Have all psychological and physiological problems been considered?

f   *Simulation.*   Have the new methods or systems been simulated in any way to ensure that they will work successfully once they are introduced?

INSTALL AND MAINTAIN.   Selling the new method is an important factor in achieving success. The basis of the sale should be to appeal to the self interest of the person buying the new method or system.

Presentation is nearly as important. A simple, well documented, easily understood solution should be made. Though most of the details in the presentation should have been discussed and as far as possible agreed with the line manager or supervisor concerned during the inspection.

Once agreed, installation should be made by a well controlled timetable with full exploitation of all available resources.

Training is an essential prerequisite to installing a better method or system. Operatives, managers, and supervisors all need to be trained in the degree and depth which will ensure installation success.

If necessary a pilot scheme should be started. If this succeeds, confidence will be gained so that full implementation can proceed.

Control can take many forms—overall cost control, labour control, output control, quality control. The controls should be such that deterioration from a predetermined standard can easily be seen by the manager controlling the personnel operating the new method or system.

8:3 Successful areas of application and examples

Any investigation tends to use methods analysis to some degree. The logic of the approach is always relevant. An example of a specific area of application is unnecessary.

8:4 Problems in the use of the techniques and conditions for success

Methods study by connotation is a method for investigation and improving systems and operations carried out by professional methods study personnel. This has certainly been true in the past and work study and O & M personnel have adopted methods analysis as their own major technique. But there seems no reason why non-MS personnel should not apply methods analysis with as much success as anyone. Though one factor must be taken into account: experience. The MS professional should have a deep knowledge of systems and methods and should quickly be able to pinpoint inefficiencies and weaknesses. He should be able to bridge the gap between examine and develop, by intuition, skill and judgement. He will know short cuts and standard problem solving techniques, indeed perhaps he will be able to apply standard solutions to problems. The work simplification approach will often produce minor (though important) methods and systems changes. Often with his knowledge of organisational precepts and business activities generally, a management services man will make radical, perhaps revolutionary, proposals. Work simplification techniques applied by line personnel will rarely produce such changes.

Work measurement is an important element in any methods analysis. One of the most powerful reasons why a new system or method should be adopted is because it will save time or labour. This can only finally be proved by work measurement. Correct manning strengths must somehow be established. Comparative costs have to be worked out.

It is rare, therefore, for methods analysis to be carried out without some work measurement being done at the same time. This tips the scales slightly against the use of methods analysis by non-MS personnel.

Methods analysis is a significant tool in the fight for profit improvement, but it will never solve problems that are not right for methods solutions. Organisational deficiencies, lack of good management and training often masquerade as methods problems and practitioners can spend many weary man-weeks working on methods solutions only to have the problem remain as formidable as ever.

All the recording techniques quoted earlier are useful in setting out what is happening in a system or in a shop-floor activity. Any recording mechanism which appears to help in deciding where improvements can be made ought to be used, no matter how unsophisticated. The author has long considered that a blackboard and chalk should be part of the standard furniture of any manager's office. Narrative recording should not be ignored if this too seems to help. It is always helpful to give a copy of the recorded situation to the line manager who is responsible for it and ask that the record's accuracy is confirmed. Job descriptions, activity lists and procedure manuals should all be used to determine what is happening.

Too much time, money and effort can be spent on finding the best solution to a problem. Extravagant use of company resources to achieve the last penny from a new system or method is completely wasted. If 90 per cent of all possible savings can be achieved quickly then an investigating team should be satisfied. The best solution this year may not be the best one next year when conditions may have changed completely.

Business skill and knowledge of how the company operates are still vital. Methods analysis alone for example would scarcely result in budgetary control and standard costing being devised for company cost control purposes, without some prior knowledge of this technique.

8:5　Conclusion

Methods analysis is one of the more important techniques in reducing costs and improving efficiency and productivity. It should be the stock-in-trade of every MS practitioner. Complete success will never be achieved, however, without considerable knowledge of business and cost reduction techniques.

Methods analysis might be the application of common sense in problem solving, but this is a clear case when common sense is not enough. Knowledge, too, is vital.

8:6　Further reading

1　A Fields, *Method Study*, Cassell, 1969
2　J O'Shaugnessy, *Analysing and Controlling Business Procedures*, Cassell, 1968
3　T J Schriber, *Fundamentals of Flow Charting*, Wiley, 1969
4　M E Spear, *Practical Charting Techniques*, McGraw Hill, 1968
5　N Chapin, *Flow Charts*, Auerbach, 1971
6　M V Farina, *Flow Charting*, Prentice Hall, 1970
7　O Gilbert, *A Manager's Guide to Work Study*, Cassell, 1970
8　A Rae, *Work Study—a Practical Primer*, Hamlyn, 1969
9　R M Currie, *Work Study*, Pitman for BIM, 2nd edition, 1963
10　A P M Purdon, *A New Approach with Method Study*, Work Study and Management Services, October 1971

Part 3

MEASUREMENT TECHNIQUES

Work measurement

9:1 Introduction

Work measurement of machine and other factory operatives was one of the cornerstones of modern management techniques. The man with the stopwatch and data board has long been a common sight on most shop-floors. Regrettably, however, work measurement has often failed to achieve any substantial improvement in productivity. (The recent vogue for productivity agreements as an alternative helps to prove this.)

At the same time clerical work measurement is being pursued more vigorously now than at any time in its history. The reasons for this apparent ambiguity will be discussed throughout Part 3.

9:2 Description

Work measurement has been defined as the systematic determination of an appropriate time for a defined task to be completed by a specific method.

The reasons why work measurement needs to be applied are largely as follows.

Manning standards need to be ascertained for either an existing department doing accepted jobs or for new work of any kind and also for general staff control purposes.

Different methods for carrying out the same job need to be compared so that members of staff, machines and their total cost can be evaluated. Similarly when new methods are introduced work measurement will help to measure improvements in performance.

Work measurement will help to control output and work loads so permitting effective planning. Output when ascertained can highlight poor operator performance, bottlenecks and ineffective work distribution. It will aid the matching of the man/machine capacity with the work to be performed. Peak-loading, panic overtime and production delays should be uncovered and eventually eliminated by work measurement.

Work measurement should be a technique closely involved in cost reduction planning and the making of man-power budgets. A work measurement assignment might be carried out as follows:

1   Define the best method of carrying out the job being studied. This, regrettably, is not very often done. It infers that method study should be a precursor to work measurement

2   Decide the method of work measurement to be used. This is more important in clerical work measurement than in shop-floor activities. The method must match the situation. The rule to follow is to apply the simplest method which will give the requisite control required

3   Plan the operation. Decide which jobs need to be measured. Lay down an appropriate timetable and inform all concerned (management and staff) of what is going to happen. A talk describing the operation could well be useful. (The behavioural situation will need to be considered extremely carefully.) The best advice to offer is to be as honest as possible

4   For each job which has to be measured, a breakdown into appropriate elements is required. An element is a part of the total job which can be measured as a part separate from the whole. Elements were first formulated by Gilbreth (one of the pioneers of this subject). He devised an element category (reach, grasp, lift, etc) which is still useful today. Elements will need to be classified, perhaps as follows:

a   Repetitive elements—those which occur repetitively during the course of several job cycles

b   Random elements—those which occur randomly during the course of several job cycles

c   Constant elements—those which are constant in the time taken to do them, no matter how long the cycle takes to complete

d   Variable elements—the opposite of constant

e   Manual and machine—it is important to distinguish the kind of elements

f   Constraint element—one which largely determines the time which the job cycle takes to complete

g   Foreign element—one which is unnecessary in the job cycle. A job cycle is a sequence which will produce the unit of output being studied

5   Carry out the study. The study will be concerned with two factors:

a   The rate of working. It is of little value measuring the output of personnel who are only working at half pace. The problem lies in determining what rate of working is actually being achieved

b   Time taken. This is usually an easy task of reading element completion times from a clock or watch. Numerous observations are taken (perhaps up to two weeks continuous activity) and the results eventually averaged.

The various element times are added together and an operational time results. To obtain a "normal" time for the operation, it is necessary to relate the observed time with the observed rating and usually a simple sum is used:

$$\frac{\text{Observed time} \times \text{observed rating}}{\text{Desired level}}$$

The study will not be complete until various allowances have been added to the normal time. These are usually concerned with fatigue (energy output) posture, motions, personal needs and general environmental conditions. The harder the job, the longer fatigue or relaxation allowances need to be.

Even simple typing jobs need personal and relaxation time allowances and usually up to 10 per cent of total time is given for such activities.

A final allowed time is calculated and this is presented to the personnel concerned or their representatives. Negotiations about the times are then usually undertaken. This can be a time-taking and frustrating activity and the whole basis of the study may be undermined during such negotiations. Even when the times have been accepted, negotiation is still not at an end, as usually a bonus scheme has to be agreed.

Several methods of bonus payments have been devised and to appreciate the various types, some comment concerning "earned minutes" is appropriate.

Usually either a 60/80 or a 100 scheme is used. In the 60/80 system standard output is based on 60 minutes. If the standard output is a 1000 products per 60 minutes any addition to 1000 products processed during 60 minutes is calculated for bonus payment. Standard output rates should be so set that 80 minutes of work should normally be earned by an operative in an hour (hence the 60/80 scheme).

		Date									
Department		Operation			Number						
					Number	of	sheets				
Part number	Operator	Machine number			Analyst						
Element		Rating	Readings								Extension
			1	2	3	4	5	6	7	8	
Allowances	Personnel		Skill:		Approved						
	Fatigue					Foreman					
	Delay		Effort:								
	Tools					Signed (analyst)					

Figure 9.1   TIME STUDY OBSERVATION SHEET

Where a 100 scheme is utilised, the standard is 100 and operatives should normally earn 133. If many operatives normally earn above 80 or 133, then the scheme is suspect.

Bonus payments are based on minutes or points earned above standard and negotiation centres on the money to be paid for these minutes or points. Many companies operate a straight-line payment method—that is, bonus is paid in proportion to minutes or points earned.

In other organisations stepped payments are used—that is, once certain output levels have been reached higher bonus per piece or product is given. This is not unrealistic. Operatives should be motivated to achieve outputs where the higher bonus is earned. (See Figure 9.1.)

POINTS WHICH DETERMINE THE USE OF A WORK MEASUREMENT METHOD. The method ought to be a simple one readily understandable by all staff.

The ability to apply the techniques well is equally important. An unsophisticated technique applied well is far better than a complicated one applied badly. Work measurement operatives need to be extremely well trained. There will be enough discussion about the results without disputing the application of the techniques concerned.

As far as possible, negotiable situations should be avoided. Direct time study will always be subject to some discussion. If union negotiators agree to element-times of a predetermined motion–time system, the areas for quibble will be much reduced. In this respect therefore, PMTS systems are to be preferred.

Environmental conditions should be taken into account—noise, dirt, depressive conditions, etc. Other conditions concerning the determination of the use of work measurement systems are quoted later. The more common methods of work measurement particularly clerical work measurement are listed in Figure 9.2

9:3   Successful areas of application and examples

CLERICAL WORK MEASUREMENT. The increasing interest shown in clerical work measurement has been largely because of the need to reduce or even contain administrative overheads. Certainly the advent of computers has so far failed in this task and as another possible method of control, clerical work measurement has increasing vogue.

Senior management may be jumping onto another bandwagon in the same way that they rode computers for a while, making the mistake of ignoring all the other O & M techniques, such as clerical method study, work simplification, etc, which could have an even greater effect on administrative costs.

Despite the problems of introducing clerical work study, which are listed later, all evidence points to the fact that most clerical activities are just as susceptible to work measurement as are shop-floor jobs.

Type	Self-recording	Activity sampling	Direct time study	Pre-determined motion time studies	Analytical estimating	Corporate estimating	Work scheduling
1 Brief description	Records of output are maintained by the staff showing total tasks performed and time taken to perform them	A technique of work measurement which uses a large number of observations taken over a long period essentially at random intervals. Each observation records what is happening at the precise moment in time that it occurs. System operates on the basis of law of probability	A method whereby the rate of work and the actual time spent carrying out the work is recorded. Actual time is usually determined by using a stop-watch	A method in which predetermined times are used to build-up total times for carrying out job elements	A method of work measurement based on the use of knowledge of past practical experience	A method in which required times are found by comparing the work content of a job being timed with others which have been previously carefully determined	Method of work control based on issuing work to staff in controlled batches. Records of average product times are taken and used for control purposes
2 Applicability	Clerical activities generally	Any area of job activity which needs broad time study, machine usage, job activity, etc	Either clerical or manual operations; but particularly where elements can be devised and where there is a large amount of repetition	Both manual and clerical activities where a sound definition and description of work methods is possible			General clerical activities
3 Advantages	Useful at the beginning of a clerical measurement assignment when an assessment of work loading and bottlenecks is required. It is useful also in confirming job duties and responsibilities	Can quickly give an indication of the effectiveness of the work distributed and the incidence of idle time etc. Does not need trained observers	Simple and easy to teach operatives to carry out the study. Can be understood clearly by job operatives	Low cost of application. Consistency between analysts and areas of application. Maximum ability to transfer data between job areas			Provides a valuable method of control for supervision
4 Disadvantages	Personnel will tend to distort the situation by amendments to times, duties and responsibilities but over a period the situation tends to average out	Merely records what is happening now, not what could or should really happen	Arguments concerning accuracy of rating and time studies with union representatives nearly inevitable	Elemental times of extreme accuracy are used. Manual jobs need to be both limited and well defined			Basis of times is not determined scientifically

Figure 9.2 TYPES OF WORK MEASUREMENT SYSTEM

Type	Self-recording	Activity sampling	Direct time study	Pre-determined motion time studies	Analytical estimating	Corporate estimating	Work scheduling
				1 Simplified predetermined motion time studies This is a simplified version of PMTS achieved by reducing many of the variables in the original method			
5 Types – use		1 Rated activity sampling uses the technique set out above but a rating factor is applied to the observations to enable times at a defined rate to be calculated		2 Basic work data This is a development of PMTS in which minor elements of work are used to build up times for major elements Used mainly for maintenance operations 3 Master clerical duties This is a method based on the Birn Organisation 4 Clerical milliminute Data (Clerical MM) Devised by PA Consultants 5 Clerical work data Developed by BR		1 Universal maintenance standards (Maynards) are similar	

Figure 9.2 (continued)

Any system of clerical work measurement, however, has to be successful in coping with the fundamentals of clerical activities:

1   *The variable nature of the duties performed.*   For example, the incidence of queries or non-routine elements in even the most routine clerical jobs are often quite large
2   *The quality of the finished product.*   Service given to customers by a sales correspondence clerk is scarcely quantifiable in a broad sense. Yet a vital factor in work measurement is that the products produced are to an acceptable standard
3   *The interrelation of the activities.*   Functions and departmental interrelation may inhibit the establishment of job duties and responsibilities which can be easily measured and controlled
4   *Discretion in clerical activities.*   This is often much higher in clerical duties than in shop-floor situations. Machine settings are standard and quantified. Credit control activities may be subject to rules concerning credit limits, but there must always be a certain amount of discretion left to the clerk concerned
5   *Defining final output.*   The output of a purchasing clerk may be orders handled. But must orders always be of the same value? Is it possible for all orders always to have the same amount of search time for suppliers and negotiations for price, spent upon them. Surely not
6   *Element breakdown.*   In most clerical jobs breaking down a total activity into elements is extremely difficult. Whilst this may be possible for say a stock recording clerk, an accountant's duties may not be so easily defined

These are valid points which need to be taken into account when choosing the type of work measurement method to be used and when applying it. They still do not invalidate the application of CWM.

To define the objectives of applying CWM is important. The obvious answer may be to reduce clerical costs, but is this enough? Is a fairly vigorous cost reduction campaign in operation or is merely a chance being pursued to relate volume of work with personnel available? Perhaps persistent backlogs or overtime need to be eliminated? More important still, is CWM to be introduced as part of a total job evaluation, merit rating and work measurement activity?

How often is reporting on clerical output performance required? What limits on the degree of accuracy are anticipated? How fine must control be? What use will be made of the data produced by budgetary control—costing of specific operations so as to determine which parts of the organisation are most profitable? How will reports be made? By individual, section, department or any other grouping. Is a bonus system to be introduced at the same time? Is any kind of payment system to be related to the CWM control?

The answer to these questions and the clerical work involved should largely determine what method of measurement will be used.

TYPES OF CLERICAL WORK MEASUREMENT. Three clerical work measurement techniques often applied in the UK are clerical work improvement (CWI), group capacity assessment (GCA) and variable factor programming (VFP). Each is sponsored by a firm of consultants:

CWI: W D Scott & Co Ltd
GCA: Arthur Young & Co Ltd and Lockyer & Partners
VFP: Wofac Corporation

A brief outline of each method follows.

Clerical work improvements (CWI). This method is based on predetermined time standards originated by Paul B Mulligan about twenty-five years ago. Mulligan determined that, like manual operations carried out on the shop-floor, clerical operations are common to the extent that standard elemental times can be established for them.

As a result of his work and subsequent applications in this field a vast amount of standard time data has been determined. Rating or levelling is not applied. The method depends upon gaining a sound average for each element. Unit element times are expressed in decimal man hours ranging from five to seven places of decimals. Fatigue and relaxation allowances are given on a basis of one hour in seven ($16\frac{2}{3}$ per cent).

It is stated by the consultants that the standard time data now covers 95 per cent of all routine clerical activities. The accent is on participation during the installation of CWI and the responsibility for the success of the program lies with line management not the analyst. First-line supervisors are given the responsibility of carrying out the survey of work in their own departments aided of course by the analyst. Members of staff take part in a discussion about the nature of the program and their role in it.

Whilst the supervisor supplies data on work activities (obtained by asking personnel to complete job activity sheets), a simple method study activity is mounted, ensuring that all possible short-term improvements are obtained. Once these operations have been completed a work measurement analyst supplies time standards for the elements of each job being performed.

Once the standards for all jobs have been established line managers are asked to confirm them and it is their responsibility to agree that the calculated standard times are really acceptable. The standards are then used to determine manning strengths after which an appropriate control can be established.

Group capacity assessment. The basis of GCA is that the clerical jobs carried out by a group of people can be broken into separate parts and then related to units of output. Work measurement and control is of the group and not of individuals.

The actual method of work measurement used may differ from one situation to another. For example any one of the following techniques could be utilised:

1   Multi-minute measurement (no stopwatch)
2   Standard time study (stopwatch)
3   Standard data (predetermined from manuals or other departments already studied)
4   Work sampling (for long cycle time areas e.g. drawing/design offices)

The constraints on the application of GCA are that the area being controlled should be relatively stable, work carried out largely homogenous and the group larger than five people. The advantages claimed for GCA are that it can apply to work carried out sequentially which has widely differing cycle times.

Following a period of discussion with staff and management, the department or group is analysed. Any method improvements which appear possible are set in train. The analysis also determines the method of work measurement to be used.

Standard work units are assessed for the group's activities and an appropriate reporting system determined. The results for approximately four weeks are used to determine an optimum group manning strength.

Maintenance is an important part of this technique when the checking of weekly performance reports and carrying out further work measurement is done.

Variable factor programming.   Variable factor programming emphasises control rather than work measurement.

The initial survey is not usually directed towards solving method's problems but to gather information on staffing, payroll costs and departmental organisation. Analytical information is gained regarding work flow to determine significant variations in work activity, bottlenecks, the dependency of one department or group on the work of another and the areas where supervision is lax or non-existent.

Activity sampling is used to determine the extent of work activity, personnel movement, etc. This survey largely determines the target improvement in manning which it is hoped will be achieved.

Staff are then asked to complete activity forms. These are forms that will list the activities carried out, volumes handled and other duties that are associate to the activity listed.

Target times for activities are then developed by the use of observation or estimations. They are generally those that seem to be appropriate and are agreed with the supervisor of the activities being investigated. Historical records, employee reporting and estimates are used to establish manning strengths which will cover normal and peak loads.

The crux of VFP lies in the batching procedures which are introduced. VFP specialists claim that staff work better when they have a limited amount of work on their desks.

Batching procedures ensures that the back-log or work-bank is held on the supervisor's desk and that only an hour's work (or perhaps more) is issued to desk personnel at any time.

The supervisor has the ability to eliminate time spent by staff waiting for work. It is also possible to choose what work is done when and by whom. Delays in work flow should be minimal. Overtime is worked only when necessary.

Management reports on individual and departmental performance are made each week and appropriate records are kept by supervisors.

CONTROL.   Among the controls that should be built into the work measurement system which is introduced are the following:

1   Clocked hours against hours or minutes earned and appropriate percentage efficiency
2   Standard hours of product produced
3   Hours spent on unmeasured work
4   Hours lost and the cause of the loss
5   Arrears of work in standard hours
6   Forward balance of work in standard hours
7   A comparison between staff calculated to be necessary to produce the standard hours achieved and those actually working

9:4   Problems in the use of the techniques and conditions for success

Two related factors which inhibit the successful introduction of work measurement have already been quoted. The first is the necessity to rate work output, the second the negotiatory element which is inevitable in the process. These factors have been positive hindrances in achieving any major productivity improvements.

Mistakes by work measurement analysts continually occur and overpayment for jobs done is often the rule rather than the exception. It is essential that method study is carried out before work measurement is started and also that analysts must be thoroughly trained before any work measurement is carried out. Short-term gains are often extremely expensive in the long run.

The major and perhaps overwhelming drawback in achieving success with work measurement lies in the motivational aspects of the activity. Direct and indirect labour has long been subjected to time study analysis. The work now being carried out by behavioural scientists suggests that the application of direct incentives may be approaching redundancy. Whilst this seems too far-fetched, there appears to be a correlation between strikes and labour unrest generally with the rigid application of time study and the neglect of job enrichment. A company with a poor industrial environment and bad management practices will rarely improve total efficiency by a vigorous application of work measurement.

9:5   Conclusion

Heading the list of problems in introducing clerical work measurement must be the psychological one. For a long time clerical personnel have had "staff

Department or section Name		Supervisor Start a.m.											Date Stop p.m.		
Activity		Number of work units in batches issued											Total issued	Target minutes	Achieved minutes
Totals															
Time out															

Figure 9.3 WORK ALLOCATION AND CONTROL SHEET

Department_____												Week ending_____
Name		Monday	%	Tuesday	%	Wednesday	%	Thursday	%	Friday	%	Weekly totals
	Units planned											
	Units achieved												
	Units planned												
	Units achieved												
Total for department	Units planned												
	Units achieved												

Figure 9.4 DEPARTMENTAL ACTIVITY SHEET

Department or section	Supervisor		Date
Activity	Work units	Equivalent in minutes	Remarks

Figure 9.5 WORK REMAINING SHEET

Department		Supervisor		Date
Name	Job	% achieved of target	Reason for failure to meet target and corrective action	
			Reason	
			Corrective action	
			Reason	
			Corrective action	
			Reason	
			Corrective action	

Figure 9.6   CORRECTIVE ACTION REPORT

status." They have identified themselves with management and not labour. They have, despite the erosion in differentials between office and shop-floor, regarded themselves as an elite, where any kind of output control has been anathema. It has long been regarded that they can work well without work measurement. The fact is that they do not. Improvements in productivity of more than 25 per cent are common when CWM has been introduced. Calibre of clerical personnel consistently declines as the potentially good senior clerks go off to university or become chartered accountants and responsibility may have declined in consequence. But a psychological problem exists, nevertheless. Most supervisors of clerical labour (unlike shop-floor foremen) bitterly resent any suggestion that they are not aware of output rates of the clerks under their command. This factor alone has been the cause of more failures to introduce CWM than any other. Somehow clerical personnel must be "trusted." A sad mistake.

9:6   Further reading

1   P M Steele, "The MTM Data System for Office Work," *Work Study and Management Services*, July 1971
2   D A Whitmore, *Measurement and Control of Indirect Work*, Heinemann, 1970
3   R M Crossman and H W Nance, *Master Standard Data*, McGraw Hill, 1968
4   H W Nance and R E Nolan, *Office Work Measurement*, McGraw Hill, 1970
5   Russell M Currie, *Simplified PMTS*, BIM, 1963
6   R M Barnes, *Motion and Time Study, Design and Measurement of Work*, Wiley, 1964
7   L H Bunker, *Measuring Office Work*, Pitman, 1964
8   E V Grillo & C J Berg, *Work Measurement in the Office*, McGraw Hill, 1959
9   W C Glassey, *The Theory and Practice of Time Study*, Business Books 1965
10   C F Graham, *Work Measurement and Cost Control*, Commonwealth and Industrial Library, 1965.
11   John Constable and Dennis Smith, *Group Assessment Programmes: The Measurement of Indirect Work*, Business Publications, 1966
12   H B Maynard, G J Stegemerten and J L Schwab, *Methods Time Measurement*, McGraw Hill

_____

Activity sampling

10:1 Introduction

Activity sampling is often linked with work measurement, being used as a technique which reinforces the application of pure time study. However, because of its ability to be used on a multiplicity of occasions, other than in work measurement operations, activity sampling has been given a chapter of its own.

10:2 Description

Activity sampling is a measurement technique which uses a large number of instantaneous and random observations to determine the characteristics of something which has to be measured.

The number of observations taken will determine the probable accuracy of the result. Each observation has to be instantaneous. A predetermined code is usually used to record what has been seen.

Activity sampling is an application of statistical sampling, the basis of which is that from the observation of a part it is possible to infer many characteristics about the whole being investigated.

The observations are carried out comparatively unobtrusively. They often provide a short cut to conclusions which only extensive work measurement might otherwise have given.

Sequential activity sampling is a derivative of normal activity sampling and is often used in quality control charting when the cumulative average of an occurrence is plotted against the cumulative number of observations. Sampling continues while the plot remains outside two acceptable control limits. When the plot becomes steady inside the limits a steady result is indicated and sampling can diminish.

Non-random sampling is a systematic, fixed interval sampling technique which makes full use of the observer. It can be used where the work being sampled is not cyclical or has no out-of-course patterns (a rare occurrence). Other varieties of activity sampling are as follows.

ACCEPTANCE SAMPLING.   This operates by taking a random sample of size *n* to confirm or deny that the total is acceptable from a quality standard viewpoint. The sample is determined statistically.

This method of quality control is appropriate where total inspection would be very expensive and time-consuming and the loss from passing some defective items would not be very great. This would be particularly true where quality control results in the destruction of the product being inspected.

ATTRIBUTE SAMPLING.   This method uses sampling criteria to grade products as acceptable or unacceptable.

10:3   Successful areas of application and examples

USES OF ACTIVITY SAMPLING.   These are manifold but are usually concentrated on the following type of activities:

1   As a means of helping to determine the activity of a clerical, shop-floor or warehouse work force
2   To determine the utilisation of machines or equipment of some kind —e.g. fork-lift trucks, special production equipment, overhead cranes, conveyor belts etc
3   Measuring the activities of a team, particularly a team that operates one piece of equipment—e.g. a steel mill or conveyor belt, etc. Some members of the team may be carrying out excessive duties, others may be idle for most of the time. The exercise could produce a new team activity situation
4   To determine the time spent on various activities. For example, a clerical work force might be employed in filing, answering queries by telephone, looking up catalogues and general clerical activities. Activity sampling can be used to determine the incidence of time spent on each activity
5   To check the quality of work. For example, it can be used to check the accuracy of invoice calculations
6   To check on lateness of staff who do not have to clock in
7   To check on factors which would otherwise be checked or controlled only through expensive procedures—e.g. checking the quality of products by total destruction testing would obviously be wrong

CARRYING OUT A STUDY.   As with work measurement, objectives have to be agreed. What is to be proved or measured?

It may be disconcerting to have an analyst appearing at irregular intervals, more disconcerting, perhaps, than a straight time-study operation. Suitable warning or discussions ought to prepare personnel for irregular visits.

The design of observation sheets may be more difficult than it sounds. For example in taking observations on a clerical work force the following aspects ought to be pre-coded:

1	Clerk working
2	Clerk not working
3	Clerk at work place
4	Clerk not at work place
5	Clerk:
a	Writing
b	Telephoning
c	Perusing documents
d	Dictating a letter
6	Clerk talking:
a	With a colleague
b	To supervisor, manager or junior
7	Clerk visiting:
a	Another section in the same department
b	Another department
c	Filing room etc

An observation sheet should be so designed and coded that it is possible to distinguish between the various factors quoted and, if possible, between apparently meaningful and non-meaningful activity. This latter point is important especially when inevitably the results will be challenged.

Establish the number of observations to be made. The higher the number of observations the greater the certainty of achieving accurate results. There will, of course, be a limit on the number of observations that can be made and 100 per cent accuracy will be impossible to achieve. It is usually acceptable to have 95 per cent accuracy or confidence limits of this amount.

A standard formula used in determining the number of observations which will have to be made is:

$$N = \frac{4p(100-p)}{L^2}$$

—where N = The number of observations which have to be made, L is the desired limits of accuracy of the results, p is the percentage occurrence of the major activity determined by a pilot survey or from an estimate.

If applied to a homogenous population and 95 per cent confidence limits the following formula should be used:

$$L = 2\sqrt{\frac{P(100-P)}{N}}$$

However there are some rough rules of thumb which might be tried. For example:

1   It may take 100 observations to reach some first conclusions about general objectives and whether a full-scale study is necessary

2   An accurate machine utilisation appraisal may take approximately 4000 observations and an accurate assessment of a clerical work force's activity about the same number

3   Accurate time standards may need 10000 or more observations

These may appear to be large numbers of observations, but if there are approximately twenty clerks carrying out activities being sampled, 4000 observations may take ten days, if twenty observations a day are possible.

4   A representative period must be found for the activity being observed. A standard occasion when peaks and troughs in workload have been eliminated is required, unless a peak or trough situation is being observed. All working hours should be covered—from starting to finishing time. If there are work cycles in the activities being observed then these need to be taken into account

5   No apparently exceptional observations should be disregarded. If all the clerks are away from their desks or all are not working, then these situations should be recorded

6   The final report should show all the observations made, the time when they were made, the date and the department, section, machine or activity being observed

10:4   Problems in the use of the techniques and conditions for success

The observations have to be random. If they are not then bias will certainly creep in.

The results of the activity may be suspect through wrong coding of activities. For example, if a clerk is at his desk and apparently looking at some papers, then in all probability he will be coded as "working." Is he? He might be idling. The papers may be his football pools. If he is talking to a colleague is it an essential conversation, vital to good running of the department or is it an inconsequential discussion?

In the hands of an inexperienced observer a totally wrong conclusion could be drawn even if an acceptable activity sampling method is used.

10:5   Conclusion

Activity sampling can be a very useful technique, either in its own right or in support of classical work measurement. It has many pitfalls for the unwary however. Juniors, without adequate training, should never be allowed to carry out observations which could lead to a deterioration in management–worker relationships, the sale or purchase of expensive capital equipment, or any other far-reaching result.

10:6 Further reading

1   R M Barnes, *Work Sampling*, Wiley, 1957
2   M J Moroney, *Facts From Figures*, Penguin, 1956
3   R S Espie and O W Metcalfe, "A Practical Technique of Sequential Work Sampling," *Time and Motion Study*, January 1962
4   A Wald, *Sequential Sampling*, Columbia University Press
5   D A C MacLaren, *Activity Sampling—a Useful Work Measure*, Rydges (Australia), June 1970

ELEVEN

Productivity measurement

11:1 Introduction

Productivity has become one of the most used and at the same time abused words in a manager's lexicon. Vital though it sounds productivity is rarely defined appropriately. This chapter defines the term and gives some examples of how the data for productivity measurements can be gathered and used.

11:2 Description

Productivity is best calculated by an assessment of the ratio between resources produced and resources used in their production, when it is possible to use the same units of measurement in each case.

Productivity cannot be equated with performance or effort. For example, one set of operatives could work extremely hard yet produce little because they are using obsolete manufacturing equipment. Another set could hardly work at all yet produce in great quantities because of the employment of expensive up-to-date production machinery.

Labour effort alone, therefore, cannot be equated with productivity. In some instances operator performance can be improved considerably yet total output could be raised only a little.

In most factories materials handling is an anathema, as it adds to cost but produces nothing. Materials handling and the transportation of products generally is eliminated as far as possible. Yet there is a growing (and flourishing) distribution industry in Britain which, on the basis just suggested, adds nothing to industrial productivity. Surely this cannot be true.

The crux of productivity measurement lies in the definition of a productivity index for the ratio between input and output. This index has to use:

1   An unambiguous measurement of input and output
2   Numerical values which are constant throughout the operation of the resources being measured
3   A comparison between a historical base and current performance (if these are in comparable units)
4   Comparisons within one measurement unit—a job, a factory, an activity, a body of men etc
5   Comparisons of actual performance with an objective

There must be consideration of the purpose of the index and who is going to use it. Personnel must know how the index is made up and how they can influence it. The index must be produced (like all management information data) in time for it to allow managerial action which will correct an undesirable situation. The index must be used as a means of measuring performance and for taking action.

11:3   Successful areas of application and examples

SOME FORMS OF PRODUCTIVITY MEASUREMENT. The simplest form of productivity is that of labour productivity. The calculation of an index uses the following simple formula:

$$\frac{\text{Standard hours of production achieved} + \text{other factors} \times 100}{\text{Clocked hours}}$$

A standard hour of production is a technically derived standard at which a machine or operative should work. The standard hours of production achieved are found by dividing actual output by the standard.

Schedules of standard times are produced for all measured activities. Output achieved is then calculated and an effectiveness ratio produced as follows:

$$\frac{\text{Standard hours of work produced} \times 100}{\text{Actual hours spent on measured work}}$$

Further ratios of hours spent on measured and unmeasured work, lost and effective time, arrears of work and current work output, etc, can all be produced.

Where a company produces only one product a productivity index presents little problem. The NCB, for example, have long used the hundredweights of coal mined per man-shift as the basis for determining productivity.

Key ratios have been used as a means of identifying changes in company productivity. These management ratios are very often financially dominated, but are still extremely useful.

CONCEPT OF ADDED VALUE. In many ways "added value" is a more useful approach to productivity measurement than the use of ratios. (An increase in selling prices, for example, can often distort a financial ratio.)

A company can be regarded as a fixed investment to which there is an input of raw materials, components, general services, etc. Output can be in the form of goods or services. Input is transformed into output by the use of capital, labour, etc. The output less the input can be measured as the added value which has been made.

Two of the most widely used methods of calculating added values are:

1   Sales value less raw material plus bought out parts
2   Sales value minus raw material, plus bought out items and factory services

The latter method should be used where factory services form a large part of total cost.

The added value should be compared with the other main cost factors within an organisation—for example, with labour costs or as a ratio of added value per employee.

Added value calculated in the way suggested has been used to form the basis of productivity agreements and in particular economists have used such measurements to determine the productivity of various industries in various geographical areas of the country. Net output per employee, for example, was used as a productivity measurement by the Board of Trade economists in the census of production statistics published in February 1966.

Part of the difference in productivity indices for various industries obviously arises from the different capital intensities employed and capital depreciation is added to the productivity equation to give:

$$\frac{\text{Added value}}{\text{Total labour cost + capital depreciation}} \times 100$$

WEIGHTING OF KEY FACTORS METHOD. Most organisations make numerous products, service two or more markets, perhaps have two or more production units. The use of a simple productivity index or the use of meaningful ratios is often difficult. A method of weighting the various factors involved is therefore used, in the hope that each factor will be reduced to a uniform base level. Work or labour content, sales value or sales cost are normally used to establish a base. A factor is determined by the sales value, sales cost, etc, contained in the product, and output is weighted accordingly.

USE OF CAPITAL AS AN INDICATOR OF PRODUCTIVITY. ROI or return on investment has nearly had exclusive use in reviewing capital spending. Despite its many detractors, ROI is an extremely useful measurement of how efficiently an organisation is operating. The efficient use of capital is dependent upon the correct deployment of labour, an accurate assessment of markets and future sales as well as overall good management.

PRODUCTIVITY COSTING. Productivity costing is a method of costing which has been developed in order to measure productivity in various types of industry making a variety of products. It can be used to determine the performance of various parts of an organisation in contributing to overall profit. It attempts to determine the rate at which products contribute profit.

Various formulas are used in which elements of cost are set against sales revenue. A primary productivity index used, for example, is:

$$\frac{\text{Net sales} - \text{cost of raw materials}}{\text{Cost of sales}}$$

A second index used in determining profit productivity is:

$$\text{Profit productivity} = \frac{\text{earnings} - \text{cost of sales}}{\text{Cost of sales}}$$

Various elements of an organisation's operations can be dealt with in the same way, for example in determining a measurement of productive work as a ratio of the cost of sales:

$$\text{Facilities productivity} = \frac{\text{cost of productive work}}{\text{Cost of sales}}$$

Such an index can be applied to various segments of the total organisation or to a particular product. For example, if a segment is S_1 then:

$$\text{Facilities productivity } S_1 = \frac{\text{cost of productive work } S_1}{\text{Cost of sales } S_1}$$

$$\text{and } \frac{\Sigma}{S_1} \text{ Cost of productive work } S_1 = \text{cost of productive work}$$

$$\frac{\Sigma}{S_1} \text{ Cost of sales } S_1 = \text{cost of sales}$$

11:4   Problems in the use of the technique and conditions for success

The value added concept of measurement of productivity will often be distorted during periods of inflation when selling prices are being constantly adjusted upwards. Value will appear to have been added, but this may not really be true. More resources are not generated.

Capital employed is important. It is imperative, therefore, that an appropriate definition of capital is made. This as most managers who have wrestled with "return on investment" and other measurements know is often difficult.

The effect of increases in raw material and component prices will also have a major effect on a productivity index. It is likely to go down if raw material prices go up and no commensurate improvement in productivity is made.

Productivity indices of any kind will always be suspect unless it is known conclusively that the base data is right. For example, the higher the unmeasured or other factor content of a labour productivity calculation, the more likely it will be to give a misleading result.

It is important that the organisation's costing system is linked with the productivity index. For example, if a labour productivity index is used, the cost per standard hour should be utilised for product costing purposes. A comparison between actual and standard cost is necessary. Control sheets should be designed to show how much productive and how much non-productive time has been spent.

The use of productivity indices in productivity bargaining has been criticised by trade unions because it is said that many of the components of the factors in the equations are not in the control of the employees whose pay is being determined by them. For example, a good costing system is essential as well as adequate or superior management. If neither of these two items are available the operation of the index may be erroneous.

To avoid trade union suspicions, it will be necessary to establish standard rules about the elements that are included in the equation and how the effect of these can be eliminated from the final result, as far as wage payments are concerned.

11:5   Conclusion

This chapter has attempted to discuss the problems of productivity measurement. Some useful examples have been given, but it is unlikely that any one of them will serve all organisations at all times.

Productivity indices which merely relate to labour output are fairly crude measurements of an organisation's real productivity.

Productivity indices tend to concentrate on total company performance not just straight labour efficiency. Anything that does this is valuable. Anything that helps in comparing comparatively diverse enterprises and how they utilise their resources is of greater value still.

11:6   Further reading

1   Gellerman, *Motivation and Productivity*, American Management Association, 1963
2   L H C Tippett, *Indices of Productivity*, BIM
3   Sir Ewart Smith and R Beeching, *Measurement of the Effectiveness of the Production Unit*, BIM
4   A R Smith, "Productivity Measurement and Wage Levels," *British Management Review*, December 1951
5   *Productivity Measurements, 1 Concepts; 2 Plant Level; Measurements and Results*, OECD
6   *Bibliography on Productivity*, OECD
7   M Fleming, "Manpower ratios and Productivity," *Management Decision*, Winter 1970

Part 4

PLANNING, STRATEGY FORMULATION AND GENERAL MANAGEMENT METHODS

Profit planning

12:1 Introduction

Profit planning in the last few years has had considerable management thinking devoted to it. Successful applications, however, are rare and many companies still consider that budgetary control is the same as profit planning. Nothing could be further from the truth. Budgetary control starts from a forecast, someone's guess about the future which may or may not prove correct. Profit planning begins with an objective which the use of profit planning techniques must help to achieve.

12:2 Description

Profit planning is a disciplined management method in which integrated plans are designed to utilise total company resources and management skills to achieve predetermined objectives. The benefits which will accrue from the application of this method could number any of the following:

1   Profit planning tends to engender discipline, professionalism and dynamism in order to achieve demanding objectives. Everyone should know where the company is going and how it will get there
2   The company business is defined. Strengths and weaknesses are recognised and appropriate steps taken to build on one and counter or eliminate the other
3   A lack of cohesion in management decision making is eliminated. The process co-ordinates management activities and helps to define priorities
4   Standards of required performance are established against which achieve-

ments can be judged. Appropriate reporting and control systems can be established

5   Opportunities for profit improvement are recognised soon enough for appropriate steps to be taken to achieve them
6   The company environment is analysed and as far as possible strategies introduced which will either help to change the environment or help the company to carry out a successful adaptation
7   The effects of situations which cannot be totally foreseen are minimised by putting the company into a posture which aids adaptation
8   Profit planning should provide a framework which will facilitate the investigation of the operations aspects of the company and ensure the optimum use of all resources
9   Though intuitive judgement is largely eliminated, the planning process need not restrict entrepreneurial flair, otherwise it could be largely useless

These points in total add up to a formidable case for applying profit planning. Once this case is accepted the following steps will have to be taken to achieve a profit plan.

ESTABLISH JOB RESPONSIBILITIES.   Often job responsibilities are too imprecise to provide the information on which performance standards can be established and then judged. It is essential to have job breakdowns in the detail which permits the agreement and allocation of appropriate objectives.

ESTABLISH APPROPRIATE CONTROL SYSTEMS.   Profit planning and control may have grown out of budgetary control systems but is now very different from those systems. It is essential to have some form of budgetary cost control, plan monitoring and management information systems generally which will serve to enable profit planning to be effective. How measurement of current and future performance can be carried out must be agreed and suitable measurement programs drawn up.

CARRY OUT A SITUATION AUDIT.   This can be done in many ways but it is largely covered by establishing the strengths and weaknesses of the company and its competitors and the competitive environment generally. How this might be done is described in *How to Apply Strategy in Profit Planning* (Business Books, 1971).

ESTABLISH APPROPRIATE OBJECTIVES.   These can be established in many ways—expectation of shareholders, cash flow needed to support future growth, past performance, taking account of management competence, competitors' activities and calibre, etc. (It is essential that a dialogue is established following which desirable objectives will either be confirmed or have appropriate amendments made to them. Once this has been done, objectives can be established at all management and supervisory levels.)

A GAP ANALYSIS. This should be undertaken at this stage. This is a method wherein the required profit, growth and other major objectives will have been established and compared with the current trend in the company. A gap will nearly certainly be obvious between the two. Profit planning is largely concerned about how the gap can be closed.

ESTABLISH APPROPRIATE PLANS AND STRATEGIES TO CLOSE THE GAP. Usually a "hierarchy" of plans is made each of which integrates with the whole. Marketing, cost reduction, R & D, capital expenditure, diversification, acquisition and merger and manpower will be the more important of the plans made, though wherever money is spent an appropriate plan to ensure that spending is related to profit earned should be formulated. Strategies are the result of choosing between alternatives in the use of company resources through which it is hoped desired corporate objectives will be achieved. They can be highly complex depending upon the situation audit. Appropriate alternatives need to be set out in such a way that a logical choice can be made.

CONTROL. Once the profit plan and its integral parts have been completed they should be appropriately controlled (though control should be implicit in the making of the plans and once they are made they should be achieved). However, action programs which show how each strategy is to be applied and each planned objective achieved should be drawn up. The quantified result, the date by which the action is to be achieved, the personnel responsible, all need to be quoted. The plans, strategies and control plans outline might suggest a complexity, even a bureaucracy which will be alien to most organisations. This is not intended. Profit planning can be introduced with a minimum of paperwork but some must exist, more in all probability than is present in a company which has a pragmatic approach to profit making.

The term "management by objectives" has been used by many as a synonym for what truly is profit planning methodology. MBO is an intrinsic part of profit planning but cannot really be equated with it. Managers are allocated objectives. Their performance is appraised. Training, guidance, perhaps rewards and punishments are metred out accordingly. But there is much more than this in profit planning, as the foregoing outline suggests.

12:3 Successful areas of application and examples

The book *How to Make and Control a Profit Plan* (Business Books, 1969) goes into this in detail.

12:4 Problems in the use of the techniques and conditions for success

The difference between forecasting and planning deserves restating. Forecasting is a guess about what might happen to the company in the future. Planning is a

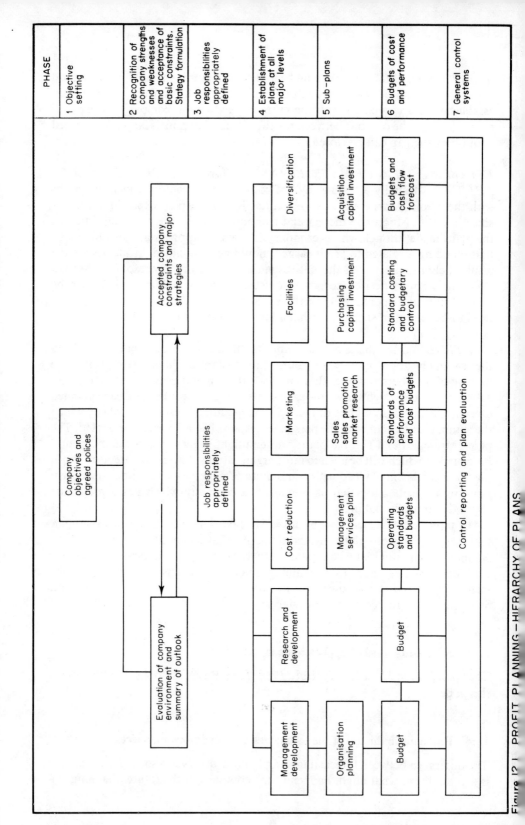

PHASE							
1 Objective setting	2 Recognition of company strengths and weaknesses and acceptance of basic constraints. Strategy formulation	3 Job responsibilities appropriately defined	4 Establishment of plans at all major levels	5 Sub-plans	6 Budgets of cost and performance	7 General control systems

Figure 12.1 PROFIT PLANNING – HIERARCHY OF PLANS

126

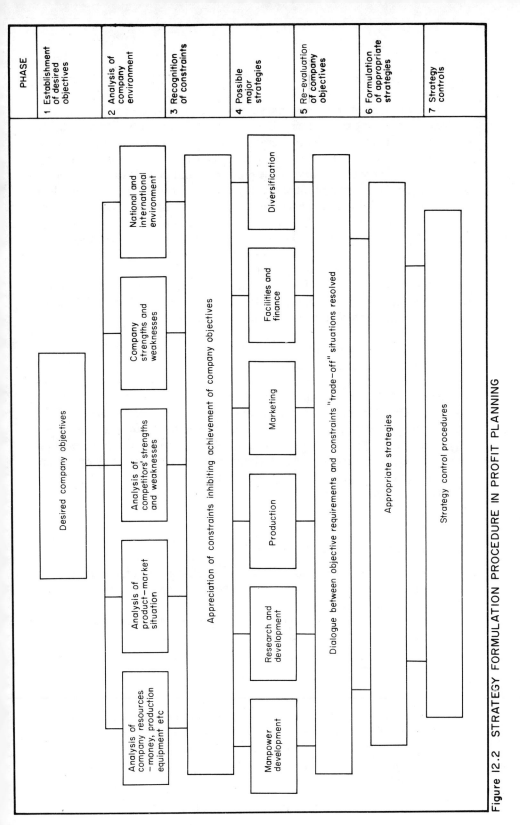

Figure 12.2 STRATEGY FORMULATION PROCEDURE IN PROFIT PLANNING

precise method and within reason controllable. It decides the way the company is to go to achieve predetermined objectives.

The role of the chief executive is paramount. He has to set demanding corporate goals and at the same time inform all personnel of the need for change within the company. He must motivate co-operation, collaboration and executive involvement at all levels. He has to encourage, warn and reward according to progress made. He must be seen to believe in the profit plan and that he wants it to succeed without question. Though profit planning will obviously help managers to achieve higher goals, inevitably company attitudes will have to change in doing this. Much improved performance may be demanded from managers. Performance will be measured and they will be judged accordingly. Without the full support of the chief executive, profit planning will die no matter how enthusiastically it is welcomed at middle management levels.

Key results should be clarified and objectives must be unambiguous—if possible, quantified. Account has to be taken of all job parameters and the various constraints which inhibit the achievement of objectives.

Control information has to be available quickly enough for a significant response to be made to an out of course situation. It is no use getting information too late to carry out remedial action.

Training and guidance need to be given in all profit planning techniques and above all in the essential company attributes which are necessary for success in profit planning. Training is often dissipated on a series of *ad hoc* subjects which usually have no relationship with each other and certainly none with long-term corporate goals. The introduction of profit planning focuses training needs on those techniques and methods which should add profit to company operations. The inadequacies in management training are soon made obvious and must quickly be put right.

12:5   Conclusion

Profit planning and control can be recommended for any organisation where there is a need to eliminate many of the weaknesses inferred earlier in this section. It works. But only if the chief executive wants it to.

If a company has long had a pragmatic approach to profit making it will hurt. It will certainly change the company style of management.

12:6   Further reading

1   B H Walley, *How to Make and Control a Profit Plan*, Business Books, 1969
2   Institute of Cost and Works, *Aspects of Corporate Planning*, ICWA, 1970
3   J Argenti, *Corporate Planning*, Allen & Unwin, 1969
4   S R Wilson and J O Tomb, *Improved Profits Through Integrated Planning and Control*, Prentice Hall, 1968

5   D R C Holford, *Business Planning*, Pan Books 1968
6   Palmer & Taylor, *Financial Planning and Control*, Pan, 1969
7   S V Bishop, *Business Planning and Control*, Institute of Chartered Accountants, 1966
8   P H Irwin, *Business Planning—Key to Profit Growth*, Ryerson, 1970
9   A Presanis, *Corporate Planning in Industry*, Business Books, 1968
10   F Gardener, *Profit Management and Control*, McGraw Hill, 1964

THIRTEEN

Manpower planning

13:1 Introduction

The idea that it is possible to plan an organisation's manpower requirements for a year, perhaps two or three years ahead, is hard to accept. The imponderables, the changing conditions, death and resignations, decline of facilities, the new recruit who turned out better or worse than anticipated, will all throw any manpower planning awry. Yet not to attempt it is to admit that it is impossible to match manpower with profit planning requirements. Surely the one vital element in any organisation—its human resources—must be planned like all lesser elements in the plan.

13:2 Description

Most pundits consider that "manpower planning should ensure that the right number of personnel of the correct technical competence will be available to an organisation in desired locations, so that corporate objectives are achieved."

Organisation theory and planning has obvious links with manpower planning but this subject will be dealt with later as it obviously extends into realms not covered by manpower planning.

The operation of manpower planning—in theory—seems perfectly straight forward. The situation and skills audit implicit in starting the corporate strategy methodology should indicate the basic weaknesses in management numbers—age, technical expertise and experience, etc. The audit should indicate current skill levels, efficiency performances, training requirements for management and overall manpower requirements.

The further analysis of desired organisational objectives, strategies and tactics to achieve them, will suggest the manpower requirements needed to achieve future profit, turnover level, etc. This should be made even more emphatic when individual marketing, cost reduction and capital expenditure plans are made.

The effect of industrial relations, trade union bargaining situations and productivity bargaining must be considered. The use of such techniques as work study and method study and their effect on manpower requirements will also need to be reviewed—so an appreciation of the future use of such techniques is vital.

The help of line managers will be needed to determine the size in the light of the company's objectives and strategies, of the manpower gap—the difference between what is required and what on a current trend basis the organisation will have. It is likely that the company may have an excess in some grades of manpower and a deficiency in others. The location (factory, site, office, etc) where the excess or deficiency is likely to occur and the skills (technical, managerial, clerical, etc) required must be known. The likely training requirements must be assessed and the possibility of training current staff then considered. It is possible that personnel employed by the company will be unable to accept the new jobs which must be performed because they are inherently of low calibre. This decision must follow an objective appreciation of current staff standards.

From the analysis detailed above should emerge a clear picture of the numbers, type, calibre and skills of personnel required at various times in the future. A manpower costs budget will perhaps have been prepared as a corollary to this.

Once a dated manpower schedule has been drawn up a *training program*, a *recruitment plan*, a *redundancy plan* and, possibly, a *long-term plan*—to introduce various wage payments, management development, management by objectives programs—need to be made. The manpower plan should aim to match manpower to the profit plan, avoiding panic redundancies and recruitment and ensuring that manpower levels will always be as near optimum as possible.

13:3 Successful areas of application and examples

The rather narrow definition of manpower planning which suggests that the use of manpower schedules can pull manpower requirements into line with a profit plan is not enough. There are a variety of basically behavioural personnel orientated techniques that should be brought under the manpower planning umbrella. Each one will probably demand its own specialism and to be applied in its own right. In total, however, they add up to a formidably powerful operation—if successfully carried out.

ORGANISATION PLANNING. The company organisation has to match the company's strategy and objectives. This could mean low-level decision making, speedy communications, close financial control of all activities. The system of organisation must provide full opportunity for each of these activities.

JOB EVALUATION, MERIT RATING, PERFORMANCE MEASURE-MENT. These factors have already been considered under the generic heading of job study. They are a necessary precursor to manpower planning.

SUCCESSION PLANNING. The organisations which have attempted to carry out succession planning have found it extremely difficult. Key people have a tendency to resign unexpectedly or someone does not live up to expectations and so the plan becomes invalid.

Integral with succession planning is career path planning (which will be discussed next) and the ability to quantify in some way a manager's attributes, potential and current job performance so that a choice can be made between competing candidates for promotion.

Usually the organisation is analysed function by function, department by department and management assessed in terms of job attributes, skills and performance rating.

Current job holders are then matched against the job they hold and their potential. The following are usually considered the key factors:

1   Age
2   Length of years in current job
3   Current job performance
4   Future potential (which could be broken down into the potential ability to do his superior's job or the ability to be promoted elsewhere outside the job holder's current function)

Some systems operate a grading method where job holders are allocated a grade from 1 (good) to 6 (bad). Once this has been done a senior manager could take a coherent and objective view of the whole of his organisation. He could compare rival candidates for promotion, consider personnel for transfer from one function to another, see which manager was apparently getting stale and which apparently needed retraining or, if necessary, demotion.

A succession chart can then be worked out. X will take Y's job in Z years and needs training in A, B and C subjects, before becoming established in the new job.

A chart of the kind outlined should give a clear indication of the potential promotion patterns by showing weaknesses and strengths.

CAREER PLANNING. Career planning should be a concomittant of succession planning, though in this field a manager's as opposed to the organisation's desires are taken into account. Each manager or potential manager has a career path mapped out for him based on his aims, ambitions, desires, qualifications and attributes. Both current job performance and the job holder's potential are discussed formally.

It is obvious that the organisation's requirements must still be paramount, but within the broad organisation strategy and manpower plan, an attempt should be made to ensure that as far as possible appropriate individual career paths are suggested.

POTENTIAL ANALYSIS. If career planning is to be successful potential analysis is required. In an era when graduates are accepted to have all the managerial talents which are apparently necessary to be successful in industry and commerce, it is becoming increasingly difficult for non-graduates or professionally qualified people to gain promotion. Despite current educational opportunities it is still possible to find managerial talent at many junior levels in an organisation. Potential analysis should unearth any unused talent that the organisation possesses.

TRAINING PLANS. This is an important aspect of manpower planning. Often training is undertaken as an *ad hoc* activity divorced from the real requirements of the company. Training ought to be carried out to cover one or all of the following situations:

1   To correct current job failures. Merit rating, performance appraisal and management by objectives will all help to indicate where job failures are occurring and where training will help
2   To improve employee potential. Emphasis has been made in this chapter on succession planning and potential analysis. Training should be used to support these activities. The training, therefore, has largely to be individually tailored. Conglomerate training courses, beloved of many personnel managers, will largely be a waste of time
3   To learn a new technique or management method. Techniques regretfully seem to be continually expanding. It is vital for an organisation's competitiveness that its managers' techniques education is constantly updated. This would indicate a constant planned education course for all grades of management, once again tailored to suit individual managers. There is little value in teaching market modelling to an engineer in charge of factory maintenance

JOB IMPROVEMENT PLANS. As part of the manpower planning process, plans to improve job performance will be required. Such improvements should not impinge on company training plans. Action plans only are required. These plans will be formulated between a senior manager and his subordinate. The substance of the plan will be a record of how the subordinate's performance should be improved. Priorities may have to be considered if any cost is to be incurred in achieving the improvement.

13:4   Problems in the use of the techniques and conditions for success

Manpower planning ought to be a team effort. The wider implications of the company policy and long-term strategy have to be taken into account at one end of the planning scale. At the other end, the often subjective evaluation of manager performance has to be made. Government action—the training, retraining and redundancy field—has also to be considered.

There is a close link between industrial relations, productivity bargaining, wages negotiations generally and manpower planning. Such planning cannot be done in a vacuum; redundancy and recruitment may be managerial failures but trade unions and staff associations have to be consulted. It is likely that of all the planning functions, manpower planning is most likely to be the close concern of the trade unions.

Wrong forecasts and poor planning of manpower could have more immediate and dangerous repercussions than any other of the planning functions. Erroneous redundancy or recruitment, training in wrong disciplines, labour unrest, poor morale and perhaps strikes may occur as a result.

Probability theory and sensitivity analysis ought to be widely used. There may be a case for backing a decision both ways. This sounds a negative, perhaps defeatist attitude, but the results of poor manpower planning could be disastrous. Unless all the behavioural attitudes quoted in the chapter on this subject are taken into account things will not go right.

Unlike many other planning functions, planning manpower is not a mechanistic process. It needs a finesse and experience which few corporate planners straight from business school will have achieved.

13:5   Conclusions

Redundancy must mostly lie at the door of senior management. The situation is often caused by the inadequacy or non-existence of profit planning and of one of the important subplans, manpower planning.

Conversely, an organisation has often had to scramble for an adequate supply of skilled personnel, the need for which any good profit planner should have foreseen. The outcome has often been recruitment of inadequate personnel at inflated wage rates.

Manpower planning should help eradicate both these painful situations. This is not to say that manpower planning is easy. It is far from that. But this is no reason why it should not be attempted. The alternatives are too unnerving for most logically minded managers.

13:6   Further reading

1   A R Smith, *Models for Manpower Systems*, EUP, 1970
2   J J Lynch, *Making Manpower Effective*, Pan Books, 1968
3   G McBeath, *Organisation and Manpower Planning*, Business Books, 1968
4   G Stainer, *Manpower Planning—the Management of Human Resources*, Prentice Hall
5   J Cox, "Manpower Planning at National and Company Level," *Long-Range Planning*, June 1971
6   J W Walker, "Models in Manpower Planning," *Business Horizons*, April 1971
7   T H Patten, *Manpower Planning and the Development of Human Resources*, Wiley

8   A R Smith, "Developments in Manpower Planning," *Personnel Review*, Autumn 1971

9   J J Lynch, "Manpower Planning from an Industry Viewpoint," *BACIE Journal*, December 1971

10   A R Smith (editor), *Some Statistical Techniques in Manpower Planning*, CAS occasional papers, number 15

FOURTEEN

PERT and critical path planning

14:1 Introduction

PERT or program evaluation review technique has many offshoots. Network analysis, critical path planning, critical path scheduling are all similar to PERT. Each formulates a major activity by making a diagram or network. All use time analysis, resource allocation, scheduling and control functions.

14:2 Description

PERT is a management method designed to show diagrammatically all the activities in a (usually) complex operation. By so doing it is hoped that management planning, scheduling and controlling of such operations will improve.

The key to network design lies in the use of arrowed diagrams to show the logical sequence of operation within the total activity. The series of occurrences are quantitatively expressed in time.

Drawing a network is not difficult. An activity—building a factory, for example —is broken down into basic operations: finding the site, obtaining planning permission, engaging an architect, laying down broad specifications for shape, size, cost, floor area, etc.

Each operation is represented by an arrow. The operation begins and ends at an identifiable time in the total activity. At the beginning and end of each arrow is a circle, representing an event (Figure 14.1). This is the simplest form of network diagram. The arrows show a relationship between events. Each arrow can then be allocated a completion time. So that once a series of activities and events have been joined together to form one continuous activity, a total time for that activity can be calculated (see Figure 14.2).

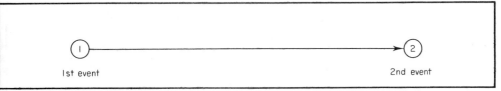

Figure 14.1 SIMPLE NETWORK

In practice a pessimistic, an optimistic and a "most likely" time are calculated and a mean of the three times is used in the network. The critical path can be recognised by the length of time it will take to complete—that is, the longest. (In Figure 14.2 the activity passing events 5, 6 and 7 is obviously the critical path.) The critical operations are then apparent and appropriate control over them can be established.

Other, non-critical, paths will have spare time or capacity. Once the amount of time to spare has been calculated and accepted as a "float" or a "spare," the paths concerned might be redrawn to ensure an overall balance in the use of resources. Start and stop dates would be amended to suit the changed resources allocation.

Often a separate resource scheduling activity is carried out to complement the amended PERT network. The resource scheduling program is designed to optimise the use of resources and provide a work program. The two are complementary—a poor work program will produce poor resource utilisation.

A work schedule is usually designed on the basis of commencing the various work activities at times which will provide an optimum usage of the resources involved. The time analysis of the network will indicate the earliest starting date possible, but this date may not always be advisable and it certainly will not optimise resources if the dates are strictly adhered to.

A trial and error rescheduling activity where start dates are altered so that they fall anywhere between the earliest and latest possible, has to be carried out. Obviously this kind of activity is best done by a computer. If the computer

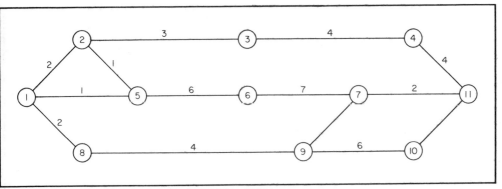

Figure 14.2 NETWORK SHOWING CRITICAL PATH

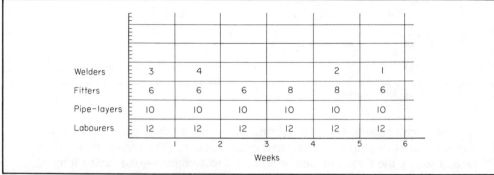

	1	2	3	4	5	6
Welders	3	4			2	I
Fitters	6	6	6	8	8	6
Pipe–layers	IO	IO	IO	IO	IO	IO
Labourers	I2	I2	I2	I2	I2	I2

Weeks

Figure 14.3 MANPOWER REQUIRED–BY SKILL

program can take into account the resource requirement for each activity, the
total resources available and any constraints on the use of resources or in time
situation, then an appropriately optimised result is probable.

The total length of the whole activity will depend upon the quantity of resources
which can be utilised. Manpower of different skills, money, machinery and
equipment generally, material and tools, all need to be programmed within the
time situation allowed.

Figure 14.3 and 14.4 indicate extremely simply the resource utilisation graphs
which are necessary—that is, those that are dictated by the network. Amendment
is obviously essential to bring resources into line with requirements or vice versa.

Usually there is a threshold level at the limit of normal working. Beyond this
limit, overtime can be worked and extra labour taken on. It should be part of the
resource–schedule operation to ensure that the threshold limit is crossed as
infrequently as possible.

Costs at the normal, beyond the threshold and extra labour situations should
emerge as part of the time–cost analysis which PERT ought to foster.

Various resources—financial or material—can be passed forwards and back-

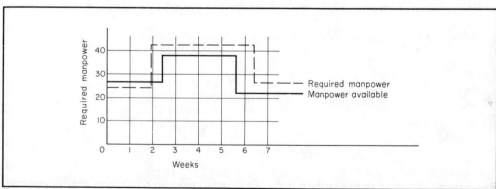

Figure 14.4 SIMPLE RESOURCE DEMAND AND AVAILABILITY GRAPH

wards between time periods and this too needs to be considered in evaluating resource utilisation.

The total cost of the project at various timescales and with the use of specified resources has to be calculated and the computer program (if one is being used) should provide such data. A cost per unit of resources used seems essential. For example, an hourly rate for certain work force categories should be calculated before the total operation starts. In this way standard costs for the whole and for segments of the total can be made.

Ultimately, the amount of work completed, its value in standard hours of cost and the actual cost can be compared in Figure 14.7.

14:3   Successful areas of application and examples

PERT or network analysis was first used with success in the USA in the space industry and Polaris development. It has since been widely used in the aircraft and building industries particularly in bridge and motorway building and it is such activities which have gained it most publicity. Other major PERT uses have been in building new factories, product changes and computer installations. This latter activity has been the subject of a network by ICL and copies of it can be obtained from that company. Comparatively small activities such as the re-arrangement of offices can be handled by PERT with a substantial probability of success.

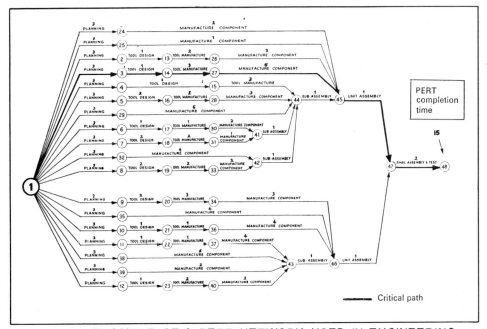

Figure 14.5   EXAMPLE OF A PERT NETWORK USED IN ENGINEERING

TIME ANALYSIS IN TOTAL FLOAT & EARLIEST START SEQUENCE

S/P CDE	PREC EVENT	SUCC EVENT	U I	REPORT CODE	DESCRIPTION	DUR	EARLIEST START	EARLIEST FINISH	LATEST START	LATEST FINISH	TOT FLOAT	FREE E FLT
P3	1	2		TEC	DESIGN	3.0	5DEC66T	22DEC66	2DEC66	21DEC66	-.1	.0
P3	2	4		TEC	PLAN CASTINGS	2.0	22DEC66	9JAN67	21DEC66	6JAN67	-.1	.0
P3	4	14		PUR	OBTAIN CASTINGS	12.0	9JAN67	3APR67	6JAN67	31MAR67	-.1	.0
P3	14	15		PRD	M/C CASTINGS	4.0	3APR67	1MAY67	31MAR67	28APR67	-.1	.0
P3	15	16		QAD	INSPECT	1.0	1MAY67	8MAY67	28APR67	5MAY67	-.1	.0
P3	16	21		PRD	MECH ASSEM	2.0	8MAY67	22MAY67	5MAY67	19MAY67	-.1	.0
P3	21	29		PRD	RUN-IN	1.0	22MAY67	30MAY67	19MAY67	26MAY67	-.1	.0
P3	29	30		PRD	FIT CONTROLS	1.0	30MAY67	6JUN67	26MAY67	5JUN67	-.1	.0
P3	30	31		TEC	TEST	2.0	6JUN67	20JUN67	5JUN67	19JUN67	-.1	.0
P1	1	2		TEC	DESIGN	5.0	5DEC66T	9JAN67	5DEC66T	9JAN67	.0	.0
P1	2	13		TEC	DESIGN BASE FRAME	10.0	9JAN67	18MAR67	9JAN67	18MAR67	.0	.0
P1	13	16		TEC	DESIGN COVERS	1.0	18MAR67	23MAR67	18MAR67	23MAR67	.0	.0
P1	16	17		PRD	MAKE COVERS M/C1	6.0	23MAR67	8MAY67	23MAR67	8MAY67	.0	.0
P1	17	34		PRD	MAKE COV M/C 1	6.0	8MAY67	20JUN67	8MAY67	20JUN67	.0	.0
P1	34	23		PRD	FIT COVERS M/C 2	1.0	20JUN67	27JUN67	20JUN67	27JUN67	.0	.0
P1	23	24		QAD	FUNCTION TEST	1.0	27JUN67	4JUL67	27JUN67	4JUL67	.0	.0
P1	24	25		QAD	ACCEPTANCE TEST	2.0	4JUL67	18JUL67	4JUL67	18JUL67	.0	.0
P1	2	6			LEAD	1.0	9JAN67	16JAN67	13JAN67	20JAN67	.4	.0
P1	6	8			LEAD	2.0	16JAN67	30JAN67	20JAN67	3FEB67	.4	.0
P1	8	9	L	PRD	TOOL MANUFACTURE	10.0	30JAN67	10APR67	3FEB67	14APR67	.4	.0
P1	10	11	L	PRD	P/P MANU	8.0	20FEB67	24APR67	3MAR67	28APR67	.4	.0
P1	9	11			LAG	2.0	10APR67	24APR67	14APR67	28APR67	.4	.0
P1	11	12		PRD	SUB-ASSEM	2.0	24APR67	8MAY67	28APR67	12MAY67	.4	.0
P1	12	18		PRD	STAGE 1 ASSY	1.0	8MAY67	15MAY67	12MAY67	19MAY67	.4	.0
P1	18	19		PRD	STAGE 2 ASSEM	1.0	15MAY67	22MAY67	19MAY67	26MAY67	.4	.0
P1	19	20		QAD	FUNCTION TEST	1.0	22MAY67	30MAY67	26MAY67	5JUN67	.4	.0
P1	20	21		QAD	ACCEPTANCE TEST	2.0	30MAY67	13JUN67	5JUN67	19JUN67	.4	.4
P3	4	13		TEC	DESIGN TOOLS	4.0	9JAN67	6FEB67	20JAN67	17FEB67	1.4	.0
P1	8	10			LEAD	3.0	30JAN67	20FEB67	10FEB67	3MAR67	1.4	.0
P3	13	14		PRD	MAKE TOOLS	6.0	6FEB67	18MAR67	17FEB67	31MAR67	1.4	2.0
P1	17	19		PRD	FIT COVERS M/C 1	1.0	8MAY67	15MAY67	19MAY67	26MAY67	1.4	1.0
P1	11	15			DUMMY	.0	24APR67	24APR67	12MAY67	12MAY67	2.4	.0
P1	15	18		PRD	SUB-ASSEMBLY CIRCUITRY	1.0	24APR67	1MAY67	12MAY67	19MAY67	2.4	2.0
P1	2	4			LEAD	1.0	9JAN67	16JAN67	3FEB67	10FEB67	3.4	.0
P1	2	14		TEC	DESIGN CIRCUITS	3.0	9JAN67	30JAN67	3FEB67	24FEB67	3.4	.0
P1	4	5		PUR	OBTAIN RAW MAT'L	9.0	16JAN67	18MAR67	10FEB67	14APR67	3.4	.0
P1	4	10			LEAD	3.0	16JAN67	6FEB67	10FEB67	3MAR67	3.4	2.0
P1	6	7	L	TEC	TOOL DESIGN	6.0	16JAN67	27FEB67	20JAN67	22MAR67	3.4	.0
P1	14	15	A	PUR	OBTAIN B.O. ITEMS	11.0	30JAN67	17APR67	24FEB67	12MAY67	3.4	1.0
P1	7	9			LAG	3.0	27FEB67	18MAR67	22MAR67	14APR67	3.4	3.0
P1	5	11			LAG	2.0	18MAR67	3APR67	14APR67	28APR67	3.4	3.0
P1	13	12		PRD	MAKE BASE FRAMES	4.0	18MAR67	17APR67	14APR67	12MAY67	3.4	3.0
P1	18	22		PRD	ST. 1 ASSY	1.0	15MAY67	22MAY67	13JUN67	20JUN67	4.0	.0
P1	22	23		PRD	STAGE 2 ASSEM	1.0	22MAY67	30MAY67	20JUN67	27JUN67	4.0	4.0
P3	2	5		PRD	PLAN COMPONENTS	3.0	22DEC66	16JAN67	27JAN67	17FEB67	4.4	.0
P3	5	7		PRD	MAKE COMPONENTS	6.0	16JAN67	27FEB67	17FEB67	31MAR67	4.4	.0
P3	7	8	L	PRD	SUB-ASSY	3.0	27FEB67	18MAR67	31MAR67	21APR67	4.4	.0

Figure 14.6   TIME ANALYSIS

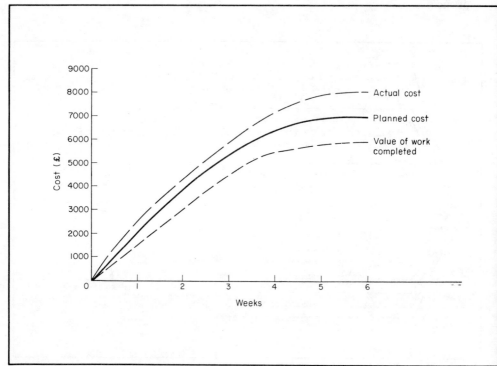

Figure 14.7 COST—WORK CONTROL GRAPH

PERT has developed (and is still developing) from its original designs and one comparatively new addition to the technique is the use of precedence diagrams. This is an alternative method of network construction, where each job is shown as a box, called a work item. The box contains a brief description of the operation to be performed and the logical work flow is shown by arrows as in a conventional network. The arrows are designated "dependencies."

This type of network can be applied to engineering subassembly or small building and many other activities in engineering, general manufacturing and construction industries.

14:4   Problems in the use of the techniques and conditions for success

For fairly small activities, it is possible to draw up and control a network manually. But for an activity which has more than a hundred separate tasks, manual methods become both expensive and inefficient. It is likely that 100 task activity is the dividing line between manual and computer-based PERT. This factor does not rule out organisations that have no computer but need to plan, schedule and control 100 plus task activities, as PERT computer program packages are available which can be run on a computer bureau. ICL markets a PERT program package handling network planning and precedence diagrams, so that control over projects and in particular resource analysis, cost control and multi-project scheduling is possible. It is suggested that this package is highly flexible and can be run with credit by both newcomers to and long established users of PERT.

Considering that PERT has been around for quite some time it has failed to make a significant user break-through. The use of charts and diagrams has had a long innings, why has PERT failed to catch fire? A PERT network looks complicated to anyone who has never used one. It seems to be a verbose way of stating the obvious. In some situations the obvious "critical path" in an operation is so well known that a PERT network is superfluous.

In small companies, particularly in building organisations there is usually no one available with the training and perhaps inherent skill to make and control a PERT chart. Like all techniques PERT needs a reasonable amount of training and expertise to ensure success.

The preparation of a network is best done by a committee or a number of personnel whose activities will be closely controlled by the network. Estimating times, for example, will be better done by specialists in the activities concerned. In making a network, it will perhaps be more easily understood if it can be broken down into trades and work groups etc.

14:5   Conclusion

The advantages claimed for PERT are as follows:

1   It helps to ensure that delivery or completion dates are achieved by establishing controllable work schedules

2   Resource allocation is improved
3   Because better resource allocation is achieved, tighter budgeting and overall lower costs are gained
4   Key activities in achieving the completion date are highlighted so that special attention can be directed towards them
5   PERT makes it possible to make a simulation of the activity being programmed, so that the effect of carrying out the activity in different ways can be discussed and the best way chosen
6   Monitoring of progress is made easier by the use of PERT. Delays which will vitally affect the completion date are seen soon enough to enable corrective action to take place
7   Expenditure can also be monitored in the same way and corrective action taken if it is necessary
8   By using PERT, better co-operation between different functions, trades and even organisations appears possible

These are advantages which ought to dictate a wider use of PERT.

14:6   Further reading

1   J D Wiest and F K Levy, *A Management Guide to PERT/CPM*, Prentice Hall, 1969
2   G Thornley (ed), *Critical Path Analysis in Practice*, Tavistock, 1969
3   K G MacLaren and E L Buesnel, *Network Analysis in Project Management*, Cassell, 1969
4   H S Woodgate, *Planning by Network*, Business Books, 1964
5   A Battersby, *Network Analysis*, Macmillan, 1967
6   J J Moder and C R Phillips, *Project Management with CPM and PERT*, Reinhold, 1964
7   L R Shaffer (and others), *The Critical Path Method*, McGraw Hill, 1965
8   C W Lowe, *Critical Path Analysis*, Business Books, 1966
9   K G Lockyer, *Introduction to Critical Path Analysis*, Pitman, 1964

FIFTEEN

Cost reduction planning

15:1 Introduction

There are various ways and means of carrying out cost reduction. The earth-quake approach of demanding huge cost reductions because the company is in financial trouble has had considerable success. Cost reduction teams have been tried, where commando units have scoured the company for likely savings. Budget validation too has been attempted to some degree, while some companies consider that containment of costs is sufficient.

All these methods have advantages and disadvantages. By far the best approach seems to be one where line managers consider cost reduction as second nature, where it is built into the job. Cost reduction then becomes day-to-day operating practice, not a once and for all situation which must be lived through and then forgotten.

The best ways of ensuring a continued appreciation of a need for cost reduction and containment so that both become a way of life is through budget validation and cost reduction planning.

15:2 Description

Cost reduction planning is one of the major plans which in total make a profit plan. The plan should be company wide, certainly not confined to production operations (though this area will probably yield most savings). The administration function should be attacked as vigorously as the shop-floor and distribution department.

The complementary activity of budget validation is stressed. Cost reduction planning, as will be seen later, has wider implications than budget validation though both could yield significant savings. The two techniques should be used as one major weapon in cost containment and reduction. The basis of planned cost reduction comes under the following four headings.

A planned approach.   Cost reduction should follow the same rigorous analysis as the marketing or R & D plan. Strengths and weaknesses need to be ascertained, objectives established and cost reduction plans made to achieve them.

Co-ordination.   Cost reduction is an important element in the total profit plan. It should be viewed as being part of the goal-orientated strategy of the company. Volume and profit margins are the key factors in earning profit. Cost reduction can improve profit margins, but so could increased volume. The complementary nature of these two factors should ensure a close link between marketing and cost reduction planning.

Continuity.   It is essential that the improvement in standards of performance and the overall cost structure of the company improves from year to year. The investment of capital to help to improve productivity should be viewed on a long-term basis. The long-term and continuous nature of cost-reduction planning is therefore stressed.

The results of assignments take many months, perhaps years to mature and come fully to fruition. Recruitment of specialist cost reduction staff should also be a long-term procedure.

All these factors pinpoint the need for continuous cost reduction planning.

Comparisons of performance.   Measurements used should all show the performance required against that already achieved and still being achieved. This should be done operating unit by operating unit, department by department. The comparisons should pinpoint out-of-course events or departments or units which should prove useful in reducing costs. Cost reduction plans have constantly to match the challenge of established or desired corporate objectives.

The discussion between marketing and cost reduction personnel (though marketing management should themselves be involved with cost reduction) should eventually arrive at the improvements needed in both spheres. A critical analysis of each area may subsequently prove that objectives of one or the other may have to change, but initially this first critical discussion should establish the degree of performance improvement/cost reduction required.

It is assumed that appropriate measurements of performance are in existence. (If not, they quickly should be.) These should be set out under the following headings:

1   Department
2   Overall activity
3   Operation
4   Current performance
5   Possible performance—that is, maximum machine speeds etc
6   Performance required by overall objectives

Standard product data sheets should be available for at least all major products.

The result of this data preparation will be a cost/performance presentation showing current standards and those required if the overall corporate objectives are to be achieved. If possible, standards achieved for the last three to four years should be prepared.

A gap between the current and required performance will be calculable. This should show where the greatest effort is required; areas where there has been no improvement or whose improvement has deteriorated over the last three to four years might be suitable for a cost-reduction attack. Area where recent improvements have been made, may not be so rewarding but should not be ignored completely.

It is at this stage that a dialogue is necessary to discover whether the gaps between current and desired performance can be closed. Some companies use a form for this purpose with headings as follows:

1   Desired corporate objective
2   Can this be achieved—state yes or no
3   Give reason for non-achievement—state whether resources, competence, strategies, other constraints are responsible
4   Quote alternative objectives
5   Quote resources, strategies, etc, necessary to achieve either initial or revised objectives

The dialogue necessary to complete such a form should establish the current situation in some depth. Particularly, key factors in achieving corporate objectives at a local level will be recognised as well as all constraints which inhibit performance improvement.

It may be necessary to call in personnel skilled in cost reduction techniques— MS personnel—to help to calculate the possibility of reducing costs and increasing performance.

It is possible to utilise a checklist for cost/performance evaluation. A suitable list is shown in Figure 7.1 in *How to Make and Control a Profit Plan*. Various headings are utilised, the first of which is *area*. It is useful to divide the organisation into areas which can be regarded as complete entities, worthy of a single assignment.

Production costs can be broken down into direct labour, indirect labour, material and overheads, for example, for departments initially and then perhaps for each production line.

The next heading should list the possible failings—for example, inefficient scrap recovery methods are increasing material costs; tolerances and quality are too tight so more products than necessary are being scrapped, etc. Many of the possible failings should already be known by line management or shop-floor personnel and their knowledge and experience should never be ignored.

The third column should show the percentage improvement or deterioration in standards which have taken place in the ones being analysed. It is likely that a figure for the past three to four years would be valuable.

The analysis carried out so far should automatically lead to the next section where possible improvement action is listed. For example, to improve material utilisation a plan for scrap minimisation should be made. Standardisation and variety reduction of the product range might be tried. Tolerances and overall quality might be lowered without prejudice to customer acceptance of the product range.

Under the subsequent heading all the management techniques which might be used should be recorded. Most are listed in Chapter 28 on budget validation or given elsewhere in the book. Techniques by themselves will not make all cost reductions possible, but they have a potent effect on the situation and non-use of a technique which would help a line manager to improve the standards of his performance, should be an anathema. The crucial problem is for line managers to know the full range of techniques and for skilled personnel to be available to apply them.

There are other ways of reducing costs apart from techniques usage. For example, financial considerations, management ability, and use of resources.

FINANCIAL CONSIDERATIONS. These are largely concerned with the differential rate of return on investment in various parts of an organisation and the use of total company financial resources.

There are numerous ways in which financial strategy can improve a company's performance and reduce costs. The use of the money market, for example, might improve a company's gearing and help to beat both taxation and inflation. The use made of money in inventories and assets should be strictly controlled and appropriate project evaluation techniques used. The use of sale and lease back of assets has had considerable attraction over the last few years.

MANAGEMENT ABILITY. The situation audit which should be an integral part of a profit planning and strategy formulation system, should have measured management ability and shown where corrective action is required. Few techniques applications or resource additions will help if line management is failing.

Line management ability and overall performance might be reviewed under the following headings:

Total ability. This should also emerge from the application of job study (particularly merit rating). Performance reviews should indicate how well or badly a manager is carrying out his job.

Organisational difficulties. These include job descriptions (which may be inadequate) as well as a poor organisation which inhibits communications and low-level decision making.

Control. Systems and procedures must be developed to enable the right speed of response to be made to out-of-line situations.

Decision making. Decision making of all kinds should be based on accurate and timely information. Is this currently available? Managers should not be blamed if they make wrong decisions based on inadequate information.

Morale and motivation. Morale needs to be checked as well. The possibility exists that insufficient resources are being allocated to morale, motivation improvement and to other behavioural problems.

An assessment on these lines should help to reduce managerial weaknesses, through the promotion of training and development programs. Suitable performance appraisal methods may have to be installed.

USE OF RESOURCES.   Resources for line managers are usually the amounts of stock, work in progress, labour and equipment and machinery of all kinds which can help him perform better.

Machinery and equipment should only be used where its value has been proved through a rigorously disciplined project evaluation method.

Normally a cost reduction plan will show many areas and activities which might benefit from the application of more resources. A full list of these ought to be drawn up, otherwise it is possible that some priority applications may not be included. All operations which could either immediately or at some time in the future need extra resources ought to be recorded. At a suitable moment in the future, a resource allocation (if proved necessary) can be made. The benefits from this approach are:

1   Priorities for capital spending can be assessed
2   Suitable time limits can be made, so that appropriate negotiations with the unions can be carried out
3   The necessary finance can be obtained and the overall cash-flow not unduly disturbed

These further cost reduction activities should support and complement the application of cost reduction techniques. All should be combined under the next heading on the cost reduction plan—to suggest whether any improvement action is possible this year and if so what improvement is planned. This latter column should show monetary savings, performance improvements and staff reductions (so that personnel departments can arrange suitable transfers, etc).

Any improvement in control systems which are necessary appear in the subsequent column.

Finally the number of the action plan which covers the improvement should be quoted. The action plan will be a timetabled list of activities, recording who is responsible for them, their cost, the gain and the time taken to implement them. It will show in detail how the proposed improvements will be achieved.

This finally will complete the cost reduction plan. A rigorous analysis will have been carried out, priorities assessed, resources allocated and control established by means of a constant monitoring of action plans.

15:3   Successful areas of application and examples

The methodology of cost reduction is standard no matter what area of an organisation is being investigated. It is not intended to quote the application of a technique, etc, as this is done throughout the book.

15:4   Problems in the use of the techniques and conditions for success

The major problem lies in carrying out a company-wide survey within a plan-formulation period, which normally might last two to three months. (The same problem arises in the application of budget validation.) If skilled MS or cost reduction experts are used to help line managers analyse their costs and potential savings, it also means that such personnel will not be available for carrying out cost reduction activities. Actual savings stop being achieved while analysis and plans are made for further assignments.

Whether and how personnel skilled in cost reduction techniques should be utilised in cost reduction planning has been discussed at length in Part 1 of this book. The author's views, briefly summarised, are that MS personnel are vital if cost reducting planning, budget validation and efficiency auditing are to be carried out efficiently.

There is good evidence that a combined project team approach which uses a balance of line managers, MS personnel and other staff specialists is an appropriate way for many organisations to tackle cost reduction planning.

The main danger in carrying out cost reduction planning lies in the process itself. There is always a likelihood that the planning process will predominate and cost reduction will be secondary. All emphasis will be placed on the paper-work and little on the actual achievement of savings.

This sounds a little ludicrous, but from actual experience tends to happen.

15:5   Conclusion

Cost reduction should be companywide. It applies equally to manufacturing, administration, distribution or marketing generally. Whether the production divisions are chosen as the main area for cost reduction will depend upon the comparative costs of production, marketing, administration, etc. As a preliminary measurement the ratio of personnel and their cost in each functional area should be obtained. The ratio will vary from industry to industry, but will give some indication of where a cost reduction program should start.

15:6   Further reading

1   B H Walley, "An Integrated Approach to Cost Reduction," *Work Study*, October 1967

2   W L Furlong and L H Robertson, "Matching Management Decisions and Results," *Management Accounting* (USA), August 1968

3   D T Welch, *Budgetary Control and Cost Reduction for Retail Companies*, Macdonald.

4   *Cost Reduction*, Institute of Cost and Works Accountants

SIXTEEN

Market planning

16:1 Introduction

Profit planning provides a framework for the motivation of professionalism in management. Where entreupreneurial flair is missing it promotes an alternative— a methodology for managerial action and decision making.

Marketing personnel (particularly the sales force) have long prided themselves on their "feel for the market." Market planning is often an anathema to them. Yet, as marketing decisions become more complex and the need grows for in-depth appraisals of markets, product life cycles, and competitors' strengths and weaknesses, a logical approach to marketing is essential.

16:2 Description

Market planning is the logical projection of an analysis of the company's market environment, its past performance and future objectives.

It is a multi-activity operation covering all the functions that are necessary to determine the customer demand for a product or service and its sale and distribution at a profit. The major functional areas covered are:

1   *Market research.*   The determination of what can be sold when all factors that inhibit sales have been diagnosed and taken into account
2   *Product planning.*   Planning the optimum mix of sales, taking account of market environment, company resources etc
3   *Sales promotion.*   All activities which will help to promote sales—advertising, public relations etc

4   *Sales and selling.*   The activities of the sales force
5   *Warehousing and distribution*
6   *Control.*   Setting objectives and their achievement
7   *Administration.*   Systems and techniques used in the control of marketing
     activities, especially in the sales order processing operation. Stock control,
     sales forecasting, competitive strategy, product pricing routines would all
     come under this category.

As with the main profit planning routines, the methodology is covered by three
main activities:

1   *Measurement.*   In the case of market planning, measurement should cover
     all aspects of the company's past performance in current market situations,
     competitors' and own strengths and weaknesses. Costs of all kinds should
     also be listed. (This largely should be covered by the term analysis)
2   *Planning.*   Once an analysis has been carried out objectives have to be
     established and appropriate plans and strategies made to achieve them.
     As part of the planning process action programs that establish individual
     objectives and courses of action need to be drawn up
3   *Control.*   All plans need control and it should be an integral part of the
     marketing plan process. Control of the sales force and the achievement
     of planned sales volume is necessary

The marketing plan has no independent existence. The concept of profit planning
presupposes that there is a complete integration of all functions in the company.
There must in consequence be complete interrelation between marketing,
manufacturing, research and development, finance, cash flow, etc. No function
should play a role or have capital and other resources allocated to it which is not
in keeping with its importance.
    The benefits of market planning are a microcosm of those of profit planning
itself:

1   The optimisation of effort
2   The best use made of scarce resources
3   The elimination of illogical decisions
4   The setting of objectives and establishment of key results making the
     best use of management time

16:3   Successful areas of application and examples

Marketing plans have been made for both consumer and industrial product
marketing, but it is obviously the latter with its comparatively long lead times
for product change which benefits from a planned approach.
    As part of the process it will be necessary to establish:

1   *Strategy aims.* These must be concerned with the strategies that the company should adopt—the number of new products to launch, how far an attack should be made on competitors' market shares etc
2   *Micro-marketing strategies.* Micro-strategies concerning pricing, levels of inventory, distribution and warehousing, sales promotion, product quality, etc
3   *Marketing objectives.* Market share, levels of profit, etc, desired
4   *Marketing information systems.* Appropriate marketing information systems should be established before planning procedures are implemented. These include the setting up of a market research activity, plus costing rates from which pricing and product market strategies can be developed

The outline of a suitable marketing plan will obviously differ from company to company, but the basic plot which must be covered is as follows:

ANALYSIS

General situation audit

1   *National and world economy.* Strategy trends and effect on turnover etc.
2   *Political situation.* How this might affect marketing
3   *Technological situation.* Technological trends which may affect company's product market situation should be quoted
4   *Market and competitive situation.* Shares of company and competitors; strengths and weakness of each are needed
5   *Skills audit.* Skills of the marketing, sales force and distribution personnel should be ascertained
6   *Vulnerability audit.* Factors which make the company vulnerable to changes in the market place ought to be recorded
7   *Organisational review*

Past and present company performance

1   *Strategies* which have been used in the past and their success
2   *Current situation* in profit, turnover, market share, for each product and family group

PLAN. The following elements of the plan should be established:

Market report. This report should list the current turnover, value and the number of items being sold by all methods.

Production plan/product mix. This part of the plan should show how far current manufacturing capacity is being utilised, the products utilising it and their profit margins.

Objectives and strategies

1   Overall objectives should be made listing turnover, market share, profit against each market segment for the next three to five years
2   Strategies whereby the company will achieve the objectives desired should be stated
3   The overall objectives quoted in (1) should be broken down into detailed objectives which can be the subject of suitable control. Individual objectives may be necessary
4   Action programs should be drawn up, which will list all the actions that need to be carried out to achieve the company's marketing activities
5   A planned future marketing organisation will be necessary whereby management development and career planning will be facilitated

Other plans including diversification, proposed product mix, etc, should be made.

Marketing costs should be known and kept under control.

CONTROL.   A comparison between objectives and their achievement will be the key control requirement. This will need to be on an overall and an individual basis to complement the way in which objectives will have been established. Costs will have been ascertained and an appropriate budgetary control system will be in operation.

While the foregoing lists the steps, data and possibly the forms that will constitute the plan, this does not provide the basic motivation or belief in the planning methodology. This can only come from commitment as there must be a belief that a planning process can improve profitability. This is not something that can easily be achieved.

TIMETABLE.   An outline timetable for making a marketing plan is shown in Figure 16.1.

16:4   Problems in the use of the technique and conditions for success

Many companies have been extremely profitable without the aid of planning procedures. There are many obvious examples where flair, even genius, has produced higher rewards than any planning system possibly could do. The danger exists that planning procedures will strangle initiative and flair. A plan should provide a framework within which management is motivated to make professional decisions. It should not impinge on entrepreneurial activities.

The protagonists of the marketing concept state that in a competitive economy, the market place provides the only real justification for a company's existence. This is a truism accepted by many companies. It could, unfortunately, lead to a

Item	Data required	Personnel responsible	Timetable	Comment
1 Establishment of appropriate job description				
2 Set appropriate ROI and turnover/profit margin targets	Network			
3 Obtain appropriate market data	Market research data by product group of self and competitors, strength, weaknesses, etc			
4 Carry out product mix exercise to ensure that items with high profit margins receive top priority in the plan. Also required will be a product-profit projection for each of the major products or product groups involved	Cost and technological data			
5 Establish requisite strategies	Appropriate marketing fields			
6 Arrange check meetings with plans co-ordinator and manufacturing division to ensure that plan embryo is in line with total company requirements				
7 Set marketing objectives for each product group, area, area manager and rep. Break objectives down into trade and industry requirements				
8 Check all marketing costs to ensure that every possible reduction in costs has been investigated. Establish budgets of expenditure	Cost information of all marketing activities			
9 Check all marketing systems to ensure that appropriate planning and monitoring information will be available on time				
10 Establish controls and action programs				
11 Correlate and present final marketing plan				

Signed _____ Director

Figure 16.1 TIMETABLE FOR MAKING A MARKETING PLAN

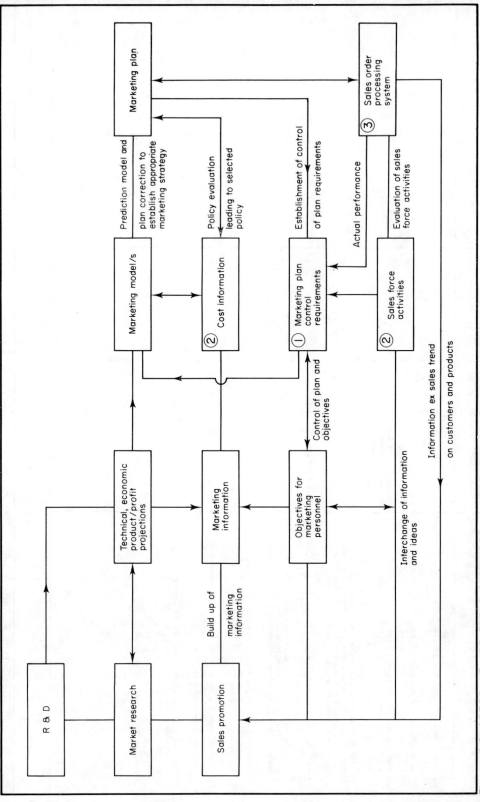

Figure 16.2 AREAS OF USE FOR A COMPUTER IN DECIDING MARKETING STRATEGY

situation where marketing will dominate all functions, especially production and research and development.

In a planning context the outcome of such company bias might be the production of a marketing plan which is not basically complementary to other activities. The cornerstone of planning is that the plans that are made are totally integrated. Unless this happens the use of company resources will not be optimised.

The dangers that plans will be made which are not compatible with company style, strengths and weaknesses, competitors' activities and the marketing environment generally will have to be faced. Planning is a complex operation in which management at all levels needs to take part and give advice. The plans have to be realistic and fully supported by the chief executive.

Behavioural attitudes will largely determine the planning mechanisms and the eventual success of the plans that have been made. Training in techniques and in establishing appropriate psychological attitudes is vital. Unless these are satisfactorily resolved, planning will fail.

Appropriate strategies will be necessary and these will have to emerge as part of the planning process. Company management may be reluctant to state strategies openly. They may want the ends or objectives, but not decide on the means—the strategies—whereby the objectives can be achieved.

Marketing personnel have often prided themselves on their flair. They are not the easiest people in an organisation to discipline by means of a marketing plan.

16:5 Conclusion

Like all planning, market plans have a definite role to play within a particular company style. Even where overall profit planning is not formalised, market plans still have considerable advantages in the optimisation of marketing resources.

Any procedure which attempts to assess priorities for profit earning must be welcomed. Market planning is high on the list of such procedures.

16:6 Further reading

1   Ralph Glasser, *Planned Marketing*, Pan Books, 1968
2   Martin L Bell, *Marketing Concepts and Strategy*, Macmillan, 1965
3   David B Montgomery and Glen L Urban, *Management Science in Marketing*, Prentice Hall, 1969
4   Philip Kotler, *Marketing Decision Making*, Holt, Rhinehàrt & Winston
5   J Stapleton, *How to Prepare a Marketing Plan*, Gower Press, 1971
6   B Taylor and G Wills, *Long-Range Planning for Marketing and Diversification*, Crosby Lockwood, 1970
7   J Siebert and G Wills, *Market Research*, Penguin
8   L Hardy, *Marketing for Profit*, Longman
9   E R Corey and E S H Star, *Organisation Strategy—a Marketing Approach* Bailey Bros and Swinfen

Production strategy and planning techniques

17:1 Introduction

This chapter covers various production strategy and planning techniques (other than production planning and control systems) which help to decide the way production facilities are first determined and then utilised. Together they should help to optimise production costs.

17:1 Description

PRODUCTION STRATEGY. Strategy is the activity of utilising and controlling company resources to achieve desired objectives. A strategy will usually result from a considered choice between two or more alternatives.

Any investigator setting out to analyse production facilities and methods and costs therefore needs first to analyse production objectives. This may be a little more difficult than it sounds. Often such objectives are obscure; more often still they are inferred rather than overt.

The main aim of such a pre-investigation analysis is to determine how far production facilities match the objectives that production personnel have accepted. A secondary aim should be to distinguish where there are incompatibilities in objective setting.

The first aim will only be achieved once a production facilities audit has been carried out. A suitable checklist is given for this purpose (page 158).

Incompatibility of production objectives often arises from an inadequate appreciation of production facilities, technical and administrative skills, and the general environment. For example, the following objectives may have been set:

1 Least cost production
2 Maximum machine runs
3 Highest possible material utilisation
4 Production within the normal working week
5 Maximum output
6 Flexibility of output—that is, it must fluctuate with sales demand
7 Total efficiency and control

While least cost production and maximum machine runs may practically be synonymous, flexibility of output is scarcely compatible with any of the other six objectives quoted. On closer investigation few, if any, of the objectives may be compatible with the equipment, general facilities and production systems of the company.

Where marketing requirements dominate the company scene, production personnel will be forgiven if they assume that production facilities must always be used to fulfil the whims of the market. This certainly should not be so. For example:

The production range. This should depend to a large extent on the available production facilities, the capital available for their management and extension, the competence of production personnel and the availability of raw material supplies as well as marketing requirements.

Customer service. This can be achieved by building up stocks and improving the flexibility of production equipment. However, such flexibility will nearly always be bought at extra production cost—setting up time, extra components and tools to be carried, etc.

Quality of products. Quality too will depend upon the type of production equipment in use and how close to desired tolerances it can be set.

Without taking such considerations into account, there is a strong likelihood that marketing personnel may make dangerous oversimplifications about their requirements and the company's ability to meet them. An investigation into production strategy and in particular production facilities should be extremely wary of a marketing dominance, which entails an extremely lopsided total company strategy and incompatibilities in the objectives which production personnel have been given.

Section 17:3 sets out the production audit and then goes on to strategy problems that need to be resolved.

PREPRODUCTION PLANNING. Preproduction planning is a methodology which entails the investigation of all production equipment, facilities, methods and systems which could be utilised in a planned production unit.

The method should ensure that ultimately, production takes place at optimum cost within the overall company and marketing strategy framework.

PLANT LAYOUT.   A plant layout study should ensure that the siting of all production machinery, production services and materials handling equipment is such that optimum cost production is substantially aided.

Examples of both preproduction planning and plant layout will be given in section 17:3.

17:3   Successful areas of application and examples

PRODUCTION AUDIT.   Once objectives have been suggested a production audit will help ensure whether or not they can be met.

Product equipment.   List each piece as follows:

1   Generic type
2   Main usage
3   Constraints in use—tolerances, quality, size of product etc
4   Designed speed
5   Current output levels achieved
6   Age
7   Supplier
8   Current utilisation
9   Machine manning strength
10   Current book value
11   Amount of maintenance required: per week, month, year
12   Modifications carried out since it was new
13   List possible further modifications

Handling equipment.   (See chapter on materials handling.)

Production services.   List all equipment under the following headings:

1   Heating
2   Lighting
3   Power—steam, gas, electricity
4   Water
5   Details as per production equipment

Production personnel.   List by number:

1   Direct operatives
2   Indirect operatives:
a   Storemen
b   Materials handling
c   Maintenance

d   Foremen/chargehands
e   Cleaners
f   General labouring
g   Clerks
h   Progress chasers
3   Tradesmen—list by trade

Utilisation of personnel. Quote:

1   Appropriate ratios
2   Production in standard hours
3   Direct time
4   Allowed hours
5   Bonus percentages for each production cost centre

Production systems. Record each system and assess its suitability for planning and control purposes.

1   Bonus and labour control
2   Production planning and control
3   Materials utilisation
4   Cost control
5   Quality control

Factors outside the control of production personnel

1   Order flow
a   Seasonality
b   Ratio big/small orders
c   Ordering patterns generally
2   Production range
a   Total number in product range
b   Product items ordered each month
c   Product items making 80 per cent of total production
d   Dependence on outside suppliers
3   Service required
a   Deliveries—days from receipt of order
b   Quality
c   Variations from standard
4   Government regulations of various kinds
5   Personnel policy
a   Production staff morale
b   Joint consultation activities
c   Flexibility
d   Training

e	Recruitment—calibre available
f	Efficiency
6	Company cash flow situation
a	Cost reduction needed
b	Investment possibilities
7	Site location
a	Is desired change possible?
8	Company style and management methods
a	Is desired change possible?
9	Efficiency of support services
a	R & D
b	Warehousing and distribution
c	Management services
d	Accounting and control

With the data collected assess:

1	Production equipment:
a	Bottlenecks
b	Replacement equipment which would improve efficiency, List:
i	Specification
ii	Price
iii	Improvement anticipated
c	Differences between current annual sales forecast (translated into production capacity) and actual production capacity
2	Handling equipment—as above
3	Production services. Consider utilisation and current sales forecast, and suggest where over capacity and poor utilisation increase costs
4	Production personnel
	Consider:
a	Utilisation
b	Motivation and morale
c	Compare bonus and pay with output
d	Skills
e	Age
f	Competence against obvious requirements
5	Production systems. Discuss adequacy for measurement, planning and control purposes

Analysis of possible and desired objectives

1	Least cost production. List how this can be obtained including:
a	Changed equipment—elimination of constraints
b	Different service requirements

c	Amended product range
d	Increased stock levels
e	Appropriate cost control systems etc
2	Maximum machine utilisation. Factors which will need to be analysed include:
a	Order flow constraints
b	Product range—standardisation and variety reduction
c	Equipment maintenance standards
d	Calibre of staff
3	Highest possible material utilisation. Possible constraints will include:
a	Equipment—possibility of operating at tolerances demanded
b	Quality required is too high
c	Bonus systems to be orientated towards output and quality, not output alone
4	Maximum output. Elements which may inhibit maximum output will include:
a	Manufacturing equipment constraints
b	Fluctuating order flow
c	Too high quality required etc

An audit on the lines suggested followed by appropriate analysis and objective evaluation will establish what production strategies and objectives are acceptable.

The subsections which follow indicate some of the strategy and planning activities which ought to follow from the production facilities audit.

PRODUCTION COST REDUCTION PLANNING. This subject is dealt with in Chapter 16 and will not be considered again—except to point out that a production cost reduction plan should have immediate priority after a production audit and analysis has been carried out.

COMPLEXITY OF OPERATION. Except for some who are bemused by engineering sciences, there is always a strong feeling among production staff that their activities should be simplified not made more complicated. This is a reasonable view for them to adopt as inevitably it should lead to decreased production costs. Among the factors which they might make a claim for are these:

1. Fewer products—perhaps following a standardisation and variety reduction activity
2. Products demanding a simple technology
3. High volume per product item
4. Long design life of products
5. Products to use only standard equipment
6. Products with standard components
7. Low quality requirements
8. Constant production levels

9   Make for stock rather than direct to a customer
10   Products demanding a minimum of engineering services

The adoption of such tactics and their combination into a "simplicity of operation strategy" might have considerable risks. Competitors may take advantage and offer customers a more sophisticated product. Technological vulnerability may ensue. But with these risks appropriately considered, there seems no reason why simple things done well should not be as profitable as difficult things done badly— if not more profitable.

MAKE OR BUY DECISIONS.   Accurate make or buy decisions are vital for the cost profit performance of the production division and also for the long-term profit health of the company in general. It is as wrong to believe that everything which is sold has to be made by the company, as to think that everything has to be made externally.

Make or buy decisions are both economic and strategic. If variable, semi-variable and fixed costs are known accurately, plus appropriate sales forecasts, then the economic decision is simple. The strategic decision is much more difficult.

Despite economics, is it desirable to provide work for production personnel? Loss of company expertise in making the products may be important. Buying from outside could militate against tight control over quality and service which may be vital competitive factors. Finally, making internally could retain product and manufacturing exclusiveness.

Where a decision to make internally has been made, opportunity cost—that is, the possibility of utilising some equipment for other more profitable items— needs to be considered.

PREPRODUCTION PLANNING.   Preproduction is an attitude of mind in technique utilisation. Often cost reduction or general production strategy is considered only once a production unit is in operation. By then it is often too late to make the significant savings that would have been made if preproduction planning had been carried out.

Management services personnel and others skilled in systems design and cost reduction techniques need to be involved in all matters relating to setting up a new manufacturing unit, especially in the application of the following techniques:

1   Methods study and procedure analysis. This will help plant layout
2   Work measurement. Where MTM or other similar techniques are used, pre-work standards can be calculated before operations are started. Appropriate incentive schemes can then be negotiated with union representatives
3   Manpower planning should start from the beginning

4   Profit planning to ensure that the operation is integrated with the company as a whole is essential

5   PERT is a useful technique in helping to ensure that critical paths are recognised and appropriate resources allocated for them

6   Production strategy (as set out in this chapter) should be negotiated

7   Systems design—appropriate systems need to be formulated and personnel trained in their use, before production starts

8   Materials handling needs to be considered

9   Plant maintenance routines are necessary

10   The logic of the learning curve will have to be taken into account

11   Project evaluation (plus risk analysis) is vital

.his is a formidable list of techniques which needs to be employed before a ʰroduction unit is established. If such techniques are not used it will be certain that productivity, machine utilisation, return on investment and profit will all be lower than they should be.

PLANT LAYOUT. Both engineers and method study personnel claim plant layout as their own. Each has believed that their special expertise will produce a layout of production equipment, production services, material handling routines and warehousing and dispatch areas which will minimise cost.

The conflicting claims of electrical, mechanical, production and civil engineers, draughtsmen, method study personnel, safety officers, materials handling specialists, operations research staff, line managers, that only they know best, suggests that a team approach to the problem is required.

These brief notes are written from the viewpoint of the contribution which a member of an MSD might make.

Benefits which should ensue from good plant layout

1   Direct

a   Best use made of shop-floor, warehousing and general stores space

b   Material savings—in electrical cable, ventilation, steam, water, gas, etc, piping

c   Saving in equipment—overhead cranes, materials handling equipment generally etc

d   Materials movement between processes

2   Indirect

a   Ease of maintenance

b   Ease of movement of staff about the shop

c   Opportunities to keep the shop clean and tidy

d   Avoidance of heat losses and ease of space heating

e   Facilitating of store-keeping and movement of stores to the line

f   Help in systems application—production planning and control, inventory control (audit) etc

g   Ease of control of labour, material utilisation, and product movement.
h   Aids to supervison generally
i   Avoidance as far as possible of fatigue or low morale inducing conditions
j   Flexibility—a need to build in the ability for change in layout at a later
     date

Safety and legal restrictions must be taken into account.

General principles of plant layout.   The production process will largely dictate
the machine—operation flow pattern. Within this framework these general
principles need to be applied:

1   Least space utilisation is obviously extremely important and any layout
     should be judged on its space utilisation
2   Working conditions must be such that an optimum working environment
     is achieved. The layout should not inhibit the good working practices which
     will motivate least cost production
3   Interdependent operations, activities and departments should be in prox-
     imity to each other
4   As far as possible the layout should facilitate flow process-type manu-
     facturing operations
5   There are various standard plant layout "plans" which need to be con-
     sidered. For example:
a   Straight line
b   *U* shaped
c   Divergent processes
d   Convergent processes
e   *E* plan etc
     The processes, the site, access to road/rail communications will help to
     determine which plan is most convenient
6   The most widely used services—maintenance, stores, etc—should be
     located centrally
7   All dangerous or obnoxious stores should be isolated
8   Adequate aisle and non-productive space for in process storage and move-
     ment must be made
9   Warehousing and materials handling processes must be considered as
     an integral part of the production process
10   The advantages of single or multistorey manufacturing processes should be
     discussed
11   Arduous or delicate work should be carried out in comparatively quiet
     parts of the factory
12   Adequate service areas should be provided:
a   Engineering
b   Tool reclamation
c   Inspection/quality control

e Dispatch
f Receipt
g Maintenance of all kinds

The least possible operative and product movement should be the major aim. Initial cost could be saved many times over by reducing product movement.

A plant layout survey. The following steps should be taken:

1 Form a plant layout team of engineering and methods study personnel
2 Collect basic data:
a Site situation
b Building regulations
c Basic constraints—money (capital) etc
d Production processes—number and type of equipment and constraints
e Volume of production—warehouse services required and proximity of supply
f Labour required
g Materials handling equipment required
h Warehouse and general stores space desired
3 Plan the operation:
   By using a three-dimensional model layout, scaled drawings or other media, choose the following:
a Type of layout—*U* shaped, straight line etc
b Direction of materials/production flow
c Position of key activities:
i Warehouse
ii Stores
iii Receipt—etc
d Considering minimum space and least cost position remaining:
i Production processes
ii Service areas
iii Labour facilities—canteens, restrooms etc
e Draw power and service lines of all kinds and at the same time locate service supply areas
f Design material handling system utilising principles suggested in Chapter 22
4 It is assumed that:
a Space required for production, materials movement and storage and service areas will be pre-calculated
b Suitable scaled templates for production processes and service areas will be made, so that layout amendment is facilitated
c Various layouts will be made and by adopting suitable evaluating criteria, the optimum one will be chosen
d At all times the various constraints will be taken into account

17:4 Problems in the use of the techniques and conditions for success

Production is only one of the functions in a company which determines profitability. It is possible that production must be subordinate to the marketing function. But normally production personnel ought to have very positive ideas about how their function is organised, the products it makes and the costs which marketing policy imposes.

17:5 Conclusion

The chapter has very briefly discussed some of the various factors that production personnel ought to be concerned with in optimising production costs.

Production personnel should have a strong influence on total company strategy. Also within the production function there are needs for substrategies. These are mostly concerned with resource allocation and make or buy decisions all of which should be considered within production planning strategies.

17:6 Further reading

1   Oxenfeldt and Watkins, *Make or Buy*, McGraw Hill, 1956
2   A M Brichta and P E M Sharp, *From Project to Production*, Pergamon, 1969
3   S Ammer, *Manufacturing Management and Control*, Appleton
4   M J Clay and B H Walley, *Performance and Profitability*, Longmans, 1965
5   D L Lock, *Project Management*, Gower Press, 1971
6   J Hollinggum, *Mass-Production With Batch Work, Group Technology Explained*, Pergamon
7   C Hardie, "Plant Layout," *Works Management*, July/August 1971
8   E S Buffa, *Operation Management: Problems and Models*, Macdonald and Evans
9   J Cantor, *Profit Orientated Manufacturing Systems*, AMA
10 D B Urman, *New product Programs—their Planning and Control*, AMA
11 R W Mallick and A T Gaudreau, *Plant Layout Planning and Practice*, Wiley

EIGHTEEN

Organisation planning

18:1 Introduction

The hundreds of thousands of words written about "organisation" by management writers describe situations which seldom, if ever, occur in real life.

Organisations are rarely planned as such. They grow around the dynamism of the chief executive. Alternatively, a series of tough uncompromising line managers arise that acquire responsibilities and personnel, because they demand them and are powerful enough to obtain them.

The neat little boxes and lines of command which are shown on many organisation charts seldom reflect the truth as it is at ground level. Status, despite level line boxes on organisation charts, is rarely equal. One man has a greater say in what decisions are made, on the committees on which he sits, on the attitudes which permeate the organisation. The rest—his apparent equals—accept his leadership.

18:2 Description

Organisation is the formal way a company projects job responsibilities and the interrelationship and communication between the members of the company having the job responsibilities.

Organisation is the arrangement which should secure the participation and co-operation of all members of a company so that corporate objectives are achieved. It should have a linking effect on everyone's efforts to secure corporate objectives.

The basis of organisational planning is the matching of the company's organisation, competence and capacity to adapt to the environment in which it has to operate in order to survive. This indicates, rightly, that an organisation must be constantly changing in order to meet the challenge of technological, competitive and general environmental change. But first of all, some fallacies and comments.

LINE AND STAFF ORGANISATION. Various organisational divisions have become enshrined in the theory of the subject. One of these is the line and staff organisation. Line organisations, it was said, were based on military precepts with separate departments commanded by line managers. Managers would be non-specialist and support was to be provided by staff personnel, each of whom would be a specialist in some field.

The advantages of such divisions of responsibility were that strict ranking was possible, delegation of authority was easy, the chain of command usually clear and well established.

With rapid technological and managerial changes—techniques, for example— this kind of organisational division is quickly becoming obsolete. The line managers—if that is what they are still to be called—need the assistance of specialist staff nearly constantly. The interchange between "line" and "staff" is taking place more often. No longer can a line manager claim that he has no specialist knowledge and still hope to retain his job.

The terms "line" and "staff" therefore are an anachronism and the sooner they are dropped the better.

FUNCTIONALLY BASED UNITS. The functionally based unit of management is rapidly gaining favour. In this type of organisation managers control a particular function in the company, which is usually largely autonomous. The

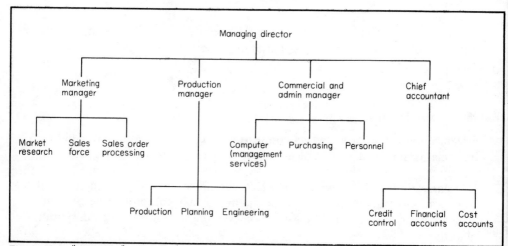

Figure 18.1 "NORMAL" ORGANISATIONAL CHART FUNCTIONALLY ORIENTATED

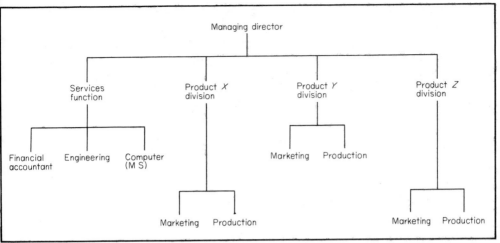

Figure 18.2 DIVISIONALISATION
An organisation, if profit centred, is likely to be more profit orientated

advantages of functionally based units are that line and staff are integrated into one unit and the specialists are constantly available as supports to the non-specialist. Everyone can specialise and gain some skill important to carrying out the function appropriately.

However, responsibility is often diffuse and discipline can suffer in consequence. Indeterminate lines of command and promotion may cause frustration and perhaps animosity. But this is certainly the kind of organisationally integrated unit that will be more adaptable to change.

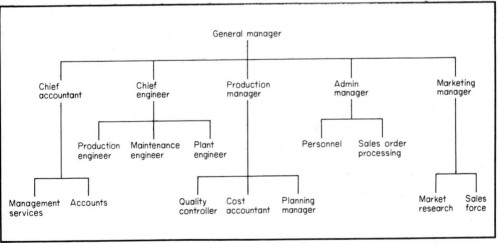

Figure 18.3 EXAMPLE OF BADLY DEFINED FUNCTIONS
An organisation not likely to be very profit orientated
or one readily usable for MBO practices

SPAN OF CONTROL. This concept was a favourite of early organisation theorists who suggested variously that five to ten or perhaps fifteen subordinates were the maximum that should report to a supervisor or manager. The duties or responsibilities that were being carried apparently had no influence on the decision. But of course this is the crucial factor in span of control considerations. A senior manager may be overburdened with four junior managers reporting to him. A supervisor in charge of a football pool vetting operation may find forty female clerks reporting to him are too few.

CENTRALISATION AND DECENTRALISATION. This subject too has caused considerable anguish to organisational theorists. The trend in the last decade has been towards decentralised units, with Drucker's profit centre idea leading to considerable local autonomy. The trend to some extent now seems to be in reverse.

Decentralisation was thought to improve local decision making—as the man on the spot knew best. Morale was supposed to be higher, span of control and communications problems were minimal.

In an age of increasing specialisation, local autonomy has often failed to produce reasonable results. When no specialist assistance was necessary, local decision making was probably no better than could be achieved centrally. But now that increasingly difficult decisions have to be made, autonomy of the kind which complete decentralisation has engendered must be wrong.

The behaviouralists that suggest that local decision taking is vital for good morale, have generally ignored the fact that many organisations using decentralisation have disintegrated into separate closely guarded units, gaining nothing from being part of a larger unit. The twin problems of management by objectives are that a manager will try to take as many of the company resources as he can, giving him a higher probability of success in achieving his objectives; at the same time he will tend to ignore total organisation requirements.

Decentralisation engenders these kinds of failings. Unless a strong and cohesive management structure and a consolidating methodology, such as profit planning, are in operation local autonomy will promote disintegration, bringing all the weaknesses of small unit operations.

Local autonomy could only be supported while local decisions could be made more speedily and accurately than was possible centrally. The use of computers, and special decision making techniques associated with them, suggests that centralised decision making must now be better.

The rise of the specialist, the increasing number of graduates of all kinds being used, will create a gulf between old and new staff, managers and managed, whether local autonomy is given or not. The problem of morale and communication is bound to worsen, unless communication of all kinds is improved. Local autonomy has still to prove that it is better in this respect than a degree of centralisation.

Lines of communication with computers and data links in operation must be reasonably short between the centre and the periphery.

The degree of reversal in the trend to decentralise will depend on the organisations concerned. Company style, tradition and the will and power of the chief
executive will aid or hinder the process but the pressure towards centralisation
is now stronger than towards decentralisation.

COMMITTEE DOMINATION.   This has long been an anathema to many
theorists. It chokes decision making—managers can shelter their responsibilities
behind its cloak—it produces anonymity and time wasting. Only weak organisation have committees, it is blandly stated.

It is only now being realised that committees play a vital role in establishing a
battleground on which managers can fight out their prejudices. If managers must
play behavioural games, then a committee is as good a place as any in which to do
it. Problems arise when one or two strong personalities combine to dominate
the committee and decision making becomes warped in consequence.

These dangers are real, but not to have a battlefield is probably just as dangerous.

OUR ORGANISATION IS RIGHT BECAUSE IT IS OUR ORGANISATION.
This perhaps is the greatest fallacy of all. It infers that it has grown with the company, personnel are used to it, it has been adapted over the years and seems to
suit the situation, therefore the current organisation must be right.

It is not surprising that many organisations are warped in favour of strong
managers or because someone once had an idea which at that moment in time was
appropriate but is no longer.

It is partly due to arrogance, perhaps lethargy or even just a lack of knowledge,
that senior managers assume that they have the optimum organisation for that
particular moment. The one thing the organisation does not know is how to change
automatically to meet changing situations. It needs regular well-informed and
deep organisational analysis to achieve appropriate change.

An organisation's appropriateness is constantly being eroded. For example
by:
Managerial change.   People resign, die, retire. One type of organisation may
not suit a changed managerial team. Calibre will dictate (to some extent) spans
of control, centralisation/decentralisation, etc.

Company style.   A new chief executive may demand a completely new
company style. The organisation has to be adapted to suit.

Technological factors.   To meet changing technological environment, the
organisation will need to recruit staff with specialist skills. At the same time long-
service members of the company will be growing obsolete despite retraining.
These factors may lead to communications problems, the need to set up new
departments and possibly new grading schemes. The new specialists will have
to be phased in so that their full potential is realised; old managers may have
to be phased out.

Social and governmental factors.   Social, economic, taxation and ecological
legislation will impose constraints on the company—how it operates generally

and in particular industrial relations and redundancy problems may become extremely important in deciding organisational trends.

Market and product changes. The product life cycle of most products is shortening rapidly. This should mean a greater amount of time and money spent in R & D, better marketing knowledge, greater rapidity in marketing resource deployment.

General manpower problems. A scarcity of specialist staff and more rapid turnover of such staff must motivate greater time and effort being spent on manpower planning, succession planning and training planning. The need for the organisation to be established accordingly is vital.

General behavioural factors. If technological change is imposing ever greater stress, then the company may have to change its style, or its management methodology. This will have an effect on the organisation.

Corporate planning. The introduction of corporate planning will certainly push the company into organisational changes that will aid it in meeting different technological and environmental situations. But at the same time there may be a need to consider the position of management and staff in the company. It has always been assumed that management and the company have identical aims. As objectives become more rigorous, performance appraisal more salutary and the personality and individuality of a manager may have to be subordinated to the achievement of corporate goals, there may be a dichotomy of views if not outright opposition by management.

A METHOD OF CARRYING OUT ORGANISATION PLANNING. The following items need to be covered if organisation planning is carried out. A situation audit:

1   Job responsibility for all personnel in the organisation.
2   Skills audit:
a   Qualifications
b   Years in current job
c   Performance audit
d   Overall knowledge
3   What work is done in each department, section, operation. Detail interrelationship with other departments and activities
4   Appraise the value of work done
5   Appraise company objectives and strategies
6   An executive questionnaire is necessary:
a   Name
b   Title
c   Location
d   Responsibilities—hiring, firing, resource utilisation etc
e   Name of immediate superior
f   Name of people who respond to executive
g   Names and duties of committees to which executive belongs
7   Management generally

a   Are all functions and responsibilities clearly defined?
b   Is there an organisation chart?
c   What management grades exist, do these appear to be appropriate?
8   Committees
a   Are there too many?
b   Do they stultify decision making?
c   Are they run badly?
d   Are there written agendas?
c   Do personal animosities intrude?
f   What executive decisions emanate from the committees?
g   What advice is passed on by the committees?
9   Record company functions needed to achieve objectives and strategies
10 In the light of the audit carried out highlight apparent weaknesses in:
a   Job responsibilities—list objectives and constraints inherent in the job and see if any ambiguity exists
b   Communications—are these poor/medium/good?
c   Working groups
d   Span of control
e   Overlapping of departmental functions (is combination possible)
f   Line and staff relationship
g   Centralisation/decentralisation
h   Decision making
j   Use of committees
11 Consider weaknesses in the light of:
a   Function, product groupings and geographical locations
b   Greater flexibility in the organisations
c   Revised status, grades
d   Authority levels—is there duplication?
e   Dissimilar objectives for similar groups of personnel
f   Training (and the lack of it)
12 What controls exist for:
a   Expenditure of all kinds including capital expenditure
b   Hiring
c   Firing
d   Making policy decisions
e   Methods and procedures
13 When all the organisational aspects are considered, does the company's organisation affect efficiency in any of the following ways:
a   Poor or non-existent decision making
b   Poor communications
c   Low morale
d   Lack of standardisation in:
i   Management methods
ii Grading
iii Any functional activity
e   Non-adherence to company policy

f   Lack of flexibility
g   Low utilisation of staff ability at all levels
h   Insufficient specialists and specialist assistance
j   Delays of any kind:
i   Order processing
ii   Recruiting
iii   Training—etc

18:3   Successful areas of application and examples

Each company needs an organisation suited to its style of management, calibre of management staff, the environment where the company operates, etc. This being so, individual organisation charts seem of little value. However, a checklist of major precepts which might be utilised to carry out organisation planning might be useful and this is now quoted:

1   A situation audit similar to the one in section 18:2 is vital.
2   Organisation structure. The organisation needs a structure which should include all the following factors
a   Job design should fit a manager to his role and to the objectives he must achieve
b   Appropriate job parameters and general constraints must be explicit and fit objectives
c   Suitable training, succession, management development and appraisal techniques need to be established
3   A sufficient identity of purpose, job responsibility and appreciation of the behavioural aspects of organising a work force, need to be built into the organisation structure. How far meaningful activities—job security, job satisfaction, ability to influence company objective setting, opportunities to express personality and be creative as well as directive—can be built into most people's jobs is very doubtful. But the dichotomy between corporate and personal objectives has to be bridged. Organisation may have to play a major role in doing this
4   A manager's authority should be limited to his ability to lead and control effectively
5   The organisation should teach managers and others to use their skills to the best purpose. Authority should be delegated in line with the objectives which have been established
6   Interdepartmental, interactivity, interfunction rivalries should not exist within a good organisation. The organisation should promote co-operation; only rivalries of achievement should be fostered.

18:4   Problems in the use of the technique and conditions for success

The major problem of organisation lies in its informal and not in its formal nature. One man may work well and conscientiously for one manager by not for another, though this latter may organisationally be his logical manager.

Companies are always in a state of flux and they are often much too complicated as organisms to have definite organisation imposed upon them. Upheavals of this kind have been known to stifle the enterprise for years until good human relations have been re-established, confidence and morale generally regained and all the multiplicity of unofficial relationships built up.

Most companies do not begin with a clean sheet of paper and say "What can we do?" They are constantly evolving (even apparently the most lethargic) and organisation planning should ensure that new organisations also evolve, perhaps comparatively slowly.

There is reason to believe that the objectives of the company plus the desired methods of achieving them are no longer compatible with desires of management and staff. There is a large body of behavioural scientists that suggests that real motivation will emerge only from job satisfaction and this in turn will evolve only from the establishment of job duties which are meaningful to the job holder. This theory is totally contrary to the "division of labour" concept and all that it implies.

The behavioural scientists' view of management is given in Chapter 35, and, if it is true, it dictates a view of organisation and job responsibilities very different from what might appear to be the most efficient organisation structure.

18:5 Conclusion

There seems no uniform or correct organisation for any company. From year to year the structure will need to change, often substantially. What may suit one company may be disastrous for another.

The factors that are now impinging on a company's organisation are many. The pressure due to rapid technological change is growing. The worst that can happen in these circumstances is to adopt a "fire-fighting" approach to organisation. Not to plan is tantamount to giving up.

18:6 Further reading

1 P A Management Consultants, *Company Organisation*, Allen & Unwin, 1970
2 J Kelly, *Organisational Behaviour*, Irwin Dorsey, 1970
3 J C Emery, *Organisation Planning and Control Systems: Theory and Technology*, Macmillan, 1968
4 E F L Brech, *Organisation—the Framework of Management*, Longman, 1959
5 G Mc Beath, *Organisation and Manpower Planning*, Business Books, 1966
6 R S Edwards and H Townsend, *Studies in Business Organisation*, Macmillan, 1966
7 Joseph A Litterer, *The Analysis of Organisation*, Wiley, 1965
8 Joseph A Litterer, *Organisation: Structure and Behaviour*, Wiley, 1963
9 R L Kahn (and others), *Organisational Stress*, Wiley, 1964
10 Joan Woodward, *Industrial Organisation: Theory and Practice*, Oxford University Press, 1965

NINETEEN

Operations research and general mathematical techniques

I: MODEL MAKING AND SIMULATION

19:1 Introduction

Everyone has used models of some kind, ever since childhood. Business models, unlike toy trains, should help to provide meaningful solutions to complex problems. That many business models do not provide such solutions perhaps reflects more on the users than the formulators. Regretfully model making seems to be largely in the hands of management science personnel and not line management. This is a situation that needs to be changed.

19:2 Description

A model, in business, is simply a representation of part or a whole of the characteristics of a real life situation. It could be a physical model such as an aircraft testing wind tunnel or a model harbour with artificial tides. But in industry and commerce a model will usually be a series of mathematical equations, which is intended, when manipulated, to simulate a larger system.

Usually a model is used primarily to predict the outcome of decision taking in a real process. It tends to answer questions which begin: "What would happen if . . . . ?" To do this a model need not represent the whole of the real life situation. If the important elements are represented then the results should, everything else being equal, be meaningful.

The advantages of simulation or answering "What if?" questions by the use of models are formidable:

1   A business model will usually be less costly to use and experiment with than a real process

2   It will give an organisation an ability to experiment with ideas and alternatives without unduly affecting or taking up the time of senior management. Normal company operations are not affected

3   The act of gathering data for a model often helps line management to rethink their problems and information requirements generally so that the overall decision making process is improved

4   The act of model making also has the effect of emphasising the interdependence of company functions. (Inventory control models are a good example of this.) This too should help co-operation and decision making

Many benefits will, therefore, accrue merely by attempting to build a model. The interaction of variables will be noted. An appreciation of regression situations should be gained. The implications of decision making in the field being modelled should also be seen more clearly.

How a model is set up and run appears very easy in theory but in practice is far from simple. The methodology used in model making is as follows.

FORMULATING A MODEL.   Model making should clarify and formalise ideas about the real-life system as well as make it possible to predict how the system probably will work when certain decisions are made. Techniques and theories used for model making in operations research include mathematical statistics, probability theory, linear and non-linear programming, Monte-Carlo technique, decision and games theories, Boolean algebra, etc.

The steps which should be used in formulating a model therefore will have to include fairly sophisticated mathematics. These should be decided before the model is made.

THE MODEL'S PURPOSE.   Establishing this may be more difficult than it sounds. What information is required and what accuracy? What variables have to be considered? What objectives must the model achieve—maximisation of profit, increased turnover, improved competitive position, etc?

CONSTRUCT THE MODEL.   The more complex the structure of the model, the more likely it will be to give erroneous information and of course it will take longer to build and be more expensive to operate. It is better to have several reasonably small models, which are constructed to solve a well-defined problem, than to attempt a model with major interaction variables. Models should be capable of adaptation and extension.

What is or is not controllable by line managers is important. The model has to be feasible, as near real life as possible. It is of little use setting constraints or parameters which are beyond the control—or even the knowledge—of line managers.

Education through discussion is vital and no model should be constructed in a vacuum. Line managers must be informed of the project and as far as possible contribute to it, especially in providing appropriate data.

The model may be derived from analogies, from implicit theories based on experiences, from analysis of historical data or from the result of experiments. Analogies depend upon the recognition of similarities between rational systems and those that are man made. The use of implicit theories has its own inbuilt danger complicated by the fact that line managers are not usually asked to think conceptually.

In many ways the formulation of a model should stem from experiments. In this way cause and effect should be proven at each stage in the model's formulation and an accurate result is nearly assured. With experimentation it is also reasonably easy to determine the relationship of variables in the model and by how much they change. Various scales—for example, ratio, ordinal, interval—can be used.

The parameters, therefore, need to be determined statistically and also their relationship with each other. Even when apparently well established, correlation and multi-colinearity may be misleading. For example, an established linear correlation between sales and advertising, when X per cent spent on advertising appears to increase sales by Y per cent, can be dangerous if taken too literally. Market factors generally, competitors' reactions and consumer resistance at particular price or quantity levels will all help to nullify such an apparent correlation. Forecasts, too, may be a problem. Short-term forecasts can be made by using exponential smoothing and a tracking signal or by lagged adaptive response rates, but longer-term forecasting depending upon market conditions and national and international situations, could be fatally inaccurate.

DERIVE A SOLUTION.   The solution obtained should be the optimum one that could be produced from all the decision variables that have been used. Analysis or simulation could have produced the result. The former is appropriate for a restricted optimal type solution; the latter is necessary where there are numerous alternative answers to the problem and the model itself is a complex one.

TEST THE MODEL.   The model's efficiency can be tested by comparing the result produced by the model with observed reality. The results have to be practical within the context of the problem which the model has been established to solve.

Building the model should have helped to identify solutions anyway, because numerous parameters, alternatives and basic decision rules will have been initially stipulated.

If the model is not too complex, various statistical tests can be made to determine the "goodness of fit."

ESTABLISHING CONTROL.   Control should be established to ensure that model amendment is carried out.

PUTTING THE SOLUTION TO WORK.   Once a solution has been obtained, it should be handed over to a line manager for implementation. Implementation can be as much a problem as when a solution has been derived by any other means.

19:3   Successful areas of application and examples

Generally the following model types are recognised.

PHYSICAL MODELS.   These have already been mentioned and two examples quoted. Generally they have little relevance in business model making.

DETERMINISTIC MODELS.   These are models where all the factors or constraints which affect the real life situation are known and are quantifiable. The use of linear programming in a production planning and control situation is usually a definitive model, in that costs, machine output rates, economic batch sizes of products to be made are all known.

PROBABILISTIC MODELS.   The type is used where the data, constraints, etc, are not fully known. Games theory models, forecasting, simulations of all kinds make use of risk or probability. Often the term "stochastic" is used to desscribe such models.

BEHAVIOURAL MODELS.   This kind of model is used where a system is dependent upon individuals. Where probabilities of the sytem's interactions can be accurately determined the model becomes probabilistic in nature. But where inputs, outputs and general constraints are difficult to quantify a behavioural model is justified.

STATIC AND DYNAMIC MODELS.   Static models do not take into account time effects; conversely dynamic models do take time effects into account. Academic though these divisions sound, models of the kind outlined have successfully been put into operation in many organisations as the following examples show:

Stock control.   Stock or inventory models are one of the most common varieties of model. ICL's SCAN 3 and IBM's OPTIM and IMPACT stock control computer packages are good examples.

These packages are optimisation models in that they attempt to take account of the customer service levels required, stock values, economic ordering quantities, sales demand, variations in lead time and market and profit considerations in order to arrive at an optimum stock level.

It is not always realised what constraints operate on stock levels and Figure 19.1 shows them and the nature of the model.

Inventory is concerned with the total value held, the number of items in the inventory range, the turnover/profit obtained from each segment of the inventory

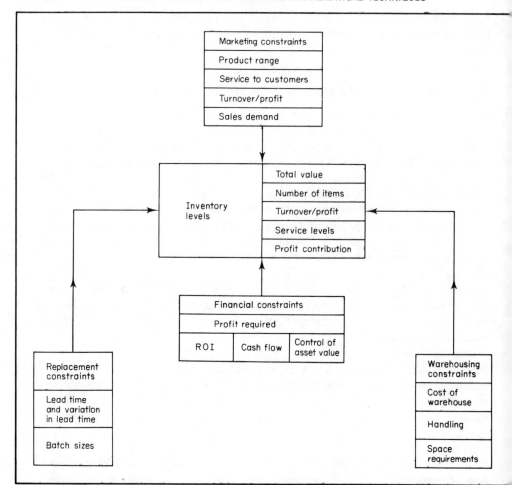

Figure 19.1 CONSTRAINTS OPERATING ON STOCK LEVELS

or perhaps each item and service levels which are achieved. All these factors are affected by the four major constraints outlined and the minor constraint elements which go to make up the whole.

Warehousing constraints, for example, include the cost of warehousing, provision of materials handling facilities, equipment and space constraints generally. There is also a limit on the amount of capital which an organisation can afford to invest in stock. The capital needs a return, and the whole asset must be controlled accordingly.

An inventory control model must attempt to reconcile the constraints quoted in the figure. Unfortunately none of the computer suppliers' packages do precisely this. They tend to optimise several—service levels, sales demand and batch sizes. Analysis of profitability of items is included in the calculations but the rest of the constraints are ignored. Anyone wishing to have the kind of model outlined as Figure 19.1 will so far have to construct it themselves.

ICL Prompt—Production control.   This is another, quite sophisticated, computer package developed by ICL's software specialists. It is concerned with the four major aspects of production planning and control—the breakdown of orders, stock control, factory planning and purchase control.

Order breakdown uses sales forecasts to review stock requirements and the order position. Future requirements are calculated as economic batch quantities. The stock control element carries out stock recording as well as reviewing requirements produced by the breakdown.

The production planning element models factory operations. It gives the location and rate at which work will be carried out, as well as having a monitoring activity. There are four stages: forward loading, short-term loading, work documentation and progress control.

The purchase control element orders from suppliers (for desired bought-out requirements) and also reports on delayed orders.

The models used in PROMPT consist of queues which require data on waiting times, productive capacity, parts breakdowns, etc.

Financial analysis—ICLs "Prosper" package.   This ICL computer package helps organisations to carry out financial analysis and project evaluation. The package sets out to analyse the forecast cash flow and associated risk in capital projects. The interactions between different risk levels and forecast cash flow, sales prices, production volume and production costs are calculated and resulting cash flows made. If necessary, trends and trade cycles can also be taken into account.

The package is a model in that it can answer questions such as: "If sales prices were consistently 5 per cent lower than anticipated, what effect would this have on the return on investment?"

Company models.   Many large oil and chemical companies have a company model. An oil company for example, by using linear programs can optimise the flow of crude oil from several sources, through numerous refineries, to make various products for different markets. This could never be regarded as a simple operation, but certainly the associated model would be regarded as reasonably simple (compared to an attempt to optimise a medium-sized engineering company an oil company's operations are simple)

Econometric models.   Various models of the economy or at least sections of it have been hypothesised, none with much success. As yet no complete model of the economy has been built which provides an accurate forecasting method of factors such as the gross national product, unemployment, changing price levels, rate of investment, etc. The interaction between such factors is still not fully understood.

Marketing models.   Various types of model have been used to represent marketing environments and many types of mathematical techniques have been applied. For example, regression analysis has often been used in forecasting market trends. Factors such as price, quality, gross disposable income are used in a linear regression and tested for significance. Differences in rates of change are found and eventually forecasts deduced.

Games theory has been used to assess the probability of the outcomes of various strategic decisions. When more than two participants are playing the game, the mathematics become exceedingly complex. Yet competitive response models appear to have a very important future and it is in this area and in marketing models generally that the use of model making should grow.

Models and computers.   It is scarcely conceivable that a model of any sophistication can be handled manually. Even fairly simple inventory control models can best be handled by a computer. Specialist computer programs have obvious attractions to computer and OR personnel but it is always best to first investigate all the program packages that are available in this field. Packages if thoroughly understood provide the basis for a short-cut to utilising the computer as a decision making aid. Once the limitations of the package are appreciated and an evaluation of the limitations and their effect on desired results is known, then the package should be used.

19:4   Problems in the use of the techniques and conditions for success

It has yet to be proved conclusively that model making will lead to better decision making.

Many models cannot be made to respond fast enough to represent real life situations. Anyone who has attempted to computerise a stock control system knows how difficult it is to give an up-to-the-minute answer on queries on stock levels, without very expensive equipment.

Models rely on data which is often difficult or perhaps impossible to obtain. If such data were available there might be no need to make a model.

A model rarely, if ever, is a true mirror of a real-life situation. The real process is usually too complicated to be simulated by mathematical equations. In particular there are always problems of building in probabilities for behavioural situations. Once this is done, the model's accuracy is dependent upon a guess about people's psychology. Even when well informed, a probability is still only a probability, not a certainty. The model will certainly simplify reality.

The antagonists of modelling suggest that every situation is unique and to impose a general version in a situation which deserves a purpose-built model will lead to totally misleading results.

One thing that both protagonists and antagonists of model making recognise is that a mature model is more likely to produce more approximately correct answers than an immature one. It takes some months of running to make essential corrections to a model. It will rarely operate correctly first time.

The type of personnel who can formulate models are extremely rare. Models need both complex mathematics and statistics, plus a detailed knowledge of the organisations, methods, systems and decision making processes in the company.

19:5   Conclusion

Both the protagonists' and the antagonists' views on model making have been expressed in this chapter. Undoubtedly model making is an aid to decision making. It is important now and will have an increasing importance in the future. Models may not become the complete decision making tools that many management sciences personnel suggest, but they will have a vital role to play in this process.

19:6   Further reading

1   J L Livingstone, *Management Planning and Control, Mathematical Models,* McGraw Hill, 1970
2   J McLeod (editor), *Simulation: the Modelling of Ideas and Systems with Computers*, McGraw Hill, 1968
3   R F Barton, *A Primer on Simulation and Gaming*, Printice Hall, 1970
4   Philip Kotler, *Marketing Decision Making—a Model Building Approach*, Holt Rhinehart and Winston, 1971
5   E S Buffa, *Models for Production and Operations Management*, Wiley, 1963
6   A Charnes and W W Cooper, *Management Models and Industrial Application of Linear Programming*, Wiley, 1961
7   F M Bass (editor), *Mathematical Method and Models of Marketing*, Irwin, 1964
8   C P Bonini, *Simulation of Information and Decision Systems*, Prentice Hall 1963
9   J L Livingstone, *Management Planning and Control—Mathematical Models*, McGraw Hill, 1970

II :   FORECASTING

19:7   Introduction

All forecasts are wrong, but some are more wrong than others. The difference in the accuracy of forecasts is usually due to the forecasting data method used and the amount of data that has been collected and built into the method.

The second part of this chapter is concerned largely with statistical forecasting. Intuition or market knowledge is mostly ignored, though these factors play a large part in arriving at an appropriately accurate forecast.

19:8   Description

The premise used here is that it is possible to use statistics to estimate the future more accurately than guessing without their aid. Of course, market knowledge is vital in forecasting but it should be allied with a statistical method.

Why forecast? Because there has to be a basis of some kind for planning, budgeting and decision making generally. When a manager states that it is impossible to forecast in his business, he means that he is taking most of his decisions in the dark.

There are, of course, both long-term and short-term forecasts. Even so, for the chemical industry a long-term forecast is ten years or more; for the clothing industry six months may be too long. Short-term forecasting—of which statictisal stock control is a good example—will be concerned with tactical decision making. Long-term forecasting—such as that needed by profit planners—will influence strategic decision making.

DATA REQUIREMENTS.   Data requirements should stem from the search for and identification of the factors that affect business decisions and activities. These factors are often variables, elements which alone and together affect the future situation of the company.

Profit planning, for example, is largely concerned with the future, determining long-term economic growth, product obsolescence, social change, technological change, and so on. Economic growth may be dependent on numerous considerations, for example:

1   World trade situations
2   Balance of payments problems
3   Inflation
4   Social problems
5   Potential factors
6   Industrial unrest—etc

The company's product obsolescence rate could be affected by:

1   Rate of economic change
2   Rate of social change
3   Growth of individual incomes
4   Technological changes of many kinds including:
a   Rate of technological progress
b   Amount of R & D expenditure committed by competitors
c   Use of alternatives and raw materials
d   Dependence on raw material supplies of certain kinds

It is necessary to first recognise all the factors concerned and then determine which of them is most important. Obviously, in long-term forecasting this comparative importance is changing all the time and an appropriate weighting factor should be made, at suitable intervals.

In short-term forecasting, data collection and its use in a statistically based methodology is just as important. It so happens that most data is collected as part of a time series and implicit in the method used.

TRENDS. Statistical forecasting largely relies upon the use of trend analysis. Every forecast has some sort of trend either statistically derived or intuitively inferred built into it. The trend could be linear. For example, sales of a particular product could be increasing at a constant rate, or the trend may be exponential— that is, an increase in sales could be by a constant ratio. There are also seasonal trends, when sales of ice cream, for example, go down in winter.

Some forecasting methods set out to measure the relationship between variable factors. The sales of electric fires go up and this in turn will have some effect on the demand for electricity.

Statisticians therefore "predict" by analysing the history of past events, either directly or by considering related events. Errors in forecasting are important, not only to the user of the forecast but also to the statistician. Errors indicate random fluctuations in a trend situation and help to make new forecasts which it is hoped will be more accurate. In stock control, errors help to determine the level of safety stock to be carried as well as future forecasts.

The use of time-series—that is, the analysis of trends over a period of time— is the usual basis for statistical forecasting. Some common types of forecasting methods follow.

Moving averages. Moving averages are the simplest form of time-series fore- casting. Usually a years' sales or data is produced as follows.

		SALES
1973	January	120
	February	135
	March	145
	April	120
	May	140
	June	160
	July	180
	August	190
	September	195
	October	205
	November	200
	December	210
	TOTAL	2000

The total data is then added together and then divided by the number of items in the series—in this case twelve. The forecast for sales in January 1974 would be $2000 \div 12 = 166$

For the forecast for February 1974, the sales for January 1973 will be dropped and those of January 1974 added. There will, in consequence be a "moving aver- age."

The failings of this method of forecasting are obvious. In the example shown, there is an upward trend in sales and it seems likely—even from a casual inspec- tion—that January 1974 sales will be in excess of the 166 calculated.

A forecast with an increased probability of accuracy could have been calculated by giving greater weight to the most recent data.

Exponential smoothing.   Exponential smoothing or weighted moving averages was a method first used in the 1950s by R G Brown to carry out the improvement quoted above. The trend weighting factor was called a smoothing constant and given the Greek letter α (alpha).

The smoothing constant is given a value from 0.1 to 0.9. Generally if the variations in past demand are slight a low value for the smoothing constant or alpha factor is given. If variation is extreme then a high value is given.

The method of forecasting must ensure that a greater weight is given to the most recent data. The formula used is:

Let $a=$ the smoothing constant and let it be between 0 and 1
Let $M=$ the month's past demand so that $M_1\, M_2\, M_3\, M_4$ are past months in order.
Then the average demand $=$

$$aM_1 = a(1 - a)M_2 + a(1 - a)M_3 + \ldots + a(1 - a)n \div 1M$$

which can eventually become:

New average demand $= \alpha\, M_1 + (1 - \alpha)$ old average demand where M_1 is the most recent demand.

It is possible to calculate a trend (if a trend is present in the series) by deducting each month's average demand from the previous month's. The trend average can be calculated by using:

α(current trend) $+ (1 - \alpha)$ old trend

A forecast can be made by adding the average demand and the trend.

The major problem in exponential smoothing is determining the value of the smoothing constant. But even if this has to be guessed (and in practice it usually is) the result will probably be better than using moving averages alone.

How exponential smoothing (plus a tracking signal which is discussed next) is used in a practical stock control system is given in section 19:9.

Bias in forecasts and adaptive systems.   Once a forecast has been made it needs to be checked for accuracy. Obviously the more accurate the forecast, the more a system is under control.

D W Trigg published a paper in 1964 which proposed a method of signalling forecasting errors. [See D W Triggs' article in the *O R Quarterly*, July 1964.]

"Biased forecasting" implies a situation where forecasts have a tendency to be too high or too low particularly when the error to some extent is dependent upon previous errors. A tracking signal which indicates the degree of error is an advantage, especially if past errors can be built into future forecasts.

The work of Box & Jenkins in the early 1960s uses exponentially weighted moving averages to achieve a forecast. [See "Some Statistical Aspects of Adaptive Optimisation and Control" by G E P Box and G M J R Jenkins, *Statistical Society*, volume 24, number 2, pages 297–343, 1962.] New forecasts, however, are up-dated by an amount dependent upon the error in forecasting in the last period. At the same time the system should be so constructed that the parameters of the forecast may be modified as each new item of data becomes available.

The manual method quoted on page 189 is adaptive. Usually a computer is used for such a system and the Box-Jenkins approach is used by ICL in their computer packages. However, the ICL model is a restricted version using recommended preset parameters in a predetermined model. Nevertheless, it has been found to give satisfactory results in many applications.

There has been further work carried out in exponential smoothing, particularly by D W Trigg and A G Leach in the late 1960s when adaptive or lagged adaptive response exponential smoothing was developed. The adaptive response rate (tracking signal) uses a variable smoothing constant in place of the constant factor. The forecasts are automatically revised if the series under consideration shows significant change.

Unlagged adaptation of the smoothing constant responds to single splash inputs and forecasts are increased or decreased accordingly. If a tracking signal is used in the previous periods instead of in the current period, the disadvantage is overcome.

The various statistical methods quoted give rise to some complicated mathematics in their more sophisticated systems. The maths used in SCAN 3, the ICL computer stock control package, should be reviewed in this context.

REGRESSION ANALYSIS. Regression analysis (usually with the help of a computer) attempts to define the movement over time of one variable such as sales, relative to other variables such as disposable income, growth in population or the sales of a complementary product. It sets out to measure the statistical relationship and indicates the degree of reliability of the data.

The statistical theory is reasonably complex and needs to be reviewed carefully. [See Norman Draper and Harry Smith, *Applied Regression Analysis*, Wiley.]

The basis of the technique, however, lies in the recognition of the reasons for trends or patterns. In exponential smoothing a trend is calculated, but no reason for it is usually suggested. In regression analysis, the reason for the trend and especially its relationship with other trends is actually necessary. The key lies in finding statistical association with one or more variables. The association then becomes the basis for the forecast.

The greater the number of associated statistical variables, the more likely that the forecast will be accurate. The RCA Sales Corporation in the USA has concentrated on identifying rather more important trends of nearly 300 variables so that more accurate sales forecasts of television sets, radios and record players are possible.

The start of a regression analysis program, therefore, begins with an attempt to recognise the variables that will affect a forecast. Sales of cars for example could be affected by:

1   Net disposable income
2   Tax reductions or increases

3   Motorway mileage completed
4   Closure of branch railway lines
5   New designs of cars
6   Advertising
7   Efficiency of local transport

The relationship between such variables and sales of cars is known as a regression coefficient. It usually needs many years' data before a meaningful relationship is established; perhaps five or more.

Gross sales of motor cars will equal the base year's sales plus the effects of all variables in the equation. The method is then to analyse past performance and plot the apparent relationship between the variables and total sales.

As each past year's data is analysed, the reliability of the initial equation and the weighting given to each variable, can be determined. A "co-efficient of determination" will indicate whether the equation needs amendment. The weighting given to the variables in the equation will also need to be verified. The lag situation in cause and effect will distort the apparent weighting necessary.

Errors will have to be calculated in order to confirm the overall accuracy of the equation. The higher the standard error, the more likely that the equation needs amendment. Changing the equation is comparatively easy, especially if a computer is used (computer packages for carrying out regression analysis are available). Sensitivity analysis can be used as a means of testing the importance of the equation's variables.

There are obvious snags in using correlation analysis. [See "How to Get a Better Forecast," George C Parker and Edilberto L Segura, *Harvard Business Review* March/April 1971, for a simple explanation of regression analysis.]

Two-way causation may be a problem. Advertising may affect sales, but extra sales itself may be a motivating factor. A simple equation of the type suggested may be inadequate.

Some of the variables may not be independent of each other and it may be difficult to calculate the effect of any one variable.

Over or under prediction often occurs when an important variable has been left out of the equation. A consistent error (as opposed to a random one) should confirm this.

Apparent association may often be mistaken. A variable may be built into the equation because of a mistaken belief that it has a direct effect on the result, but this may not be true.

19:9   Successful areas of application and examples

Profit planning and stock control are two of the more important areas where forecasting is particularly important. The book has fully covered profit planning and strategy application. The example chosen to illustrate statistical forecasting is taken from a practical inventory control system.

STOCK CONTROL

Forecasting.   In most cases, stock requirements are composed of two separate parts. Stock is needed to satisfy the estimated demand on a designated future time period and some additional "safety" stock is held to cover unexpected demand.

Initially, therefore, it is necessary to calculate a forecast of likely demand. This is done by taking the average of past sales and weighting it by adding or deducting a factor for the trend that should have been calculated.

Safety stock.   The amount of safety stock that should be carried depends upon a number of factors. Stability of demand is paramount. The less stability, the greater the amount of safety stock which must be carried. If it seems possible to forecast very well, then little or no safety stock need be carried.

Service levels.   The service level requested by sales staff will also influence stock levels. A service level is a measurement of the probability of being able to satisfy a customer's demand from the stock held. If 100 customers order products from stock but only 95 per cent can be supplied, then the service level is said to be 95 per cent. Less stock is needed to give low service levels and of course the converse is true.

Lead time.   Lead time is the time taken from placing an order to the receipt of the goods. This, too, must be taken into account. If goods can be obtained very quickly then the stock to be carried should be small as less safety stock needs to be carried.

The method.   In designing a stock control system it is necessary to include all the factors quoted extremely briefly above. Deciding on the parameters and what weighting should be given to them is important.

The following method takes account of these parameters and uses the exponential smoothing system of forecasting, but also includes a method of building into the equations previous forecast error. This method is more usually referred to as a "tracking signal" and many sophisticated statistical methods can be used to indicate out of course events through tracking signal analysis.

A sheet as shown in Figure 19.2 was used as the basis on which to record the appropriate data. Completion of the sheet was undertaken as follows:

1   The appropriate date was entered in column 1
2   The withdrawals from stock during the month (called demand from now on) was noted in column 2
3   A weighted average demand was calculated and put into column 3

As previously suggested trend is extremely important in determining future demand and it is necessary to "weight" current demand so that it has a greater influence on the forecast for the next period.

Description	(No.)	Nov 69	Dec	Jan 70	Feb	Mar	Apr	May	June	July	Aug
Action	(20)										
Tracking signal	(19)										
Mean deviation (actual)	(18)										
Ordered on factory	(17)	1550	1770	4040	270	9950	5590	3090			
New requirement	(16)	1548	1773	4043	266	9948	5590	3094	4096		
Total stock	(15)	36940	32200	30980	32870	23190	25780	26600	23260		
WIP	(14)	26180	1550	1770	4040	270	9950	5590	3090		
Free stock	(13)	10760	30650	29210	28830	22920	15830	21010	20170		
Stock requirement	(12)	30488	33973	35023	33136	33138	31370	29694	28086		
L × forecast	(11)	20648	19518	17114	14730	15666	15480	14354	14016		
K × deviations = safety stock	(10)	17640	14455	17909	18406	17472	15890	15340	14070		
Weighted deviations (absolute)	(9)	5040	4949	5131	5259	4992	4540	4383	4020		
Error	(8)	8670	4130	6770	6410	2590	470	2970	750		
Forecast	(7)	10424	9759	8557	7365	7833	7740	7177	7003		
A × trend	(6)	+1350	+ 963	+ 342	− 243	− 9	− 54	− 315	− 378		
Weighted trend	(5)	+150	+107	+ 38	−27	− 1	− 6	− 35	− 42		
Current trend	(4)	−670	−273	−561	−607	+234	− 48	−302	−106		
New mean	(3)	9074	8796	8215	7608	7842	7794	7492	7386	7444	
Demand	(2)	3040	6290	2990	2150	9950	7360	4770	6430	8160	3770

Weighting is carried out by multiplying current and previous demand by a weighting factor. The current demand is given a higher weighting than any past demand.

The weighting factor (or alpha) can range from 0.1 to 0.9 (in total 1.0). The less volatile sales demand happens to be, the lower the weighting factor used for current demand. In the example the smallest trend (or alpha) factor has been used as demand from month to month has been reasonably stable.

The current month's demand, therefore, was multiplied by 0.1. The previous months' average demand was multiplied by 0.9 (making the total of 1.0). The results of both of these multiplications were then added together and put into column 3

4   A trend factor was found and put into column 4. This was achieved by subtracting from the latest weighted average

5   The trend was "weighted," in the same way as for the average demand. The result was put into column 5, i.e. the current month's trend factor from column 4 was multiplied by a smoothing factor and added to the previous months' average trend which had also been multiplied by a second smoothing factor. Again 0.1 and 0.9 respectively were used

6   The total trend was found by multiplying the weighted trend from column 5 by a constant which is related to the first smoothing factor. This was equal to 9 when 0.1 was used. The total trend so found was entered in column 6

7   The forecast was found by adding the total trend in column 6 to the weighted average in column 3. This was put into column 7

8   The error between previous months' forecast and the current month's demand was found and put in column 8. This was calculated by subtracting the previous month's forecast from the current month's demand (in column 2 and column 7). If the value was negative it was noted

9   A weighted average value of error was found in the same way as in the case of the average demand and trend, i.e. the error in the current month (column 8) was multiplied by a smoothing factor (0.1) and added to a second smoothing factor (0.9) × the previous months' weighted error (column 9) This was put into column 9. It was assumed that the error was positive i.e. a minus sign, if there, was always ignored

10   The safety stock needed was calculated by multiplying the weighted average error (column 9) by a factor which is known as K. (This is determined from a relationship which states that the safety stock is equal to 1.25 times the square root of the lead time × a statistical constant for the appropriate service level × the mean average error.) For this exercise $K = 4.3$ for a three month lead time and 3.5 for a two month lead time. The service level used was in the region of 98 per cent. The value found was put in column 10

11   The total stock required must be sufficient to satisfy the forecast demand multiplied by the appropriate lead time. For a three-month lead time the forecast made and put in column 7 was multiplied by 3 and put in column 11. (If the lead time is two months the current figure in column 7 is multiplied by 2 and shown in column 11)

12   The total stock needed was found by adding the safety stock (column 10) to the forecast needs (column 11) and this was put in column 12

13   The total free stock is obtained by subtracting the present month's demand (column 2) from the total stock which was available at the start of the month and noted in column 13

14   The work in progress figure is brought forward from the previous month's requirement on the factory (column 17) and shown in column 14

15   The total available stock is found by adding the current month's figures in column 13 to column 14 and shown in column 15

16   Actual requirements are found by subtracting the stock available (column 15) from the theoretical requirements (column 12) and then put into column 16. Zero to be used in the case of a negative requirement

17   It was advisable to check the accuracy of the forecasting system. This was done by calculating the smoothed error in the same way as was done for column 9 but on this occasion, allowing for the sign of the error—i.e. negative errors were subtracted. The smoothed mean error was the current error (column 8) $\times$ a smoothing factor of 0.1 plus a second smoothing factor of 0.9 $\times$ the previous months average error (column 18). The result was written in column 18

18   The tracking signal was calculated by dividing the mean average error in column 19 by the mean average absolute error from column 9. If the tracking signal is greater than $\pm$ 0.54 the situation is acceptable, *but* if the tracking signal is in excess of this value it may be necessary to bring this item before the manager responsible for stocks

19   Column 20 is used to mark the sheet if any action is required. In the majority of instances this column will be left untouched

Comment. It takes some time for such a control system to "settle down." Several periods may be required before the safety stock and forecasting procedures have reached their optimum values. An exponential smoothing system should be run in parallel with existing systems until stability has been attained.

No cognisance was taken of factory constraints. The existence of minimum batch quantities or capacity constraints may affect the ordering pattern against the factory.

While in the medium-term production will equal demand, in the short term there may be some instability with irregular order sizes in each time period.

No forecasting system is capable of anticipating "splash" demands. These are unusually large orders placed unexpectedly. If accepted, such orders will reduce safety stocks and service levels until the deficiency can be made good.

Some stockouts are inevitable if any service level less than 100 per cent is aimed for. High service levels will lead to high stocks and high stock holding costs.

Automatic forecasting systems of the type described will function only with "fast moving" stock. This may be defined as stock with an average demand in each period of at least ten units and at least six movements in every twelve months —i.e. 50 per cent chance of stock movement in each time period.

Such a system is no substitute for managerial information suitable for sound inventory control procedures. Managerial judgement will still be required in some cases.

It is recommended that a tracking signal is used to monitor the forecasts. This will minimise any danger of stock instability as well as identifying problem references.

A regular system's audit should be conducted to ensure that systems are functioning satisfactorily and that the systems used for each reference are most suited for it.

19:10   Problems in the use of the techniques and conditions for success

Must managers rely totally on statisticians? To do this is to infer that all management can be passed into the hands of operations research and other management sciences personnel. Obviously this is nonsense. But it would be equally nonsensical not to rely to some extent (even a large extent) on statistically derived forecasts.

The fundamental problem is how to marry market knowledge and expertise with the statistical forecast. Ultimately every manager must decide how much reliance he can place on a forecast. Therefore past forecasting accuracy must be considered.

Should market knowledge be ignored? It would be folly not to include market knowledge or any other information that would affect a trend. Stock control methods that do not take account of market planning can be nullified. It is essential, therefore, to take account of:

1   Buyers' intentions—these can be construed from market research
2   What has happened in the past—analysis of past purchasing attitudes is essential
3   Sales force and other appropriate opinion. Never ignore the man who has had contact with potential buyers or the market generally. Salesmen may be biased witnesses, but an aggregate opinion can be useful
4   Expert opinion should not be ignored. Economic forecasts by government or trade bodies should always be taken into account.
5   Environmental conditions of all kinds should also be utilised

Dangers in statistical demand analysis. The predicative reliability of an equation depends upon excess of observations over variables.

Dangers also exist of multi-colinearity when it is possible to mistake one parameter's effect with another's. Both may "risc" for example, but only one may be significant.

Two-way causation may be possible. Marketing activities may help demand, but demand may also help marketing.

It may be as hard to determine the parameter variables as demand itself.

Statistical demand forecasting obviously works best in reasonably non-dynamic situations. It works well where markets and also sales are reasonably stable. It becomes increasingly ineffective as demand fluctuates. It may be slow to take account of changing market situations—the input of a new computer, a changing economic situation, the level of advertising and marketing generally used by competitors, etc.

Once explicit marketing objectives have been set and a considerable knowledge about markets built up, then not to use such knowledge to determine product ranges, stock levels, etc, is wrong.

Data is obviously the key to good forecasting. If this is difficult to obtain, or is not presented in an appropriate way, a first priority must be to organise a system to catch data.

Forecast errors ought to be stated very clearly as well as the reasons for them. Only in this way will a method of self-correction be built into the forecasting method. Normally an error of $\pm$ 5 per cent is "normal." Anything outside this limit needs an explanation.

Forecasting effort and total costs, should always be related to results.

19:11   Conclusion

A forecast must be viewed as a dependent variable which is affected by company plans and planning activities. One activity interacts on the other. Without forecasts of some kind being made managers will often be making blind decisions. At the same time forecasts are always wrong in some degree. Like every other management technique, forecasting has to be tempered with management flair and judgement. It is an aid to, not an alternative for, management decision making.

19:12   Further reading

1   Frank Broadway, *Industry Week*, 27 June 1969, 11 July 1969, 25 August 1969
2   G G C Parker and E L Segura, "How to Get a Better Forecast," *Harvard Business Review*, March/April 1971
3   James Morrell, *Business Forecasting for Finance and Industry*, Gower Press, 1969
4   R G Brown, *Statistical Forecasting for Inventory Control*, McGraw Hill, 1959
5   G E P Box and G M Jenkins, *Time Series Analysis, Forecasting and Control*, Holden-Day, 1970
6   A Battersby, *Sales Forecasting*, Cassell, 1968
7   G A Coutie and others, "Short-term forecasting, ICI Monograph number 2," Oliver & Boyd, 1964
8   D W Trigg, "Monitoring a Forecasting System," *OR Quarterly*, volume 15, pages 271–4, 1964
9   P R Winters, "Forecasting Sales by Exponentially Weighted Moving Averages," *Management Science*, volume 6, number 3, 1960

10   A Muir, "Automatic Sales Forecasting," *Computer Journal*, volume 1, number 3, 1958

11   J C Chambers, "How to Choose the Right Forecasting Technique," *Harvard Business Rewiew*, July/August 1971

III : OPTIMISATION TECHNIQUES

19:13   Introduction

The third part of this chapter is mainly about mathematical programming, though there are other optimisation techniques—for example, model making helps this process.

Optimisation in this context is the creation of the most favourable situation from a series of alternatives. It demands that a decision maker's objectives are set out in a mathematical form, the value of which is to be optimised. Various constraints can be accommodated in the equation or equations.

The constraints will affect the possible best alternatives, which when found will optimise the value of the objective function.

Linear programming will be considered in particular.

19:14   Description

LINEAR PROGRAMMING (LP).   This is a mathematical technique for determining the optimum allocation of resources such as capital, raw materials, labour or plant to obtain a desired objective such as minimum cost of operations or maximum profit, when there are alternative uses of the resources in question. LP can also help to analyse alternative objectives—the economics of alternative resources, etc.

Linear programming is only one (though the most important one) of a series of techniques given the generic title of "mathematical programming." All the techniques help in handling optimisation problems. In linear programming the objectives function and the associated constraints are expressed in a straight-line form, whereas in non-linear programming these two factors are not linear or straight line. An example of this latter form of programming is quadratic programming which uses a second degree curve in the solution to an optimisation problem.

Integer programming handles optimisation problems where all the variables are integers or whole numbers. Normally where the integer restriction does not exist, the method of solution will be linear programming. It is possible to have an integer quadratic programming method.

Dynamic programming is a technique for optimising certain decisions which must be made sequentially.

If the series are independent—that is, they have no influence on each other—linear programming could probably be used. If the series has dependence it is more than likely that dynamic programming will have to be used.

Each decision is usually made in the light of the decision variable associated with it. Buying decisions, for example, are made throughout the year, but each decision must be taken with the last and the next decisions in mind. The aim of the decision policy will be to minimise total cost. The mathematics used in such situations involves the theory of functional equations and usually requires a computer for its solution.

The objective function is usually determined along with the constraints imposed upon it. Nearly inevitably, the function will be financial—least cost, return on investment, profit, maximised sales revenue, etc.

The constraints will be mainly concerned with the fundamentals of the problem, the resources which are available—for example, men, machines, maximum output, carrying capacities, etc.

Some way must then be found to arrive at a policy that will determine the kind of solution required from the possibilities available.

Once the optimum or best solution has been determined re-runs of the total problem may be required, if constraints or data change. To this extent the LP equations need to be a model which can be used to answer "what if" questions.

Nearly always large-scale problems are best solved by using computers and an investigation of the available LP program packages would be useful. Small-scale optimisation problems will probably be solved manually, without using LP at all.

Types of linear program. There are two basic types of linear program as follows.

Simplex or general method. This method will solve all linear programming problems but entails more work than the usually specialised applications of the transportation method. The constraints are written in the form of equations by adding (or subtracting) different non-negative variable slacks to each. The contribution to the objective function from these variables is zero.

A table (a coefficient matrix) of the coefficients of the constraints is then constructed.

A first feasible solution is found by making one variable in each equation non-zero and the other variables zero. A test can then be made to determine whether the solution is an optimum one.

Further tables can be constructed to test the results of varying data and constraints. Solutions can be iterated until optimality is determined.

Transportation method. This method can be used to minimise the transportation of goods from one point to several receiving points. The amount of goods to be transported from one point to another has to be known, as does the cost of doing this. The total of goods dispatched equals the amounts received.

The information concerning costs, capacities and distances, are set up in the form of a table. A first basic, feasible solution is found by assigning loads from the top left corner of the chart, allocating as much as possible by each route—this is called the "north-west corner" route. The costs and distances will be calculated.

Each empty cell is inspected to determine whether costs would be less if it were used. The totals are then added. A recalculation is attempted until a least cost situation is determined. (See Chapter 25 for details of this technique in greater detail.)

COMPUTER PROGRAM PACKAGES. Both ICL and IBM produce data books describing the use of linear programming by computer. ICL have a linear programming package for their 1900 series computer issued as technical publication 4147, second edition July 1969. Since this time various amendments have been made. The package solves problems with upper bounds, lower bounds and ranges using the revised simplex algorithm. A "report writer" provides the computer users with convenient access to LP problem files and solution files, but the program needs a computer central processor with at least 48 000 words of core store.

Though a user is not required to write sophisticated computer programs, the problem must be formulated appropriately for a linear programming solution. Input data is particularly important.

19:5   Successful areas of application and examples

One of the first applications of linear programming was in the blending of animal feed-stuffs. This is now a fairly standard type of application in any manufacturing process which needs to utilise the cheapest combination of raw materials. I   the animal feed-stuffs industry the various components of the feed—soya bean, corn, vitamins, etc—are constantly adjusted to take account of price fluctuations, and in order to maintain predetermined levels of nutritional value.

As a corollary of the previous paragraph another use of LP is in defining an optimum product mix. This activity should ensure that a manufacturer who makes a number of different products, each using the same production resources will maximise his total profit by constraining the amount of each product he makes.

The oil industry has used LP considerably. The optimisation of the use of oil-fields, refineries, types of product produced and markets served has now been established as an LP case study.

Transportation problems have also been solved by the use of LP (see Chapter 25).

In marketing, optimum advertising media decisions have been made by the use of mathematical programming. The application of the simple linear programming model requires a number of very restrictive conditions. The number of problem "insertions" are fractional. Theoretically this can be overcome by the use of integer programming.

19:16   Problems in the use of the techniques and conditions for success

Unlike many techniques LP and OR in general are not based on common sense. Conflicting aims of the type of mathematical programming mentioned, cannot be resolved without the use of some mathematical knowledge. It is possible to go some way towards the optimising of a problem's solution by intuition or experience alone. A definitive answer will almost inevitably not be derived. Emotion and prejudice have to be eliminated. LP helps to do this.

It is difficult occasionally to determine what is an OR problem. Stock control, particularly the forecasting element, has been so called for a number of years. Yet many people who have designed and implemented such systems (which have sophisticated forecasting techniques) do not regard themselves as OR practitioners. The fairly simple mathematics needed should be within the competence of most line managers.

It is important to recognise that OR people have tended to absorb a wide range of simple problems which by definition have nothing to do with OR.

Many OR applications have now become routine. The product-mix or blending of animal feeding stuffs routines, for example, could be applied comparatively simply by line management.

It is such standard routines that should be utilised as far as possible.

The problem of communication is strongly stressed. In no other technique or series of techniques is the psychological problem so severe. As will be emphasised again in the conclusion, understanding and appreciation of mathematical programming will be at a premium.

Line manager reaction may be of two types:

1   Total surrender to the OR or MS practitioner and at the same time total abdication of responsibility and involvement in the project
2   Total rejection, claiming that neither LP nor any other mathematical technique can be of the slightest use in solving line management problems

Both points of view could be disastrous. It should be essential that MS personnel in this field are competent behaviouralists, otherwise little or no progress will ever be made.

Like all fairly sophisticated mathematical techniques, correct and sufficient data is essential. There is nothing so frustrating as applying LP and arriving at an apparently optimised solution only to realise that the data which has been used is invalid.

An LP problem must have a quantified goal. There must be separate and identifiable activities. The level of each activity must be known (and quantified). The activities must be interrelated and the constraints explicit and their effect must be known in measurable terms. All activities must appear only in linear form.

19:17   Conclusion

The danger in employing OR people is that often they cannot communicate with non-mathematicians and particularly line managers. In most problems the psychological content far outweighs the mathematical. This is certainly true with linear programming. It is a technique that should not be shrouded in mystery. The more line managers can be exposed to the general applications which are now standard, the better.

Any further extension from the standard applications should be viewed with some caution. Inevitably there will be communication and educational problems. These could dissipate any savings which the use of the technique might engender.

The applications of LP should be done by personnel with a strong business instinct, otherwise there is a chance that overriding considerations will be given to sophisticated maths and little to profit improvement.

Linear programming is a powerful technique but it is not a cure-all. It does have limitations and these should be studied before an attempt to use the technique is undertaken.

19:18   Further reading

1   K Williams, *Linear Programming—the Simplex Algorithm*, Longmans, 1969
2   N J Driebeek, *Applied Linear Programming*, Addison-Wesley, 1969
3   A Battersby, *Mathematics in Management*, Penguin, 1966
4   G Hadley, *Linear Programming*, Addison-Wesley, 1962
5   G B Dantzig, *Linear Programming and Extensions*, Princeton, 1963
6   W W Garvin, *Introduction to Linear Programming*, McGraw Hill, 1960
7   White, Donaldson and Lawrie, *OR Techniques*, Business Books, 1969
8   R L Ackoff and B H P Rivett, *A Manager's Guide to OR*, Wiley, 1963
9   C W Churchman, R L Ackoff and E L Arnoff, *Introduction to Operations Research*, Wiley 1957
10   H A Siman, *The New Science of Management Decision*, Harper & Row, 1960
11   D J White, *Dynamic Programming*, Oliver & Boyd, 1968
12   O L R Jocobs, *An Introduction to Dynamic Programming*, Chapman & Hall, 1967

TWENTY —————————————————————————————

Systems analysis

20:1 Introduction

There is no ideal way of carrying out systems analysis, nor is there an ideal set of documentation standards which systems analysts might use.

The job title "systems analyst" seems to have as many definitions as there are organisations that install computers. The range of titles is nearly overwhelming —procedures analyst, systems engineer, systems designer, computer systems coder, etc.

This chapter, therefore, sets out some of the job duties of a systems analyst, but largely concentrates on the type of work which may be performed—depending upon the employing organisation.

20:2 Description

A simple definition of a systems analyst is that he is a member of a computer or management services department. He is responsible for the preparation of a series of descriptive documents concerning potential computer systems from which programmers can code, so that the systems can be run on the computer.

This is an oversimplified general definition, but a discussion of how a system is computerised will help to expand it. There are ten definite stages of computerising a system:

1   The systems survey
2   The systems definition
3   Data collection and analysis

4 File content design
5 Input/output requirements
6 Program specification
7 Programming
8 Program test
9 Program and systems evaluation
10 General maintenance

The systems analyst is totally concerned with items 1 to 6, and also in large part with items 9 and 10.

Alternatively, some analysts define their role in computerising systems under four main headings:

Analysis. This covers the preliminary study of the system's area under review. A decision is made on whether it will be worthwhile computerising the system— that is, whether it will be profitable.

Planning. This heading covers systems planning and general design of the computer system. Data collection, specification of goals, design of files and input and output documentation and general technical design will all be tackled.

Implementation. Programming or systems coding plus all the problems of systems conversion make up the activities under this heading.

Maintenance. Systems control, maintenance and future systems development are the functions covered.

A division of responsibilities is important if there are two or more analysts or programmers working on one system's application. It will be easier to timetable the operation as well as to define job responsibilities.

DOCUMENTATION. During the documentation of systems, paperwork might be viewed from the angle of five potential uses and users:

The analysis. Documentation is orientated towards providing a complete analysis of what is currently happening.

Systems design. Paperwork covering this activity should ensure that all elements in the systems design have been covered in order to facilitate programming.

Programming. Computer documentation should ensure that file structures, input and output documentation, plus the calculating/sort activities, will be appropriate.

Operational activities. Operational activity will cover the physical running of a system on the machine—i.e. data control and security, data preparation, machine running, etc.

User documentation. Users need to be informed of the way information should flow to the DP section and how they can best help in ensuring that systems are applied and then run appropriately on the computer.

GENERAL SYSTEMS ASPECTS. As well as documenting systems for computer application, a systems analyst ought to be concerned with five other important factors to ensure that the computer is a viable unit. These factors suggest that systems analysis is far more than a rigid documentation of systems and that serious psychological problems must be overcome during the course of carrying out the activity.

Gaining management commitment.   This is an obvious task that many systems analysts do not do well. Unless management is committed, a computer system's application is likely to fail. Managers must feel that they will gain from the application, they must understand what is happening and know that the systems personnel are competent.

Communication.   Once a study is under way, it is necessary to keep line management informed of its progress. A timetable is valuable. Regular meetings between computer, systems and line management are also necessary. But the meetings must inform.

Management education.   It is essential for line management to know enough about the computer to be aware of its potential use in their activities. How computers might help them is vital knowledge and systems analysts must play a leading role in this educational process.

Psychological environment.   It is always necessary to adapt computer applications, and the speed of change generally, to match company style and the overall psychological environment. Systems analysts should be competent to respond and adapt their approach to the company environment. They are "change agents."

Technical competence.   Technical competence needs to be of a high order. Knowledge of business systems design and hardware and software is essential. Expansion of such knowledge should be the constant concern of the systems designers. They must keep abreast of new developments.

20:3   Successful areas of application and examples

THE ASSIGNMENT.   Normally a systems analysis assignment will take the following course:

1   The assignment area will be chosen and agreed with local line management. The problem will be defined, constraints suggested and the scope of the study made explicit

2   The assignment will be planned, roughly in the phase stages which have already been quoted

3   Personnel will be nominated to carry out the assignment. A mix of senior and junior personnel may be necessary

4   A timetable will be drawn up and the man/weeks of activity necessary will be assessed

5   A budget for the assignment will be required and a cost benefit analysis should be carried out

6   Once started a control and reporting mechanism will be required, perhaps under the headings of "findings," "recommendations" and "action plans."

Design alternatives may be called for rather than one single solution. The whole assignment may have been designed around a pilot investigation carried out by a single member of the EDP team. The use of project teams for the total investigation should not be overlooked. The complexity, length and the environment associated with the assignment will largely determine the man-weeks of effort required and the method of actually carrying it out

FORM DOCUMENTATION. The systems documentation largely stems from the standard forms used by the National Computing Centre.

Overall systems design. Flow charting is a key part in describing current and proposed systems. (Standard symbols have still to be defined.) Systems designers usually use symbol templates provided by the supplier of the computer. However, narrative reporting should predominate.

Figure 20.1 shows the symbols suggested for users of IBM equipment.

Analysis

File structure. The configuration has to accommodate file sizes which are likely to be used in the running of the system. Their size may be crucial and an initial assessment of the numbers of characters required is essential. (A detailed examination of file requirements will be done later on the kind of format shown in Figure 20.3 but this should take place as part of the systems design.)

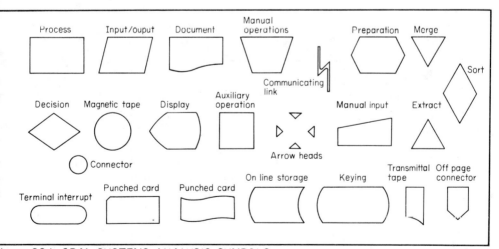

Figure 20.1 IBM SYSTEMS ANALYSIS SYMBOLS

Number	File content (description)	Random/ sequential	Number of items	Alpha/ numeric (characters per item)	Fixed variable length	Total possible characters per file	
F1/	Customer order file						
01	Account number		9999	A/N 11		109989	
02	Credit reference		99	A/N 11		1089	
03	Date of order			A/N 16			
04	Order number		9999	A/N 17		169983	
05	Date of dispatch			A/N 17			
06	Invoice number		9999	A/N 17		169983	
07	County/country classification		121	A/N 7		847	
08	Agents classification		99	A/N 7		693	
09	Industrial classification		50	A/N 6		300	
10	Customer classification		600	A/N 8		4800	
11	Project classification		99	A/N 7		693	
12	Invoice amount		4000	A/N 19		76000	
13	Cash		1500	A/N 15		22500	
14	Other sales ledger ⎱		1000	A/N 15		15000	
15	Information ⎰						
16	Ledger balances		2000	A/N 19		38000	
17	Invoices outstanding		39565	A/N 24		609877	

Figure 20.2 POSSIBLE FILE-SIZE SUMMARY

Input-output analysis. Each document used in a system should need to be analysed as in the outlines shown in Figures 20.4 and 20.5. Volumes are important (see Figure 20.2).

Flow charts will also be required.

File name			Date		Issue number				Card/disc	
Programs using this file					Issued by					
									Page____of____	
Entry number	Field description	Range	Card columns	Data levels	Field name	Picture	Usage	Length CH	WDS	Remarks
							Totals c/f			

Figure 20.3 FILE SPECIFICATION

I	Project/system						
2	Document title				Form number		
3	Prepared by						
4	Method of preparation				Number of copies		
5	Purpose						
6	Sequence						
7	Frequency						
8	Volume		Maximum	Minimum	Average		Absolute
9	Records affected						
10	DATA CONTENT						

Item location	Columns from to inclusive	Item name	Picture	Origin of data	Range, checks notes, etc

II	General remarks	Name
		Date
		Sheet of
		Reference number

Figure 20.4   INPUT DOCUMENT ANALYSIS

The analysis will determine the value of running the system and a final report listing problem definition and a computer systems solution should be made. The report should form the basis for a decision on whether the system should be run on the computer. It should be free of jargon and it should also suggest how the system could be handled and the benefits which should ensue.

Systems design.   Logically, system design should start with the output which the computer can provide and which is acceptable to line management. This should begin a process that gives in non-technical terms how the systems design will be carried out so that they can participate fully in the application. As far as possible, therefore, narrative and not flow charts should be used.

Once "output" has been designed and agreed, the rest of the system can be designed to match the output.

Files have to be specified as well as input. If punched cards are used, card formats similar to the one shown in Figure 20.6 are needed.

1	Project/system				
2	Document title				
3	Distribution				
4	Purpose				
5	Frequency				
6	Volume	Maximum	Minimum	Average	Absolute

7					DATA CONTENT					
Line number	Slew	Total line	Average frequency	Source	Field/ area reference	Field position	Field name	Frequency or volume	Maximum number of characters	Editing

11	General remarks	Name
		Date
		Sheet of
		Reference number

Figure 20.5 OUTPUT DOCUMENT ANALYSIS

Normally the interrelationship between output, input and files and the calculations which the central processor will be asked to perform will be gained by using a series of high-level flow charts which show the interrelationship, as in Figure 20.7.

Normally the output specification is first established by using a form similar to that shown in Figure 20.8 and then carried on to a tabulation with spaces similar to that on the line printer of the computer. The result of systems design will be a fully documented program specification which a programmer can code and then run on the computer.

Programming. The programmer will code the program specification into the program language being used. He should have no need to contact users during the programming period. The systems analyst should have cleared all the outstanding

Program	Description		Project	Application	Procedure	Program
Date type 36	Card title Ledger analysis card		Location	Department	Section	Stage

1) CARD LAYOUT

| Key to symbols | ← Left justified | → Right justified | If no arrow is present, field is of fixed length | ═ Field to be gang-punched | wwww Card columns to be skipped |

2) CARD CONTENT

Field	Description	+Type	Columns		Field	Description	+Type	Columns	
1	Card code 36	N	1	2					
2	Description	A	3	36					
3	P and L code	N	37	39					
4	Product code	N	40	43					
5	Detail code	N	44	46					
6	Spare								
7	Designation Doc C	A	-	70					
8	Value	S	71	80					

| Data must be present in these fields | + A = Alphabetic N = Numeric | S = Sterling A/N = Alpha/numeric |

Figure 20.6 OPERATING MANUAL—CARD SPECIFICATION

problems before the program is written. Therefore program specification should contain:

1 Output specification
2 Input specification
3 File specifications

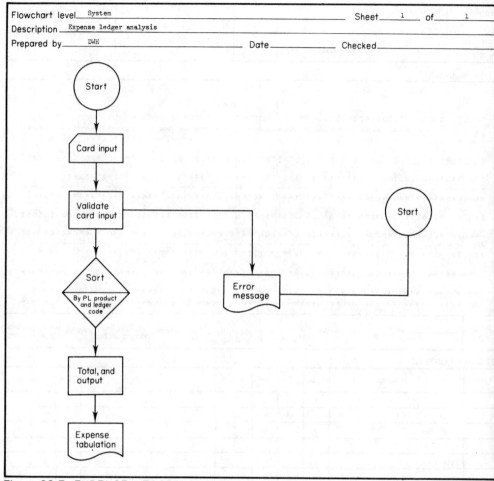

Figure 20.7 EXPENSE LEDGER ANALYSIS

4   Linking mechanisms with previous programs
5   The calculating or processing functions to be performed
6   Validation and edit criteria
7   Special tables, formulas, logarithms etc

Examples of an RPG control card and file description specification and a calculation function are shown as Figures 20.9 and 20.10.

Operational activity.   The two main sets of documentation covered by this heading are the program testing instructions and the computer operating procedures.
      The first document set helps to make a comparison between what the program-
mer intended to write and what actually takes place when the program is run on
the computer.

RPG OUTPUT - FORMAT SPECIFICATIONS

| Punching Instruction | Graphic | | | | | | |
| Punch | | | | | | |

Page 1 2

Program Identification 75 76 77 78 79 80

	Filename		Space	Skip	Output Indicators			Field Name		End Positon in Output Record		Edit Codes							Sterling Sign Position

Edit Codes

Commas	Zero Balances to Print	No Sign	CR	-	X = Remove Plus Sign
Yes	Yes	1	A	J	Y = Date
Yes	No	2	B	K	Field Edit
No	Yes	3	C	L	Z = Zero Suppress
No	No	4	D	M	

Constant or Edit Word

gure 20.8 REPORT PROGRAM GENERATOR FORMAT SPECIFICATIONS (IBM)

The computer operating procedures or operations manual should be used as operating instructions for the computer department. The manual's content might take the following form:

1 A title page giving systems references
2 A contents list
3 Systems review—a brief review of the systems being run
4 Procedure flow charts of the systems
5 Timetables
6 Computer requirements—priority ranking, use of peripherals etc
7 Input data—source, samples, average quantities, punching, verifying instructions etc
8 File data—size, type, identification etc
9 Output data—samples and document specification
10 Programs—identification etc
11 Operational activity—normal
12 Operational activity—in case of problems

This document should be prepared by the systems designer.

RPG CONTROL CARD AND FILE DESCRIPTION SPECIFICATIONS

Date _____

Program _____

Programmer _____

Punching Instruction	Graphic					
	Punch					

Page | 1 2 |

Program Identification | 75 76 77 78 79 |

Control Card Specifications

Refer to the specific System Reference Library manual for actual entries.

File Description Specifications

Figure 20.9 RPG CONTROL CARD AND FILE DESCRIPTION SPECIFICATIONS (IBM)

User documentation. This heading should cover summaries which inform management about current EDP developments in their line area. Reference manuals and guides to data processing services need to be prepared.

These examples of systems analysis documentation are merely the tip of the iceberg of the forms needed. Documentation standards need to be formulated and then rigorously followed. One certain way to cause chaos and confusion is to have no, or ill-defined, documentation standards.

Document checklists need to be developed to ensure that all documentation has been carried out. A library of documentation is not out of the question.

SYSTEMS SPECIFICATIONS. The first part of this section has outlined some of the many forms and procedures necessary when computerising a manual system. A large EDP department with numerous staff (and probably a turnover problem) needs well documented systems design.

However, in a small department, implementing a small machine, the rigorous document by document analysis may not be necessary. But even so, a moderate degree of discipline is required.

RPG CALCULATION SPECIFICATIONS

Punching Instruction	Graphic				
	Punch				

Page [1 | 2] Program Identification [75 76 77 78 79 80]

Figure 20.10 RPG CALCULATION SPECIFICATIONS (IBM)

20:4 Problems in the use of the technique and conditions for success

The increasing failure rate of computers, the tendency towards greater complexity of hardware, the proliferation of software packages, operating systems, etc, puts communications at a premium.

This problem seems to be worsening with the increased scepticism of line managers. The more computers fail to make an impact on company profitability the greater the gulf between line managers and the computer department will grow. Why should line management be involved in failure?

In these circumstances, good communication is vital. An absence of jargon, a desire to explain what the computer can do and basic humility are all required.

Systems analysts have been criticised for getting far too involved in the sophistications of data processing while ignoring company profitability.

Business training is essential. If a division has to be made between business and computer orientated individuals, then having business systems analysts and computer analysts might be a useful first step.

Business systems analysts help determine systems which will be computerised, communicate with line managers and generally take responsibility for the profitability of systems analysis.

Computer systems analysts will write program specifications from which coding can take place. They will be machine, not business, orientated.

20:5 Conclusion

The way in which manual systems are translated into computer based activities is through systems analysis and programming. With the increase in high-level languages and program packages, programming is becoming progressively easier. The difficulty of systems analysis remains.

The message given in this chapter is that techniques of a good systems analyst are not too difficult to learn. It is, however, essential that disciplined analysis, design and amendment of systems is carried out, leading to a standard use of systems documentations. Without it, in complicated design, there will be chaos.

20:6 Further reading

1   A Daniels and D Yates, *Basic Training in Systems Analysis*, Pitman, 1969
2   M Gray & K R London, *Documentation Standards*, Business Books, 1970
3   A Chandor and others, *Practical Systems Analysis*, Hart Davis, 1969
4   H D Clifton, *Systems Analysis for Business Data Processing*, Business Books, 1969
5   B Rothery, *The Art of Systems Analysis*, Business Books, 1969
6   S L Optner, *Systems Analysis for Business Management*, Prentice Hall, 1968
7   R J De Masi, *An Introduction to Business Systems Analysis*, Addison-Wesley, 1969
8   F Greenwood, *Managing the Systems Analysis Function*, AMA, 1968

TWENTY-ONE

Use of computers

21:1   Introduction

There was never a better example of pride going before a fall than in the use of computers in the last decade. Stories are legion of disillusioned line management angrily demanding to know why their computer has not resulted in considerable profit improvement.

This chapter, therefore, does not set out to record the techniques of computer applications except by inference. What is obviously more important is to discuss the reasons why computers have failed to live up to their expectations and how this failure rate can be reduced.

21:2   Description

The successful application of a computer depends upon four main factors:

CHOICE OF CONFIGURATION.   Much has been written about making a choice. [For example, *Choosing a Computer*. D Shirley, Business Books, 1968.] Obviously the machine must do what the company wants it to do; whether a configuration is obtained that will carry out only designated systems or whether a margin for running time error is taken into account is worth a debate. If a considerable equipment enhancement is made initially, it may take a long time for it to be fully utilised. If no margin for error or expansion is given then, perhaps sooner rather than later, an enhancement will have to take place.

A checklist for equipment evaluation purposes might be:

1   Does the configuration do the jobs required?
2   What apparent spare capacity is there?
3   What is marginal in the configuration in terms of capacity?
4   How much is the next enhancement?
5   How long is it likely to be before an enhancement is required?

Consider:

6   Ease of installation and running
7   Packages available—proved and running
8   Ease of operating the configuration
9   First cost of the configuration
10   Possible subsequent cost
11   Delivery, maintenance and second shift costs
12   How easy is it to expand?
13   Minimum core store to carry out the systems designated including operating
     systems, program area, overlay area and data area

As well as the hardware, the evaluation ought to include all the customer support
services given by the computer supplier—training, systems and programming
support, and general help in getting the machine operational, including planning
the installation, for example:

1   What other machines are there of a similar type in the area, which could be
     used for back-up facilities?
2   Space and general environmental considerations
3   Service bureau assistance for program testing

Software
1   Languages:
a   Assembly·
b   High level (e.g. Cobol)
2   Operating system—how good is it?
3   Housekeeping and utility routines
4   Linkage and integration of systems

Systems loading and timing.   An exact assessment of the full capacity of the proposed systems for each main application is necessary. Timing should distinguish
between productive and set-up time. The amount allowed for contingencies
should be stated. Summaries of daily, weekly and monthly times should be required.

Economics of the computer.   A configuration best able to carry out the applications required over the next four to five years should be chosen. Quotations

should give:

1   Purchase price
2   Retail price
3   Rental price
4   Lease price plus any other terms the computer supplier might operate

How many shifts are planned will help to determine prices so the timing of proposed systems applications is important.
  The cost of the configuration should be broken down as follows:

1   Computer equipment
2   Data preparation equipment
3   Options
4   Suppliers—cards, discs, tapes etc
5   Air conditioning
6   Power supply
7   Delivery costs
8   Maintenance costs
9   Shift premiums
10   Program testing time—where this is not free
11   Cost per hour of service bureau facilities
12   Cost of training

Computer suppliers are now "unbundling"—i.e. selling rather than giving their
services (IBM are leading the way in this respect).

Reliability.   Statements on down time for individual pieces of equipment in the
configuration should be called for.
  Contractual terms.   A copy of the proposed contract should be carefully studied before it is signed. Copies of blank contract forms should always be called for
when hardware requirements are being discussed.
  These are the main items that should be considered when the computer configuration is discussed. More important, what the computer must do must be
specified and a discussion on this point follows.

CHOICE AND DESIGNATION OF SYSTEMS.   Basically, this means what
the computer will be asked to do. A computer is a piece of equipment, of no more
nor less importance than a new production machine of some kind. Its relationship
to profit should be exactly the same. The worst view taken about computers is
that they are an "act of faith." Somehow (so it is stated) a computer will be a
catalyst for vast improvements in company efficiency. How wrong that view can
be. By themselves computers tend not to motivate action of any kind. Managers
will not use them if they have been left unaware of the machine's potential and,
more important, of changes in management methodology that will improve
profit, and which the computer can aid. (See the example on page 223.)

It is highly dangerous, therefore, to ask line managers to state what they want from a computer. What they need is to have a management method defined for them which demands the use of a computer to carry it out: evaluation of the use of resources by linear programming, for example, or the processing of vast amounts of data that will permit the complete match of order input with factory capacity in standard hours.

This situation might be discussed by considering the past and current uses of computers. Computers have generally been used for three types of data processing:

1   The simple clerical or clerical/machine activities such as payroll, invoicing and sales analysis
2   Marginal optimisation systems such as stock control or increasing machine utilisation
3   Total resource utilisation—budgeting and budgetary control, control of company performance in all activities, modelling of company activities, in finance, marketing etc

For some organisations—gas and electricity boards, for example—invoicing customers has always been a problem and a computer has been well utilised in processing the vast amounts of data concerned. For these organisations, stage 1 alone has produced benefits in plenty—though some consumers may not agree.

For other organisations, like supermarkets or warehousing organisations, stock control has been a key results activity. A successful inventory control operation has paid for the computer handsomely.

But for the many manufacturing companies stages 1 and 2 should merely be stepping stones leading to stage 3, as in Figure 21.1. Unless computers operate in this area they will never pay for themselves and certainly will never have any fundamental effect on the way a company is being managed. Far from being a catalyst, computers have set back systems design—by absorbing scarce systems personnel and company finance—by perhaps a decade in some organisations. Their use of company resources has possibly prevented companies from extending into corporate planning and other systems development. Money has had to be spent lavishly in order to mechanise simple clerical routines.

The use of a computer is not warranted in most companies for stages 1 and 2 only. Will management decide on systems that will lead the implementation towards stage 3?

Most will certainly not.

With this situation, the computerising of systems currently extant in the company will certainly not produce an installation with a high probability of success.

APPRECIATION OF THE BEHAVIOURAL PROBLEMS OF INTRODUCING A COMPUTER.   It is axiomatic that change is often resented. When the change is likely to produce redundancy as well, behavioural stress is inevitable. Even when a "no redundancies" notice is issued the advent of a computer will bring personnel problems. The best people will sometimes leave. Unrest is caused. Line managers feel threatened, from status loss if not from redundancy.

Redundancy problems must be met immediately. Management must communicate as much as possible. The likely effects of having a computer must be made known immediately they are agreed. The timescale between starting a feasibility study and making a pronouncement of its findings should be as short as possible.

To combat implementation stress as few outsiders as possible ought to be recruited. Most programmers ought to be recruited internally—programming is becoming a fairly routine operation, not the intellectual exercise it used to be. Even systems analysts should be recruited from inside the company if this is possible.

There are, however, dangers in recruiting internally. Line managers may be able to browbeat the computer team, ultimately making it non-operative. Professionalism may be at a premium; the motivation and experience of "change" in the company may be non-existent. Computer operations will be mundane, and probably extremely slowly implemented.

Recruitment from outside may produce line manager animosity. A gulf between the computer and line staff quickly grows; co-operation is minimal if any exists at all. High pay scales, plush offices, one apparent law for computer staff and another for the rest of the company produces resentment and tension.

With the computer team under pressure to get results tension will increase within the computer department. Morale may sag if things go wrong. If it is found that personnel have insufficient expertise this, too, will have a deleterious effect on the situation.

Finally, when the computer systems start to bite and redundancies occur, a new wave of antagonism towards the machine may break out. If, however, the computer fails to produce significant savings, reliable information flow or provide the ability to make better decisions then the whole enterprise may attract ridicule from line management and co-operation of any kind may cease.

So long as mundane jobs have been put on to the computer, the risks of failure have been minimal. With more sophisticated system's application a challenge to line management's ability will be made. Organisational changes may be brought about. In these circumstances, it would be naïve not to expect psychological clashes within the company.

RECOGNITION OF THE TRAINING NEEDS FOR BOTH EDP AND LINE STAFF. Education must be directed as follows:

1   To ensure that senior management are aware of the potential of the computer, how in theory it works, what it can contribute and what changes in management style and method will best help it to make a significant impact on company affairs

2   To ensure that senior management provides the dynamic, leadership and control needed to make computer applications a success. They must not

abdicate their responsibility to computer staff. They must always be in control of the EDP situation

3   To ensure that middle management can play their full part in developing computer systems with EDP staff. Unless they are educated to do this, the computer personnel will inevitably design their own versions of company systems. Joint action of this kind must follow fairly intense computer education—what the computer can do, systems design and perhaps even programming

4   To ensure that EDP staff are fully and completely competent to carry out their role in the computer installation. But perhaps of equal importance, EDP personnel must be educated in the "business" of the company. Unless computer staff are aware of the problems of the company, of making profits, of running the factory, of selling the company products they are unlikely to help to pull the computer into operation to improve profitability

These then are the four main factors on which a successful computer installation depends. Inevitably there must be good overall management. The organisation of the EDP department must be well founded. Resource constraints must be contained if not eliminated. But essentially, the choice of configuration, the systems chosen to be computerised, the psychological situation and training in all its aspects are the real key to success.

21:3   Successful areas of application and examples

When it has been established beyond all doubt that a computer is not performing as well as it should, then an audit of the installation is required.

This can be carried out by MS personnel, the computer supplier, outside consultants or even a team picked from among line management. Regrettably, each of the groups mentioned will have an axe to grind and is unlikely to produce a totally unbiased report. The questions to be asked, therefore, are vital.

RESPONSIBILITY FOR THE INSTALLATION.   Where does the computer department fit into the overall organisation of the company? Who has responsibility for saying what the computer does? Who has had control over its activities, timetables, etc, so far? This should start a "blame trial" if one is to be followed.

THE MACHINE AND ITS ASSOCIATED HARDWARE.   What is the technical specification of the equipment being used—the machine and peripheral speeds, capacities, constraints, bottlenecks should be quoted. The supplier's initial specification should be compared with what has actually been found to be accurate subsequently. Any shortfall in the supplier's specifications should be quoted. The reasons for any enhancements that have been made subsequent to the initial installation need to be known.

PERSONNEL. An organisation chart of the EDP department is required. Each member of the department should be described as follows:

1   Name
2   Job title
3   Job description quoting responsibilities and to whom he responds
4   Years with the company
5   Years in current job—departmental turnover rates would be useful
6   Training undergone
7   Competence measurement—a 1–10 scale is suggested: 1 = good, 10 = bad
8   Salary being paid
9   Potential of the individual

Comment on the numbers of personnel involved and how these compare with installations of similar size and systems complexity in other organisations.

ORGANISATION, PLANNING, DATA CONTROL AND MACHINE CONTROL. How in effect are these functions carried out? What methods are utilised to control data preparation? What control over machine utilisation exists?

SYSTEMS AND PROGRAMMING RESOURCES. The questions to be asked under this heading should lead to an appreciation of the organisation of systems and programming personnel. What control over their activities is carried out? What proportion of analysts are controlled by users and what by the EDP installation? What analysts are truly business analysts and how many are purely machine specification orientated?

CURRENT MACHINE ACTIVITY. Describe the current machine activity and how much machine time this absorbs.

Record current activities at all levels in the department and compare these with the timetable that was envisaged when the machine was first implemented. Ascertain why there is a difference if any exists. Indicate the man months spent in getting systems operational and compare these with initial estimates.

Compare current machine activity and utilisation for the systems being run, with the run times envisaged. If there is a difference, detail the reasons.

SAVINGS. Compare the savings originally envisaged at this stage of the machine's life and compare with those actually achieved. If there is a difference discuss in detail.

SYSTEMS AND PACKAGES IN OPERATION. These should be shown by means of a high-level flow chart. A brief history of each application and its impact on company profitability would be valuable. The cost of running each system

Phase	Items	F I team header	Systems definition Date comp	Man days	Who resp	Data collection Date comp	Man days	Who resp	File content Date comp	Man days	Who resp	Input/output requirements Date comp	Man days	Who resp	Program specification Date comp	Man days	Who resp	Programming Date comp	Man days	Who resp	Testing Date comp	Man days	Who resp	Parallel running Date comp	Man days	Who resp	Training Date comp	Who resp
Phase I	1 Load capacity planning	Mr Smith	10.1 72		BS	10.1 72		LM	10.1 72		BS	14.1 72		BS	30.1 72		BS/GEH	1.3 72		GEH	15.3 72		GEH	16.4 72		GEH		
	2 Weekly load matching orders v machines and machines v labour	Mr Smith	10.1 72		BS	10.1 72		LM	10.1 72		BS	14.1 72		BS	30.1 72		BS/GEH	1.3 72		GEH	15.3 72		GEH	16.4 72		GEH		
	3 Calc of prod ach'd in std hrs	Mr Lawrence	10.1 72		BS	10.1 72		LM	10.1 72		BS	14.1 72		BS	30.1 72		BS/GEH	1.3 72		GEH	1.3 72		GEH/GH	16.4 72		GEH		
	4 Labour and machine eff reporting – planned and achieved	Mr Lawrence	10.1 72		BS	10.1 72		LM	10.1 72		BS	14.1 72		BS	30.1 72		BS/GEH	1.3 72		GEH	1.3 72		GEH	16.4 72		GEH		
	5 Wage and bonus calcs	Mr Lawrence	20.1 72		VL	20.1 72		LM	20.1 72		VL	20.1 72		VL	30.1 72		VL				28.2 72		VL/IBM	16.4 72		ST		
	6 Prep ware sheets	Mr Lawrence	20.1 72		VL	20.1 72		LM	20.1 72		VL	20.1 72		VL	30.1 72		ST	1.3 72		IBM	28.2 72		VL/IBM	16.4 72		SW		
	7 Labour cost integration with SC and BC	Mr Coen	20.1 72		Mr C	20.3 72		LM	30.3 72		BW	30.3 72		BS	30.4 72		BS	3.6 72		IBM	13.6 72			1.7 72		SW		
	8 WIP record	Mr Heath																				1.3 72							
Phase II	Stock recording		20.1 72		BS			LM			IBM/BS	20.1 72		IBM/BS	30.1 72		IBM/GEH	30.3 72		IBM/GEH	15.4 72		IBM/GEH	30.4 72		GEH		
	Raw materials	Mr Temple	20.1 72		BS	avail		LM			IBM/BS			IBM/BS			IBM/GEH	30.3 72		IBM/GEH	15.4 72		IBM/GEH	30.4 72		GEH		
	WIP		20.1 72		BS	-		LM			IBM/BS			IBM/BS			IBM/GEH	30.3 72		IBM/GEH	15.4 72		IBM/GEH	30.4 72		GEH		
	Finished goods		20.1 72		BS	avail		LM			IBM/BS			IBM/BS			IBM/GEH	30.3 72		IBM/GEH	15.4 72		IBM/GEH	30.4 72		GEH		
	Stock control		20.1 72		BS	- ?		LM			IBM/BS			IBM/BS			IBM/GEH	30.3 72		IBM/GEH	15.4 72		IBM/GEH	30.4 72		GEH		
	Stock analysis sheets		20.1 72		BS			LM			IBM/BS			IBM/BS			IBM/GEH	30.3 72		IBM/GEH	15.4 72		IBM/GEH	30.4 72		GEH		
	ABC analysis		20.1 72		BS			LM			IBM/BS			IBM/BS			IBM/GEH	30.3 72		IBM/GEH	15.4 72		IBM/GEH	30.4 72		GEH		
	Re-order requirements		20.1 72		BS			LM			IBM/BS			IBM/BS			IBM/GEH	30.3 72		IBM/GEH	15.4 72		IBM/GEH	30.4 72		GEH		
	Consumable stores control		20.1 72		BS	avail		LM			IBM/BS			IBM/BS			IBM/GEH	30.3 72		IBM/GEH	15.4 72		IBM/GEH	30.4 72		GEH		

Figure 21.1 PROPOSED TIMESCALE — INSTALLATION OF 3SGG

Phase	Items	FI team leader	Systems definition			Data collection			File content			Input/output requirements			Program specification			Programming			Testing			Parallel running			Training		
			Date comp	Man days	Who resp	Date comp	Man days	Who resp	Date comp	Man days	Who resp	Date comp	Man days	Who resp	Date comp	Man days	Who resp	Date comp	Man days	Who resp	Date comp	Man days	Who resp	Date comp	Man days	Who resp	Date comp	Man days	Who resp
Phase III	Accounting and conversion except where done in Phases I & II	Mr Breen			BS			LM			SW			SW	15.2 72		SW	1.4 72		ST	30.4 72		ST	16.4 72		ST			
	Summary direct debits	Mr Breen			BS			LM			SW			SW			SW	1.4 72		ST	30.4 72		ST			ST			
	Sales and production summary	Mr Copper			BS			LM			SW			SW			SW	1.4 72		ST	30.4 72		ST			ST			
	Orders on hand summary	Mr Copper			BS			LM			SW			SW			SW	1.4 72		ST	30.4 72		ST			ST			
	Journal entries, trial balances etc	Mr Breen			BS			LM			SW			SW			SW	1.4 72		ST	30.4 72		ST			ST			
	Cost of sales	Mr Breen			BS			LM			SW			SW			SW	1.4 72		ST	30.4 72		ST			ST			
Phase IV	Material utilisation and control	Mr Breen			BS			LM			SW			SW			SW	30.3 72		SW	25.4 72		SW	1.6 71		SW			
	Rejection listing	Mr Heath			BS			LM			SW			SW			SW	30.3 72		SW	25.4 72		SW	1.6 71		SW			
	Quality control data	Mr Heath			BS			LM			SW			SW			SW	30.3 72		SW*	25.4 72		SW						
	Re-cycled material	Mr Heath			BS			LM			SW			SW			SW	30.3 72		SW	25.4 72		SW	1.6 71		SW			
	Other items to be listed after a systems definition is prepared	Mr Heath																30.3 72			25.4 72								
Phase V	Sales and market data	Mr Copper			BS			LM			SW			SW			SW			SW			SW			SW			
Phase VI	SOP	Mr Copper			BS			LM			SW			SW			SW			SW			SW			SW			
Phase VII	Standard costing and budgetary control (await systems definition)	Mr Copper			BS			LM			SW			SW			SW			SW			SW			SW			

Figure 21.1 (continued)

might also be useful. For this machine running cost is needed plus any potential system and programming amendment cost.

Packages analysis should include a record of packages that might have been run in place of home-developed systems and the reasons why it was found necessary to develop own systems.

CURRENT AND POTENTIAL PROJECTS. These should be so listed that the man-months of systems programming effort being or to be used can easily be compared with their potential impact on company profitability.

Detail the timetable envisaged for the implementation of new systems. Give reasons why this cannot be done more quickly. Why have the projects been chosen? (See Figure 21.1.)

EDUCATION AND TRAINING OF EDP STAFF. The courses EDP staff have attended and will attend should be recorded. The course duration, its content and the staff member's score, if this is possible, should all be quoted. Some indication of the competence level of EDP staff should appear, but the record should also help to determine the value of such courses as EDP staff have attended. List what else needs to be done in this field.

EDUCATION AND TRAINING OF NON-EDP STAFF. This is an important factor in getting the computer accepted. List all courses given to non-EDP personnel, their type and duration, who attended, what apparent result accrued.

What further needs to be done in this field?

EDP STANDARDS. What formal standards have been implemented in the EDP department?

COSTS. Record, where these have not been listed already. Details of machine-running-hour cost, cost of programming, systems analysis, etc.

Record total budgeted cost of department and how this compares with the actual cost. If there is a difference explain why.

OVERALL EFFICIENCY. Indicate overall efficiency of the department and suggest causes for this. Ask user's opinion for information concerning EDP contribution to company affairs. Determine potential user opinion about EDP usage.

LONG-TERM PLANS. Give long-term plans for computer development—in hardware, software and systems development. Detail anything that will affect cost and performance of the installation over the next two to three years.

An audit carried out on these lines should indicate how effectively the computer is being operated and where improvements can be made. The following questions should also be answered:

1   Is the EDP installation failing?
2   If so what is the basic cause:
a   Hardware
b   Software
c   EDP staff competence
d   Lack of understanding by line management
3   What is being done to correct the situation:
a   Hardware
b   Software
c   EDP staff competence
d   Line manager training and attitudes
4   What could be done (under the same headings)?
5   What are the cost/saving implications of correcting the situation?
6   Is the computer viable?

21:4   Problems in the use of the techniques and conditions for success

The major causes of computer failure and how a situation audit might be carried out on a failing unit have been discussed.

What needs emphasising still is that computer installations are usually no better or worse than the company as a whole. It is hard for a computer unit to be very efficient while the rest of the company wallows in inefficiency. Company style and attitudes will quickly contaminate even the most enthusiastic professional EDP personnel.

Enthusiasm and dynamic leadership must stem from senior management in the company—it cannot be self-generated by computer staff.

21:5   Conclusion

It is my considered opinion that in many companies systems development has been decisively slowed by the installation of a computer. All effort has gone into getting the machine running. Computers have put systems development back many years.

The failures in computer applications are worrying. It is hoped that the comments made in this chapter may help to stop even more money being wasted.

THE APPROACH TO COMPUTER USAGE IN XYZ Co Ltd

The feasibility study began on the premise that it was not sufficient for a computer to pay for itself, but that also it must have an influence on how the company is managed and so ultimately on profitability. It is on this criterion that computer usage in the company will be finally judged and it may be interesting for computer suppliers to understand the management method which has been evolved during the feasibility study.

The system is one of profit planning and is a logical extension of the budgetary control system that has been in use in the company for some years. It is designed to plan to achieve a specific return on investment. The gap between what is required and what is currently achieved is the gap that XYZ Co Ltd must close.

Two new concepts have been introduced. These are that managers will manage by objectives and then once objectives have been accepted, action programs setting out how the objectives will be achieved and what managers are responsible for achieving them, are made out.

Marketing has been strongly stressed within the scope of this kind of planning process and much of the management information which a computer could initially help to obtain, must be marketing orientated.

The feasibility study, therefore, has been considered on the basis that a computer must help to improve the company's profitability within the method outlined. To do this an integrated company system has been produced and each part has been investigated, to ensure that the "key results" areas in the company have been identified and possible computer applications designed to help in these areas.

It is hoped that a computer could provide information on which:

Profit plans and marketing plans and other major and sub-plans can be:

1   Made (and appropriate strategies adopted)
2   Tested
3   Co-ordinated
4   Implemented
5   Monitored
6   Revised on a sound and practical basis

Objectives can be:

1   Assessed
2   Implemented
3   Monitored

Action programs can be:

1   Assessed
2   Monitored

For the complete profit plan to be made, tested and monitored is very much a long-term proposal, but a manual application has already started and a computer, within three years of the installation, should provide the majority of the information for planning and control which is required.

The study has been used to carry out a redefinition of the information which is required to undertake the method of improving profitability outlined and as the manual method proceeds, further adaptation will be necessary.

21:6   Further reading

1   Brian Rothery, *The Myth of the Computer*, Business Books, 1969
2   Brian Rothery, *Installing and Managing a Computer*, Business Books, 1970
3   R Stewart, *How Computers Affect Management*, Macmillan, 1971
4   W H Desmonde, *Computers and Their Uses*, Prentice Hall
5   B de Ferranti (editor), *Living With the Computer*, OUP, 1970
6   M Rose, *Computers, Managers and Society*, Penguin, 1969
7   T L Whisler, *The Impact of Computers on Organisation*, Praeger, 1971
8   E A Tomeski, *The Computer Revolution*, Collier Macmillan, 1971
9   I Taviss, *The Computer Impact*, Prentice Hall, 1970
10 Enid Mumford, *Living With a Computer*, The Institute of Personnel Management, 1964
11 W Buckingham, *Automation: Its Impact on Business and People*, Harper Row, 1961
12 W H Scott, *Office Automation: Administrative and Human Problems*, Organisation for Economic Co-operation and Development, 1965

TWENTY-TWO

Materials handling

22:1 Introduction

This and the following two chapters form a coherent whole for anyone wishing to investigate the materials handling, warehousing, distribution and transport fields.

This chapter is concerned with the general problem of materials handling—a function that has produced the truism "handling adds nothing to value but only to cost."

Unfortunately, many organisations' accounting systems ensure that the materials handling cost is rarely accurately known. This fact, and the apparent lack of materials handling specialists in many companies results in the cost of handling being too high.

22:2 Description

Materials handling is a term that embraces all aspects of material movement, other than when an actual production process is occurring.

"Materials" is used in its widest sense to cover raw materials, part finished products (work in progress), components, subassemblies, etc. "All aspects" are the physical transportation, equipment, methods, personnel and systems used in materials handling.

Mechanical handling, though often misleadingly used as a synonym for materials handling refers only to the mechanical processes and their associated equipment for materials handling.

MATERIALS HANDLING COSTS.   It is fallacious to assume that materials handling costs have to be minimised. They should be optimised—that is, they should be such that an appropriate service will be given at a minimum cost for that service. It seems easy to reduce materials handling costs, but often at the expense of good materials movement—a good service.

Various information is needed to determine materials handling costs. An analysis checklist is given later; what is now suggested are some first measurements that will help to determine the efficiency of a materials handling situation.

ACTUAL COSTS   NUMBER YEARLY £ COST

Materials handling
equipment operatives
Fork-lift truck drivers
Tractor drivers
Pedestrian platform and pallet trucks
Mobile cranes
Cranes, hoists and other overhead equipment
Interplant trucks
Interplant railways
Lifts
Manual handling

Operatives involved in:
Receiving
Shipping
Raw materials storage
Finished goods store
Scrap and salvage
Maintenance of equipment

TOTAL

The following ratios ought then to be used:

1   Materials handling staff/operating work force
2   Time lost because of materials handling by direct labour/total time of direct operating
3   Total number of material and product movements/total number of production operatives
4   Total operating time/total time taken to complete a product
5   Total effective possible utilisation of materials handling equipment/actual utilisation
6   Total transportation costs/per cost/product/ton/gallon etc

A physical model of the materials movement throughout the production process, warehousing and loading areas is obviously an advantage. This should be a scaled representation of actual performance and among other things might show:

1　Where delays occur
2　Back-tracking and cross traffic—coloured tape representing movement might be tried
3　Disorderly storage
4　Cluttered aisles
5　Manual loading operations
6　Poor location of service areas
7　Rehandling
8　Operatives walking for supplies of raw material and components
9　Idle labour
10　Lack of standardisation of equipment

Such costs, ratios and plans will help to pinpoint current weaknesses and where improvements might be made. Once service levels are firmly agreed and a full appreciation of the products and their qualities is established, the basis for costing alternatives has been reached.

"Service" need not remain an inviolate activity. A considerable decrease in cost at expense of a slight decline in service might well be worthy of exploration.

MATERIALS HANDLING CHECKLIST.　The further analysis of a materials handling situation can be helped considerably by the use of an appropriately designed checklist. The answers will help to modify or improve an existing handling situation. At the same time the checklist might be used to help design a new system from scratch.

Data required.
　Products/item handled

1　Size
2　Frequency and variety (types and subtypes)
3　Quantities in numbers
4　Weight
5　Unit load capability
6　Product characterisitcs:
a　Breakages
b　Toxic or noxious
c　Solid, fluid or gas
7　Bulk to weight ratio
8　Perishable or shelf life
9　Value to size ratio

10   Types of product
11   Vulnerability to theft

Equipment used

1   Types in use
2   Load capacity
3   Speed
4   Age
5   Replacement cost
6   Depreciated value
7   Breakdowns
8   Percentage utilisation
9   Bottlenecks

Flow chart and factory layout
Flow chart to scale of production warehouse and loading areas
Labour utilised

1   Work study standards
2   Utilisation
3   Average wage and bonus
4   Numbers
5   Gangs or working groups
6   Skills
7   Age and apparent competence

Constraints analysis.   List constraints in:

1   Floor area
2   Structure of buildings
3   Production facilities
4   Load bearing
5   Pillars, retaining walls etc
6   Factory Acts

Basic analysis

1   Are flowline principles used?
2   Is all possible handling and rehandling avoided?
3   Are materials and products always deposited as near to the point of use
     or storage as possible?
4   Is materials movement, both in times and distance, reduced to a minimum?
5   Is movement continuous as far as possible?

6a Is manual handling eliminated or as limited as possible?

b   What can be done to reduce manual handling if it exists?

7   Are all manual operations recorded in detail so that appropriate analysis can be carried out?

8   Does the system set a uniform pace which optimises the use of both equipment and handling personnel?

9a Do bottlenecks or peak period loading situations exist?

b   If so why?

c   Can they be eliminated?

10a Is the utilisation of all equipment fully known?

b   Is any piece of equipment underutilised?

c   Why?

11a Are definite routes for all handling activities set out?

b   Are such routes followed at all times?

c   If not why not?

12a Is the simplest kind of equipment used?

b   For example, are gravity or roller conveyors used when possible, and not powered conveyors?

13 Are "unit loads" the rule rather than the exception?

14a What product breakages occur?

b   Why is this?

15a Have work simplification principles been applied to materials movement and equipment?

b   What was the result?

16 Could package redesign help material flow or unit-load concept?

17a Is the system of materials handling flexible—i.e. can fork-lift trucks be utilised for pulling trolleys, etc?

b   Has variety reduction and standardisation been applied—in equipment, pallets, cranes, etc?

18 Are all costs known—of handling, depreciation rates, breakages, etc?

19a Is it possible to suggest any "trade off" which would decrease cost of materials handling—for example:

b   In use of greater EBQ v cost?

c   In increased inventory v cost?

d   In production constraints v cost of handling?

20 What can be done to increase manpower productivity—increased equipment, revised bonus system, etc?

21 Do the paperwork systems inhibit materials flow in any way?

22 Does materials flow hinder accurate counting and checking of production?

23a What in-transit manipulation is required?

b   Is this necessary?

24 Are all precautions taken against fire, theft, etc?

25 Where has special equipment been bought?

26 Would special equipment of any kind help?

27 Are working conditions for materials handling personnel adequate?

22:3   Successful areas of application and examples

DETERMINING MATERIALS HANDLING REQUIREMENTS.   Materials handling consists of movement and support equipment.

A precursor of a materials handling service is to know current and future product loads and costs for comparison purposes. It is assumed that such data is available.

Equipment ought to be bought, leased or rented (leasing and renting are of increasing importance) on the following assumptions:

1   Do not mechanise for the sake of mechanising—use gravity wherever possible
2   New equipment has to fit in with that already in operation
3   Always attempt to replace old equipment with new types that yield greater immediate efficiency
4   Use equipment that is flexible and requires no fixed floor space—as far as possible
5   When unloading or loading, plan to use equipment where the power unit is separate from the load unit
6   Provide alternative equipment for breakdown situations
7   Plan an effective maintenance program

MAJOR TYPES OF EQUIPMENT.   Only a very brief outline of the major types of equipment will be given. Supplier's catalogues and materials handling magazines should be reviewed for more detailed descriptions.

Fork-lift and other trucks.   Electric fork-lift trucks are becoming more important than petrol driven types. The benefits of electrically driven units are their cleanliness, lack of noise and fumes and less complicated driving motor. Their drawbacks are their cost, limited range, speed and general lifting capacity.

Various subtypes have been developed as follows:

Straddle trucks can pick up timber or other bulky products by first straddling the load, clamping onto it, then picking it up and carrying it.

Pedestrian controlled power-trucks (usually electrically driven) are handled by one man and are capable of controlled lifting and carrying of palletised loads. They usually have prongs to fit inside a pallet.

Industrial tractors have been developed for handling loads of equipment, products, etc. They are either petrol, diesel or electrically driven.

Hand-operated trucks capable of lifting a palletised load and then having it man hauled are frequently used.

Pallets.   Pallets were one of the first means of operating on a unit load principle. Usually fork-lift trucks have been used to lift and transport them and their loads.

A pallet is a portable platform on which products can be stacked. It can be made from wood, metal or even (in some cases) papiermâché. A "stillage" is a cheap form of pallet and is usually disposable.

The top and bottom of a pallet are usually called "faces" or "decks." "Bearers" support the top deck and are spaced on the "entry sides" to permit the entry of the forks of a lift truck. Stringers connect the bearers supporting the deck.

There are both single- and double-decked pallets, some of the latter being reversible. Wing pallets have either a top or perhaps both decks extending beyond the bearers. Post pallets have a superstructure of posts which permit other pallets to be superimposed.

Box pallets have at least two vertical sides and are used to carry loose or unpacked products such as books or foodstuffs.

Conveyors

1   The simplest type of conveyor is a gravity chute. It can be built of wood, steel, aluminium etc
2   Conveyors are either fixed or free-standing, powered or non-powered
3   The simplest form of non-powered conveyor (except for the gravity chute) is the roller conveyor. It can be used wherever gravity can help materials movement—often as part of a powered conveyor unit. The "rollers" can either be rollers or wheels
4   Belt conveyors can either have plain rubber or fabric belting. Slats can be attached—these ensure an even spaced flow of material and assist the load to climb an inclined plane
5   Drag-link conveyors are formed by an endless line enclosed in a trough to which loads are fastened
6   Screw conveyors are rotating screws usually enclosed in a tube which carry chemicals or fuel
7   Other types of commonly used conveyors are:
a   Drag-line conveyors
b   Pneumatic conveyors
c   Vibrating conveyors
d   Mono-rail conveyors

Hoists, Lifts and Cranes.   This is an important equipment type and covers the following subtypes:

1   Hoists can either be power or manually operated and are based on the rope and pulley principle. Normally an overhead rail provides a traversing facility
2   Lifts for goods or personnel
3   Cranes are of three main types:
a   Portable or mobile, which have a prime mover as part of the crane's construction
b   Travelling cranes—usually on a gantry or fixed tracks
c   Fixed cranes

Other materials handling equipment which needs to be considered in a materials handling assignment are:

1   Lorry floor conveyors—inset rails on which pallets can be pushed along the lorry floor
2   Platform "trolliloaders"
3   Lifting tail gates—a hydraulic hoist fitted to the back of lorries onto which a load can be put at ground level and is then lifted to the height of the lorry floor
4   Vibrating screens
5   Hydraulic bridges
6   Earth-moving equipment

GROUP TECHNOLOGY. Group technology is an interesting materials handling development, concerned with the flow of interprocess materials. It is based on the principle that each machine operation should be linked by roller and other types of conveyor to transport materials to the next stage.

The production personnel are flexible and move from machine to machine depending upon the work flow. Group technology, therefore, tends to largely eliminate work in progress and convert jobbing shop activities into flowline processing.

22:4   Problems in the use of the techniques and conditions for success

The general principles of materials handling have already been stated. A point that needs to be fully considered is safety.

The safety officer should be consulted at all stages of a materials handling assignment particularly concerning:

1   Safety of equipment generally
2   Floor loadings
3   Possibility of overloading equipment beyond its designed capacity
4   General equipment maintenance and breakdown procedures
5   Possibility of bottlenecks and congestion of all kinds which will lead to unsafe practices
6   Safety precautions of all kinds: painting white lines, mirrors on dangerous corners, training staff in safety practices, satisfactory lighting etc

As far as general use of equipment is concerned the following factors may aid the choice of new equipment:

1   Conveyors are usually cheap to install and run. As far as possible gravity roller conveyors should be used. If fixed conveyors are used, they often restrict future plant layout changes and changing materials handling practices generally

2   Training and education is important. Electronically guided transfer
     equipment and fully mechanised flow lines are important and potentially
     could achieve great savings—if personnel could be trained to operate them
     successfully
3   Aerial ropeways and cableways are useful where difficult terrain has to be
     crossed
4   Cranes that are capable of having multi-attachments fixed can be purchased
     or leased. This flexibility should be pursued

General checklists are given in this chapter concerning materials handling
principles, but each organisation will usually have a unique materials handling
situation of its own. Inevitably considerable study of equipment suppliers'
catalogues, type comparisons, and how well a "fit" with specialist equipment is
achieved, is necessary.

The rising trend in renting and leasing equipment is emphasised.

22:5   Conclusion

The benefits of improving materials handling are not confined to cost reduction.
They should include all of the following and some measure of their importance
should be made.

1   Improved customer service
2   Decreased breakages
3   Improved safety
4   Better quality of product
5   Increased production—labour flexibility
6   Decreased work in progress
7   Increased product output rates
8   Reduced fatigue
9   Better utilisation of production and warehouse storage capacity
10   Increased speed of handling

22:6   Further reading

1   Survey in the *Financial Times* of 9 May 1972
2   G C James, Mechanical Handling Equipment, Works Management,
     July/August 1971
3   D Rogers, Systems Design in Materials Handling, Works Management,
     July/August 1971
4   D Foster, Automatic Warehouse, Butterworth
5   R Mather and K Haganas, *Systematic Handling Analysis*, Industrial
     Education Institute
6   H A Bolz (editor), *Materials Handling Handbook*, Ronald Press
7   *Mechanical Handling Directory, Iliffe*

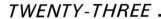

TWENTY-THREE

Warehousing and distribution

23:1 Introduction

Materials handling, warehousing and distribution are the composite items in physical distribution management. To these three major elements, inventory holding and packaging are sometimes added.

Each element ought to be the subject of a trade-off or an evaluation of the alternatives between cost and service. Increased costs will give a better service, lower costs the reverse. Some of the major factors in determining the trade off in warehousing and distribution are given in this chapter.

23:2 Description

"Warehousing and distribution" covers all the activities between the end of the production line and the physical delivery of a product into the hands of a customer.

Materials handling and inventory control are discussed in other chapters. This chapter concentrates on the physical elements that are necessary to control product flow to the customer after the manufacturing process. Product movement will depend upon:

1   *Product characteristics*—its weight, size, value, fragility, density, toxicity, liquid or solid state etc
2   *The movement channels*—warehouse, agent wholesaler, retailer etc
3   *The marketing environment*—competitive high service rates; single/multi customer; after-delivery service requirements

4   *Physical environment*—types of equipment in use (fork-lift trucks, etc), own transport, warehouse space etc

The optimum physical distribution system will, therefore, be one that:

1   Takes account of the constraints above
2   Moves the product from the point where it completes its manufacture to a customer at least cost, when giving the service demanded by marketing personnel, having taken account of all possible trade-offs

COSTS OF PHYSICAL DISTRIBUTION.   Physical distribution is the most costly function most organisations have, following production and general administration. As such it should be a potent area for cost reduction or, at least, cost justification.

Costs have to be related to the service being given, unless current service levels can be maintained and costs reduced. Costs should be ascertained as follows:

	Current		Future	
	£	%	£	%
Mode of transport				
Road				
Rail				
Water				
Air				
Road transport				
Lorry drivers' pay				
Equipment/lorry cost				
Depreciation				
Operating costs—petrol, oil, maintenance etc				
Fixed costs				
License fees				
Taxation				
Private warehouse costs				
Rental/lease				
Depreciation (if any)				
Delivery costs				
Occupation costs—heat, light, insurance etc				
Own warehouse costs				
Rental/lease				
Depreciation				
Delivery costs				
Heat				

	Current		Future	
	£	%	£	%
Light				
Insurance				
General maintenance				
Other changes				
General handling costs				
Labour				
Equipment depreciation				
Maintenance				
Supplies				
Running costs				
Administrative expenses				
Order processing				
Warehouse control				
Transport control				
General supervision				
Management				
Miscellaneous expenses				
Damaged products				
General supplies				
Carton and other packaging				
Strapping				
Pallets				
Packaging				

WAREHOUSE AND DISTRIBUTION PRINCIPLES. It is possible to lay down basic principles against which a warehousing and distribution system can either be analysed or established. The major factors are as follows:

1 Any equipment should show a reasonable return on investment after discounting cash flows or any other suitable project evaluation method has been used
2 The system should provide the service required. If not there should be good cost reasons for not doing so
3 Materials handling (see Chapter 22) should be suitable for handling the products and give the service required
4 A trade-off or cost/service comparison of all alternatives in warehousing and distribution should have been drawn up utilising full cost data. These comparisons should be kept up to date.
5 The total system should be designed to give:
a Appropriate product flows
b Flexibility—to give improved service or increased warehouse capacity etc

c   Unit load handling should have been considered at the systems design stage

d   The system should have been designed to cope with the transport mode being used. If not it should have been suitably adapted

6   The warehouses in use should have been designed to:

a   Take advantage of lease/rent situations

b   Take account of the interrelationship in distribution

c   Provide suitable space and material flow to suit materials handling equipment in use

d   Provide for peak loads and safety stocks

7   Space requirements can often be judged by converting average stock-holding requirements (taken from the inventory control system) into pallet loads. If products are in family groups and require segmented areas, an initial space requirement appropriate to segmented areas is needed. Actual space can be calculated by multiplying pallet or other unit loads by the inventory and adding 10 to 20 per cent for contingency purposes. Space usage should always be judged by using the ratio of total space to space being used. "Space" should be in cubic rather than square metres (or feet) so emphasising the three-plane idea of stacking and space utilisation. A future load pattern is, of course, essential. Space is also required for:

a   Aisles and general movement

b   Materials handling equipment

c   Loading facilities

d   Offices

e   Rest rooms and other facilities

f   Product assembly areas

g   Maintenance-shop (for equipment)

h   Equipment storage

8   General equipment considerations should include:

a   Transport mode

b   Handling equipment

c   Storage equipment—racking, shelving, tote bins etc

d   Special storage equipment—glass lined vessels drums, tanks etc

e   Packaging

PACKAGING. Packaging can help or hinder physical distribution activities. Principles which might apply are as follows.

Packaging should suit the methods of storing and distribution. For example, if cartons are used, these should be of a size that will fit easily into any unit load that is in operation. Cartons should interlock on pallets, for example.

Containers should, if possible, remain within a size range that will facilitate the use of conveyors, fork-lift trucks, etc. Fewer mistakes in counting packages will occur if cartons of a standard size are in use.

Damage because of inadequate packaging should be minimal.

Packaging will also be affected by :-

1   Customer acceptability
2   Competitors' packaging
3   Cost per unit shipped

Types of packaging include: boxes, crates, sacks, (paper, plastic, film, jute) cartons, etc. Each may be the subject of a "trade-off" (see section 23:3).

PICKING METHODS. The method of picking will help determine the physical stores layout. There are various selection methods, notably:

1   Individual selection where one warehouseman picks one complete order
2   Area selection—a certain area of the warehouse is allocated to one picker

Most warehouse layouts can be improved by studying warehouse picking methods. More important items (in terms of turnover and picking activity) can be stored together, so facilitating speed of order picking and bin or space replenishment. Congestion of pickers has to be considered.

CUSTOMER SERVICE. Customer service will often be the deciding factor in choosing a physical distribution system. The problem will be in defining a customer service level that truly represents what the company needs to achieve. An optimum cost of physical distribution can then be considered. Service will depend upon:

1   Competitors' service level. This must be defined. Often salesmen suggest that it is better than it actually is
2   Delivery times—from receipt of order to delivery. Often delivery is only a minor part of the time span. Order processing times need to be checked
3   Warehouses should be located at prime customer areas. All customers need not have the same customer service. Profit gain has to be related to money spent in warehousing
4   Other factors may be more important than service—quality of products, their price, after-sales service, etc. Why spend lavishly on customer service when it is not the key result in achieving business?

DAMAGE TO PRODUCTS. The breakage/deterioration of products stored will provide a valuable aid in determining whether the physical distribution is an optimum one. The cost of breakages and products thrown away for some reason ought to be known at all times. The causes of breakages are usually:

1   Mishandling, double handling
2   Bad warehouse planning
3   Poor warehouse layout
4   Inadequate or inefficient materials handling equipment
5   Poor packaging

Training of warehouse staff will improve the breakage situation, but a re-evaluation of materials handling equipment is obviously necessary.

23:3   Successful areas of application and examples

Warehousing and distribution systems will largely be dictated by marketing strategies. As such, warehousing and distribution will conform to established preconditions and not have an independent existence of its own. For example:

1   Type of product handled, its variety, weight/volume ratio and vulnerability to breakage will help dictate vehicle types or transport mode generally, packaging and intermediate werehousing
2   Production—centralised/decentralised, flexibility of production units and location of production sites will help dictate warehouse location, distribution mode and stock levels
3   Marketing considerations—speed of service, volume and total number of deliveries will help dictate level of customers' service, direct or distribution flexibility and total cost of distribution
4   Local carrier effiiency will help dictate whether own or local carrier service is used
5   Labour efficiency and supply will help dictate transport modes and warehouse site

These basic marketing factors will help determine:

1   Transport modes
2   Own or other transport
3   Warehousing decisions—location, dispersion points
4   Stock situations—products stocked, service given
5   Handling equipment
6   Types of distribution channel—agents, wholesalers, brokers etc

TRADE-OFFS.   The basis of choice in distribution systems will largely be determined by the marketing strategy of the company. The various subelements of the system will be determined by trade-offs.

A trade-off is a considered and (hopefully) quantified appreciation of two or more factors that could be mutually contradictory or exclusive. A considered choice has to be made between them.

The major trade-offs that are relevant in warehousing and distribution are:

1   Selling direct to the customer *v* selling to the retailer or wholesalers
2   Total cost *v* service which must be given
3   One transport mode *v* any other transport mode or combination
4   One type of distribution channel *v* any other type of distribution channel

5   Low inventory levels *v* service to customers
6   Specialised handling and storage equipment of all kinds *v* non-specialised equipment
7   Expendable pallets, containers, etc, *v* returnable empties, containers etc
8   Use own facilities as far as possible *v* use agents, private carriers as far as possible
9   Centralisation *v* decentralisation
10   Flexibility *v* rigidity in operation
11   Speed of service *v* cost

TRANSPORT MODES.   The four basic transport modes are air, water, road and rail. The basic advantages and disadvantages of these are:

Air.   Advantages are speed, insurance is cheaper, packaging possibly cheaper, less loss by pilfering or damage, smaller inventories needed, possible elimination of warehousing. Export market testing is comparatively easy.
    High cost is major disadvantage, but containerisation has brought costs down where this method of packing is possible.

Water.   Cost is the greatest advantage. It is useful for container operations. It is slow and has limited accessibility in Britain.

Road.   Road offers flexibility, with good access for loading and unloading. High utilisation is possible with high area penetration. Low cost for short- and medium-length journeys. Special lorry construction is possible. There are legal restrictions, traffic congestion and high cost for long hauls. Own transport fleet advantages include: specialised vehicle building, marketing advantages (advertising, etc) staff loyalty, hygiene is controlled and there is a twenty-four-hour availability.
    Disadvantages include capital outlay, maintenance problems, management distraction and the public's antagonism to goods vehicles which may bring about government action to divert more traffic from road to rail.

Rail.   Advantages include speed, comparatively low cost over long distances, (especially with containerisation) and cutting down on pollution and traffic jams.
    Disadvantages include inflexibility, low loading gauge and comparatively high cost over short journeys.

CONTAINERISATION.   Containerisation is the logical development of the unit load philosophy which started with the introduction of palletisation. It permits the use of intermode methods of transport—ship–road–rail etc—attracting handling economies in each mode.
    Costs could be reduced by less handling, no deterioration of product, little or no pilfering or loss (so lower insurance), speedier turn-round and faster journey times generally. Paperwork should be simplified.
    The freightliner rail–road service operates on a containerisation basis and

provides speed, comparative immunity from weather hazards, cheapness, reliability and security.

Undoubtedly the spread of containerisation will continue. Bulk break methods of distribution where a bulk load travels a major distance and then is broken down into unit components could be fitted into this form of distribution.

WAREHOUSING.   The major consideration that will help to determine the location and type of warehouse to use are as follows. Warehouses may be necessary where:

1   Fast deliveries are required at sites, a long way from manufacturing centres
2   Stocks are needed to cover emergencies, sales promotion activities, fluctuating demand etc
3   Temporary storage—repacking etc
4   Deliveries are beyond the daily delivery range of lorries
5   The cost of the warehouse is less than of deliveries even though the site is within a day's journey from the manufacturing unit
6   Improved customer service is required

Warehouse site location will be helped by considering:

1   Proximity of competitors' warehousing—do they have the best sites?
2   Transport facilities—motorways, container depots, ability to unload and load easily in mode of transport being used
3   Cost consideration—the distance travelled from production to warehouse and the distance to deliver are vital considerations; general site costs must be added to transport cost
4   Proximity of services—water, power etc
5   Government aided site development
6   Waste disposal
7   Fire risks and legal requirements
8   General surroundings—environmental, climatic, social etc

The aim of good warehousing will be to provide an appropriate service at adequate cost. A functional organisation will help in this operation. Division of labour will also help. However, the smaller the warehouse, the greater its problem of having functional responsibility. There is a case to be made, therefore, for large warehouses which, because of overheads and functional efficiency, should be more effective than small ones.

An intelligent warehouseman is needed in a small warehouse because of the multiplicity of activities that he must perform. He will obviously gain in job enrichment, however. Small warehouses will suffer from:

1   Inability to install modern materials handling due to economic considerations

2   Absenteeism
3   Management generally—which may be a problem

The possibility that large public warehouses could handle the stores of a small warehouse more efficiently than the small unit could operate, needs to be reviewed.

23:4   Problems in the use of the techniques and conditions for success

Transport and warehousing has been included as a technique because it is frequently a subject for analysis by MS personnel.

In effect it is a series of techniques—site location, storage, transport allocation, plant maintenance, warehousing principles and practice, materials handling, etc. It is often made the subject of cost-reduction exercises, probably because it is an activity which is tending to cost proportionately more and more. This is due to increasingly sophisticated marketing, which in turn is dictated by increased competition.

It would be wrong to view warehousing and distribution without first fully appreciating the marketing strategy demanded by the company. The worst terms of reference given to an analyst involved in this activity might be that a least cost system is required.

Warehousing and distribution is at the end of a long line of order processing which begins when a salesman gains an order. It is an integrated part of the total company—customer relationship. Anyone who investigates warehousing and distribution without considering the paperwork system will obviously miss out one of the most vital elements in the situation.

The following paperwork systems and subsystems, therefore, need to be incorporated into the assignment:

1   Sales order processing
2   Stock control
3   Lorry routing
4   Dispatch
5   Handling of returnable empties
6   Warehouse—product location records
7   Maintenance of equipment
8   Personnel records—especially bonus/wages payments

23:5   Conclusion

As competition grows, so does the cost and increased specialisation of warehousing and distribution. The future in part must lie in the increased use of the unit load principle which containerisation has helped to foster. The movement of smaller loads will only be carried out by specialised vehicles and transport modes for short distances.

It is certain, however, that warehousing and distribution will grow ever more costly so analysis should be on a cost-justification basis not a least-cost operation.

23:6   Further reading

1   Felix Wentworth, *Physical Distribution Management*, Gower Press, 1970
2   B M Deakin and T Seward, *Productivity in Transport*, Cambridge University Press, 1969
3   P Attwood, *Planning a Distribution System*, Gower Press, 1971
4   J L Blackbourn, "Principles of Materials Storage," *Works Management*, July/August 1971
5   J Warman, *Warehouse Management*, Heinemann, 1971
6   H K Compton, *Storehouse and Stockyard Management*, Business Books
7   H K Compton, *Supplies and Materials Management*, Business Books
8   G H Jenkins, *Modern Warehouse Management*, McGraw Hill

TWENTY-FOUR

Distribution networks

24:1 Introduction

Sections 19:13 to 19:17 discussed optimisation techniques, in particular linear programming. Some mention was made of the transportation method that helps to determine least cost distribution methods.

This chapter suggests how linear programming can be used in optimising distribution networks.

24:2 Description

Distribution networks cover the activities of depot siting and vehicle scheduling. In the former activity the problem to be solved is to locate either one or a number of depots in order to ensure the minimum ton-mileage of lorry usage in delivering products to customers. The cost of savings in lorry usage has to be more than the cost of establishing one or more depots. The problem can be extended to include which depot shall make deliveries once locations have been established.

Data is extremely important in solving the problem. Over a year's operations data will usually be necessary before a definitive solution can be recommended. It will be particularly difficult where there are strong seasonal factors or where the pattern of distribution is changing substantially. Both these situations are more common than appears at first sight.

The solution of vehicle scheduling problems has received considerable attention in the last decade. It was one of the first uses of linear programming and the "transportation technique" has now become one of the established textbook routines. Normally the capacity of vehicles in relation to delivery points is taken into account, and the associated costs have to be minimised.

As vehicles have different running costs and capacities, the size (volume and weight) of deliveries, has to be included. It has to be assumed that depots have been sited in an optimum position and that delivery points will remain fixed.

Given that the total demand will not be more than the capacity of depots and vehicles, routes are chosen which minimise overall costs.

Transhipment problems can be handled in a similar manner to a normal vehicle routing solution. In general vehicle routing, the route is a straight one; in transhipment, the necessity to pass through an intermediate point has to be included.

Linear programming will either provide a number of best solutions or prove that the constraints in the problem are such that an optimum solution does not exist.

24:3 Successful areas of application and examples

DEPOT SITING.   As an example of the use of a computer package in this field ICL's 1900 series distribution network computer package is used to describe how depot siting problems can be solved by computer. In the ICL package it is necessary first to distinguish between the number of depots involved and their location.

A graph of transport costs against depot location and running costs can be established by carrying out a number of depot siting runs on the computer. Once the number of depots has been determined, their position is calculated by using a program that utilises the radial distance from each depot in conjunction with known vehicle mileage to determine depot delivery boundaries and so locations.

Where only one depot is to be sited it is usually first placed in an arbitrary position and by using a calculated vehicle route-mile cost, the site is gradually moved until an optimum position is determined.

The problem grows considerably more complex when two or more depots have to be sited. Two subproblems exist: where the depots should be sited to minimise vehicle mileage costs and from what depot deliveries are to be made.

The computer is fed delivery-demand statistics and initial depot sites are determined on the basis that vehicle mileage will be minimised. Delivery locations are then allocated to each depot site following the same principles.

Each depot is then relocated within a constrained area until total least vehicle mileage is obtained. Delivery points can be reallocated to new depot locations where this helps to minimise total distribution costs.

The use of a computer facilitates the heuristic approach—that is, by constant adaptation an optimum situation is derived. It is possible to build in such constraints as river crossings or mountains, etc. Data requirements are considerable:

1   The number and position of fixed depot locations
2   The number and position of variable depot locations
3   The number and position of any geographical constraints (up to twenty are possible)

4   The number and positions of pass points
5   The number of delivery locations, their position and the amount delivered

The example shown is of East Anglia and it is assumed that there are forty-five delivery locations to be served from three depots. Depot 1 is variable, whereas depots 2 and 3 are fixed. The constraints or barriers are an estuary (1) and a curved obstacle made up of barriers (2, 3, and 4). The estuary has one pass point; the curved barrier has two.

The map is divided into ten-mile squares and each depot is assumed to be in the middle of one of the squares. In the same way all delivery points in each ten-mile square are also assumed to be exactly in the middle. Squares are numbered from one onwards commencing at the bottom left hand corner of the map. The location of each fixed depot is indicated. Each centralised delivery point is also

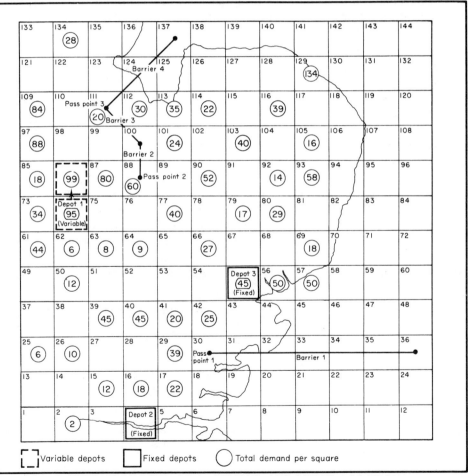

Figure 24.1 DISTRIBUTION NETWORK – DEMAND AND DEPOT LOCATION

shown with its total demand. An estimated position for a new depot location is indicated by giving it a new square number.

The computer program repetitively modifies until no further reduction in vehicle ton mileage appears possible. Where constraints occur the computer calculates mileages based on the passpoints. This is done in two stages. The first is one where deliveries are allocated to depots and in the second each variable depot is moved until its allocated vehicle ton mileages are minimised.

The first stage is then repeated on the basis of the new position of the variable depots. The second stage is then again run and the cycle repeated until no signifi-cant reduction in vehicle ton mileage is possible.

VEHICLE ROUTING. The application of the transportation technique fol-lows the same basic pattern as the depot siting problem solved by the ICL pro-gram package, and recourse might be had to this package. However, a simple example that can be handled manually can serve as an example. Three factories supply the same product as follows:

Factory *A* 10 units
Factory *B* 12 units
Factory *C*   6 units
Total $\overline{28}$ units

Receiving points need:
1 to   8 units
2 to 10 units
3 to 10 units

The cost of transporting the products is as shown in Figure 24:2. How can a least cost distribution method be evolved? The initial step in solving this problem is to design a matrix that allocates as much as possible by each route. A solution must take account of capacities and dispatch requirements using the following criteria.

Cost is to be minimised from a number of dispatch points (*D*) to a number of

	Factories	A	B	C
	I	10	12	8
Receiving points	2	12	8	6
	3	10	6	6

Figure 24.2 COST OF TRANSPORTING PRODUCTS (in £'000s)

Factories Receiving points	A	B	C	Total
1	10	12	8	8
2	12	8	6	10
3	10	6	6	10
Total	10	6	6	28

Figure 24.3 DISTRIBUTION NETWORKS—FACTORIES AND RECEIVING POINTS

receiving points(R). The quantity of products sent must equal those received. The quantities dispatched and received must be known. The cost of transporting must be known. The solution must take account of the capacities and requirements by the use of $D+R-1$ routes (see Figure 24.3). The factories send 8–10–10 units. Receiving points take 10–12–6 units.

By applying the north-west corner rule, where as much as possible is allocated to the square at the top and left of the matrix, etc, so that all columns still add up correctly, Figure 24.4 emerges, Using the $D+R-1$ route, there are five routes suggested, the total delivery of which costs is £280 000. (This is a multiplication of the two figures shown in the squares.)

It is possible for the cost of transporting to be made up of two parts: costs of sending and receiving. A position might occur where the receiving cost at 1 is zero, so that the cost of sending from A to 1 must be 8.

Where costs have been allocated in each cell, the same procedure is followed. The cells where no costs have been allocated can now be considered. Where the sum of receiving and sending costs for any cell not being used exceeds the true cost which is marked within the cell there is saving to be made by using that cell.

	A	B	C	Total
1	8 10	12	8	8
2	2 12	8 8	6	10
3	10	4 6	6 6	10
Total	10	12	6	28

Figure 24.4 DISTRIBUTION NETWORKS—ROUTES AND DELIVERY COST CALCULATION

So products can be transferred to it. While this happens the correct row and column totals must be maintained.

When all real costs in the cells either equal or exceed the sum of the part costs for sending and receiving, an optimum solution has been achieved.

24:4 Problems in the use of the technique and conditions for success

The components of a physical distribution system are order processing, inventory control, packaging, warehousing, shipping, general transportation, customer service, field warehousing and accounting procedures covering the physical distribution activity.

Physical distribution is only one part of the total package covered by marketing.

Vehicle routing procedures have to take into account vehicle capacities. Capacity can be assessed as weight, volume, "handlability" or volume of goods carried: or perhaps a combination of all four factors. Maximum weight of lorry loads is defined by law. Volume may be extremely important where bulky, light-weight goods are carried. While a driver must be able to gain access to his load and offload as necessary, statistical analysis of past load data may be needed to determine what is realistic loading practice.

Another practical problem arises from the speed the vehicles take (or are scheduled to take) when following the routes that have been planned. While being the shortest, they may not be the fastest. Unloading time, too, needs to be included in the time taken to carry out one transportation activity.

Once a route has become accepted and perhaps standardised, it might be unwise to change it because of some minor alteration to the drop-situation.

The main problems associated with the techniques outlined, therefore, are concerned with the practical application of the results. A transport manager will ensure that a balance is made between operations research and hardheaded common sense.

24:5 Conclusion

The optimisation of distribution networks will not solve all distribution problems. The techniques outlined in this chapter, however, could significantly reduce the cost of distribution—perhaps as much as 20 per cent of the total delivery cost could be saved. The individual benefits will be:

1 *Transportation and transhipment.*   The optimising of routes and the determination of which warehouses will serve which delivery points will save both overall cost and time. Customer service should, therefore, be improved
2 *Vehicle routing.*   By determining the least mileage for the vehicles of known capacities, transport cost will be reduced
3 *Depot siting.*   Depot siting will also reduce vehicle mileage costs by determining the most efficient number of field warehouses and where they should be sited

24:6 Further reading

1 B M Deakin and T Seward, *Productivity in Transport*, Cambridge University Press, 1969
2 L R Carter, "A Scientific Approach to Dispatch Scheduling," *Work Study and Management Services*, February 1971
3 F G Unwin and J D H Weatherby, "Improved Route Planning," *OR Quarterly*, volume 20
4 J E Sussams, *Efficient Road Transport Scheduling*, Gower Press, 1970
5 V J East, "How to Reduce Distribution Costs," *Purchasing Journal*, August 1971
6 *Computers in Vehicle Scheduling*, NCC

TWENTY-FIVE

Plant maintenance control

25:1 Introduction

The maintenance department is a unique part of most organisations. It usually has the highest ratio of skilled personnel to its total labour force. It often also has the highest wage bill per man employed and at the same time its output rate is usually the lowest in the organisation.

It would be wrong to say that all maintenance departments are out of control, but a majority are in such a sad state.

25:2 Description

Maintenance control means, in effect, that maintenance work must be measured. The difficulties in attempting to do this are considerable:

1   There are a large variety of skills involved and jobs to be performed at a multiplicity of sites in the organisation
2   Most jobs tend not to be truly repetitive (the basis for accurate work measurement)
3   Most jobs occur in site conditions that are not ideal—where weather, fumes, dust, dirt, etc, impinge. The contingency factors to be included in work measurement are obviously high
4   Most work cannot be directly supervised. The work force by its nature, operates in small groups at indeterminate distances from the main maintenance workshops
5   Many jobs that are undertaken have an indeterminate work content when

they are first started. A machine breakdown, for example, may take one hour or ten hours to put right. It is difficult to decide exactly how long it will take when the repair men leave the control maintenance area

These difficulties only make the application of a control system more difficult, they do not invalidate it. The first problem is to decide what improved control is required:

1   Reduced total manpower
2   Increased activity—job maintenance time
3   Greater flexibility
4   Less walking and general non-working time
5   Improved work planning and scheduling

The second problem will be to decide on the method or methods which will ensure that the objectives are established.

The type of work measurement systems and method of maintenance control generally that should be introduced will largely depend upon the organisation of the function. What follows is a brief discussion of various maintenance organisations and associated factors that will help determine control procedures.

KINDS OF ORGANISATION AND SYSTEMS NEEDED IN MAINTENANCE CONTROL.   It would be interesting to quote in checklist form the job activities, systems, etc, needed in a maintenance division:

1   Workshop organisation systems: production planning and control, inventory control, quality control, workshop practice
2   Work orders (and priority systems for them): workshop control, site maintenance
3   Allocation of maintenance men and scheduling of job duties generally—daily, weekly, monthly and annual work programs
4   Evaluation of work content of jobs being performed
5   Work ticket completion and control
6   Material requisition and material utilisation and control
7   A work force disposition/control
8   Work methods—the standard method of carrying out various maintenance activities
9   Records of:
a   All plant, its age, capacities, utilisation (plant register)
b   Activities previously performed, times taken
c   Spares—an appropriate control, including issue-receipt and reordering procedures
d   Maintenance carried out on all major machines and buildings; their cost, man-hours used
e   Monthly and annual work programs

f   Job standards—where these have been calculated
g   Wages payment
10   Instructions: Safety, standard practices

DIVISIONS OF MAINTENANCE ACTIVITY.   Normally a maintenance department will have four separate and identifiable functions:

1   General maintenance—heating, lighting, ventilating, painting, plumbing, minor construction etc
2   Plant maintenance—maintenance of plant and equipment, machines, furnaces, compressed air equipment, meters, gauges, dust extraction and workshop heating, maintenance of materials handling equipment, cranes, forklift trucks etc
3   Electrical equipment maintenance—electric motors, electric rewiring, electric lighting, battery charging
4   Workshop activities:
a   Fitters and welders shop
b   Tinsmiths
c   Joinery shop
d   Millwrights' shop
      —or any combination of these.

TYPES OF MAINTENANCE ORGANISATION.   Various forms of organisation have been tried for maintenance departments and men. The major ones are listed below.

Devolution of activity.   Maintenance personnel are so far as possible seconded to production divisions. The men grow accustomed to the machines in the divisions. They develop specialist skills and can on the whole carry out corrective action faster than if they were centralised and only had intermittent experience of the division's equipment. If they have a bonus system allied to the production division, they have a suitable incentive to make corrections quickly.

The main disadvantage of this system is that it loses the flexibility in job allocation which a centralised activity could give. Personnel become too specialised.

Flying squad maintenance gangs.   Teams of mixed skills are formed to carry out maintenance requests, "heavy gang" removals, etc.

Centralised control.   In this situation all maintenance personnel are centralised in the work-shop area and, as far as possible, maintenance is carried out in the shops. For example, materials handling equipment is brought to the shop to be maintained. The engineer does not visit the site.

The advantages of the system are that the maintenance men are under close scrutiny by foremen and supervisors. Work output and quality can be checked. The disadvantage is that men must be sent to sites for the repair of buildings, steam lines, etc. If they only have one central site, then they spend a considerable number of their clocked hours walking to and from site and central workshop.

Intercraft exchange.   Some productivity bargains have included an intercraft exchange, with little or no job demarcation. This is fine when skills truly are interchangeable.

A mixture of devolution and centralisation (above). This seems the ideal approach if it is possible to have an integrated maintenance plan. The production division's maintenance personnel respond to the line production manager. Their activities need to be integrated with those of the central services if an optimum situation is to exist.

PLANNED MAINTENANCE.   This is an activity that has fallen into some disrepute as the effort has not apparently achieved suitable rewards.

A maintenance control list is designed listing activities to be performed, when they should be performed and how long they should take. The apparent *advantages* of this system are:

1   Breakdowns are forestalled by preplanning
2   There are many operations which need to be done at regular intervals—oil change, filter change, etc—and an added service to surrounding areas is worth while
3   Time to be spent on operations can be calculated, personnel allocated and a plan made for the utilisation of workshop facilities

The *disadvantages* have been:

1   Maintenance is carried out on non-essential equipment and parts of equipment by highly paid individuals with no corresponding improvement in efficiency
2   It is often desirable to allow something to "break" before it is replaced rather than replace it beforehand
3   Potential major breakdowns—metal fatigue, or breaking of a major component—are rarely found by planned maintenance and it is this type of occurrence which causes most lost machine time

GENERAL INSPECTION.   Though planned maintenance has become less popular than it was there are still a considerable number of activities which need to be inspected closely on a routine basis. These are:

1   Where corrosion is likely to occur and metal or wood is damaged in consequence
2   Where vibration is likely to weaken structures or machine parts
3   Where abuse of equipment and machines is likely
4   Where stress may weaken structures and machines

5   Anywhere fumes and toxic conditions may occur due to a lack of maintenance
6   Anywhere where hazards could occur due to wear and tear of machinery and equipment

MAINTENANCE COSTS AND APPROPRIATE RATIOS. Before a productivity bargain or a new work measurement system is agreed, cost and other appropriate data will have to be obtained. Often the costs listed below will not be available from a normal standard costing and budgetary control system.

Costs.   All factory/production services as under:

1   Water
2   Steam
3   Power
4   Light
5   Per division
6   Per production line
7   Per machine (perhaps if it is important enough)

Costs of the toolroom as under:

1   Direct wages
2   Materials
3   Machines (depreciation)
4   Tools
5   Power—heat, light, steam also

Costs of vehicle maintenance.

1   Materials handling equipment
2   Production equipment
3   Service equipment
4   Building and land
5   Administrative buildings—building services equipment

Costs of various trades and their activities:

1   Electricians
2   Joiners
3   Painters
4   Tool makers
5   Sheet metal workers
6   Fitters and turners
7   Welders

Total value of:

1   Administration
2   Production
3   Warehouse buildings etc
4   Production equipment
5   Materials handling and distribution—including vehicles
6   Services facilities

Ratios appropriate in analysing maintenance work force should also be determined:

Cost of maintenance/production (for the factory per production unit):

1*a*   Cost of maintenance per £10 000 of plant in own organisation
 b   Same in other organisation of comparable size with similar plant
2   One trade/other trades
3   Machine utilisation/incidence of breakdowns due to poor maintenance
4   Cost of maintenance/production value in each division or production activity
5   Maintenance operatives of all kinds/production personnel

Some figures have been made available which indicate the cost of maintenance when viewed against value of plant. For example, modern chemical plant has a ratio of approximately 1 to 20 or less.
   The higher the plant value, the higher should be the maintenance costs involved depending upon:

1   Plant complexity
2   Age of plant
3   Corrosive nature of products made
4   Intensity of plant usage

Comparing plant value with maintenance costs therefore may be uninformative. It would be more meaningful if similar companies were compared with each other. American practice and results seem particularly valuable.
   All maintenance activities should be recorded so as to provide an accurate picture of work done, time spent and area or unit worked upon. To achieve this an appropriate coding system seems necessary so as to record:

1   Area of company activity worked upon:
a   Production
b   Non-production
c   Plant and equipment
d   Buildings

c	Services etc
2	Time spent:
a	Total hours
b	By trade
3	Type of maintenance carried out:
a	Planned or routine on production facilities
b	Breakdown on production facilities
c	Accident maintenance—improving safety
d	Cleaning
e	Painting and general repair of buildings
f	Service maintenance
4	Cost in each case:
a	Labour
b	Spares
c	Power
5	Reasons for maintenance
a	Negligence
b	Routines
c	Extra accommodation etc

25:3   Successful areas of application and examples

The key to successful maintenance control will generally lie in a productivity bargaining activity, where personnel are asked to participate in improved maintenance methods which will be followed by the introduction of improved control. A simple system based on this premise follows.

MAINTENANCE CONTROL SYSTEM

Introduction

  Objectives.   Covers all maintenance staff. Savings of 30 per cent to be made by natural wastage over next twelve months. The first priority will be to set up an effective progress and control system after which measurement activity can commence.

  Reasonable times will be established for most jobs. Job descriptions for repetitive jobs will be made. Maintenance budgets by cost centres will also be established.

  Prior to the introduction of the systems, agreements will be made with all craft unions.

Outline of system

1   A maintenance control function will be established and will be manned by a senior foreman and a male clerk

2   An authorised person (who will be designated) will prepare a maintenance requisition

3   The requirement will state:

a   Cost centre

b   Location

c   Cost code

d   Equipment

e   Date requested

f   Description of work to be done

4   An estimate of skills, by trade, in hours and total cost will be made by the foreman supervisor. An assessment of material requirements will also be done

5   Agreement that the maintenance can go ahead will then be obtained from the maintenance manager

6   Once agreed the control clerk will load the skill times required onto a planning board, informing the person who prepared the maintenance request of the date maintenance will be carried out—if this differs from the original request

7   Priorities will be assessed on all requests. This will help to determine forward planning. Priority numbers will be issued

8   The work to be done should be described in sufficient detail to provide maintenance control with the ability to give time standards for the work to be performed. If these are not known from previous jobs of the same kind, an on-site inspection should be made and an assessment calculated

9   Each request should indicate whether production is stopped or where production is not affected but dangerous conditions are present. Equipment availability must also be stated. Requests which can be delayed provide another category

10   Telephoned requests are necessary when urgency dictates them, but in each case a requisition must also be completed to ensure a suitable record is maintained and a job number issued.

11   Tradesmen will be informed of future work loads by a forward load schedule which will be on show in the maintenance department. This schedule will record:

a   Job numbers

b   Man hours and trades involved

c   Days

d   Small and emergency job allowance

    They will also receive a job card on which the activity to be performed will be listed in detail, plus material to be used, time to be taken, date issued and completion time

12   Once the work has been done the tradesmen concerned will complete the job card by inserting time spent on the job

13   The maintenance department clerk will then:

a   Compare actual time spent on the job with estimate and calculate difference

b   Code the job carried out

c   Calculate the cost of the job

d   Amend job records, after consultation with senior foreman if this is demanded—times particularly might need amendment

e   The card will then be processed to provide overall control and analysis of maintenance department activity

14   Records will be maintained of:

a   Departmental efficiency in labour/skill utilisation:

i   Against a budget

ii   Against estimates

iii   Total utilisation

b   Daily assignment logs listing

i   Jobs carried out

ii   Job numbers

iii   Estimated hours

iv   Actual hours

c   Job records—work performed and standard times

d   Back-logs—work due but no tradesmen available to carry it out

e   Cost centre—maintenance cost

f   Material requirements

g   Tools requirements

h   Plant inventory

25:4 Problems in the use of the technique and conditions for success

Time study is not always applicable to maintenance activities. Very often it is extremely difficult. The wide variation in types of maintenance require different scheduling skills.

Planned maintenance and routine activities have been measured by the use of synthetics. MTM2 (see Chapter 9) has been used for this purpose.

Simple and reliable observation techniques using coded motion sequence recording have been used. With the classification of tradework into "data-blocks" a new system of job slotting has been evolved.

The job slotting technique was developed from analysis of patterns of repair work. Small orders of less than one hour's duration tend to predominate. Supervision is asked to "time band" such small jobs, keeping a record of them.

The standard time or data block is subjected to control limits to check that on average the foreman is guessing—within limits—correctly for all minor jobs in total. (The percentage number of small jobs is found from analysis and total times assessed.)

The advantages claimed for MTM2 include the simplicity of auditing procedures and the well-defined validation procedures.

Job estimating or analytical estimating has been developed for use in situations where tasks and work involved are not standard. Estimates are made from experience and previous knowledge. To provide against occasions when extremely high bonus may result, performance is usually "geared." The bonus earnings drop sharply once "time and one-third" has been earned. A ceiling bonus figure is usually put into the system.

It is still said that a practical working estimator with detailed records to back him up can be as good as the use of synthetics.

25:5   Conclusion

The aim of maintenance control should not be to reduce maintenance costs. This can be done very easily, but production units will eventually grind to a halt.

Maintenance costs are a trade-off. Higher service will produce higher costs and vice versa. What is inexcusable is the lack of control found in many maintenance units. Maintenance is expensive and techniques now available can bring it under control.

Unfortunately the effort may be expensive. Estimates of one clerk or administrator per fifty to seventy maintenance men are usual.

25:6   Further reading

1   Roy Grant, "Motivating the Maintenance Men," *Business Management*, October 1968
2   J K Hildebrand, "Maintenance Turns to the Computer," *Industrial Education*
3   A K S Jardine (editor), *Operational Research in Maintenance*, Manchester University, 1970
4   H M V Stewart, *Guide to Efficient Maintenance Management*, Business Books, 1963
5   E T Newborough, *Effective Maintenance Management*, McGraw Hill, 1967
6   L C Morrow, *Maintenance Engineering Handbook*, McGraw Hill
7   G C Corder, *Organising Maintenance*, BIM

TWENTY-SIX

Design of
management information systems

26:1 Introduction

The role of information is obviously to help the profitability of a business. By definition information is concerned with knowledge about events. In the case of management information, the definition will include knowledge required to measure, plan and control company activities.

26:2 Description

Designing management information systems (MIS) is often a long and fruitless task. But there are basic principles which should influence the design of MIS as follows. Utilising such principles will help to avoid many pitfalls and time-wasting assignments, common in this field.

As was said above, information should be used to measure, plan and control company activities. If it does not do these things it should be ignored. Only relevant information should be presented, if possible on an exception basis.

Information needs should be related to the resources which a manager controls. This will be as true for salesmen who should be measured on the sales/turnover they achieve as for shop-floor supervisors who have labour, machinery, material and factory services to control. This factor leads automatically to the formation of a pyramid information structure (see Figure 26.1) broken down as follows:

1   The board or chief executive—information concerning profit and loss, turnover, return on investment and supporting data
2   Divisional managers—divisional profit and loss, divisional return on · investment, turnover and supporting data

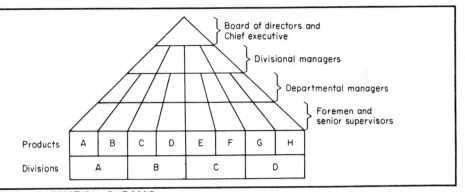

Figure 26.1 INFORMATION PYRAMID

3   Departmental managers—departmental operating statements, material
     and labour utilisation and all supporting data
4   Foreman and supervisors—material, labour and machine utilisation under
     their control and any other factory resources for which they are responsible

It is possible that an information pyramid of the type outlined, will need to be
split vertically where product divisionalisation has been introduced.

To review management information systems from a total company viewpoint
often overwhelms the information analyst. It seems appropriate that the company
should be fragmented for this purpose and while the integrated whole must not
be forgotten, segmentation ought to be followed (see Figure 26.2).

Figure 26.3 shows a typical management information system outline which
quotes appropriate company segmentation.

DEFINING INFORMATION NEEDS. The discussions implicit in preparing
information schedules will largely have determined the information that a line
manager needs. However, it may be necessary to prepare further schedules.
Each manager should review his role in using company resources and prepare
an information requirement as follows:

1   List the area, function or department that will supply and receive the
     information
2   Record the purpose of the information—to control a profit plan or a budget
     or to measure performance etc
3   State the unit of measurement to be used—money, standard hours, actual
     v standard performances etc
4   Suggest the format the information might take
5   Determine the frequency of the information—daily, weekly, monthly,
     randomly etc
6   List the date of availability of the information and also that of the action
     being controlled or planned
7   Suggest how the information might be processed

Major element	Sub-elements	Data for other purposes (planning and control etc) and links with other systems	Files for data
1 Order translation/sales input	1 Order document production 2 Record of order entry 3 Classification of order type	1 Comparison of forecast (plan) and actual 2 Evolution of order input with factory capacity	1 Customer file 2 WIP production file
2 Credit control	1 Credit check 2 Credit improvement systems 3 Debtors ledger	1 Establishment of credit limits Amount Length of credit period by product group by market segment	1 Customer file
3 Stock control	1 Stock recording 2 Stock forecasting 3 Stock analysis of various kinds 4 Stock audit 5 Performance review of stock carried	1 Cash flow planning 2 Production planning and control 3 Performance review 4 Market planning	1 Stock control and record file 2 Demand history file
4 Production planning and control	1 Evolution of order input with factory capacity 2 Plant loading 3 Machine loading 4 Labour control 5 Material control 6 Efficiency reporting and cost control 7 Raw material purchase and control	1 Budgetary control and standard costing 2 Cost control 3 Plant renewal and new investment 4 Raw material requirements	1 Production or WIP file
5 Distribution home	1 Transport & warehousing control 2 Lorry routing 3 Depot siting & control 4 Stock control (service levels) 5 Document preparation	1 Transport costs 2 Total data for optimisation of transport review	Customer file

Figure 26.2 SALES ORDER PROCESSING SYSTEM

Major element	Sub-elements	Data for other purposes (planning and control etc) and links with other systems	Files for data
6 Distribution export	1 Transport & warehousing control 2 Stock control (service levels) 3 Document preparation	1 As in 5	Customer file
7 Invoicing	1 Sales data analysis	1 Control for sales/market planning	Sales ledger
8 Sales ledger	1 Data for standard cost of sales & budgeted sales comparison		Sales ledger
9 Comparisons of sales achieved with budget	1 Budgetary control 2 Profit planning		Budget
10 Cost control	1 Budgetary control 2 Profit planning		Budget

Figure 26.2 (continued)

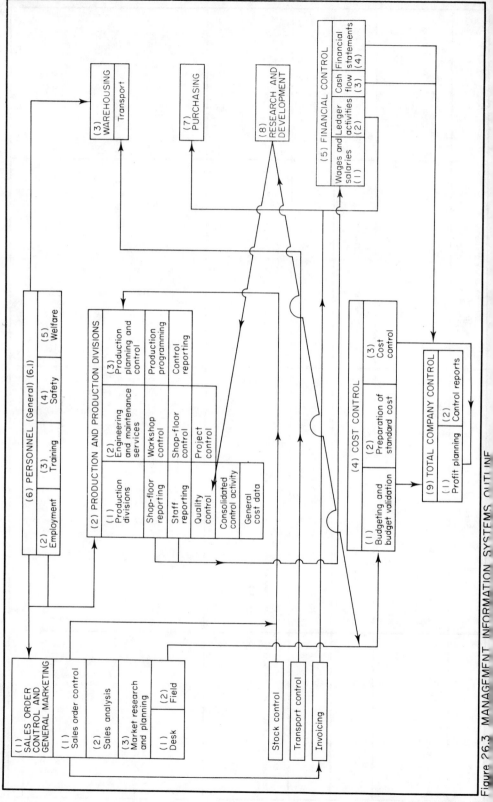

Figure 26.3 MANAGEMENT INFORMATION SYSTEMS OUTLINE

The information analyst should determine:

1   Whether the information will be timely
2   Whether he considers that the information required by the line manager is really what he should require
3   Whether the information format is appropriate
4   Whether the cost of producing the information is worth while—a definite calculation of cost *v* value obtained should be made

INTEGRATED SYSTEMS.   There are obvious advantages in having integrated systems. Once written or produced in a form acceptable to line managers, information should not be reprocessed. The speed of data handling is improved and errors in transcription and transmission avoided (see Figure 26.2).

All data does not have the same value. In every company there is a main stream of management information and many substreams joining to make the whole. Systems componenents act and react on each other and unless the design of each component is undertaken with the total system always in mind inefficiency and possibly friction will occur.

26:3   Successful areas of application and examples

The information analyst could follow the rules for designing management information systems set out in 26:2 and evolve an appropriate framework. It would take a long time and might in the end miss out certain vital components.

To speed up the process and ensure that both analyst and line manager know that they have discussed, considered and possibly included every aspect of a system a checklist is invaluable.

Technical systems will always provide problems. It is unlikely that an analyst will include every possible factor in a standard costing and budgetary control system for example. For this he will need a checklist that records all the system's elements which should be taken into account when designing such systems. He should consider each factor quoted, weigh its importance and decide how best it might be fitted into a total company system and then design accordingly.

The same methodology should apply when designing most major systems in a company. For example, the system's checklist quoted in the section on production planning and control should be utilised for a company design of that system. Similarly the stock control checklist (see page 292) is a necessary requirement for the design of a stock control system.

Each major systems area might have its own checklist. A management information control system for profit planning and control is shown as Table 15.1 in *How to Make and Control a Profit Plan* (Business Books, 1969).

The following organisational divisions seem appropriate in ascertaining information requirements:

1   *Marketing and order control*
a   Sales order control
b   Sales analysis
c   Market research
i   Desk research
ii   Field research
2   *Production and production divisions*
a   Production divisions
b   Engineering and maintenance services
i   Workshop control
ii   Shop-floor control
c   Production planning and control
3   *Warehousing and transport*
4   *Cost control*
a   Budgeting and budget validation
b   Preparation of standard costs
c   Cost control
5   *Financial control*
a   Wages, salaries payment
b   Ledger activities
c   Cash flow
d   Financial statements
6   *Personnel control*
a   General personnel
b   Employment
c   Training
d   Welfare
7   *Purchasing*
8   *R & D*
9   *Total company control*—integration of divisions 1 to 8 including documentation
a   Profit planning
b   Control reports

SYSTEMS FLOW OUTLINE.   For each area a systems flow outline, covering all information requirements, is necessary. For a production division this might be as follows:

1   *Shop-floor reporting*
a   Production records
b   Material usage records
c   Stock and WIP returns
d   Bonus calculation and labour usage reporting
e   Machine utilisation and down time reports
2   *Staff reports*

a   Absenteeism and lateness
b   Accident reports
c   Trainee and training reports
d   Termination of service
e   Engagement notifications
f   Medical centre reports
3   *Production planning activity*
a   Production programming
b   Control reports
4   *Stock recording*
a   Control report
5   *Quality control*—reports at appropriate stages of production
6   *Consolidated control activity*—daily, weekly and monthly. Information covering actual costs compared with standard labour, material and machine utilisation and sales volume
7   *General cost data*
8   *Returns* sent out by divisional production departments
9   *General information* received by division

All forms covering each operational area should be collected, analysed and recorded. The information currently available should be listed under the following headings:

1   Activity
2   Activity elements
3   Measurement used—hours, tons, gallons etc
4   Recipients
5   Time/data required
6   Control apparently established
7   Form title and number
8   How and when prepared
9   Comment

This should then be recorded against the job responsibilities of those concerned. (It may be necessary to review job responsibilities and record them appropriately if this has not been done in a way that will facilitate a correlation between information available and responsibilities.)

The name of the individual should be recorded, also his/her area of responsibility—for capital expenditure, for achievement of listed objectives etc. Cost centres should be quoted where relevant.

The information that the information analyst and the line manager together think is necessary to enable the listed responsibilities to be controlled should then be stated, preferably under similar headings to those used initially.

The exclusion of information currently available is as important as the inclusion of information which is required.

Once a rapport between the information analyst and line management has been achieved, it will be necessary to authenticate the data source, and evaluate the methods of data capture, processing and presentation. Recommendations concerning the methods of data processing need to be made including potential changes in:

1   Location of data processing procedure
2   Manual to semi-automatic or automatic production
3   Forms design to restrict or expand the information given

Once this stage has been successfully completed a program for the implementation of the changes which have been agreed, needs to be drawn up. Appropriate timescales and manpower allocations will be necessary.

26:4   Problems in the use of the technique and conditions for success

The basic principles for designing management information systems have been stated in this chapter. Ignore these and systems will be inappropriate, often over elaborate and costly.

There is a myth that a total company-wide management information system is possible. This is a holy grail, often sought but rarely, if ever, found.

26:5   Conclusion

Without management information systems a company has no life blood. With one it may bleed to death because of bad design and over sophistication.

26:6   Further reading

1   R O Boyce, *Integrated Managerial Controls*, Longmans 1969
2   A E Mills, *The Dynamics of Management Control Systems*, Business Books, 1968
3   D Rogers, *Creative Systems Design*, Anbar Publications, 1970
4   V Lazzaro, *Systems and Procedures*, Prentice Hall
5   R N Anthony, *Planning and Control Systems*, Harvard University Press, 1965
6   A Rappaport (editor), *Information for Decision Making*, Prentice Hall
7   B L J Hart, *Dynamic Systems Design*, Business Books, 1964

Part 5

CONTROL OF PERFORMANCE

Standard costing and budgetary control

27:1 Introduction

No claim can be made that standard costing and budgetary control reduces costs or even saves money, but if action is taken as a result of differences arising between predetermined standard and actual results then substantial benefit can accrue. Emphasis must be placed, therefore, on using the information thrown up as a spur to management action.

27:2 Description

Most standard cost systems are based on budgets of "normal" expenditure, which have been set following the establishment of standards of operating performance and material usage by technical personnel. The "normal" budgets of expenditure combined with these standards produce costing rates. This information can then be used to give a service to management for the following activities:

1   Control of performance
2   Control of expenditure
3   Control of material usage
4   Cost of individual products on a clearly defined basis
5   Analysis of selling values for guidance in the development of policy
6   A basis for estimating
7   A complete and practical accounting record regularly and promptly presented to all levels of supervision with the limits of the expenditure which they control

COST CENTRES AND ACCOUNT NUMBERS.   Before an expense budget can be made, appropriate cost centres and account numbers must be established. Too few cost centres and account numbers will not provide the necessary cost control. Too many will burden down the company with paperwork. The cost accountants will usually suggest too many rather than too few.

For each cost centre it is necessary to have records of:

1   Output achieved
2   Time utilised

The output standards are assessed by technical staff and expressed as "units per standard hour." Direct expenses for running the cost centre can then be budgeted on the basis of the standard output. Standard output is a calculation of what the normal cost should be under normal efficiency and output.

When budgets for all other expenses (other than direct manufacturing expenses) have been calculated, they can be spread over the manufacturing cost centres. The method of spreading should be the one which best relates the non-direct expense with the manufacturing operation.

Before the expense budgets are completed all relevant data on which initial standards can be based should be collected. The data will be provided by technical and production personnel. It should include:

1   Material—material usage, raw materials and components bought out
2   Labour—machine manning strengths and a breakdown of labour in the company by cost centre and department
3   Machine speeds at each operation

SCHEDULE OF CALENDAR FACTORS.   As the number of days in each month vary from the monthly average of working days (because of the length of the month and holidays) a weighting factor has to be applied to ensure that each month is standard.

BUDGET PREPARATION

Sales budget.   It will first be necessary to make a sales plan or forecast for each product or product range the company makes and sells. Because of the likely fluctuations of production during the year, it is wise to make a monthly breakdown of the annual forecast. This not only helps to control cost but assists production planning personnel in optimising production facilities. Data might be built up under the following headings:

1   Product type
2   Products within product type
3   Any components necessary
4   Forecast per annum

5   Forecast per month—seasonal fluctuations shown
6   Total sales of product with components
7   Various machine speeds involved
8   The normal standard hours involved—i.e. a division of machine speed into
    products required

Expense budgets

Types of expense.   Once the sales budget has been set, appropriate expense budgets can be formulated. To enable expenditure to be controlled with a fluctuating production output rate, each kind of expense which will be incurred in meeting the sales budget must be reviewed separately. Generally three broad classifications are used:

1   *Fixed*—these are expenses that do not vary whatever the level of production
    —e.g. rates, insurance, rent etc
2   *Variable*—expenses which will vary directly with production levels—such
    as direct labour
3   *Semi-variable*—expenses which are partly fixed and partly variable. Such
    expenses might be storemen and indirect labour

Normal standard hours.   The next step in the process is to establish a normal standard hours sheet. This is a budget of normal output expressed as the number of standard hours of activity required at each cost centre to achieve the sales budget. This is done by estimating the hours available for production during each month (normal capacity hours) and comparing this with the standard or required production hours. It is usual not to expect 100 per cent efficiency from each machine and some lower figure—90 per cent, for example—is often used to calculate the normal standard hours for each cost centre.

Budget detail sheets.   Once an appropriate sales budget has been agreed, and the schedule of normal standard hours compiled, etc, budget detail sheets can be made out. These sheets will show all expenses to which the company will be committed in achieving the sales budget. They are usually set out on separate sheets for each cost centre in the company. Related normal standard hours are also shown so that a standard cost for the budgeted output at the cost centre can be calculated.

From the budget detail sheets, budget schedules are completed to summarise the various types of expenses and used as a means of spreading the accumulated cost.

The allocation of general works, administration and direct expenses should be on as direct a basis as possible. The basis should be laid down early in the exercise to establish a standard costing and budgetary control system.

Budget summary.   Totals of anticipated expenditure are transferred to a budget summary sheet which should show the total cost of direct labour at each cost centre with direct expense, general works and administration expenses added. It should also show the total expense which is fixed in the budget.

Once budgets have been fixed, they should, as far as possible, be static. If minor fluctuations in labour or expense budgets occur, it is better to allow the variance to appear in the cost and variation statements or the final accounts. Each of these sheets has a revision variance column—this column should be used to signify minor changes from standard.

Costing rates.   Once the budgeted expenditure has been allocated to cost centres —including general works, direct expense and administration expense—the total expenditure can be divided by the budgeted standard hours to give the standard hourly costing rate. Each costing rate produced is the total cost for running the cost centre for one hour under normal operating conditions.

The standard unit cost of each product, therefore, is the hourly costing rate divided by the speed of the machine in units per hour. So that if the speed of the machine in the cost centre is 1000 units per hour and the hourly costing rate £50, the standard unit cost is £0.05.

Product costs.   With the material standards which the company's technical staff should have formulated and the costing rates—the calculation of which has been previously described—it is possible to build up the standard cost for any product or component which the company's equipment can manufacture.

The range and variety of products made may prohibit the production of individual product costings. In those cases individual costs for a few high value/fast selling items can be made. The remainder, the low value/slow selling items, can be put into product ranges—size, product, type of material used, being the usual criteria. An average costing rate is then given for each product devised.

The foregoing outlines show very briefly how a standard costing and budgetary control is established. Once budgets have been set and data obtained on which control can be established emphasis must be on the reporting procedures essential to a standard costing and budgetary control system.

EFFICIENCY REPORTING.   In controlling production costs it is important to report in the fullest but simplest possible way. The following rules seem to govern the presentation of efficiency reports:

1   The exception principle should apply—i.e. only the significant results should be brought to the attention of management
2   Results should be given at a time which will permit rapid correction of adverse trends
3   The figures used should have a direct relationship between the efficiencies produced and the cost of product and, eventually, the price being charged to the customer

LABOUR CONTROL SYSTEMS. These control systems should:

1 Provide a means of checking labour usage
2 Enable a financial evaluation of labour usage to be made and with the assessment of material usage, provide the basis for a simple, monthly financial appreciation of the company's manufacturing operations
3 Establish a base from which improvements in labour productivity can be started

The data required for labour control will include:

1 Current output performance for all operations in the area being controlled
2 If there is an incentive scheme in operation—the "normal" performance at each operation
3 The labour manning at each operation

Information required from the factory for control purposes will be:

1 The amount of production at each operation, stage or cost centre where control is required
2 This production converted into standard hours
3 The labour hours used at each of the operation stages or cost centres, which can be attributed directly to production

MATERIAL CONTROL. A method similar to the labour control system can be used for material control. This system provides:

1 A means of checking material usage and correcting overusage
2 The means for making a financial evaluation of material usage

The following data will be required in order to create the system:

1 The total weight and type of material used for each batch of products or for each product
2 The number of products expected from each batch. The materials and quantities which constitute each batch
3 The standard losses at each operation which it is desired to cover have to be discounted in determining any departure from standard

STANDARD AND ACTUAL COST COMPARISONS. Standard and actual cost comparisons are usually carried out each month. Working papers are first prepared for each cost centre as follows:

1 Budgets—direct labour and direct expense cost multiplied by the month's calendar factor

2   A summary of output expressed in:

a   Standard hours—the number of hours which the month's production should have taken, calculated from budgeted standards

b   Allowed hours—the standard hours of output achieved after making some permitted variation for unavoidable lost efficiency to the original standard of speeds

c   Actual hours—the operating hours available for production—i.e. clocked hours

3   Ratios for standard, allowed and actual hours of budget can then be calculated. Efficiency achievement can be calculated by dividing allowed hours by actual hours and multiplying by 100

4   Each cost centre cost will have to be factored by the actual hours worked to achieve a true standard cost—that is, the proportion, fixed or variable, will have to be multiplied by the actual hours, to allow a true standard cost to be calculated for the output achieved

5   Appropriate costs for each cost for standard and allowed hours can then be calculated. Where there are no variable or semi-variable costs (such as administration) this standard cost can be transferred from the cleared-in-cost sheet directly

6   In total, therefore, an appropriate standard cost for the standard and allowed hours will have been calculated. It should then be compared with the appropriate actual cost and a variance produced

Cost and variation or operating statements can also be used to control material usage and the figures built up on the cost and variations sheet can eventually be transferred to departmental operating statements.

STANDARD COST PROFIT AND LOSS ACCOUNT.   This monthly statement sets out the standard profit or loss for each department or profit centre in the company. It is broken down to give the actual or net sales, and the standard cost of sales. The difference between these two is the standard profit or loss.

To this figure are added or deducted the variances from standard—materials, labour and overhead, transfers and profit on sales of scrap. A deduction of delivery, packing and other expenses and an addition of miscellaneous credits produces a net profit. Usually cumulative totals for the year to date are added.

OPERATING STATEMENTS.   The standard costing profit and loss statement is usually retained by the chief executive and his board of directors. Senior managers and their staffs often use the summary operating statement, supported by materials and departmental operating statements, to measure their performance.

An operating statement summarises the company's monthly performance and compares actual activity and efficiency with "normal" or budgeted. It compares actual cost with standard cost and gives an analysis of the variances. This is an important measuring document for senior managers for it shows clearly what the costs of running the departments in the company are compared with what the costs should have been. The analysis covers the various causes for failing to achieve or overachieving "budgeted standard." The variances can be divided into two groups:

1   *Non-controllable variances* which have had an effect on the actual results, but which are not the responsibility of local management
2   *Controllable variances* which local management has the responsibility for controlling

MANAGEMENT RATIOS AND PROFIT MARGINS.   To ensure that trends in costs can be seen, management ratios should be used to indicate cost performance not shown by the standard costing and budgetary control systems.

INTEGRATION WITH THE FINANCIAL ACCOUNTS.   Having produced the cost and variation statements, the details should be capable of transfer to the financial accounts. Appropriate systems of journal entries, control accounts and entries into the nominal ledger need to be built up.

     Financial and cost accounts personnel should not follow parallel lines, duplicating work.

27:3   Successful areas of application and examples

Standard costing and budgetary control has been particularly useful in flow-line and job production industries where forecasting for a year or more ahead has proved to be realistic.

     Some examples of forms which are normally in use in such a system are given in *How to Make and Control a Profit Plan.*

27:4   Problems in the use of the technique and conditions for success

The problems implicit in achieving successful applications of standard costing and budgetary control are so many that Chapter 28 is devoted to budget validation systems. This should help to eradicate many of the problems associated with the systems.

     The control of the tactical or annual plan of the company is usually done by a system of standard costing and flexible budgetary control. The details of the system used will vary from company to company and industry to industry.

     The inherent dangers of such a system are strongly stressed. Budgetary control without profit planning tends to develop into a method for justifying inertia and poor performance. The failings are obvious:

1   A lack of will to do better. Budgets are increased each year to take account of rises in labour, material and other costs. Rarely are attempts made to reduce them
2   The control is arbitrary and ineffective. Monthly accounts are often late and line managers may be "too busy" to take action from them

3   The system is dominated by accountants, and is not orientated towards helping line managers to set and achieve their objectives

4   The main purpose of any standard cost system is to establish an adequate yardstick against which costs can be measured and control facilitated. It should also stimulate cost consciouness and encourage action to reduce costs and increase profit. The link between the system and the cost reduction/ production plan is emphasised

There are also intrinsic parts of the system that cause some concern. For example, the spread of overhead could obviously be a dangerous exercise. Occasions have occurred where it has become "too expensive" to operate a machine because it carries too high an overhead burden. This is obviously ludicrous, but absorption costing has this basic weakness, which line managers should always have in mind when cost accountants produce costing rates appearing to be too high.

27:5   Conclusion

Standard costing and budgetary control has many failings, but it is still a potent method of controlling company performance. Linked with profit planning, the system has an important role to play in ensuring that plans are achieved.

27:6   Further reading

1   J Batty, *Managerial Standard Costing*, Macmillan, 1970
2   J A Scott, *Budgetary Control and Standard Costs*, Pitman, 1962
3   R E V Duck and F R J Jervis, *Management Accounting*, Harrap, 1964
4   J Batty, *Management Accountancy*, Macdonald Evans, 1963
5   R W Dobson, *Management Information Accounting*, Gee, 1964
6   F C de Paula, *Management Accounting in Practice*, Pitman, 1964
7   D F Evans, *Flexible Budgetary Control and Standard Costs*, Macdonald & Evans.

TWENTY-EIGHT

Budget Validation systems

28:1 Introduction

In most standard applications of budgetary control there has always been a significant concentration on the control element in the systems but scarcely any challenge to the budget quantities themselves. Often there have been considerable post mortems on a variance of, say, 1 per cent of a departmental budget of £100 000, but only a cursory evaluation of whether the budget should have been set at such a figure in the first place.

The setting or establishment of budgets has largely been left to line managers. The subsequent validation of the budgeted figures has frequently been ineffective. There has been too little time for the budgetary control staff to carry out the operation; often there is a lack of competence and more especially there have been no yardsticks with which to measure whether a budgeted amount is valid or not. An arbitrary cut of 5 per cent all round or a slight reduction in a glaringly out-of-line budget is usually all that line managers have to accept.

Usually only when budgeted profit is far below the figure that is required is a serious attempt made to reduce budgeted costs and an across-the-company cost reduction activity mounted. Only if a detailed and analytical review is built into the budgetary control system, so preventing the restoration of original out-of-control situations, will a satisfactory reward be forthcoming.

28:2 Description

Though not an accepted benefit of budgetary control it is interesting to see that the budget validation method will tend to increase the professionalism of line managers in the company. If a challenge is made to a budgeted amount, the response must be a professional validation. For example, in an administration budget one evaluation procedure should lie in the recent application of work simplification to the functions contained in the budget. The line manager, therefore, has to know of and be able to apply such a technique.

The key to the proposed procedure obviously lies in the method of validation. If the methods are accepted then budget justification is comparatively simple. It seems essential, therefore, for a series of evaluation or justification procedures, similar to those listed in Figure 28.1, to be drawn up and accepted by appropriate line managers.

USE OF CHECKLISTS: A short checklist should be used by those made responsible for the budget validation procedure and a dialogue with the manager responsible for the budget, carried out as follows:

1   What functions are covered by the budget?
2   Are these functions really necessary in achieving company objectives?
3   Is the amount of money spent on the function commensurate with the return which it achieves?
a   How is the return measured?
b   Is it valid?
c   Is the amount of money to be spent on the function out of proportion with other functions?
d   Can the use of management ratios show that the function is apparently utilising more resources than necessary?
4   Does the amount of budgeted expense compare well or badly with that of other companies?
a   Can management ratios be used to prove this?
b   Is there any reason why this should be so?
c   Is the company's working environment so different that out-of-line expense is necessary?

A written comment on the answers to this simple checklist might accompany each budget proposal. It may be preferable for line managers to write it. Budgetary control personnel will then only need to check that the procedure has been fully carried out.

28:3   Successful areas of application and examples

BUDGET SCHEDULES.   These schedules should set out the budget item, the department covered by the budget item and the proposed budget. One department could have several budgets and these could be shown together.

The suggested justification or validation procedure is then shown in the next column. The procedures are the methods which line managers should have used

Budget item	Department	Total budget amount	Justification Procedure	Time-scale	Control mechanism	Person responsible for budget	Justified yes/no	Comments
1 DIRECT COSTS 1.1 Direct material	A division		Materials analysis	Annually	Material utilisation & control system	Divisional manager		
	B division		Value analysis	Every 3 years	Quality control			
	C division		Scrap analysis	Annually				
	D division		Standardisation & variety reduction	Every 3 years				
			Review of material standards	Annually				
			Resource utilisation by O R techniques	Randomly				
			Optimisation reviews (O R)	Randomly				
1.2 Direct labour	A division		Work measurement/appropriate incentive scheme	Reviewed annually	Comparison between standard hours produced, clocked hours and bonus hours paid (labour control system). Production planning and control and inventory	Divisional manager		
	B division		Method study	Every 3 years				
	C division		Standardisation and variety reduction	Every 3 years				
	D division		Review of production and planning and control systems (including inventory control)					
			Queueing theory, linear	Randomly				
			Programming,					
			Plant layout review	Randomly				
			Fatigue study	Randomly				
1.3 Power (gas, electricity, steam)	Divisional breakdown		Measurement of usage under standard conditions	Annually for standards establishment then perpetually metered	Budgetary control and divisional control performance sheets	Divisional manager		
2 ADMIN COSTS Direct clerical	Accounts		Work simplification	Every 2 years	Clerical work/output control	Various departmental managers		
	Cost-accounts		Detailed job descriptions	Randomly	Budgetary control			
	Purchasing		Activity sampling	Randomly				
	Cashiers		Use of EDP equipment and other labour-saving equipment where this is available	Randomly				
	Sales (1) (2)		Office layout study	Randomly				
	Employment		Office functions study	Randomly				
	Personnel		Training and education	Randomly				
			Method study	Randomly				
			Forms control	Randomly				

Figure 28.1 BUDGET VALIDATION SYSTEMS

	Budget item	Department	Total budget amount	Justification		Control mechanism	Person responsible for budget	Justified yes/no	Comments
				Procedure	Time-scale				
3	MANAGEMENT STRUCTURE			Organisation structure analysis Job descriptions, responsibilities and objectives Work simplification	Randomly Reviewed annually Randomly	Not applicable	Chief executive and functional executives		
4	OFFICE EXPENSES Rent, rates, lighting, insurance, heating etc	All departments		Metered or actual performance against calculated standard		Budgetary control	Office managers		
5	CANTEEN	Factory staff		Cost per meal per person/cost charged per meal Cost per meal: food labour overhead Number of meals served Review on the above lines	Annually	Annual budget and appropriate control mechanism	Canteen manager		
6	INVENTORY	Sales department		An appropriate inventory control system in use which will include: Stock recording, inventory assessment by value, replacement warehousing, financial and marketing constraints, audit routines, forecasting and the interaction of the system with others	Annually and perpetually	Statistical inventory control including standards of performance which will be required to be achieved	Sales manager		
7	WAREHOUSING AND DISTRIBUTION	Warehousing general transport		Work measurement of all personnel concerned including lorry drivers Vehicle routing plans, and schedules Distribution system is completely in line with marketing plan requirements Materials handling survey	Three-yearly check Randomly. At least every three years	Budgetary control	Warehousing distribution manager		
8	INTERNAL HAULAGE	Divisional managers		Activity sampling/work measurement Materials handling	Randomly, at least every second year Randomly at least every third year	Budgetary control	Divisional managers		
9	MAINTENANCE & OTHER ENGINEERING SERVICES	Electricians Fitters Tool shop Gen div Maintenance teams		Work measurement and establishment of standard times for all repetitive jobs. Material usage predetermined for each standard job	Randomly updated as necessary	Maintenance control Maintenance budget	Factory engineer		

Figure 28.1 (continued)

	Budget item	Department	Total budget amount	Justification Procedure	Time-scale	Control mechanism	Person responsible for budget	Justified yes/no	Comments
10	GARAGE SERVICES	Garage		Vehicle servicing rate compared with that accepted by makers. Cars controlled by usage/function. Comparison between car use and other transport costs	Annually	Annual budget and appropriate controls	Garage foreman		
11	QUALITY CONTROL	Manufacturing division		Detection rate of faults		Budgetary control			
12	SCRAP COLLECTION	Manufacturing divisions		Usage of scrap once collected		Budgetary control	Scrap controller		
13	WELFARE & SURGERY	Personnel department		Relationship of cost to direct and indirect operatives. Activity sample to check use and abuse of services	Annually	Budgetary control. Approporate issue controls for welfare supplies	Personnel officer		
14	RESEARCH & DEVELOPMENT			Annual review of progress which outlines department's activities in detail and which forms the basis for a marketing plan effective product screening committee	Annually	Control of annual R & D plan, which must be orientated towards providing product dominance in the market place	R & D manager		
15	SALES EXPENSES	Sales/marketing department		Sales obtained as % of market	Annually	Marketing plan controls	General sales manager		
	Reps			Value analysis of items	Bi-annually	Marketing plan controls	General sales manager		
	Packaging			Marketing plan requirements	Annually	Marketing plan controls			
	Warehousing & distribution	Distribution department		Marketing plan requirements. Vehicle & driver utilisation. Vehicle routing. Drivers incentive scheme. Standardise package and packages	Annually	Distribution budget	Distribution manager		
	Market research	Sales/ marketing department		Marketing plan requirements	Annually	Market research plan	Market research manager		
16	SALES	Sales/mktg department		Marketing plan requirements	Annually	Advertising plan	Advertising manager		
	Advertising								
17	CAPITAL INVESTMENT	All		DCF, risk analysis, break-even analysis	As necessary	D C F control sheets	As deputed		
18	PURCHASE OF SUPPLIES	Purchasing department		Annotated purchasing requirements various production and other plans	Annually	Purchasing control and budget	Purchasing officer		
19	TRAINING	Personnel department		Validation should stem from an appropriate management development plan and total manpower plan. Training must be related to the requirements of the plans. Individual training fees required to be assessed as standards	Annual plans constantly updated	Training budget and report on personnel trained. Measure of effectiveness required through a management and staff audit	Personnel manager & training officer		

Figure 28.1 (continued)

(either themselves or in conjunction with personnel skilled in the use of such techniques) so that their budgets are valid.

A difficult example to take to explain the procedure might be the R & D budget. A first breakdown of the budget could be between money for pure research being carried out and cash allocated for development work requested either by the manufacturing or marketing divisions. The former expense might only occur once a rigid diversification and new product development routine has been formulated and utilised. Failing this a project screening committee needs to have vetted and agreed to the expenditure. Money spent on development work seems easier to control. For example, the development of a product in order to achieve a greater market share should have development costs directly related to the extra sales revenue it will earn. Not only will this procedure validate the amounts to be spent but also provide a working method for priority assessment. The R&D budget should be viewed in total against the requirements of the marketing and production plans. A rigid control of expenditure is then required.

If these various procedures are followed, a validation for the R&D budget has been made. The weakness in the procedure is that it is unable to state categorically what the budget should really be—for example, R&D expenditure might need to be double what it actually is. This can only finally be established through a profit planning routine. Nevertheless, a reasonably tough series of criteria for judging proposed budgets will have been established.

MANAGEMENT RATIOS.   In determining the validity of budgets the use of management ratios seems obligatory. The schedules do not quote such ratios as each company will need to compare different functions with one another to determine suitable criteria. An appropriate management ratio schedule, therefore, needs to be developed to accompany the validation schedules.

28:4   Problems in the use of the technique and conditions for success

Few people are well versed in all or even a majority of the justification procedures listed. Such competence is certainly required before the system can get off the ground. How such competence is obtained will largely be a matter for the training officer.

There are bound to be organisational problems concerned with carrying out such a procedure. Must it be left totally to the budgetary control department which in turn is a limb of the accounting function? Or is budgetary control to be divorced from its origins and become a dynamic function in its own right with personnel of wide ranging expertise, not necessarily confined to standard costing and budgetary control systems?

This later proposal has been taken up by several companies, but even so the possible clash between it and management services personnel is very real.

The similarities between budget validation and cost reduction planning are very great and there may be something to be gained by joining the two functions together.

28:5   Conclusion

Standard costing and budgetary control without budget validation is largely meaningless. Regrettably budget validation is rarely, if ever, carried out appropriately.

28:6   Further reading

1   G H Hofstede, *The Game of Budget Control*, Tavistock Publications, 1968
2   B H Walley, "Effective Budgetary Control Through Work Study," *Work Study*, July 1969
3   W R Bunge, *Managerial Budgeting for Profit Improvement*, Mc Graw Hill, 1968
4   W D Knight and E H Weinwurm, *Managerial Budgeting*, Collier-Macmillan, 1964
5   J Sizer, "Budgetary Control is not Obsolete," *The Accountant*, October 1968

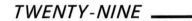

TWENTY-NINE

Stock control

29:1 Introduction

The UK has one of the highest stock to sales ratios of any advanced country. This cannot merely be that an island people has to have stock as an insurance against erratic deliveries from other countries. The import delivery situation is no worse for Japan or Sweden. Certainly too much is stocked, and too much of that is obsolete or, at least, obsolescent. An improved stock control system can make an immediate impact on an organisation's profitability.

29:2 Description

The development of inventory control practice has been aimed at reconciling the interests between the production, sales and accounting functions. Stock is required to buffer production facilities from erratic sales demand. It should enable a reasonable ex-stock delivery service to be given so that a turnover of X is gained. The accountant, by contrast, requires the absolute minimum. As well as these constraints there is a limit on warehouse capacity.

Largely mathematical forecasting has been used to determine future stock levels and the dangers of the procedure have already been pointed out—particularly in the inventory control strategy section of *How to Apply Strategy in Profit Planning*.

29:3 Successful areas of application and examples

The most useful method of either auditing a stock control system or designing a new one is to use a checklist of the type shown on page 292, recording most factors to be taken into account.

OTHER CONSIDERATIONS IN SYSTEMS DESIGN. An important distinction which must be made is between those systems which operate on a reorder level basis and the systems which utilise periodic review techniques.

Reorder level systems. The reorder level is the point to which stock must fall before a replacement batch is ordered. A replenishment order could be calculated by using lead time, sales demand, forecasting routines, safety stock, etc, but normally standard replacement quantities of a predetermined amount are ordered.

Periodic review systems. In this system stock levels are reviewed at fixed times and if a replacement order is required it is calculated by referring to past demand, safety stock, service levels, lead times, etc. This latter system is often referred to as cycle ordering. The cycle is always the same—two weeks, four weeks, etc—the quantity ordered nearly always differs.

Where supplies are obtained from outside the company, the reorder level system has obvious attractions. If supplies are obtained from the company's factory, the periodic review system is preferable, as weekly, monthly, etc, factory demands are required. The difficulty will be in reconciling factory capacity with stock-replenishment demand.

Types of stock. A stock control system should assume that usually there are three classes of stock items of descending importance. These are:

1   Fast-moving, high turnover, high stock value items, which cover about 70 per cent of all inventory carried
2   Medium turnover, medium stock value items which cover about 25 per cent of all inventory carried
3   Slow-moving items which cover the rest of the inventory range

Classification 1 items. Normally a sales department will wish to hold stocks of items in all classifications but especially classification 1 items where most turnover is obtained. For these fast-moving products a service-level figure which the sales department expects to be achieved is often nominated. The service level could be as high as 98 per cent for class 1 items but much lower for slower-moving types. For the fast-moving products a self adapting system based on mathematically derived demand-forecasting is usually tried. The system envisaged would take account of or include:

1   Sales demand patterns
2   Service levels
3   Safety stocks
4   Lead time and variation in lead time
5   EOQs or any other method of economic production required by the factory

Classification 2 items.   These items which constitute a smaller proportion of the total inventory often need a less rigorous system of control. However, a routine check on reorder points is obviously valuable and an average monthly demand (AMD) might be calculated clerically to determine whether the reorder points quoted are still valid.

Classification 3 items.   A maximum/minimum system seems appropriate with such products if items are to be carried as stock, but a continued check on class 3 stocks is desirable as well as a more detailed control of slow-moving items.

29:4   Problems in the use of the techniques and conditions for success

Obviously demand forecasting has many failings, not least that it pays no attention to a market demand which may be known. With the greater use of market planning and forecasting techniques, it seems desirable to try to link stock forecasting with the sales forecasts that are made. Any system which relies solely on statistically derived demand forecasting as a means of optimising capital spent on stock, will inevitably produce suboptimum results.

Stock analysis is an extremely important factor in indicating to stock control managers where stock-capital can be utilised better. Time and effort spent on this kind of analysis is always well spent.

Before a conversion from one system to another is made, it is recommended that a simulation of the proposed system is carried out and the results compared with those that have been achieved with the current system. Such computer packages as ICL's SCAN 3 have simulators which can be used to ascertain the type of forecasting system service level, etc, which gives an optimum stock holding.

There are few computer installations that have not seriously considered a stock control system as a key candidate for machine time, yet the result is often a poor stock recording system. The reason is obvious. Devising a system and taking account of all the factors previously listed stretches the competence of most systems personnel. At the same time it seems important not to invent the wheel again. Most computer suppliers have a stock control program package and though they will never "fit" absolutely, there is a probability that a user will gain a great deal from them.

Warning of some weaknesses should be given. For example, IBM's production information and control system operates a reorder level system, so poses obvious difficulties for companies which replenish stock internally. ICL's SCAN 3 operates both a reorder point and a cycle system, but lacks a facility to build in lead time variations. NCR's inventory management system uses a reorder level method and also utilises average lead times to help determine stock replenishments.

Cash flow forecasts should take account of all future company activities including inventory level fluctuations. Unless, therefore, some estimate of future inventory levels can be determined on a rational basis, cash flow forecasts can be invalid.

Stock is usually treated as working capital. In many ways, however, it has a closer relationship to fixed capital. It is a permanent item on the balance sheet. It usually absorbs a high proportion of the total capital available. It is rarely reduced. Sampling has shown that stock investment is usually as high as 25 per cent of total company capital; often it is 33 per cent depending upon the industry concerned.

A project appraisal method such as DCF is now fairly standard in most companies—and risk and sensitivity analysis are now being added to make the appraisal even more meaningful. But stock, which can account for up to one-third of total company capital, has no such appraisal. Stock can be increased on the plausibility of the marketing force without any detailed appraisal whatsoever.

On the basis that stock carrying costs are, on average, 20 per cent a year, a stock increase of £100 000 should produce either an increase in profits of at least £20 000 or the prevention of a profit decline of at least this amount and should be seen to do so.

If it is accepted that stock is a means of raising turnover or reducing costs, it should be treated in the same way as a new warehouse or a new production machine and charged against users. For example, an area sales manager who agrees to an objective of £1 million sales in the financial year, should be debited with the stock which he needs to obtain such a turnover. Accountants, therefore, might need to consider the management accounting procedures associated with profit centres, cost allocation and profit forecasting.

The accountant's main role in inventory control ought to be the justification of the stock levels and values which the company carries. A prerequisite for this role is categorisation of stock into functional/purpose groups. For example:

Category
A   Stock required to buffer production facilities
B   Stock required to service customers
A1   Stock required to buffer production facilities in X shop
B1   Stock required to service customers in market segment X

The stock group category, etc, should be part of a stock's identification code. It is only by making such categories that a valid comparison between values carried and the benefit intended to accrue from them can be made.

As already suggested, stock value and levels should be targeted in the same way as machine output standards or any budgets of performance. Stock levels should be forecast in total as well as in product groups. The targets should help to justify the money invested in stocks.

Inventory controllers should be responsible only for maintaining the levels of stock (including service levels) which have been agreed between the marketing, production and inventory functions. The inventory controller should maintain systems which will achieve the required service and stock levels.

Financial/management accountants should be responsible for operating systems to facilitate the appropriate debiting of stock carried.

The initial analysis of the system in use and its effects will largely determine what new system or amendment to the old is necessary. A long and hard manual data collecting operation may be necessary for this, perhaps as proposed in the following example.

STOCK CONTROL

The objectives of a stock control system should be the responsibility of the board of directors. These can vary from company to company. For example, financial constraints may be the most important element in one company; service requirements may dominate in another.

Once objectives have been defined, the following fourteen factors should be considered in the optimisation of the system: stock recording, inventory assessment by value, replacement constraints, financial constraints, warehousing constraints, marketing constraints, audit routines, forecasting, automatic stock allocation, interaction of system with others, analysis, standards of performance, inventory control system as a model, and assessment of standards capability. These factors are dealt with individually in the following pages.

A : **Stock recording**
1   Company's reference number (part number)
2   Supplier's reference number
3   Parts of which the reference number is a subassembly
4   Parts which may be substituted for the reference
5   Units of measure of the reference received
6   Units of measure of stock issued
7   Cost of stock—FIFO, LIFO:
a   Average or standard cost system
b   System should take account of problems of invoice delays—pricing stock received which has not been invoiced
8   Selling price including market segmentation discounts etc
9   Units and value for stock at depots, export, future allocations and in total
10   Transactions:
a   Receipts from suppliers:
i   Supplier code
ii   Part number
iii   Quantity
iv   Price
v   Order number
vi   Date when order was placed, promised and received, difference between each

b   Warehouse—depot
c   Depot—warehouse } Part number quantity, from,
d   Depot—depot   } to, date, etc
e   Company to supplier—as for receipts
f   Sales   } customer number, part number, price, quantity,
g   Returned sales   } date, from, to, order number
h   Stock adjustments:
i   Stock-taking
ii Scrap/breakages
iii Others
i   Bulk order record code number/depot/quantity/value/date
j   Back orders (deliveries) records
k   Forward orders (with date) record
11 Visual records for management information—must be an improvement on current system
12 Timescale—delay in updating computer records must be considered
13 Measurement of accuracy or degrees of error permissible
14 Appropriate explosion breakdown needs to be provided

B : Inventory assessment by value

It is axiomatic to allocate most resources to those items contributing most profit to the firm. Factors to be considered are:

1   A break-down of the inventory by item contribution to turnover/profit. In ascending or descending importance
2   Method to ensure allocation of resources to the most important stock items
3   Control and re-evaluation of all references on a continual basis

C : Replacement constraints

Four major areas require attention:

1   Lead times and variations:
a   Evaluate and monitor performance of suppliers, especially lead times in excess of the standard. A factor to compensate for changes in lead times should be available to alter safety stock requirements in the light of experience. This factor is derived from the square root of the lead time
b   The safety stock required to compensate for erratic lead times should be calculable, in addition to that required to cater for deviations in sales demand
c   Compare and evaluate alternative sources of supply, where possible
d   The system must take into account holidays and other factors—e.g. strikes—and these should be considered in the evaluation of expected lead times

2   Economic and production constraints:
a   EOQ's
b   Price break quantities
c   Production bottlenecks—e.g. machine and equipment overloads
d   Total production constraints
c   Quality constraints
f   Priority factors
g   Raw material constraints
h   Bought out components constraints

3   Factory loading:
a   Finished goods replacement requirements should be evaluated against total factory capacity, individual operational or machine capacity, as standard labour hours, machine speeds and operational cycle times. Where stock replenishment requirements are in excess of factory or machine capacity, the system must have the capacity of:
i   Reprocessing the stock requirements run and producing a match of requirements with capacity on an agreed basis—i.e. on some priority rule
ii   Calculating the machine/capacity overload
b   Where there is an excessive machine or general load capacity the stock requirements procedure should be rerun and the extra requirements needed to produce a full factory load should be made on an agreed system of priorities. The extra requirements must be calculated and issued as a management report

4   Automatic placement of orders:
       Final order placement/confirmation should be in the hands of local stock control managers. Particularly management should be made aware by the system where a splash demand could lead to a temporary increase in lead time. If built into the system this could automatically produce increased order requirements, leading to further increases in lead times. This vicious circle should be highlighted by the system for management action

The ability to work a maximum and minimum system for slow moving items should be available.

D :   Financial constraints
1   The following financial details concerning stock should be available:
a   Cost of each item
b   FIFO, LIFO, average or standard cost whichever is appropriate
c   Selling prices including discounts
2   Cost price value of stock held at HO and depots by:
a   Products
b   Product range

c   Turnover category
d   Total
3   Stock profitability by:
a   Product
b   Product range
c   Turnover category
d   by depot
e   by company
f   gross margin/turnover
4   Stock should be categorised by turnover and profit achieved. Number of items to be shown in each category
5   Value of stock to be shown by:
a   Safety stock carried to cover variations in sales demand
b   Safety stock carried to cover variations in lead times
6   Marginal and average total cost of holding stock by depot

E : **Warehousing constraints**
Warehousing considerations are an essential element in a stock control system. The effect of the following constraints should be included in the inventory control system:

1   Necessity of regional warehousing
2   Siting/location of warehouses
3   Usable floor space and cubic capacity
4   General materials handling and physical environment
5   Transportation and overall distribution, including packaging
6   Warehouse control procedures

F : **Marketing constraints**
The system should be capable of taking cognisance of the following constraints:

1   Service levels:
a   By product group
b   By product
c   By geographical location
d   By market segment
      Standard service level groups will probably be most useful—i.e. 99, 97, 95, 90, 80 per cent etc. It should be possible to calculate the effect of changing service levels on total inventory
2   It must be possible for factors derived from market planning and market research to be included in the stock requirements calculation:
a   Planned increases in sales, including effects of promotional activities
b   Trends
c   Seasonability

d   Competitive response
3   The system must recognise splash demand which must not be treated as a normal part of demand pattern
4   Analysis to aid marketing activities. The analysis must be of positive use in setting, achieving and budgeting marketing objectives (see section *L*)

G : Audit routine
1   Perpetual inventory. Regular physical stock check. Comparison at regular intervals between recorded and actual stock and investigation to discover causes
2   Audit reports on the following:
a   Variances
b   Causes
c   Dead stock
d   Write off stock
e   Stock adjustments

H : Forecasting
A stock control system must have some means of forecasting future demands on the stock held or required. Attention to of the following factors is essential:

1   Environment and expected market growth
2   Expected market share and effect of promotional activities
3   Analysis of past sales demand patterns
4   A tracking system and error analysis used in monitoring forecast systems
5   Reorder points
6   Frequency of forecast required for stability, in recalculating reorder requirements
7   Service level considerations to estimate safety stock requirements
8   Lead times and their variability due to the existence of production constraints
9   Desired accuracy of forecasts—must be better than any other available system
10   Forecast must be based where appropriate on explosion breakdown of parts

J : Automatic stock allocation
Automatic allocation of products to warehouses should be carried out on the basis of desired service level and the most recent demand history. In the event of a shortage, stock should be allocated in the appropriate ratio. The system should also provide the following:

1   Location demand stock adjustment routine. To transfer stock in the event of a build-up of an interdepot stock imbalance and to adjust the interdepot demand record

2   Slow-moving stock return routine. To transfer slow-moving stock to main depot
3   Printout of required stock movements

K : Interaction of stock control system with other systems

The stock control suite must be compatible with the following EDP systems in the company:

1   Sales analysis and sales statistics
2   Sales ledger:
a   Customer type
a   Customer value/profitability
c   Customer discount structure
3   Purchase ledger:
a   Supplier
b   Supplier value
c   Supplier pricing structure
4   Invoicing and statement production, credit notes, credit control
5   Cost control—budgets and expenditure, data for standard/actual performance comparison
6   Any data based system which the company builds up including the use of interrogation packages

L : Analysis
Much of the information required has been listed separately but the following is a summary of the analysis that should be available:

1   Stock recording:
a   Quantities
b   Value at cost
c   Value at selling price(s)
d   Stock
e   Allocated stock
f   Sales and sales trend
g   Date of last movement
h   Date of last order on suppliers
    All information by product groups, item, category (ABC), depot and company as applicable
2   Suppliers:
a   Performance
i   Lead times, standard deviation of lead times, means of avoiding snow-balling effect of increased L-T reorder interaction
ii   Number of orders delayed and value:
       Ref number
       Quantity

      Date order placed
      Date order due
      Number of weeks overdue

iii   Number of price changes
iv   Average percentage price change
v   No. of quality defects
vi   Percentage of quality defects
vii   Number and percentage of invoice errors
b   Automatic ordering:
     Analysis of orders placed
3   Finance:
a   Cost of stock holding:
i   Average
ii   Marginal
b   Return of investment on stock
c   Cost of:
i   Obsolescence
ii   Dead stock, for write off purposes
iii   Stock adjustments, losses, breakages etc
d   Range of stock and service levels that could be provided for a specific
     stock investment
4   Profit analysis:
a   Per item, group, stock category (*A*I etc) where applicable:
i   Quantity sold
ii   Cost price
iii   Selling price
b   Gross margin:
i   Average turnover
ii   Average stock
iii   Stock/profit ratio
c   Per customer, by stock category (ABC) and in total:
i   Total turnover
ii   Total margin
iii   Average order size
iv   Average delay in invoice payment
d   Per depot, by product, group and category:
i   Total stock
ii   Total turnover
iii   Total margin
iv   Average order size
v   Total depot profit
5   Estimated profit:
a   Per depot
b   Per product group
c   Per category
6   Objectives set and achieved

M : **Performance standards**

Performance comparison of the following activities must be carried out:

1 Stock allocation (automatic)
   Achieved/desired service level at depots?
2 Warehousing constraints
   Has the standard cost/gross profit ratio been achieved?
3 Marketing:
a Have standard service levels been achieved?
b Has target market penetration been achieved (dead stock level)?
4 Replacement:
   Lead time standards
5 Stock recording
   Accuracy of records
6 Forecasting:
a Development of forecasting and alternative systems
b Measurements of performance (forecast errors)
7 Financial:
a Percentage of desired stock level achieved
b Gross profit/stock ratio (rate) compared with required rate of return
c Turnover/stock ratio
d Total expenditure, comparison with budget

N : **Inventory control system as a model**

System should be capable of acting as a model i.e. the interaction between component factors should be immediately discernable. The basic factors are:

1 Stock and stock types
2 Warehousing
3 Finance
4 Replacement
5 Marketing

P : **Assessment of standards capability**

The system should be capable of deriving future standards for the following stock control elements:

1 Turnover in group
2 Stock value
3 Stock/turnover ratio
4 Percentage margin
5 Gross profit
6 Profit/stock ratio
7 Approximate percentage variation in lead times
8 Service level required

Actual performance should be compared and deviations calculated. A summary sheet might be used.

29:5 Conclusion

The use of the list of systems elements which have been quoted plus the use of standards and appropriate debiting methods should help to ensure that stock is fully controlled and above all is justified. Analysis of various kinds will assist in judging whether this is so. Particularly a breakdown of items by turnover/ profit may be valuable. A large number of items in the low turnover/profit/ stock ratio might indicate the wrong use of stock and the need for policy decisions concerning standards.

Before any accountant or auditor confirms that the value of stocks shown in the balance sheet is correct, he should carry out an appropriate audit. This would include obsolescent/obsolete factors and stock/profit ratios.

29:6 Further reading

1   B H Walley, "Inventory Control Systems," *Work Study*, February 1970
2   B H Walley, *How to Apply Strategy in Profit Planning*, Business Books, 1971
3   R G Brown, *Statistical Forecasting for Inventory Control*, McGrawHill.
4   G Hadley and T M Whiting, *Analysis of Inventory Systems*, Prentice Hall, 1963
5   E Naddor, *Inventory Systems*, Wiley, 1966
6   J F Magee and D M Boordman. *Production Planning and Inventory Control*, McGraw Hill, 1967
7   R G Brown, *Smoothing, Forecasting and Prediction of Discrete Time Series*, Prentice Hall, 1963
8   A B Thomas, *Stock Control in Manufacturing Industries*, Gower Press, 1969
9   D A Barrett, *Automatic Inventory Control Techniques*, Business Books
10   R G Brown, *Decision Rules for Inventory Management*, Holt Rinehart

Production planning and control

30:1 Introduction

Production planning and control systems have been in operation for a long time. From the start of the industrial revolution, and before, some method of regulating supply from the manufacturer to meet demand of the market place must have been devised. Yet the problems of oversupply, overstocking and products being delivered consistently late are still with us. With the manufacture of more and more complex products the problem has grown increasingly complex. However, the principles of production planning and control are really basically simple.

30:2 Description

A description of one system of production planning and control is nearly as meaningless as describing one production operation. There are as many types as there are subjects. As with stock control, however, there are certain basic system's principles which need to be taken into account when a production planning and control system is either being audited or designed from scratch.

Production planning and control is an integral part of a total operating system which includes stock control, quality control, general performance control (often through a standard costing and budgetary control system), incentive payments and, probably, planned or some other kind of maintenance. Linking between these systems is extremely important and any new production planning and control system must provide data for system requirements other than production control.

DEFINITIONS. Production planning and control covers the following loading and scheduling aspects:

1   Plant loading is the matching of customer demand to plant/machine capacity. The basis of comparison can be machine or man hours—usually machine hours

2   Scheduling determines the priority which is accorded to orders

a   Master scheduling is the determination of a production plan when the latest delivery date is made and priority of operation organised to ensure that this date is met

b   Job scheduling is concerned with the order sequencing at each machine or operation

SYSTEMS CONSIDERATIONS. It is assumed that appropriate objectives will be established for the production planning and control system. These may vary from specified production cost situations to the completion of *X* per cent of all orders on time, and the maintenance of stock and WIP at a predetermined level.

The systems checklist on page 305 assumes that there will be, as a first stage, an order translation process when customers' requirements are translated into production units or manufacturing capacity. A check should be made to determine that:

1   The factory is capable of making the products required

2   Appropriate jigs and tools are available or can be acquired cheaply

3   Raw material is available

4   Machine capacity is available and can produce the customers' requirements to the appropriate specifications

The further ahead in time that sales personnel can establish their requirements, the more likely that production personnel will be able to optimise their production situation. A good sales forecast will be an aid in establishing the balance between demand and capacity to manufacture.

The use of linear programming (LP) is growing slowly, though with the eclipse of OR techniques, speed of implementation is not very fast. Optimisation of orders/machines is important and the use of LP to achieve this is obviously one answer. Again there are computer packages which carry out LP and it is worth while testing such a package before a home-designed system is attempted. But most production planning and control systems are still largely manually operated. Various subsystems operate, for example:

Contract scheduling. Usually this type of production planning and control operates in the construction industry when PERT or network analysis is used to ensure that a predetermined finishing date is met.

Manufacturing to order. This kind of system affording no make-for-stock buffer is a difficult one to design. Inevitably, without considerable flexibility

Machine or activity	Monday		Tuesday		Wednesday		Thursday		Friday		Saturday	
	Pieces	Standard hours	Pieces	Standard hours	Pieces	Standard hours	Pieces	Standard hours	Pieces	Standard hours	Pieces	Standard hours
Mixing	14/621 4	8										
Forming			14/621 620M	8								
Baking					14/621 800	8						

Figure 30.1 PROGRAM OF FACTORY LOADING

in labour and machine utilisation, there will be a constant crisis situation.

Stock manufacturing.   If cycle-stock control is in operation the difficulty of matching requirements and capacity will still need to be overcome.

Single product manufacture.   The easiest form of production and consequently only a simple production planning and control system is required.

Multi-assembly processes.   These are among the most difficult production operations to control and likely to cause considerable headaches. ICL's PROMPT was designed to cover this kind of situation.

Various manual methods are still used to carry out production planning and control, for example:

Planning boards of various types.   These are used for both scheduling and control purposes. However, it is difficult to operate on an exception basis psychologically if planning boards are in use.

Programs.   These are a good method of machine loading and order-flow control. One difficulty in their use lies in the number of copies which need to be issued. Must each operative have a copy or only the foreman? (See Figures 30.1 and 30.2.)

Labour utilisation	Hours available	Monday	Tuesday	Wednesday	Thursday	Friday	Saturday
Mixing	60	60	60	40	40	40	
Forming	48	48	40	48	48	48	
Baking	88	80	88	72	72	72	

Figure 30.2 LABOUR LOADING PROGRAM

| Date_____ Order_____ Part number_____ |
| Description_____ |
| Delivery date_____ Tools_____ |
| Drawing number_____ Specification_____ Number required_____ |

Activity	Time allowed	Time taken	Operator	Quantity passed

Figure 30.3 JOB PROGRESS CARD

Network analysis.   This technique has already been quoted for use in contract scheduling. Planning boards and network analysis are a useful means of planning and controlling complex operations.

Gantt charts.   These are charts where planned and actual production is plotted against a timescale and shown as a "bar."

Reporting documents.   These are more fully covered in the performance reporting of standard costing and budgetary control. However, various reports only appropriate to production planning and control are required. These include:

1   Operation load summaries which indicate capacity, current load and over- or underload
2   Tool availability and status check. This is often needed to determine not only the availability but also the condition of the tools
3   Parts processed records
4   Material and product failures and failure rates—to check on percentage for rejection being allowed on orders

PRODUCTION PLANNING AND CONTROL SYSTEMS CHECKLIST

The aim of production planning and control systems is to enable sufficient products of the right quality and cost to be produced at the right time. Customer service, manufacturing cost and stock levels should, therefore, be optimised. It is possible to improve one at the expense of the others. To this extent production planning and control systems should act as models.

Systems can vary between highly complex and extremely simple. Largely the complexity will be determined by:

1   Type of production: job shop, batch, flow line etc
2   Complexity of the products produced: unitary, with one or more components/complex assembly

3   Relationship with other manufacturing operations for supplies
4   Production skills and whether production is man or machine dominated
5   Customer services, cost and inventory levels demanded by company policy constraints

The systems should provide unambiguous working instructions which achieve the PP&C objectives.

Basic data

1   Material utilisation:
a   Standard material per *X* products in weight at the beginning and end of the operation cycle
b   Weight of *X* products after each operation
c   Standard material losses expected at each operation
d   Raw material availability (comment)
2   Labour utilisation:
a   Standard labour hours for each operation for each product or each major product group
b   Output rates and bonus payments
c   Absenteeism, labour flexibility, turnover and availability
3   Machine output rates:
a   List all machine and other operations necessary for production in sequence
b   Machine manning strengths
c   Machine output rates—standard and actual with bonus in units per standard hour
d   Down-time and causes
e   Layout of factory
4   Costs:
a   Costs per standard machine or operation hour:
i   Direct labour
ii   Indirect labour
iii   General works overheads
iv   Admin overheads
b   Standard material costs per *X* products
c   Raw material costs
5   Product costs and specification—parts, dimensions etc:
a   Standard material
b   Machine hour output rate at each operation or cost centre standard hourly cost
c   Cost details of the expense of running alternative machines where this is possible
6   Like machines or operations which can be linked together to form a cost centre or controllable unit
7   Economic constraints:
a   EBQ's

b   Price break quantities
c   Production bottlenecks—e.g. machine and equipment overloads
d   Total production constraints
e   Quality constraints
f   Priority factors
    Expected capital expenditure requirements should be quoted
8   Factory loading:
a   Equipment constraints
b   Priority rules
9   Stock-holding constraints:
a   Stock profitability
b   Cash-flow constraints
c   Stock details—values held, T/O etc
10 Component part break down—part explosion
11 Level-by-level assembly—appropriate coding required
12 Flowchart of sales order processing system
13 Sales:
a   Distribution of customer lead times, by product-type
b   Present and projected annual sales, by product-type

Order input breakdown
and basic decision rules and planning principles

1   Time to effect a change in production levels
2   Length of time order cover will be provided to cover machine/labour utilisation
3   Length of time change will remain static once made
4   Acceptability of delivery/performance standards (98 per cent, 90 per cent etc)
5   Lead time for individual time, delivery purposes, broken down into:
a   Order processing time
b   Order queueing time
c   Manufacturing or through factory time
d   Degree of factory flexibility in standard hours
6   Method of giving delivery promises:
a   By actual date
b   Week ending
c   Week number
7   Method amending specifications and operation layouts (route cards). Filing and control of specifications

Loading and batching
1   Method machine loading:
a   By all machines—calculating standard hours for each order and each machine

b	By key or bottleneck operations or operation
c	By key or bottleneck operation, plus a zone for other like or adjacent operations
2	Zone control—a method of production planning and control whereby predetermined through zone manufacturing times are calculated, for various manufacturing zones and appropriate control systems to check on order progress are instituted. A zone is part of the manufacturing processes comprising three or four machine operations. In each zone detailed machine loading may be attempted depending upon:
a	Practicality of loading
b	The necessity of loading only the number of products each zone can accommodate in terms of man/machine availability. Each zone will have one or more bottleneck (critical) operations, and machine loading of these must be considered
c	The possibility of making significant improvements in overall through factory time, productivity and decrease in work in progress
3	Order flow determinant (scheduling) by:
a	Priority label
b	Zone date
c	Program issued for each bottleneck operation
d	Re-batching procedures, to amend sequencing of order flow at various stages in the manufacturing process
4	Machine loading:
a	100 per cent of normal time
b	95 per cent or less of normal time
c	100 per cent of normal time plus overtime
5	Rebatching:
a	Through partly finished stock
b	By delaying product item identification as late in the manufacturing process as possible
c	General rules of running like with like
6	Urgent orders:
	Method of identification—quantities
7	Information required from load-building files:
a	The level of factory activity (in standard hours at bottleneck or each operation) needed to complete current and future order load
b	The degree of sectional overtime needed to complete the order load
c	Where increases/decreases in the labour force will be required
d	Where machine/tool overloads are likely to occur
8	Delivery promises:
a	From state of order load files
b	From a priority system
9	Programming:
a	Amount factory can handle only will be programmed

b Daily, shift, weekly, monthly—set out in daily or shift requirements

c Active factory management co-operation that lends its technical know-ledge and agrees with final program

d Sequence of orders remains PP&R prerogatives

e Once agreed the program is inviolate or change rare

f Factory undertake to make what is required

g Shift/daily checks made on achievements

Production planning and control and shop-floor documentation

1 Production and planning records
Product, product code, type, etc, EBQ lead time:

a Date

b Order number

c Customer reference

d Quantity ordered

c Delivery dates/dates final and at intermediate operations

f Bought out parts—quantities supplier delivery date

2 Material control records
Material type, code:

a Batch number

b Weight

c Standard usage

d Actual usage

3 Order product card (or route sheet):

a Company's reference number

b Parts to which this part is a component or subassembly

c Parts which may be substituted for this item

d Dimensions and weight

e Quantity to be made

f Order number

g Manufacturing operations—quoting operation dimensions

h Customer

i Customer code and order number

j Delivery completion date at all operations and final completion date

k Sequence of operations—especially zone sequence if this method of planning is in operation

l Time allowances for production

m Spoilage allowances

4 Material control order cards:

a Material code, reference

b Quantity

c Material for which this material is a component

d Products which will be made—quantity, type, code

e Standard batch weight for anticipated X products at each operation

f Recycling

Control and feedback

1 Method of controls:
a By exception throughout factory
b By exception at stipulated zones, cost centres or machines
c All orders at stipulated stages, no matter whether order is late or early
d All orders at stipulated zones, cost centres or machines
e Time
(Exception—items not adhering to a predetermined production plan which facilitates rapid reporting of out of course orders)
2 Performance reporting:
a Items delayed at any stage or stipulated stages
b Percentage achieved against plan—at each operation, at each zone, totally etc
c Data: orders in standard hours planned, current machine manning, machine utilisation
3 Rescheduling of delayed items (repromising routines):
a As an emergency where overtime or extra time is utilised
b Items are rescheduled through the normal loading and scheduling systems
c Items are held back until a gap in production occurs
4 Progressing:
a Calculated delivery dates
b Exception reports
c Re-establishment of delivery dates via order card
d Delay lists beyond two to three days' delay
5 Responsibility for delays:
a Factory
b Production planning and control department
c Indeterminate
d Delivery/dispatch department
e Redeployment of labour (when absenteeism or machine breakdown has occurred) to ensure deliveries are still made on time
6 Delay reporting:
a To hands and zone production foremen daily
b To production planning and control personnel daily
c To senior factory and planning personnel weekly
7 Balance delivery problems:
a Full balance quantity—rescheduled normally
b Full balance quantity—given priority
c Balance plus margin for rejection—given priority
8 Item load location:
a Work areas
b Awaiting inspection areas

Recording and planning systems required

1 Recording on receipt of order, check on production ability, order document production
2 Delivery promising
3 Loading and scheduling
4 Reject, amendment and reprocessing of orders
5 Control and performance reporting
6 Raw material issues and control
7 Links with other systems
8 Management information reporting

Planning department functions

1 Technical:
a Specification and layout
b Tools and equipment
2 Recording of orders, order document checking tool, machine, raw materials availability
3 Loading and scheduling
4 Typing of order sets and other documentation
5 Progressing and delivery promising
6 Stock control and miscellaneous activities

Links with quality and reject control report on rejects

1 Cause, quantity and rectifiable action to avoid further rejects
2 Type of reject:
a Rectifiable by hand
b Rectifiable by machine
c Non-rectifiable
d Use for other purposes—cut down modify etc
3 Method of reprocessing
4 Basic causes of rejection

Links with other systems

1 Bonus payments
a Verification of hours/minutes of work earned against actual hours produced
b Quality and production
c Clocked hours *v* bonus hours earned—machine downtime calculation
d Use of personnel in control activities—same personnel to calculate bonus and control production
2 Stock control
a Stock levels by product, giving free and allocated stock, on order, w.i.p. etc
b Stock forecasting system
c EBQs
d Stock replenishment, systems, ROL etc

Management information

Sufficient information should be produced to give a clear picture of:

1 The level of order intake in total and by product group, in standard hours etc
2 Rate of order issue to the factory (in standard hours)
3 Balance of orders to issue to the factory including arrears
4 Order progress in the factory including delays in each zone
5 Delayed order situation
6 Raw material stocks—shortfall and stocks in excess of authorised stock
7 Dispatches made
8 Number of orders handled

Order progress control will need orders delayed:

1 Waiting processing in planning department
2 Waiting raw material
3 Waiting tools
4 Orders not located—etc

30:3 Successful areas of application and examples

It may be interesting to discuss trends in production planning and control rather than individual systems.

Some years ago it was thought that the computer would quickly be applied to production planning and control systems. Instead there have been more failures in attempts to computerise production planning than in any other system's application. Systems personnel have lacked the competence and production experience to design and implement an appropriate system.

Various computer packages have been marketed for production planning and control application. ICL, for example, have POWER, PROMPT and also NIMMS production planning and control. The danger with packages is that they are not totally relevant to the system being computerised. This may not be disastrous in a stock control situation, but could be in a production planning and control system.

Even when computer packages are used, training and education of line staff in their use is extremely important. Lack of training has caused repeated failures of even package applications.

Production modelling has had several theoretical discourses given to it, but so far little practical experience has been gained in this field.

30:4 Problems in the use of the technique and conditions for success

Discipline is the obvious missing ingredient in most production planning and control systems. Given, say, 1000 orders and twenty or more operations, it should be possible to so organise the order sequencing and the use of men and machine capacity as to optimise their manufacture.

The method of order scheduling and machine loading is, however, irrelevant if everyone either consciously or subconsciously tries to subvert the system, by ignoring the rules.

Systems are often dominated by one of the main functions of the company. Sales department for example, swamps the system by demanding orders to be produced with utmost speed regardless of machine or labour utilisation.

Psuedo control only may exist. A galaxy of planning boards, where every order is itemised and scheduled, often gives only an illusion of control as it is physically impossible to update each order as it moves from operation to operation, in the time needed for it to be under control.

For some puzzling reason training in production planning and control systems is never as rigorous as say marketing or accounting. Somehow production planning and control philosophy is "picked up." Yet production planning systems, with their link to other systems and possible impact on production costs, need a high degree of training.

The key decision of giving a delivery date is often made too early in the order processing system. Later a lack of tools or a production bottleneck prevents the delivery promise from being met. In consequence the system gets into disrepute or the order is scheduled out of priority.

30:5 Conclusion

The overall problems in the design of production planning and control systems are the establishment of objectives and discipline.

Objectives are comparatively easy to lay down once the bias in either sales or production personnel is recognised. Discipline is much more difficult to achieve. Without it any system is defeated. With it a merely moderately good system can be successful.

30:6 Further reading

1   J F Magee and D M Boodman, *Production Planning and Inventory Control*, McGraw Hill
2   J E Biegel, *Production Control: A Quantitative Approach*, Prentice Hall, 1963
3   J D C Trusler, *Production Control by Computer*, Machinery Publication
4   S Ammer, *Manufacturing Management and Control*, Appleton
5   J L Burbridge, *The Principles of Production Control*, Macdonald and Evans, 1958
6   D K Corke, *Production Control is Management*, Arnold
7   F G Moore, *Manufacturing Management*, Irwin
8   J H Greene, *Production and Inventory Control Handbook*, McGraw Hill
9   N V Reinfeld, *Production Control*, Prentice Hall, 1959

THIRTY-ONE

Credit control

31:1 Introduction

As with many other techniques, credit control is subject to the pulls of rival functions. Salesmen usually require the longest possible credit period; accountants the shortest. Neither may be right.

Credit and credit limits are an intrinsic part of marketing strategy. But equally the company's cash flow situation will dictate the credit limits which are possible. Where cash flow is limited, a trade-off between stock levels and credit may be necessary. Increased stock levels will decrease credit limits and vice versa.

32:2 Description

Credit is deferred payment. Credit control is a method of ensuring that previously determined credit levels are not abused. Marketing strategy should decide the following.

CREDIT PERIOD. This should be determined by considering:

1   Turnover profit desired
2   Market share
3   Product qualities which will help to gain turnover—quality, price etc
4   Other service aspects—such as stock availability—which will also gain turnover
5   Competitor's credit limits
6   Customer loyalty
7   The market and product generally

This latter point may be extremely important. There are products and markets which traditionally operate on long credit periods. To break such historical precedents may only produce a steady drift of customers to competitors who are prepared to maintain traditional credit time spans.

CREDIT LIMITS.   Credit limits equate to the amount of money outstanding which a company can (and should) afford in order to fund its sales operations. The limits will usually be set by:

1   The financial situation of the company. This in part will be determined by a cash flow forecast, when forecast sales revenue is matched against planned costs of all kinds, taking into account the planned/desired use of the difference between the two
2   The use of funds allocated to marketing activities. The trade-off between improving customer service by increasing stock levels as against increasing credit limits has already been mentioned. Increased advertising should also be seen in the same context

Credit control, therefore, has to enable the company to ensure that both the credit period and the credit limit are not abused.

   While the limit has a total monetary value, how the total is spread over markets, market segments and customers may have to be based on a differential application.

DIFFERENTIAL CREDIT PERIODS.   Where a company operates in different markets with different products, undifferentiated credit periods are mistaken. What is competitive in one market segment may not be so in another.

   Even in a highly competitive market, it may be desirable to differentiate in the credit period offered to different customers—indeed in the whole range of marketing activities.

   In these circumstances it is strongly recommended that actual and potential are graded after considering the following factors:

1   Turnover being obtained or offered by a customer
a   From x to $3x$
b   From $3x$ to $10x$
c   Over $10x$
2   Type of customer
3   Actual/potential credit worthiness
a   High risk
b   Medium risk
c   Low risk

A potential customer could possibly have a high turnover and a low risk of bad debts. He could also be potentially a high credit risk with a high probable turnover.

Each situation needs to be carefully examined. Market research will help to determine the potential turnover of a new customer. It may also assist in establishing credit risks, but credit-rating agencies may do this more accurately.

A coding system that can be used to indicate the factors quoted needs to be determined. Once this has been done, each order gained needs to be coded and an appropriate credit period allocated.

Overall company and marketing objectives will help to determine the credit periods allocated. Total sales potential and the cash flow forecast will dictate credit limits. The coding system can then be used as a differential-allocation method which will allocate the "credit limits" to where they should gain most marketing leverage.

OBJECTIVES. Credit and related objectives will need to be allocated as follows:

1   To the sales manager. Credit of £X000s.
2   To various brand or market managers—credit periods by code of Y days
3   To representatives—to gain orders of £Z in customer codes agreed with the marketing and sales managers

BAD DEBTS. Credit control has also the important task of avoiding bad debts altogether. The same preorder investigation is required for both control of credit and of bad debts.

Bad debts regretfully seem to be part of the pain of carrying on a business. Minimisation rather than cure is the best that can usually happen.

31:3   Successful areas of application and examples

The outline of credit control activities briefly given in section 31:2 necessitates both an organisation and system which will carry out an adequate control function.

ORGANISATION. Normally credit control is part of the accounting function. There seems no particularly good reason why this should be so, except that it may be wise to separate credit control from the establishment of credit limits and credit periods.

The sales order processing system usually allows a credit check. Where speed of delivery is an essential part of the marketing situation, an order diversion procedure to the accounts department will militate against quick service.

The sales order processing system, therefore, is often amended to follow this pattern:

1   Representatives who gain a "first" order are asked to comment on the potential customer's creditworthiness. Their evaluation is important and eventually used to help to assess their performance in this field
2   Any new customer is vetted with a credit evaluation organisation

3   If there is any doubt a banker's reference is requested, minimum goods are
     dispatched and the shortest credit period offered
4   General order receipt. On the receipt of orders, each day, order translation
     and company order set production is carried out. A copy of the order set
     is sent to the credit control section which should vet all orders within two
     hours of their receipt. If any doubt exists about a potential customer a
     telephone call is made by the credit control manager to the sales order
     office and the appropriate order is held up until it is checked
5   This process is helped considerably by the coding system which designates
     the credit period each customer should be given

CREDIT CONTROL SYSTEMS

Objectives are an essential element in providing close control.

Analysis of order types. Where numerous orders are received each day
(perhaps 300 plus), a computer would be useful in carrying out this analysis.
Order types should be coded and the total of each code compared with the
original planned order mix.

Credit intelligence. One member of the credit control section should be
responsible for building up a dossier on the financial situation of customers—
both actual and potential.

A list of bad risks should be issued to representatives and sales order office
personnel so that no order is accepted which will not be paid for within the
credit limits acceptable by the company.

An order received from a customer on a "stop" or "caution" list should
immediately be routed to credit control personnel, either for clearance, following
discussions with the customer, or complete cancellation.

Age analysis. This is a usual accounting procedure whereby the company's
computer (or accounting machines) is harnessed to show outstanding debt by
multiples of 30 days—that is, less than 30 days, 30 to 60, 60 to 90, over 90, etc.
The results can be compared with the credit period allocated and variances shown.

An open ledger type of book-keeping is ideal for the extraction of this type of
information if no EDP or accounting machine equipment is available.

Credit limits. While the age-analysis method will indicate where the credit
periods are being abused, credit limits must be assessed. Total outstanding credit
should always be the first valuable calculation. The credit coding method will
help to determine the future rate of monies outstanding. While the credit limit
may be passed today, it may well be within limits by the end of the month. The
coding method will help to indicate this possibility. A report is required listing:

1   Total amounts outstanding
2   Amounts outstanding in each age period
3   Amounts outstanding against each customer code in each age period

The trend of debt increase or decrease is important and for this the percentages
outstanding in each age-analysis period are required. The relationship between

debt and sales is perhaps more important still. A ratio of one with the other will indicate trends and general credit performance.

A weekly or perhaps monthly list of credit performance is needed. This should be issued with the monthly performance report and treated with the same importance. It is of little value making products at standard or lower cost if payment is not forthcoming.

Debt chasing. While prevention is better than cure, there are occasions when debts have to be chased. Often this chore is given to sales representatives. This may be a salutory experience for those who glibly accept each and every order irrespective of whether payment for goods will be forthcoming.

Sales credited to representatives should always be sales less bad debts with some percentage deducted for late payers. A "correct" attitude to debt and long term credit is vital.

Other methods which might be tried to induce payment or reduce bad debts are:

1   Cash discounts for payment within X days
2   Charging interest on outstanding debts
3   Placing unreliable customers on a COD basis
4   If the aggrieved supplier is also a customer of the same company, contra ledger entries are possible
5   Debt collection agencies may be useful
6   Insurance against bad debts can be taken out
7   Specific routines for non-payment of invoices need to be fully defined
a   Reminder to pay
b   Letters of increasing severity
c   Visit from representative or member of the credit control staff
d   Litigation

31:4   Problems in the use of the technique and conditions for success

Where credit control is rigidly enforced by a blinkered accounting department, a too rigorous enforcement of credit control will often result.

Credit is a marketing technique. It should be viewed in the same light as advertising or customer service generally.

Every month's credit which a customer is given is equivalent to approximately 1 per cent decrease in profit margins.

31:5   Conclusion

Credit control is an important technique in maintaining or improving company liquidity. The benefits which can be achieved by good credit control are such that money spent on the technique is usually repaid many fold.

A good credit control system will diagnose and isolate credit control problems. Danger signals for deteriorating credit performance must be built into the system.

31:6   Further reading

1   R G Breadmore, "Sales Accounting Checks and Controls," *Office Methods and Machines,* June 1968
2   R A Chestnut and E G Enkel, "Credits and Collections," *Cost and Management,* Canada, October 1968
3   "Credit Control," *Work Study,* April 1969
4   F J Bergin, "The Control of Credit," *Secretaries Chronicle,* December 1969
5   L K Scott, *Better Credit Control to Maximise Sales,* Rydges (Australia) February 1970
6   T N Beckman, *Credit and Collections: Management and Theory,* McGraw Hill

Quality control

_____

32:1　Introduction

Quality is not an absolute. What is a necessary quality for a space vehicle will
be too costly for a mass-produced car.

Quality has a price. Quality control is about controlling quality at a level
determined by production and marketing personnel. Establishing the quality
level can be a decisive factor in controlling costs.

32:2　Description

The definition of quality is very important. The quality of a product should be
of a standard which is acceptable to customers at the price they are prepared to
pay. Standards that are too low will not gain the sales required. Those that are
too high will cause unnecessary costs.

Quality control and inspection are not the same. Inspection is the process of
examination of production which determines whether the production is at a
desired quality level. To achieve this, measuring techniques and equipment
needed to carry out the process are devised. Inspection, therefore, is only a part
of the quality control activity. It should detect manufacturing failures to meet
quality standards, so protecting consumers from receiving products that are
below agreed quality levels. At the same time the inspection process should
accumulate data about the degree of quality variations and failings. This should
help to promote adjustments in production processes (both in the immediate
and medium-long term) that will ensure that quality standards are more rigidly
maintained. Inspection, therefore, should have a strong feed-back correction
factor built into the system, if it is to be truly effective.

Quality control, on the other hand, is concerned with the establishment and maintenance of quality standards. The standards can be dimensional, or an analysis of a raw material, appearance or design—anything, in fact, that will enable a judgement to be made which will determine whether a product has been produced to an appropriate standard.

Once quality standards have been set, quality control covers the following procedures:

1   When to inspect—at what stage in the production process
2   How to inspect—visual control, process measurement, etc
3   How often to inspect—for example, is 100 per cent needed or is inspection at specific times or even at random intervals sufficient?
4   What to do when a substandard product has been found. Must the whole batch be thrown away or just the faulty item? Will finding a fault trigger off greater inspection activities?
5   What control is economic? How much money is it economic to spend to ensure that quality standards are being maintained? This point will largely determine the kind of quality control (and so inspection) routines that need to be established

32:3   Successful areas of application and examples

SAMPLING v 100 PER CENT INSPECTION.   There is still a hoary attitude in existence that only 100 per cent inspection will find all rejects. Contrary to popular opinion, this has proved to be fallacious on most occasions when an experiment has been carried out.

Despite the careful selection of inspectors, it is almost inevitable that a reject or substandard item will be allowed to pass. The sheer monotony of measuring or looking at every item (the majority of which are standard) will eventually allow a non-standard product to slip through. However, where physical measurement is done, especially on a "go, no-go" gauge principle, there are greater chances that all substandard items will be found.

Because 100 per cent inspection will not find all faults, many, if not most, companies adopt a sampling technique method and statistical quality control is now the most common method of carrying out the quality control function.

STATISTICAL QUALITY CONTROL.   Two basic statistical laws apply in quality control.

The law of statistical regularity.   This states that if a fairly large number of items is taken randomly from a much larger group, the items taken will tend, on average, to possess the characteristics of the larger group.

The law of inertia of large numbers.   This states that where one part of a group varies statistically in one direction, it is likely that the other part of the group will vary in the opposite direction. The total change, therefore, will be slight.

From these laws stems the concept of statistical quality control, largely based on the activity sampling concept. Samples of finished products are measured to find how far they have deviated from a predetermined level of acceptance.

Normally a "standard deviation from the arithmetic mean" is used. This is a statistical method which is used as follows:

1 Obtain a sample of production—say 10 items
2 Find the arithmetic mean of the sample of the crucial quality measurement
3 Find the deviation in each item which goes to make up the sample, from the arithmetic mean of the total sample
4 Square each deviation and calculate the arithmetic mean of all the squares
5 Calculate the square root of the mean

This statistical calculation (which is more commonly known as the root mean square deviation) measures the dispersion of values about an arithmetic mean and provides a useful method of discovering variability from standard.

The standard deviation is used in statistical quality control as the standard error of the mean and a formula as follows is used:

Where S = standard error of the mean
     SD = standard deviation of the products in the sample
     N = Number of products in the sample

$$S = \frac{SD}{\sqrt{N}}$$

Sampling has to be random and usually confidence or control limits are placed

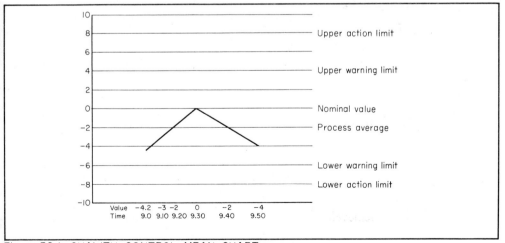

Figure 32.1 QUALITY CONTROL MEAN CHART

on the result. This is particularly important when an absolute measurement is being taken—the size of an opentop can seam lap over, for example.

Control charts are normally used for the purpose of plotting variances from quality standards. Figure 32.1 show an extremely simple version of the genre. The various limits indicate the tolerances and action limits which have been established.

Normally a sample is taken at either regular or random intervals as determined by the statistical method used. A process average is first determined, then deviations from the average are established. The first is usually a warning limit; the second an action limit, when corrections to equipment/machines are required.

The charts should be placed near the production operations they are reporting upon and production personnel need to inspect them regularly. In this way explicit reporting of quality control tests should be unnecessary. Production personnel should see when the quality of their production starts to drift.

ESTABLISHING QUALITY CONTROL. The difference between inspection and quality control will be more apparent still when comment on establishing quality control is made.

Objectives. Precisely what objectives are to be achieved by quality control? The essential one may be to produce at a predetermined quality. But is "least scrap" also a feature? The total cost of quality control must also be taken into account, while production personnel will insist that production is held up as little as possible.

Such objectives may be contradictory and will need to be reconciled within the total system.

Standards and basic data. Once objectives have been set, the standards by which quality can be measured must be formulated. These can be quantifiable, by attribute or by appearance. Basic data about these aspects must be gathered. The standards will be agreed, perhaps even stated categorically by marketing personnel.

Whether machines and production processes are capable of producing at the quality requested, will need to be tested by production personnel. It is likely that improved maintenance and production supervision will be necessary. Achievement of quality standards will need to be considered from an incentives viewpoint. Incentive schemes may have to be changed to build-in quality as well as quantity achievement.

Types of inspection. The initial considerations concerning types of inspection systems will be concerned with the 100 per cent inspection *v* sampling controversy. The latter has many advantages if appropriate statistical techniques are used. Fewer products are tested to destruction (if this is what is entailed in inspection), quality control costs are less, fewer staff are involved and production hold-ups will be minimised.

The standards of product acceptance will determine in part the equipment, inspection methods and general control principles utilised. For example:

1   Dimensional accuracy required will determine whether jigs, micrometers, plug gauges (go, no-go) or other equipment is utilised
2   Attribute testing may need colour-spectrometers or other instruments. Training to carry out visual inspection may be necessary
3   In high-speed mass-production, such as can making, the use of process average charts will be required. There will also be a need to calculate the process average, warning and action limits to make the charts viable
4   Statistically derived sampling techniques (numbers taken for inspection and intervals between sampling) are needed to ensure that statistical quality control will provide appropriate quality confidence limits
5   Where in the production process inspection should take place will have to be decided. Final inspection is usual but this is not very valuable if most quality defects occur after the first operation when there are about twenty production operations altogether. One major aim of quality control should be to improve material utilisation. This is not helped much by having only a final inspection
6   Patrol inspectors who can carry out tests for quality at any operation have considerable advantages
7   Once inspection has been carried out control reports are required. These should be of two types. Immediate control of the quality of products, perhaps through control charts of various kinds. Then short to medium-term analysis is required of all the reasons for quality defects. Monthly and annual reports of reasons for poor quality ought to be prepared
8   The essence of good quality control is to ensure that corrective action is carried out to achieve and then improve on quality standards—if this is justified economically. At the end of the operation, therefore, the economic trade-off between quality and the investment needed to achieve it or improve upon it, is still paramount. Improvement studies are obviously essential; the investment which these may suggest may not be
9   The customer is the final arbiter of quality control. Customer reports on quality defects should be routed via the quality control section. It may still, however, be a marketing problem.

COST OF QUALITY CONTROL.   Various ratios as well as actual measurements might be used to confirm that quality control costs are reasonable:

1   A budget is essential
2   The ratio of quality control to production staff is useful
3   The cost of products scrapped through quality control routines ought to be known
4   Cost to the company of rejects and customer complaints is valuable
5   Material utilisation planning and how quality control can affect it is vital

6   Cost of quality control *v* rejects found is not very meaningful. The basic idea of quality control is to prevent rejection not just to trap subquality products

QUALITY CONTROL CHECKLIST.   As with most functions quality control can be reviewed by means of a checklist:

1   What is the level of rejection—in items, in cost?
2   At what level is material utilisation—as a percentage of total raw material issued to the factory?
3   How many customer complaints are received each month?
4   What complaints about quality in general are received (from representatives, for example)?
5   How does company quality compare with that of competitors?
6   If the company's is worse, is it possible to quantify by how much?

What defects are apparent in the quality control system, for example:

1   Too few inspections?
2   Not enough people?
3   Insufficient and inadequate quality control equipment?
4   Are the functions of quality control personnel well defined?
5   Does production predominate at the expense of quality?
6   To whom do quality control personnel report?
7   Is this appropriate?
8   What type of inspection is used—100 per cent or sampling?
9   Is sampling statistically appropriate? Has it been checked?
10   What equipment is used?
11   Is there better on the market? If so, should it be bought?
12   Are sufficient/too many inspections carried out?
13   Are they carried out at the right production locations?
14   What procedures for reporting quality drift are used?
15   Are these appropriate?
16   Are they effective?
17   What has quality control done to improve material utilisation over the last three years?
18   What training is done?
19   Is it adequate?
20   Are staff appropriately competent?
21   Is inspection work programmed?
22   Is it a bottleneck operation?
23   Do production personnel try and circumvent it?
24   Is inspection time allowed in production schedules?
25   If so is it adequate?
26   Who develops new quality control routines?

27   Is R & D involved?
26   Does R & D suggest new tests?
29   Are standards too tight, too slack, appropriate?
30   Are they known by all inspection personnel, and appropriate specifications, drawings, etc, always available?

32:4   Problems in the use of the technique and conditions for success

An important factor in establishing appropriate control of quality lies in its place in the organisation. On slight reflection, it is obvious that the function should probably not report to the production manager. An independent check on quality is highly desirable.

The major objective of the production department will be to produce *X* quantity in *Y* hours at *Z* cost. The fact that some production may be substandard will only detract from achieving this objective. Putting quality control under the R & D manager takes away the temptation of allowing some substandard production to be sent to customers.

32:5   Conclusion

Quality control is not just a factory operation. Its techniques can be applied in office routines where sampling can be used to judge the quality of clerical work being produced. Raw material receipts can also benefit from the use of statistical quality control.

If quality is controlled, undoubtedly a long way has been covered in controlling costs. But it has to be dynamic. Once it has reached a stage where it merely stops reject product being sent to a customer and does no more, then quality control hardly exists. It must play a positive role in the overall improvement of product standards and material utilisation generally.

32:6   Further reading

1   J F Halpin, *Zero Defects,* McGraw Hill, 1968
2   R Thomason, *Introduction to Reliability and Quality,* Machinery Publications, 1969
3   S Weinberg, *Profit Through Quality,* Gower Press, 1971
4   D S Desmond, *Quality Control Workbook,* Gower Press, 1971
5   E G Kirkpatrick, *Quality Control for Managers and Engineers,* Wiley, 1971
6   A Hurtson and J Keen, *Essentials of Quality Control,* Heinemann
7   R Gedge, *Quality and Reliability,* Wiley
8   R H Caplen, *A Practical Approach to Quality Control,* Business Books.

THIRTY-THREE

Purchasing
control and materials management

33:1 Introduction

With techniques such as value analysis and material and quality control, purchasing control should ensure that purchases of raw materials, components, finished products, spares and service stores of all kinds are bought as cheaply as possible, while an acceptable quality and supplier service is maintained.

It is perhaps surprising that in most organisations where purchases from outside suppliers constitute from 20 to 60 per cent of total operating costs, so little is done to check that purchasing is carried out at optimum cost.

A planned attack on raw material, stock and materials management, generally, should be at the forefront of every cost reduction campaign.

33:2 Description

Purchasing is the obtaining of raw materials, tools and equipment, machine and service supplies which help to ensure the successful operating of the company. Purchasing control should, therefore, ensure the following:

1 All supplies are bought as cheaply as possible
2 The quality of such items should be such that inspection and quality control are minimised
3 Purchases are bought to a prescribed delivery date and goods are delivered accordingly
4 Quality and inspection are made so that few if any, substandard purchases have to be rejected

5   Purchasing research is organised so that all possible sources of supplies are regularly contacted, and that purchases are made only from suppliers that can deliver at the lowest price for the quantities, quality, delivery date, etc, required

6   Economic quantities are bought when necessary

7   Long-term contracts are established when these are deemed essential

8   Standardisation and variety reduction is in force wherever possible

9   Quotations are obtained wherever necessary—i.e. except for very low-priced purchases

10 Tests of the market are taken at all times

11 Suitable stock recording and control systems are in operation for raw materials, components etc

12 Relative cost advantages of buying out as opposed to making internally are known

13 Specific terms of purchase are always quoted on orders

14 All paperwork systems associated with purchases, quotations, order progressing, inspection and quality control, return of empties, etc, is simplified and efficient

15 Tests on purchasing efficiency are carried out

PURCHASING RESEARCH. The opportunities to reduce material cost lie in two areas:

1   In improving material utilisation

2   In purchasing at less cost

Purchasing research is a process whereby all possible suppliers are regularly contacted, so that company purchases are made at the lowest possible cost consistent with quality and delivery required. A systematic search of all alternative sources of supply with the possibility of using alternative materials is made. A calculation of what the material or article should cost might be made by the company's technical personnel.

SUPPLIER EVALUATION. If it is essential to carry out R & D in purchasing, and also to ensure that the activities listed at the start of this section are carried out appropriately, two checklists are essential. Their application would ensure, very largely, that purchasing control is being pursued. The two checklists refer to:

1   Supplier evaluation

2   Buying activity evaluation

Every supplier used should undergo the following evaluation:

1   Has the supplier any edge in price or discounts and how do his prices compare with other suppliers?

a   More
b   Less
c   Same
d   If more or less, by how much
2   Has the supplier's quality always been appropriate? What has been rejected—how much, how many times?
3   Does the supplier always keep to deliveries that have been promised? If not, by how much have deliveries been delayed? Is this consistent or rare?
4   Is communication with the supplier always good and response accurate? Is the supplier always obliging?
5   Does supplier always help in emergencies—when supplies are needed urgently, for example?
6   Are labour problems (strikes, etc) rare at supplier's works?
7   Is invoicing always carried out correctly?
8   Are the company buying terms always accepted without question?
9   Are rejected quantities always replaced as soon as possible?
10 Are all technical questions dealt with efficiently? Are supplier's technical personnel of a high calibre?
11 Is the packaging used by the supplier always good?
12 Are credits and other financial considerations always handled expeditiously, usually favourably?

BUYING ACTIVITY EVALUATION

1   Does buyer always know what he is buying? Is he technically competent to discuss his purchases with both supplier and departments ordering the purchase?
2   Are a sufficient number of potential suppliers contacted and quotations gained?
3   Are orders over £X000 always agreed by the chief buyer?
4   Are suppliers asked for a cost breakdown of purchases?
5   Does the buyer understand fully the discounts, price breaks, economic order quantity situations which apply?
6   Would it be advisable for the buyer to gain some cost analysis information from company sources?
7   Is the company's legal department always asked to comment where necessary, particularly on contracts of major importance?
8   Has a make/buy decision been made after due calculation?
9   Are buyers always aware of past performance of suppliers when placing orders?
10 Will any development carried out by the supplier be charged to the company? If so will the buyer be aware of this when a replenishment is ordered?
11 What special handling problems exist in:
a   Quality?
b   Inspection?
c   Dispatch?

d Transport?

e Packaging—etc?

Are buyers aware of these and can they take appropriate action?

12 Do buyers co-operate well with:

b Warehousing and delivery personnel?

b Stores and stock personnel?

c Quality control staff?

d Engineering departments?

e All ordering departments?

PURCHASING BUDGETS AND FINANCIAL CONTROL. It is important that the purchasing department conforms to strict budgetary control practice. Monthly, annual and, perhaps, project purchase budgets need to be established. Possibly these should be broken down by departments requesting purchases. Cost centres may also be a useful means of allocating purchase control. Monthly additions of purchases need to be made and the value allocated to departmental and cost centre budgets accordingly.

One important analysis that ought to be carried out to help budgeting is in product classification. Coding of product and raw material should help to assess budget requirement and budgetary control.

A significant coding system will often help this procedure. (A significant coding system is one that indicates the product's type, quality, size, use, etc.)

To help in the budgetary control procedure, a purchase requisition vetting procedure is essential. Unless some validation of purchases is carried out, it is likely that budgets will be overspent.

It is in this activity that a purchasing department's technical know-how, knowledge of standardisation and variety reduction, value analysis, etc, will be at a premium. A challenge ought to be made of everything that is requisitioned.

PURCHASING ORGANISATION. Decentralisation *v* centralisation problems will inevitably arise in purchasing. Local purchases will take place because they are urgent and local suppliers are capable of giving the service required.

Local initiative, therefore, may save machine breakdown time or some other emergency can be tackled effectively. Where local equipment, etc, is unique, buying locally may be relatively harmless. Going through a centralised purchasing unit will proliferate paperwork and extend purchase time, often considerably.

Where there is basic homogeneity of purchase requirements at several locations, centralised purchase is desirable. Uniformity of supply, supplier discounts, leverage of all kinds, which can be pressured by bulk purchases, can all ensue.

Centralised purchasing, therefore, ought to be the rule rather than the exception. Buying prices should be lower. Suppliers should be pleased to negotiate with one rather than several customers.

Where localised purchasing is allowed, strict rules about purchasing procedures particularly prices to be paid, amounts to be ordered and the fact that all transactions should be reported to a control authority, should be in force.

PURCHASING POLICY.   To optimise purchase costs and inventory holdings various purchasing methods should be tried as follows:

1   Long-term buying policies—these should be based on statistical analysis of past demand
2   Inflation buying—frequently the rate of inflation or an imminent price rise indicates that a purchase should be made, despite the fact that no immediate use for the purchase warrants it
3   Seasonal trends—seasonality in price, delivery, and availability will dictate seasonal purchasing
4   Commodity futures—raw materials and commodities generally often have violently fluctuating prices. Buying futures or forward commitments are part of optimising purchase costs and costs of inventory holding
5   Other purchase methods include:
a   Purchases for specific periods in the future
b   Marketing purchasing (as in 4 above)
c   Group purchase of small items
d   Scheduled purchasing

PURCHASE ORDERS.   Purchase orders should state simply and clearly what is required. The following information should be shown:

1   All details in recognised national or international terminology which is acceptable in the trade
2   Tolerances for all items
3   Brand or trade names, where applicable
4   The catalogue number, if buying from a supplier's catalogue
5   Specifications should be sent to their supplier when necessary. They should show:
a   Physical characteristics of purchase
b   Chemical analysis
c   Other technical/analytical contraints
6   A blueprint or sample, if necessary
7   Description of use of the purchase will always help to identify the item being bought
8   Packaging may be important and this should be quoted
9   Where inspection has to take place on the supplier's premises—for example, in the case of steel making—then appropriate arrangements for this need to be stated on the order

GENERAL DECISION MAKING.   The use of economic batch quantities is often desirable in purchasing. The rules covering make/buy decisions also ought to be well known.

PURCHASING SYSTEMS.   Another useful area for investigation in reducing purchasing costs is of the systems in use. These include:

1   Purchase requisition and requisition validation
2   Stock recording
3   Returnable empties
4   Stock reordering
5   Goods received
6   Ordering from suppliers—usually two systems are used, one for casual orders and another for order repeats from the same customer when pre-printed orders can be used

33:3 Successful areas of application and examples

Purchasing control, as the name implies, can be applied to any purchasing department or purchasing routine in a non-specialist purchasing department.

It seems important to know that purchasing control is successful. To do this a variety of measurements of performance are required. The major ones are listed below:

1   Net purchases as a percentage of the sales value of production
2   Price reductions or discounts obtained/total order value

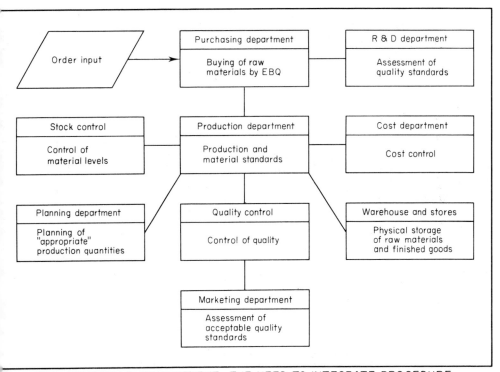

Figure 33.1 MATERIALS MANAGEMENT—THE NEED TO INTEGRATE PROCEDURE

3   Late deliveries—as a percentage of total deliveries
4   Value of rejected material due to bad purchasing
5   Purchasing department cost/number of orders placed
6   Value of stockholding/value of production

MATERIALS MANAGEMENT.   A more useful way of looking at purchasing control is to link it with all the other functions which should ensure that materials management is effective. There has to be total control. An investigation into purchasing alone will rarely yield high rewards. An analysis of materials management will be far more worth while (see Figures 33.1 and 33.2).

The functioning of an appropriate material utilisation system is an essential prerequisite to materials management.

Activity analysis	Purchasing	Marketing	Quality control	Production department	Cost office	Stock control
1 Stock levels	1 Buying procedures					1 Stock control – demand forecastin
2 Material utilisation	2 Buying procedures			2 Use of a MU system with feedback	2 Design and control of appropriate system	
3 Use of EBQs	3 Buying procedures					2 Stock control mechanism
4 Least cost purchasing	4 Purchasing control (supplies research)					
5 Material standards		5 Competition in the market place	5 Quality control standards		5 Embodied in cost control systems	
6 Scrap control				6 Scrap control as part of production process	6 Cost control systems	
7 Value analysis		7 Competition in the market place		7 R & D and production		
8 Minimum work in progress				8 Production planning and control system		

Figure 33.2 METHOD OF ANALYSIS OF MATERIALS MANAGEMENT

33:4   Problems in the use of the techniques and conditions for success

TECHNIQUES ANALYSIS.   As with every major function purchasing personnel need to be skilled in a wide range of cost reduction and other techniques.

The base for this activity lies in the generic term "materials management." This should cover all aspects of the buying, storing and use of materials. The subelements are therefore:

1   Purchasing analysis and control
2   Value analysis
3   Quality control and inspection
4   Stock control—in its widest definition
5   Material utilisation systems

Further useful techniques are:

6   Standard costing and budgetary control—in order that purchasing plays
    its full role in this system
7   Standardisation and variety reduction
8   Warehousing and stores control
9   Legal aspects of purchasing

Training in these techniques is extremely important. Purchasing is still not recognised in many companies as an important and potentially high profit making area.

Many buying departments still operate on the principle that they are merely clerks who progress an order from a user who has already nominated what he wants, the price he will pay and the supplier from whom it will be obtained. Where this situation occurs the role of purchasing as defined in this chapter is largely non-existent.

33:5   Conclusion

The aim of purchasing control should be to:

1   Buy from cheaper sources
2   Obtain agreed cheaper materials
3   Gain bigger discounts

In so doing the following further benefits should be gained:

4   Lower buying costs per £ of purchases
5   Lower stocks held
6   Less inspection
7   Fewer production delays
8   Less scrap

These are worth-while savings. Purchasing control, therefore, is a worth-while technique which ought to be vigorously pursued.

33:6   Further reading

1   J Cantor, *Evaluating Purchasing Systems*, IUC
2   "Materials Management (a policy paper)," *Purchasing Journal*, February 1972
3   D Ryder, "Corporate Strategy and Purchasing," *Modern Purchasing*, August 1971
4   S Ammer, *Materials Management*, Irwin
5   P J H Bailey, *Purchasing and Supply Management*, Chapman & Hall
6   J H Westing, *Purchasing Management Materials in Motion*, Wiley
7   P Bailey and D Farmer, *Purchasing Problems*, Chapman & Hall
8   P J H Bailey and G Tavernier, *Design of Purchasing Systems and Records*, Gower Press
9   B H Walley, "A Plan for Scrap Minimisation," *Time and Motion Study*, November 1962

Part 6

MOTIVATION AND COMMUNICATION

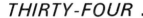

THIRTY-FOUR

Productivity bargaining

34:1 Introduction

Chapter 9 suggested that disenchantment with direct payment schemes has led many organisations and trade unions to believe that productivity bargaining is a superior wages payment system. The review of productivity measurements is another obvious factor in productivity bargaining.

The history of productivity bargaining is fairly well known. During the 1960s in Britain a series of schemes were introduced which included multi-factor considerations—output, material utilisation and quality of product among them. But it was the Fawley Agreement that really set the tone for them.

Esso Petroleum, which ran the refinery at Fawley, brought in American consultants to appraise refinery activities. The radical outcome of this operation was that with the active co-operation of the trade unions (which were consulted at all stages) far-ranging changes in intercraft flexibility, manning levels and of course wages payment were introduced.

At that time the National Board for Prices and Incomes encouraged such agreements and, for a while, productivity bargains were the only legal way a wage rise could be given.

34:2 Description

By definition a productivity bargain is an agreement, usually in the form of a contract, whereby workers agree to forgo certain working practices, thereby ensuring increased productivity in return for higher rewards.

Various general principles were laid down by the Board which had to be included in a productivity bargain. These briefly were as follows:

1   It had to be proved that the workers had made a valid and measurable contribution to the bargain. Work practices which had in the past inhibited increased productivity had to be seen to have been abandoned
2   The future outcome of productivity bargains had to be calculated by appropriate work measurement methods
3   The calculation of the gains in cost due to the increase in productivity had to show how much total unit costs had fallen, even when the costs of associated investment had been taken into account
4   The bargain had to be appropriately controlled once it had been implemented. The controls had to show by how much productivity had increased and only then should extra payment to the workers be made
5   The bargain had to show that the consumer will gain from it either from a reduction in prices or at least price stability
6   One agreement in an organisation had to bear any consequential cost elsewhere in the same organisation if any occurred
7   In all cases negotiators had to beware of any extravagant settlements which would have been resented elsewhere.

Steps towards a productivity deal generally follow this pattern:

1   Before the bargain is made the following data should be gathered:
a   What and how many job rates exist?
b   What and how many incentive schemes exist?
c   What results are being achieved? For example what percentage of all schemes are giving poor results?
d   Are there problems in recruitment of certain trades, skills, shift workers, etc?
e   How much overtime is worked?
f   Are restrictive practices a problem—if so, define in detail and suggest effect on productivity?
g   What demarcation problems exist—also detail?
h   Is timekeeping bad?
j   Is absenteeism bad?
2   Rewards given to employees. What rewards are required by the workers if a bargain is to be made? Usually all or most of the following are demanded:
a   Increases in basic pay and removal of the incentive/bonus element entirely
b   A more equitable wages structure
c   Stability of earnings
d   A no-redundancy situation when the agreement is made—or, as second best, a highly remunerative redundancy scheme
e   Sick leave with pay

f Increased holiday entitlement

g A shorter working week—i.e. the basic hours to be worked

h Reduction or perhaps elimination of overtime

j Different shift systems

k Different status—staff etc

l Improved joint consultation schemes and greater participation in management decisions

m Trade unions to be included at all times in discussions about future changes

3 Changes required by management. What does management want out of the deal? Obviously higher productivity but there are many other considerations as well:

a A simpler wages structure to stop wages drift and leap frogging

b A direct reduction in manning strengths

c Flexibility in the use of labour and an end to demarcation squabbles. Included in this will be mobility of labour, giving management the freedom to move employees around as circumstances dictate

d A reallocation, perhaps a reduction of restbreaks, make-ready times, etc. Tea breaks to be taken on site

e The uninhibited use of work measurement, method study and allied techniques which may result in changed working practices

f Giving management the right to manage

4 Various other factors may have to be negotiated as part of the deal including:

a Ability to recruit labour at any time

b Increased co-operation

c Better communications

d Sickness payments—including industrial injuries

e Safety, health and general conditions

f Disciplinary procedures and grievance systems

g Use of contractors in peak-labour demand times

h Treatment of elderly and disabled

j Renegotiation of the deal at a specific time in the future

PRODUCTIVITY BARGAINING PROCEDURE. There are three basic elements in carrying out a productivity bargain: planning and negotiation, design, and installation.

Planning and negotiation. It is usual for the two sides—management and trade unions—to both appoint a negotiating team acceptable to the other side, following an intimation from either that they are interested in negotiating a productivity deal. (It is possible that one side may reject the proposal.) The teams then draw up two lists:

1 What do we want out of the deal

2 What can we afford to give away

At the same time data concerning the operations/activities under consideration will be collected. The requirements of each side will centre on the list drawn up previously.

Negotiation.　Normally an initial meeting is held where two teams discuss what they want and what they might give. This is usually done in very broad terms. The teams will then withdraw and consider the broad-based requirements in detail. Management has the advantage in that it should have considerable operational data.

It is difficult to know where major problems will emerge. Often a seemingly impossible proviso will be accepted with alacrity while a comparatively minor factor will provoke the stubbornest of reactions. It is impossible to give any worth-while guidelines—except that it is better to have no deal at all than to buy dearly some minor working amendments.

Installation.　The criteria for installing a productivity deal and controlling the results have been listed previously. The most important factor is communication. All employees should receive minutes of the team meetings, so that a step-by-step communication is kept up as the negotiations proceed. This not only helps workers to know what is being negotiated, but, hopefully, it also engenders a feeling that they too are taking part in the negotiations.

As many people as possible should actually take part in the negotiations for the deal. If possible, unofficial leaders of working groups should be included as well as trade union officials.

Communications, about the progress of the deal, must also be given to managers and supervisors who will have to operate it. It is obvious that the usual methods of communication may not be good enough for this purpose.

ADVANTAGES OF PRODUCTIVITY AGREEMENTS.　Productivity agreements are a logical way of tackling wage–job condition situations. They seem a much more civilised way of bargaining than the brinkmanship usually associated with wage negotiation. They should lead to a breaking down of barriers between management and workers. Ultimately more trust on both sides should be generated.

The rewards being earned by blue-collar workers in productivity agreements are those that traditionally have belonged to white-collar workers and management. This in the long run should help to improve industrial relations generally. Improved security and increased job satisfaction for workers should also result.

For management, a period without strikes is certainly one thing to look forward to.

34:3　Successful areas of application and examples

A report from the former National Board for Prices and Incomes provides many details about some of the earliest and more important deals, particularly the Esso–Fawley agreement and agreements in ICI, the electrical industry, Alcan and BOC. These agreements are available on request and some are noted in the further reading list (34:6).

The factors for evaluating a productivity agreement are as follows:

MANPOWER LEVELS. In the following categories a calculation of the pre-deal and post-deal numbers of employees should be made:

PROCESS	ENGINEERING	SUPERVISION	GENERAL FACTORY
Direct process	Mechanical	AND CONTROL	SERVICES
Spares and relief	Electrical	Supervision	Fire
Laboratory	Instrument	Management	Security
(Quality control)	Central services	Planning	Internal
Supply	Semi-skilled	Control	transport
Distribution	Labourers and	Technical	Canteens
Clerical support	Assistants	Investigation	etc
etc	Contract labour	etc	
	Apprentices		
	etc		

EXPECTED SAVINGS. The effect of the agreements on the following factors should be assessed:

Manpower savings   (by function and trade)

1   Reduction in management and supervision
2   Elimination of work
3   Increased performance—measured appropriately
4   Any work that has been reallocated
5   Changes in labour mobility and breakdown in demarcation rules

General savings.   Quote savings gained in:

1   Product quality and efficiency of production—i.e. increased speed of orders through the factory etc
2   Lower overtime
3   Material utilisation improvement
4   Machinery and general plant utilisation and efficiency
5   Work measurement and bonus calculations
6   Sickness leave
7   Absenteeism

NON-QUANTIFIABLE IMPROVEMENT. Comment should be made on improvements resulting in the following:

1   Co-operation of workers
2   Worker commitment
3   Better operation of company systems—e.g. production planning and control, labour control etc
4   More effective management
5   Better deliveries, better customer service

ANALYSIS OF COST OF AGREEMENT.   As well as calculating the direct cost of the agreement (£s per week/month/year etc) the following costs should be known:

1   Cost of the total investigation
2   Retraining of operatives etc
3   New equipment and tools
4   Ancillary service costs
5   Costs associated with implementing the agreement

INDEX OF PRODUCTIVITY. Productivity indices (some of which are quoted in the Chapter 11) should be utilised to ensure that productivity has improved appropriately.

34:4   Problems in the use of the technique and conditions for success

It has been the practice of both management and trade unions to view the negotiating table as a battle field. Many people who have taken part in such negotiations as those leading to a productivity agreement can ruefully testify to this assertion. Yet, unless there is a certain amount of trust between the two sides, no agreement worth anything will be negotiated. The importance of communications at all stages of negotiations has already been stressed in section 34:2.

A productivity deal should not be handled solely by the personnel department. It is usually so important and its effects so far reaching that senior management (perhaps the chief executive himself) should lead the management negotiating team.

A positive response is needed by management. A negotiating plan should be framed, complete with phased targets, negotiating limits and alternative courses of action. This is in marked contrast to the more familiar management response of trying to secure the minimum concession to claims made by the trade unions

34:5   Conclusion

The negotiation of a productivity bargain is one of the last in the line of activities that should start with a "situation audit" and the establishment of corporate objectives. However, if it is assumed that a productivity bargain will always lie at the end of the line, there could be some disillusionment.

Without a reasonable code of industrial relations practice and adequate, if not good, worker–management regard, bargaining will scarcely be successful.

The approach needed rarely reflects the current state of the industrial relations art. It has little in common with the horse trading where management's role is usually defensive and negative. Settlements should not take the form of a reluctant compromise at the final stage of an exercise in brinkmanship.

If a deal has been made and the underlying worker–manager relationship is still poor, the union side may resent the fact that they cannot get another wage rise until the agreement expires.

The signing away of long-standing work practices may not give the union a bargaining counter in the future and consequently the deal itself may be attacked especially the interpretation of points that have apparently been agreed. The fundamental question of the worker–management relationship may remain un-solved.

34:6 Further reading

1   E J Robertson, *Productivity Bargaining and the Engineering Industry,* Kogan Page, 1969

2   Jones and Golding, *Productivity Bargaining,* Fabian Research Series, London.

3   Alan Flanders, *The Fawley Productivity Agreements,* Faber 1964

4   National Board for Prices and Incomes, *Productivity Agreements Report* number 36, HMSO

5   M Harris (editor), *The Realities of Productivity Bargaining,* Institute of Personnel Managers, 1969

6   T Cliff, *The Employers Offensive,* Pluto Press

7   S Cotgrove and others, *The Nylon Spinners,* Allen & Unwin

8   W W Daniel, *Beyond the Wage-Work Bargain,* Allen & Unwin

9   N Stettner, *Productivity Bargaining and Industrial Change,* Pergamon

THIRTY-FIVE

Behavioural attitudes

35:1 Introduction

An organisation is an entity of human and non-human resources which have been joined together to achieve a predetermined objective or objectives.

The organisation will be characterised by patterns of human relationships—status, job responsibilities, rewards and rights, etc—that will either help or hinder the achievement of corporate goals. It is reasonably certain that each member of the organisation will have personal objectives, often tangential to those of the organisation as a whole.

This chapter discusses behavioural attitudes generally and in particular the job enhancement theories propagated by leading behavioural scientists.

35:2 Description

Behavioural sciences, motivation theories or general behavioural attitudes, cover the behavioural/psychological aspects (at least as far as industry is concerned) of worker–management relationships and how best to motivate people to work.

There have been various "authorities" that are usually quoted in connection with the behavioural sciences—McGregor, Maslow, Herzberg, Lickert, Klein, etc. It would be interesting to quote some of the theories that have been propounded and on which behavioural scientists base their suggestions about motivation.

MOTIVATION. Man's primary wants were apparently identified by early psychologists and are stated by such people as Dashiell and Munder. [J F Dashiell,

Fundamentals of Objective Psychology, Allen and Unwin, 1927. A E Munder, *Psychology for Every Man*, Watts & Co, 1935.] The main body-tissue needs are concerned with the satisfying of basic wants: hunger, sex, comfort, warmth, rest and exercise. But apart from these there are further primary wants concerned with the social world—a sense of security, a wish to be noticed and admired, to feel superior in some respect to other people, to have companionship and human relationships (especially among people of a similar kind) and to possess and store up possessions.

Both McGregor and Maslow have defined man as a wanting animal and Maslow has built up a "hierarchy of needs," for which he owes thanks to earlier psychologists. The needs he suggests are:

1 Physiological needs—hunger, thirst etc
2 Safety and security, law and order
3 Belongingness and love needs—social group needs, identification and affection
4 Esteem needs—success, self respect, status
5 Self actualisation—a desire to express one's capabilities

The behavioural scientists state, perhaps correctly, that the earlier management science protagonists such as F W Taylor and Gilbreth have led industrial management to concentrate solely on the first two of the needs quoted and to ignore the rest. They go on to suggest that once man's primary wants have been settled (and this, it is stated, has now happened in most of the Western world) the remaining items in the need hierarchy are the ones that will help to motivate a work force.

TYPES OF PEOPLE. Douglas McGregor propounded a theory about types of people. He recognised two main types and suggested two theories to describe them: theory X and theory Y. Applied to management styles, the theories work out as follows:

Theory X. A theory X manager is one who believes that the average human being will not work unless he is driven to do so. Because of this most people have to be dragooned, controlled and motivated by financial gain. Security looms large and ambition very little. Decisions have to be made on their behalf, as responsibility is rarely, if ever, sought.

Theory Y. The theory Y manager is the converse of his theory X colleague. He believes that most people do not readily respond to threats of dismissal or punishment generally. People search out responsibility and want to use a high degree of imagination in their job. They want recognition and status and will not happily work if they are closely directed.

Theory X is an authoritarian style of management; theory Y is based on participation.

McGregor is merely using Maslow's hierarchy of needs to suggest two extreme management styles. His approach seems an oversimplification of a complex situation. People are rarely so extreme that they are totally X or Y. Some environments (both technical and competitive) need different management styles. X may be totally relevant in some circumstances; Y necessary in others. More often than not a compromise somewhere on a scale between the two will be most suitable.

INFLUENCING PEOPLE TO WORK. Herzberg's theories concerning motivation followed an analysis of the results of a statistical sample of 20000 people from all walks of life. Each person was asked to describe the conditions appertaining in his life when he was most and when least happy, especially in relationship with work. From the results Herzberg determined his "motivation–hygiene" or two-factor theory. It has engendered considerable research in the field of motivation and has gained the most attention of all the motivation theories. Herzberg draws a distinction between what he calls motivating and hygiene factors. The former are more important than the latter in motivating personnel.

Only the motivational aspects of a man's job, states Herzberg, will have any sustained impact on his work performance. There are six of these aspects:

1   Achievement
2   Recognition
3   Advancement
4   Work itself
5   Possibility of growth
6   Responsibility

However much the hygiene or maintenance aspects are improved they will only induce an "absence of dissatisfaction"—they will in effect prevent him from becoming bored and totally unhappy. The factors recognised under this heading are:

1   Company policy and administration
2   Technical supervision
3   Personal relationships with supervisors
4   Personal relationships with equals
5   Personal relationships with subordinates
6   Salary
7   Job security
8   Personal life
9   Working conditions
10   Status

Maintenance factors, it is stated, will never be positive in motivating personnel to work harder or more purposefully.

JOB ENRICHMENT.   The theories propounded simply above have culminated in suggestions that job enrichment is the real key to worker motivation.

A rather long-winded definition of job enrichment is: "It is the constructive alteration of jobs which will give a worker more responsibility, reduce control over him, make him accountable for his own work. It gives him, as far as possible, responsibility for a significant part of the total organisation and so allows him to become a specialist in some field."

Jobs that have been established in this way should provide growth, advancement and responsibility. They should (it is stated) provide recognition and give opportunity for achievement. The worker will, in effect, be on the way to self actualisation.

PRACTICE.   Section 35:3 suggests some of the ways in which job enhancement might be applied in practice. Undoubtedly even a partial acceptance will have some effect on all of the following:

1   Organisation structure, organisational development, the management of organisational change
2   Incentives, wages and salary schemes, job evaluation, fringe benefits, productivity bargaining and work measurement techniques
3   Analysis of skill requirements, manpower planning, training and job allocation
4   Job descriptions, performance appraisal, links between performance and rewards
5   Methods of consultation and communications, employee attitudes and opinion surveys

JOB ENHANCEMENT AND MANAGEMENT SERVICES.   The application of job enhancement will affect the work of the specialist in MS particularly in the following:

1   In fitting new methods and the application of techniques to job enrichment
2   Recognition that individual skills and the maintenance of them by specific individuals must be fostered even though division of labour would apparently be more profitable
3   Greater recognition of personality in job study and methods analysis
4   Greater emphasis on participation in project teams and general consultative /decision making practices in problem solving
5   Realisation that maximum profitability in terms of mechanistic practices, may not achieve the profit calculated
6   Delaying introduction of change until staff are ready for it and accept it. Impose little or nothing

35:3 Successful areas of application and examples

If the foregoing is accepted how can it be applied in management style, in job design, and worker–management relationships? The following may help.

GENERAL JOB DESIGN. The design of a job must if possible include:

1   A job from a beginning to an end must be established with a visual end result
2   The job should be completed with as little supervision as possible, preferably none
3   There should be a performance appraisal that will enable the job holder to match his performance against that required and to know why he failed —if he does so
4   The job should, if possible, be capable of change. The same routine should not be followed day after day
5   The implication of the job and general duties should not be so fully defined as to prevent improvement by the job holder
6   The job description should be so established, that it will be easy to see how it links with everyone else's job in the department etc

PARTICIPATION. The job holder should be allowed to contribute ideas about how his job should be done and how the overall efficiency of the organisation might be improved.

Problem solving should not be the sole prerogative of management—or even senior management. Decisions ought to be made jointly with those who will be affected by them. Personnel should not be consulted by management, they should participate.

To achieve participation of this kind personnel must be trained in specialist techniques, in company activities, in management and in problem solving generally.

RESPONSIBILITY. The worker must be given responsibility and allowed to develop it.

1   He must be given clear responsibility for a well-defined job, tools, equipment, new materials etc
2   He must be given an opportunity to look after and develop other people
3   If possible he should be given the responsibility of carrying out research and development into his job and the wider aspects of the activities he is performing
4   He should be asked to contribute ideas and thoughts about his job

RECOGNITION AND ACHIEVEMENT

1   Pay and other rewards should be related to the results which are achieved The results should be quantifiable if possible
2   Promotion should be made on the same basis
3   Success should always be recognised, never ignored

INTERDEPENDENCE AND WORK HABITS. It is important to develop an interdependence among employees which becomes employee and not job centred. A manager ought to concentrate on building effective working groups, setting objectives and then allowing the working group to achieve them. He should be concerned that the objective is met but not wholly how appropriate performance is achieved. This means:

1   Work habits must change
2   Organisation precepts have to be altered
3   Management style must change from being authoritarian to being participative

35:4   Problems in the use of the technique and conditions for success

Section 35:2 briefly outlines some of the more important theories which behavioural scientists are now propagating. Are they true?

A casual glance through a psychology textbook will show that as many psychological factors have been excluded as included. For example:

1   The conditioned response
2   The formation of habit
3   Instinctive action
4   Acquired behaviour
5   Impulses and social behaviour, allied with education, class and economic considerations etc

Do none of these have any effect on motivation?

Why is it that some countries have a better strike record than others, some industries have a better strike record than others and why do some companies have, apparently, better relationships between those managed and managers? Why, for example, is Dagenham more strike prone than Ford of Cologne? It is surely as hard to introduce job enrichment on one conveyor belt as it is on the other.

History, class consciousness, the kind of society, general social attitudes are all extremely important. Where do they stand?

Sometimes paternalism goes wrong—witness the savagery of the Pilkington Strike in 1970. Often it has gone right. Rowntrees, Bibbys, Cadburys have had little strike activity, yet "paternalism" would certainly be listed as one of Herzberg's hygiene factors.

The factors listed by Herzberg are in real life difficult to disentangle. The protagonists of job enrichment generally have failed to recognise that the work itself has always been tied up with salary, job security and personal relationships. It is difficult to define achievement if status is not part of it. Equally, recognition is often associated with status and working conditions—a better office, a carpet on the floor, etc. Most jobs, particularly management jobs, have a mixture of motivating and hygiene factors and it is nearly impossible to recognise which is which.

Setting up jobs, so that job enrichment can take place, is obviously a tremendous task. Even if it is necessary—i.e. if the behavioural scientists are correct—are there sufficient numbers of trained social and behavioural scientists to help to do it? Is it possible anyway? For many managers job enrichment in the Herzberg style is already an established fact. For many shop-floor workers is it practicable? Again, communication is a major factor. Once again new management theories have developed and attracted disciplines that have built up vocabulary barriers with line management. Jargon, no matter who uses it, will induce resentment not co-operation, particularly among middle-aged line managers who think that they know best when it comes to talking to the shop-floor. If this is what they think they have done (and done well) all their lives, a few bright social scientists are not going to make much progress with them. A line manager who is being judged on the profitability of his organisation is not going to take too happily to someone who talks about devolution of decision making.

The most logical interpretation of Herzberg's two factor theory is that motivators are more important than hygiene factors in gaining overall job satisfaction. Some research studies refute this view in certain cases where a "less-ego situation," exists. [Quoted by Wall and Stephenson in "Herzberg's Two-Factor Theory of Job Attitudes," *Work Study and Management Services*, September 1971.] Job enrichment can in many ways be equated with job enlargement, particularly vertical enlargement. There is a distinct probability that while job enrichment of this kind may produce more satisfied employees, overall company efficiency will decline. From a profit/efficiency viewpoint it may be more desirable to allow division of labour or job poverty to exist with all its human difficulties than to introduce an organisationally disastrous alternative. Job enrichment implies that each and every worker wants responsibility, authority and participation in decision making. This is far from proven. Like the Hawthorn experiments, it is too easy to conclude that experiments with job enrichment have succeeded. Sympathy and involvement with the experiment alone help in achieving higher efficiency. Moves towards job enrichment provide problems for trade unions. Where strict demarcation has existed, there are difficulties in enlarging jobs to include other trade skills. Job enrichment will lead to demands for higher pay to match the new responsibilities. Job enrichment for shop-floor personnel might lead to job impoverishment for supervisors and managers. This could cause resentment and stress, leading to an overall decline in efficiency. Job enrichment will fail unless the supervisors role, too, is changed. Managerial and supervisory resistance to job enrichment may be very real. Applied psychology and the attitudes of senior management will be vital in getting any job enrichment scheme started.

35:5   Conclusion

This brief outline of a highly complex subject serves only to indicate that motivation, in its widest sense, can no longer be served by financial "carrots" alone. If the behavioural scientists are right (and the moves from straight work measurement to productivity bargaining, etc, indicate that to some extent they are), the whole pattern of past management styles, attitudes towards profit making at the expense of labour, the total lack of participatory activities and decision making must go. If they are wrong, management might climb onto a new and potentially dangerous situation where anarchy may rule and companies quickly go bankrupt because their profit making potential has been totally undermined. The political implications involved in participatory decision making must also be considered. The experiments, carried out in such countries as Yugoslavia where "workers' control" has been tried, have produced only partial success. The political overtones of demands for similar types of control in the UK are not to be ignored. Equally there are economic considerations to be taken into account. Capitalism has been based on "risk capital." Is "labour" now to predominate and "capital" become even more of a risk, so altering the whole concept of the profit motive? Greater total participation in decision making is necessary. This will dictate a degree of sophistication in management to which few companies could aspire. Inevitably there will be failures. But at the same time, ultimate control must lie in the hands of senior management. How participation and responsibility can be equated has still to be satisfactorily worked out. My contention is that behavioural scientists (like most exponents of new management theories) have had too much exposure and too little critical analysis. From experience, the application of a rigorous method of profit planning often provides much of the motivation as opposed to maintenance, which Herzberg considers necessary. Without such a methodology much of a social scientist's activities in introducing job enrichment will be wasted. With such a method, the social scientist if often unnecessary.

35:6 Further reading

1   W J Paul and K B Robertson, *Job Enrichment and Employee Motivation*, Gower Press, 1971
2   Douglas McGregor, *The Human Side of the Enterprise*, McGraw Hill
3   C L Hulen and M R Blood, "Job Enlargement," *Psychological Bulletin*, 1968
4   F Herzberg, *Work and the Nature of Man*, World Publishing Co
5   A H Maslow, *Motivation and Personality*, Harper
6   R Likert, *The Human Organisation—its Management and Value*, McGraw Hill
7   I S McDavid "People, Participation and Motivation," *Work Study and Management Services* September 1970
8   Little and Warr, "Who's Afraid of Job Enrichment?" *Personnel Management*, February 1971
9   P P Schoderbeck & W E Reif, *Job Enlargement*, Michigan University 1970
10   M M Scott, *Every Employee a Manager*, McGraw Hill, 1970
11   G F Thomason, *Experiments in Participation*, IPM, 1970
12   Lynda King Taylor, *Not for Bread Alone*, Business Books, 1971

THIRTY-SIX

Incentives and payment schemes

36:1 Introduction

One realisation that has struck most of industry in the last few years is the state of disorder that most payment-by-results schemes has reached. In some organisations time study men are still used as rate fixers and they argue interminably about rates of pay with local unions. In other companies payment by results has been rejected altogether and some form of merit rating substituted. Linear premium bonus schemes were first invented about seventy years ago. Pioneers such as Halsey and Rowen appreciated the inherent dangers in loose rate-fixing and suggested payments methods which they hoped would prevent abuse and offer some protection against rewards for work not done. Despite this there is now wide dissatisfaction with payment-by-results systems in most companies from both unions and management. The current dilemma concerning incentives and payment schemes has resulted in a field day for the advocates of productivity bargaining and job enrichment. Protagonists of such methods state that direct payment-by-results systems provide an undignified scramble for monetary reward with both sides trying to cheat the other. To some extent they may be right, but payment by results is still widely applied, often demanded by the unions and likely to have considerable currency for a long time.

36:2 Description

An incentive is a motivation to produce action. A wages payment incentive scheme is one which it is hoped will achieve greater output for the payment of increased wages. A correlation is made between effort and reward. It is hoped (at least on the management side) that payment will be made only for extra effort over that conceded as normal. The employees, however, usually try to lower the threshold of "normal" production as far as possible and hope from then on to gain payment in direct proportion to output achieved although effort may not be proportional. Herein lies the basic problems with which all incentive plans have to grapple. Three major areas of contention therefore exist:

1   The establishment of normal production rates—often these are called base rates
2   Standards of performance—the relationship at various incentive levels with the base rate
3   The formula for incentive application

Output is normally measured in units made per hour. Cost, budgeted or standard cost, might also be useful in measuring output or performance. If the work done has an unmeasurable content, then this has to be taken into account in some way.

BONUS SYSTEM PRINCIPLES
1   Reward should be proportional to effort, not necessarily to output
2   Output should not be permitted at the expense of unbalancing order flow. The easiest and most highly rated work should not be done first and the most urgent and least rated left
3   The scheme should be easy to understand. Operatives should be able to calculate their own bonus earnings and compare the results with the company calculation
4   As far as possible jobs should be equal. There should be no "good" or "bad" jobs where incentives are large or small which will cause dissension among operatives
5   The right atmosphere should be created. If morale is low or union–management relations are poor, it is unlikely that an appropriate incentive will result
6   Method study should be carried out before time study is instituted. If an obvious method improvement is ignored, then it will certainly be exploited by the operative. Once method study has been carried out, there should be one prescribed method of carrying out the job. The operator should stick to this method
7   Non-financial incentives such as improved working conditions or less stringent control activities should always be considered when financial incentives are being applied. They are often useful as bargaining counters against inflated union demands
8   Where possible job description and job evaluation should be linked with the incentive payment. The application or reapplication of incentives should provide an opportunity to rationalise pay structures, and to gain equity between jobs
9   An appropriate scheme should be chosen. Some of the various types of in-

centives are quoted in this chapter. Some will apply to the situation being studied, others will not

10   All factors other than output, which in total affect company profitability, should be considered closely when the scheme is being sold. Quality should not suffer when an incentive is introduced (any subquality production should be debited against the operative) and neither should machine maintenance or good housekeeping. Production planning and control should apply strictly, even though this may dilute operatives' earnings

11   The incentive rate will often be compared by operatives with that of other factories in the area where they live, even if this is only done on a take-home-pay basis. To some extent therefore this must influence the incentive rate, otherwise recruitment will drag and turnover will increase

12   Non-productive or non-measurable work must always be allowed for in the scheme

13   Control over the plan must be effective. A productivity index is a useful way of measuring the result

14   The shorter the assessment period (incentive time span), the greater the incentive

15   Any disagreement over the incentive should be settled by means of basic principles, not through the strength or bargaining position of the negotiating parties

SIZE OF INCENTIVES.   Much has been written about the size of incentive that can be earned by a good operative. The extra payment varies throughout the world. Average bonus payments of 20 per cent on base rates were common for a long time in the USA. This percentage is still fairly common in Europe. In Britain a $33\frac{1}{3}$ percentage has been accepted as normal.

Elements other than the size of the bonus payment have to be taken into account. These include the level of the base rate, the efficiency of supervision, the non-financial incentives, etc.

PRODUCTIVITY MEASUREMENTS.   It is always useful to measure the effect of incentives by means of a productivity index. Often incentive payments are made for all types of consolidation and hours worked instead of for actual output. Machine down time, waiting time, cleaning and general maintenance time are all usually given "average bonus." If this figure is considerable, and it often is, the amount of money paid as an incentive will have little or no relation to effort expended on units manufactured.

A productivity index which measures clocked hours, bonus hours paid for and output achieved in standard hours would be a check on whether money expended is earning appropriate units of production.

GROUP AND INDIVIDUAL INCENTIVE SCHEMES.   There has always been some contention about the merits of individual and group incentive schemes. It would appear that if monetary reward is the motivating force for higher per-

Job Description

Number

Name

Week Ending

Shift Worker's
Rest Day

FOREMAN'S INITIALS

Mon		Tues		Wed		Thur		Fri		Sat		Sun		Hours Worked		B P or T	Job No
N/T	O/T	N/T	O/T	N/T	O/T	N/T	O/T	N/T	O/T	N/T	O/T	N/T	O/T	N/T	O/T		

Total Normal Hours

Total Overtime Hours

Hours Payable

Rate	Clocked		Extra	Total	Amount		Premium Time			Bonus				Total	
	N/T	O/T			£	p	Hours	£	p	Hours	Piece or % Rate	£	p	£	p

SPECIAL INSTRUCTIONS

PAYE
Tax Weeks
In Advance

G C
No. of Weeks

HOLIDAY PAY – 9345

VARIABLE DEDUCTIONS

	£	p
FOOT WEAR		
ADVANCES		

GROSS SICK PAY – 3555½

LESS N H I BENEFITS

TOTAL TAXABLE PAY

NON - TAXABLE EXPS (GEAR MONEY)

Figure 36.1   INCENTIVE SCHEME CALCULATION DOCUMENT

formance then individual schemes must always be preferable. In practice, group incentives often have much to commend them, as the following factors suggest.

Performance.   Individual schemes should motivate higher individual performance. In a group scheme a "levelling effect" might be noticeable. Yet the opposite is often true. The group pressures individuals who alone might be satisfied with relatively moderate performance to increase their standard. The result is that average group performance is often the same as an average individual output rate would be. Individual earnings are often preferable, but a group scheme provides greater consistency in earnings.

Co-operation.   Co-operation is often destroyed by individual incentive schemes. Operatives become self-motivated, to the extent that their actions could have a general deleterious effect.

WEEKLY FACTORY REPORT					Week number _____ Week ending _____			
Line :					Date prepared:			
Cost centre operation or machine	Earned hours	Planned standard hours	Achieved standard hours	Planned efficiency %	Labour efficiency %	Lost time analysis		
						Reason(s)	Amount hours	Amount of standard hours achieved
	1	2	3	4	5	6	7	8
Comments								
						Signed _____		

Figure 36.2   INCENTIVE SCHEME DATA COLLECTION DOCUMENT

Quality. It has been found that quality standards can often be more readily enforceable with a group than individually.

Administration and planning. This is obviously more difficult when individual incentive schemes apply. The smaller the number of schemes the less paperwork and general administration.

Training and recruitment. The group scheme often helps the training and recruitment of new personnel. Individuals will rarely be happy to train or help new recruits.

Supervision. This is obviously much easier with group schemes, where an unofficial group leader often helps supervision.

Social consciousness. The group activity often helps group consciousness leading to social improvements. The individual scheme is really appealing to man's most basic and individualistic instinct.

APPLICATION OF INCENTIVES. The steps to be taken to introduce incentives are as follows:

1 Assess the current psychological attitude and emotions extant in the company. Consider whether incentives will be acceptable and beneficial to the company—i.e. can an appropriate bargain be struck
2 Create (if one is not already in existence) bargaining machinery appropriate for the task
3 Define the objectives of incentive application—rise in productivity required or anticipated reduction in direct labour costs per piece etc
4 Consider financial and non-financial incentives. Can both be included?
5 Choose key jobs for first applications. Agree these first applications with union representatives. Agree whether individual or group bonus is to be applied
6 Choose method of measurement to be carried out—straight time study, PMTS etc
7 Choose method of incentive, for example:
a Direct piecework
b Standard time incentive
c Geared schemes
d Progressive incentive
e Regressive incentive
    The incentive formula is extremely important. No one formula can be applied to all situations. Skilled activities, looseness of standard, environmental conditions will all have some effect on the formula chosen
8 Assess how much non-productive time is involved in the jobs being studied and consider how this will be handled
9 Carry out the study and collect all appropriate data relevant to the job— material usage, quality, costs etc—if these are not available already
10 Standard times should then be established. In time study the first calculation is of "allowed time." This is determined by using a stopwatch and

taking readings at carefully defined breakpoints. Rating—assessing the
pace the operator is working at—follows next. Due recognition is then
given to the weight lifted, tedium of the job, working conditions generally
etc. The resulting standard time is then presented to the union negotiators.
Rarely, if ever, is it accepted. Most problems or discussions occur over
rating. More often than not the standards are diluted during negotiation.
It is suggested that the application of PMTS systems avoids much of the
squabbling that takes place over standards. This is not entirely true

11   The full scheme is then calculated and agreed with the union representatives
     —the standard time, incentive method, bonus calculations formula etc
12   The administration procedures are then established. Normally standard
     times, etc, are calculated by the work study/management services depart-
     ment. They are agreed with the union negotiators and line management, with
     the personnel department playing a leading role in the negotiating pro-
     cedures. Once agreed, calculations of bonus earnings are normally done by
     the wages department or time office with the work study practitioners
     carrying out control studies.

36:3   Successful areas of application and examples

APPLICATIONS.   The application of incentives has grown recently in non-
industrial applications. Local government service jobs have been the subject of
considerable incentive investigation—refuse removers, road sweepers, am-
bulance men have all been the subjects for incentive payments. Some areas of
office work too, have been the subject of incentive applications. For example:

1   Typists
2   Calculating machine operators
3   Punched-card personnel
4   Duplicating and copying staff

Supervisors or indirect operatives can be included in incentive schemes by paying
a pro-rata amount of bonus earned by their staff or staff associated with them.
However, incentives are often the converse of those which might be expected. For
example, in some organisations machine down time (which is included in a direct
operator's scheme as part of bonus payment) is a deduction for a supervisor,
whose responsibilities include that of avoiding machine stoppages for any reason.

TYPES OF INCENTIVE.   The payment-by-results incentive schemes can be
divided up into two main types:

1   Mono-factor types
2   Multi-factor types

The mono-factor type concentrates solely on wage incentives. A bonus scale is constructed between the established base rate and a standard output rate. A graph is usually drawn between the two and payment paid accordingly. The simplest method is where the base rate is a 100 and the standard output rate is 133. Various graph-forms have been used to join these two points—straight-line, curve, ellipse, hyperbola, etc.

Multi-factor incentives include various other factors in the incentive such as:

1   Quality
2   Material utilisation
3   Data recording of some kind
4   Machine utilisation
5   Punctuality
6   Absenteeism etc

It will be seen that such inclusions are leading incentives towards productivity bargaining. Mono-factor incentives can be subdivided into three main sub-types, as follows.

Piece rates.   Usually straight piece rates or Taylor or Merrick differential piecework schemes are utilised. This is the oldest type of incentive payment where output is directly related to payment.

Standard time payment schemes.   Psychologically, the standard time payment schemes are superior to the straight piecework schemes as standards are disguised as hours instead of money. This is an effective point in selling a scheme but probably makes it more difficult for operatives to assess themselves and calculate how much they have earned. The usual practice is for a minimum low base rate to be guaranteed up to a standard output level after which the operative is paid in direct proportion to his output. Various types of standard time payment schemes operate. For example, where there are no steps in the payment-graph; steps as in the Gantt method; fixed percentage saved paid to the worker as per Halsey; various percentages paid to the worker as by Rowan and Eineson.

Points earned payment schemes.   Under these schemes the operative is paid a base rate up to the standard rate of output after which any gain in production is shared between the operative and management. Both Halsey and Bedaux (after whom schemes were named) introduced points-earned systems of this kind.

Measured daywork.   The dissatisfaction with payment-by-results schemes has resulted in a swing towards measured daywork—a half-way stage between daywork payments and payment by results. Much pioneer work was done by the Glacier Metal Company, Mullard and Philips. Each job being performed is allocated a payment category and operatives are paid a consolidated hourly rate between an established maximum and minimum. At fixed regular intervals, the operative's performance is assessed by his superior. The basis of the assessment can include work output, good timekeeping, absenteeism, co-operation, etc. An output rate is established which the operative must achieve, otherwise he is in danger of being taken away from the job. The advantages of measured daywork are that a stable weekly wage is established with a minimum of administrative paperwork. An element of mutual trust is built up which should improve overall morale. As in any other scheme, measured daywork will only be as good as the work measurement which has been undertaken.

36:4   Problems in the use of the techniques and conditions for success

No incentive of any kind will work if it does not motivate people to improve their performance. It is possible (the behavioural theorists say highly probable) that wage incentives alone will not produce desired improvements. The percentage of incentive systems that fail is extremely worrying. The general causes of failure are:

1   Lack of good work study men
2   Lack of an appropriate psychological situation
3   Loose initial standards
4   Changed methods but no change in the scheme
5   Change in conditions which affect the scheme but no change in the scheme itself
6   Inadequate control of quality built into the scheme
7   The excessive payment of "average" bonus for non-earned performance
8   Extravagant allowances for down time, delays, fatigue allowance etc
9   Failure to correct incentive schemes which are obviously not giving appropriate results

To re-emphasise the points made above, wherever the character or nature of the job changes the incentive should be renegotiated.

Once introduced incentive schemes tend to stifle methods study improvement. Technological changes are resisted and the atmosphere created is often one where restrictive practices thrive. There will often be an erosion in supervisory attitudes when incentives are introduced. Incentive schemes tend to produce their own disciplinary element. Machine utilisation, production control, quality may all suffer in consequence. Flexibility should be built into the system. If a factor which was considered important has been built into the system—for example, quality or order priority—but subsequently has grown less important, it should be capable of being struck out of the scheme.

Trouble will certainly accrue if craft differentials are substantially eroded. Each scheme introduced should be unique to the job to which it is applied.

36:5   Conclusion

Many organisations are now looking very critically at their incentive schemes. The achievements of payment-by-result schemes have often been very unsatisfactory. As every scheme has to be supported by an efficient recording and administrative procedure, the burden of clerical and machine work is often considerable. If a multi-factor scheme is in operation this administrative procedure is even more complicated.

The scheme chosen must be appropriate to the work to be performed but more and more the desire to improve morale and to promote good industrial relations leads away from premium bonus schemes towards some form of measured day work. There must be a serious desire by most organisations to stop wages drift and avoid debased standards. The key to improving the basis of incentive schemes lies in a genuine attempt by management to provide an opportunity for employees to earn the same for the same effort. Job evaluation, job descriptions, merit rating and management by objectives, might all have a significant part to play in achieving this happy situation. Straightforward payment by results seems to be on its way out.

36:6 Further reading

1   R M Currie and J E Faraday, *Financial Incentives*, Management Publications, 1970
2   R Marriott, *Incentive Payment Schemes*, Staples Press, 1969
3   LAMSAC, *Questions and Answers About the Introduction of Work Study and Incentive Schemes*, LAMSAC, 1969
4   E C Aylward and J A Mead "What are we paying for? *Work Study and Management Services*, October 1969
5   J E Faraday, "Some Thoughts on Incentives," *Work Study and Management Services*, December 1969
6   V G Reuter, "Misconceptions on Work Study and Wage Incentives," *Journal of Systems Management*, December 1969
7   R Balyeat, The Case for Direct Incentives, *Industrial Engineering* (USA), December 1969

Part 7

AIDS TO
DECISION MAKING
AND PROFIT IMPROVEMENT

Marginal
costing, contribution
analysis and pricing policies

37:1 Introduction

On an apparently diversionary note, some of the characteristics of standard costing and budgetary control need to be first discussed. The basis of normal standard costing systems is that a sales forecast or plan is made, against which a budget of forecast costs is calculated. These costs are usually divided into four distinct types:

1   Direct costs—the costs of machine manning and material etc
2   Indirect costs—costs similar to charge hands, foremen, storemen etc
3   General works overhead—all the costs associated with running and maintaining the plant—insurance, heating, lighting etc
4   Administrative overhead—all costs other than the ones listed above

To oversimplify the situation further, the quoted cost divisions can then be divided between variable and fixed costs. Variable costs are those that vary in some way with the level of output. (Direct labour and material are obviously a good example of these.) Fixed costs are those that remain fixed no matter what level of production is achieved (within limits). Normally an administrative and most of the general works overhead are fixed, within certain policy constraints. The fixed overhead that a company has to bear in order to produce, is absorbed by the cost or production centres which have been set up.

This is total absorption costing. Its major weakness is that if a forecasted level of production activity is being achieved and the total overhead being absorbed, it is likely that extra output will be charged at the same overhead rate. Conversely, and perhaps more important, if a plant is operating at a level of 80 per cent of budget, any new output (sales) gained will automatically carry the fixed overhead rate which has been calculated.

This factor has an extremely important effect on product costing and pricing. Though such costs need not necessarily dictate prices to be charged, in effect they often do. Flexibility in pricing can be inhibited by absorption costing.

37:2   Description

MARGINAL COSTING.   Marginal costing is not a method of costing similar to job or operating costing. It is a technique of looking at fixed and variable costs and seeing how they can affect business operations.

A simple example will show how fixed and variable costs affect company profit.

PRODUCT	SALES	SALES PRICE £	SALES REVENUE £	FIXED COST £	VARIABLE COST £	TOTAL COST £	PROFIT/ LOSS £
1	100	10	1 000	500	600	1 100	− 100
2	100	20	2 000	800	1 200	2 000	—
3	100	30	3 000	1 000	1 800	2 800	+ 200
4	100	40	4 000	1 400	2 400	3 800	+ 200
Total			10 000	3 700	6 000	9 700	+ 300

With a cost evaluation where fixed and variable costs have been ignored, there is a possibility that both products *A* and *B* would be under a sentence of death. Product *A* makes a loss of 10 per cent on its turnover.

The problem is changed significantly when contribution to fixed overhead is considered. Products *A* and *B* contribute £1300 to fixed overhead. Unless such overhead can be eliminated (and in the short term this may be impossible) or if other new products or greater sales of old ones cannot absorb the fixed overhead of £1300, it would be wrong to eliminate products *A* and *B*. A more significant breakdown might be:

	PRODUCT *A* £	PRODUCT *B* £	PRODUCT *C* £	PRODUCT *D* £
Sales revenue	1000	2000	3000	4000
Less variable cost	600	1200	1800	2400
Contribution	400	800	1200	1600
Less apportioned fixed costs	500	800	1000	1400
Operating revenue	− 100		200	200

The apportionment of fixed costs is often an arbitrary decision. The costs rarely relate directly to the products or cost centres which are bearing them. Looking at costs from a contribution analysis viewpoint, therefore, may significantly improve decision making concerned with product change.

The significance should be even greater if a contribution–volume analysis is carried out. For example, the following volume situation might apply in the case of the four products.

ITEM	PRODUCT A		PRODUCT B		PRODUCT C		PRODUCT D	
	£	%	£	%	£	%	£	%
Volume of current production		10		20		30		40
Volume of total factory capacity		8		16		24		32
Contribution	400		800		1200		1600	
Fixed cost	500		800		1000		1400	
RATIOS								
Volume of current production/ contribution		40		40		40		40
Volume of total factory capacity/ fixed cost		62		40		33		36

If one objective of costing is to enable measurements to be made which will help to optimise the use of production capacity, then until such figures (especially the ratios) are available an appropriate appreciation of how production volume generates contribution will be lost.

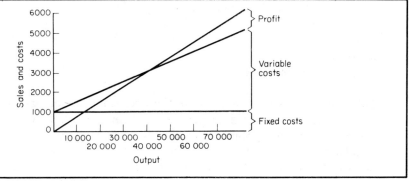

Figure 37.1 BREAK-EVEN GRAPH

Product *A*, which from a standard cost situation might be removed from the product range altogether, actually gains an equal contribution for the company as the other products. The fixed costs allocated in proportion to volume of total factory capacity taken up are nearly twice as much as those given to product *D*.

This is a considerable oversimplification of a complex situation. For example, in the simple illustration given, the allocation of overhead to product *A* may be justified—management skill and time may be being spent at the financial rate shown. The converse may also be true—the method of allocating overhead may be completely unjustified when seen from the viewpoint shown in the illustration.

The break-even analysis graph technique uses a similar approach.

Figure 37.1 shows a normal break-even graph. Fixed costs are first covered, then variable costs. Figure 37.2 conversely covers variable costs first and only then takes account of fixed costs. This will show more clearly that below the break-even point it is fixed costs that are not being covered.

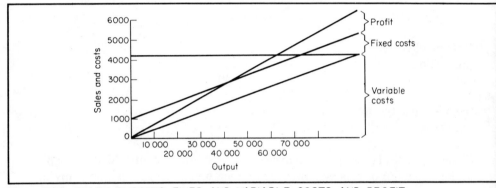

Figure 37.2 GRAPH SHOWING FIXED AND VARIABLE COSTS AND PROFIT

PROFIT—VOLUME RATIOS.   One of the more important ratios to consider in costing is the profit—volume ratio:

$$\frac{S - V}{S} \times 100$$

where S = sales

V = variable costs

The ratio expresses the relationship between contribution and product sales. It measures the change in percentage contribution in relationship with sales volume. The profit—volume ratio, therefore, is the margin left after deducting variable costs from sales volume. The "margin" is expressed as a percentage of the sales value which then becomes the profit—volume percentage of sales. For example:

	PRODUCT A £	PRODUCT B £	PRODUCT C £	PRODUCT D £
Selling price per 1 000	20 000	10 000	200	2 500
Variable cost	12 300	6 750	144	1 625
	7 700	3 250	56	875
P/V ratio	38.5%	32.5%	28.0%	33.5%

Assuming these items represent 90 per cent of the total sales for the month of say £1 000 000 the following method would apply

P/V RATIO

Product A	250 000	38.5%	96 250
Product B	35 000	32.5%	113 750
Product C	100 000	28.0%	28 000
Product D	200 000	33.5%	67 000
	900 000		305 000

$$\text{Average P/V ratio} = \frac{305\ 000}{900\ 000} \times 100$$

$$= 33.9\%$$

Sales for month say	£1 000 000	100%
P/V ratio at 33.9%	339 000	
Less fixed overhead	210 000	
Net profit	129 000	12.9%

As a means of checking on selling prices it is suggested that records should be maintained of past variances of the ratio of the percentage of total standard overhead/sales volume variance. A six months moving average might be useful.

37:3 Successful areas of application and examples

The application of the general principles quoted should help in the following decision making areas:

1   Deciding on products which are making a loss and which in consequence should be eliminated

2   Grading products in terms of their contribution and profitability, so a league table is possible

3   Pricing products generally

4   Helping in marketing decisions, particularly in the allocation of marketing resources, to promote sales. (Differential use of such resources is obviously required)

PRICING.   Pricing is one of the most important factors concerned with marginal costing and contribution analysis. Marketing personnel often suggest that pricing has nothing to do with costing. "The 'market' sets the price" is a common statement.

Pricing cannot be looked at, purely as a means of recovering costs, but equally costs cannot be ignored. Economists have oversimplified the situation by suggesting that sales ought to go on being made (at lower prices if necessary) until marginal cost (the additional cost of producing one extra product) equalled marginal revenue (the additional sales revenue gained by the last item). Where these two factors equate both optimum prices and manufacturing quantities have apparently been established.

Elasticity of demand is the other vital aspect in pricing which classical economists formulated. Elasticity is expressed as $D \div P$ where D = demand motivated by change in price and P = price of one unit of sales. If demand is greater than 1, price elasticity is considered to be good; if less than 1, poor. If a product has good price elasticity, a higher price may decrease total revenue; if poor, higher revenue may be earned.

However, both the MC = MR and the elasticity concepts can rarely be applied to a single company or a single product. Market forces will dictate otherwise. (Is the market competitive or non-competitive?) Even so, the maximisation of sales revenue and minimisation of cost is the simple main aim of pricing strategy.

A good estimation of future demand is vital to any product pricing decision, particularly the demand curve at various price levels. Experimentation may be the only way of achieving such data, though on a large scale such experiments may produce retaliation from competitors.

Such demand–price equations can also be determined statistically and the least-squares and multiple-regression-analysis techniques have been utilised for this purpose.

However, the marginal cost approach comes closest to providing an answer to pricing problems. In the long run, contribution theory should probably be utilised as a means of optimising the situation.

CONTRIBUTION PICTURES.   Contribution pictures is a program package developed by the Central Management Services department of ICI. [See article by T E Heywood: "Contribution Pictures Can Tell the Basic Story," *Management Accounting*, November 1971.] It produces graphically, financial data for use in marketing and financial control. Two log scales are set up as axes, the Y scale represents the contribution per unit and the X axis represents the volume sales in whatever units are used. Against these axes profit contours can be drawn as straight lines at 45° to the X and Y axes. (If log scales were not used these profit contours would be hyperbolas.)

So using the log scales, the total contribution from any product can be represented on the graph by a single point. The effect of increasing sales or contribution by a fixed percentage can be immediately seen. This could save long arduous arithmetic calculation.

Also on the contribution picture produced by the computer, various lines have been added. These lines indicate the various aspects that may be considered important by management. For example, the minimum profitability indicator which will show the minimum contribution from a particular product may be demanded; or upper profitability indicator which indicates those customers generating more than 80 per cent of the total "contribution" of the company.

Whether contribution pictures are used or some other method is devised to show contribution factors the contribution/production volume ratio is the key both to assessing product profitability and testing prices which are being changed. However, the market and competitive situation will determine how far price changes can be pushed. Change may be impossible. The ease at which change can take place will depend upon:

1   Whether the product is a price leader
2   The price/promotional situation. Has the product any intrinsic qualities that will induce purchase despite price (quality is one, advertising, the sales network, service are others)?
3   How competitive is the market? Market research should help to determine how much business could be gained or lost through price changes—elasticity of demand is a factor
4   What pricing strategy is required? Is it to maximise sales revenue, optimise profit, undercut competition, skim various segments of the market etc?
5   Credit terms and pricing are often complementary. A high price may be offset by a long credit period. (With interest rates at, say, 10 per cent, a three month credit period is equal to a price discount of 2.5 per cent)
6   If a product is to be dropped or its volume reduced can the freed resources be used to bring about a much higher total contribution
7   Are all resources being used to produce maximum contribution now. If not pricing changes may help

37:4   Problems in the use of the techniques and conditions for success

The application of the principles discussed in this chapter will in many circumstances be extremely difficult. If a good system of process or operating costing is in existence, especially if it is based on standard costs, the basis for marginal costing and contribution analysis will have been made. But to be completely accurate may be impossible. Even so it will be very useful to attempt the exercise as in no other way will an appropriate view of contribution be gained.

The value of the techniques will depend upon the situation in the company. For example, has all production been absorbed or is a percentage unused which could be usable in the near future. The former situation will demand a product mix review; the latter might motivate pricing policies which gain marginal revenue.

The break-even chart lacks precision as a decision weapon, but should be used as an overall view of possible product–profit performance. The factors which need to be considered in such charts are:

1   That all costs—fixed, variable, semi-variable and also revenue are linear, throughout the entire range. This is untrue in most cases
2   Similarly, the chart assumes that variable costs vary in direct proportion with fixed costs. This is unusual
3   Selling prices, production efficiency and productivity should also remain static no matter what production levels are reached. Not a probable situation
4   The analysis should be of a single-product company or a company where the sales mix will remain unchanged during the life-span of the chart
5   In total, volume is the only variable on the chart

Contribution analysis is stressed as being a useful way of determining product profitability and the start of an amendment to pricing strategy.

37:5   Conclusion

It is much too easy to utilise a "full" costing system and make decisions concerning product profitability, etc. This outline suggests that such a system is weak when making decisions concerned with product pricing and pricing strategy generally.

Utilising marginal costing alone for this purpose could be just as dangerous. In the long run, selling prices must cover not only marginal costs, but also fixed costs and profit.

37:6   Further reading

1   Marginal Costing, *Institute of Cost and Works Accountants*, 1961
2   *Profit Volume Decisions*, Queensland University.
3   S A Tucker, *The Break-Even system*, Prentice Hall, 1964
4   H Dugdale, "Marginal Costs and P/V Analysis." *The Commercial Accountant*, January 1971
5   H Dugdale, "Aspects of Marginal Costing," *The Commercial Accountant*, August 1969
6   R May, "Pricing Policies and Corporate Strategy," *Long-Range Planning*, June 1970
7   T S Dudick, "Alternative Costing Methods for Reporting and Pricing Purposes," *The Journal of Accounting* (USA), October 1969
8   A J Bergfeld and others, *Pricing for Profit Growth*, Prentice Hall, 1962

Decision theory

━━━━━━━━━━━━━━━━━━━━━━━━━━━━━━━━━━━━

38:1 Introduction

A decision is usually a conscious choice between one or more alternatives. Decision theory has been developed (and is still developing) to help in this choice.

Most techniques aid decision making in some way. Few help in formulating a decision making framework that will guide managers in arriving at optimum solutions to problems in general.

Regrettably, emotional and environmental conditioning tend to destroy objective decision making. Against such pressures, decision theory battles in vain.

38:2 Description

Decision theory is a technique of structuring problems so that managers are helped in choosing between alternatives. The structure is basically a simple one which most line managers ought to utilise, though it should not be necessary to structure all problems in the way proposed. Most minor problems can be left to intuition and experience often constrained by the limited data which is available. But there are large numbers of decisions which should be so structured. For example, all major tactical and all strategic decisions should utilise the technique.

The proposed structure (now generally accepted) is as follows.

Define the problem. This may be more difficult than it sounds. What objectives are to be achieved? Do any of these clash with each other? How will the solution be judged? Is it possible to judge it quantitatively and not emotionally?

Obtain all relevant data. Once objectives have been decided appropriate data will be necessary. As constraints and other aspects of decision making are recognised, data requirements might change.

Data collection could be an extremely lengthy process, often expensive and on most occasions boring. If senior personnel are concerned with it, it could be the most expensive part of the decision making technique.

Identify all the constraints which will inhibit decision making. These will largely be concerned with company style, past decision making techniques, the risks which it is reasonable to take considering the company's environment and the competence of the staff involved with the application of the decision. Resources and the lack of them will also have a potent effect on the decision; as will the state of technology especially inside the company.

Record the decision alternatives in as much detail as possible. Creativity may have to be used (and so creative people must be involved with the decision making process). Conversely if the decision alternatives are well known and of a standard technological base, then decision makers can remain non-creative.

Calculate the value of the alternatives, recording the probable outcome of each one. During this process the key uncertainties should be recognised. Each outcome will depend upon chance variables—which may or may not impinge upon the result of the alternative being taken.

If possible these variables should already have been subjected to sensitivity and risk analysis (see Chapter 44 for a description of these techniques). Each outcome can then be assessed probabilistically, perhaps with a risk profile.

Choose one alternative from the several that have been stipulated. The choice should be made by using some decision making criteria. The best fit between decision and objectives to be obtained, when all constraints and probabilities have been taken into account, is usually the alternative to take.

The important factor in decision theory is that the process is formalised. Each step is recorded in detail. As far as possible, emotion and prejudice are eliminated.

38:3   Successful areas of application and examples

Decision theory has had a far from universal application. It has been mainly used in capital investment and marketing decisions. In marketing, new product development, sales promotion alternatives, pricing and test marketing decisions have mostly been covered. Decision making is developing into two different branches.

Behavioural decision theory. This focuses attention on how decisions are made in real-life situations. This part of the main theory attempts to include all the behavioural problems with which decision makers are faced. Situations which have been recorded include two people bargaining over a price and the betting activity of a group of people. As such case histories are built up it is hoped that behavioural decision theory will become more practical.

Normative decision theory. This branch deals with the decision making that should lead to the optimisation of situations. Whether such decisions can be wholly normative, as mathematicians suggest, is doubtful. All problems seem to have some behavioural content and ignoring this will lead to a biased result. The fact that even in normative decision theory, most solutions are probabilistic—i.e. the outcome is probable not certain—and not deterministic, only adds more confusion.

Model making in its widest definition has been the tool most used in solving problems by the normative method. Mathematical programming will usually give apparently optimum answers in normative decision theory. Linear programming has been used in transportation and depot siting problems. Integral equations and Markov chain analysis has been developed to solve queueing problems. Dynamic programming has been used for problems involving the optimisation of functions with many variables.

Decision trees have been used where a series of segments make up a total decision. This is a useful graphical technique which provides flexibility in situations that demand the structuring of problems in the form of numerous branch alternatives. The alternatives are usually quoted on the left side of the chart. Branches are then used to show the possible events which could follow the making of a decision. Where each branch leaves a main stem, a decision node occurs.

Where the comparison between alternative decision probabilities is required, the outcome can be assessed by adding together all the decision node results. This will usually be done by "rolling back" from the terminal decision and adding together all the benefits of making the decision.

38:4   Problems in the use of the technique and conditions for success

Despite the use of more and more techniques in management theory, decisions, regretfully, are still mostly the result of conditioning by history, environment and company style. The following situations are examples of the behavioural problems that bedevil decision making of any kind:

1   Organisational influences.   An organisation is a social institution with its own concepts of right and wrong, of what must be said and not said, of how far risks can be acceptable and what risks are unacceptable
2   Company style is a powerful pervading constraint on decision making. If "we don't operate that way" is an order from the chairman, it is not really worth pursuing a course that will meet such a rule head on
3   Competence, though not entirely behavioural, has a large behavioural content
4   Habit is a significant factor in making a "programmed decision." Judgement, intuition and creativity are not often allowed full rein
5   Most fairly routine decisions are conditioned by the operating systems that are in existence

Decisions are still likely to be dependent upon the subjective analysis of the likely outcomes of making the decision. This is not a particularly scientific way of deducing the results of an alternative. The line managers who have always made poor guesses at decision outcomes, will probably go on making poor guesses despite the addition of quantification.

Data must be adequate. Any solution can be invalid if insufficient or wrong data has been collected.

Decision theory will not work where senior managers are not convinced of its value. Decision making has long been the prerogative of the intuitive manager or the "guestimator." Any change that introduces constraints on decision free-wheeling will generate some resentment.

38:5   Conclusion

This brief review of decision theory indicates that a structured approach to the problem should aid managers. It is certainly one technique which needs more development. As pointed out in 38:4, decisions are still largely emotionally motivated. Any formalisation of decision making should be of benefit.

Competing alternatives should be discussed more objectively in decision theory. It should also motivate a desire—and action—to obtain all relevant data before a decision is made.

38:6   Further reading

1   *BBC Decision Making*, transcript of a BBC Third Program series, 1969
2   H Biermann and others, *Management Decision Making*, Penguin, 1969
3   R B Bannerjee, *Theory of Problem Solving*, Elesevies, 1969
4   W T Greenwood, *Decision Theory and Information Systems*, Edward Arnold, 1969
5   E W Martin, *Mathematics for Decision Making*, A Programmed Basic Text, volumes 1 and 2, Lyon and Grant Ltd, 1969
6   P G Moore and S D Hodges (editors), *Programming for Optimal Decisions*, Penguin, 1969
7   Rex V Brown, "Do Managers Find Decision Theory Useful?" *Harvard Business Review*, May–June 1970
8   M Alexis and C Z Wilson, *Organisational Decision Making*, Prentice Hall, 1967
9   W Emory and P Niland, *Making Management Decisions*, Houghton Mifflin, 1963

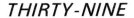

THIRTY-NINE

Management by objectives

39:1 Introduction

Management by objectives is a method of management and not a technique as such. It has been and still is confused with the system of profit planning. A better term for the method might be "management accountability."

39:2 Description

Management by objectives has been described as a management method whereby the main corporate objectives of the organisation—profit, growth, market shares, and major standards of performance—are set out in such a way that individual management objectives can be established which will ensure that the main corporate objectives are achieved. Many organisations believe that they already operate in this way. What MBO does is to formalise the whole procedure.

The objectives of each manager are generally agreed once appropriate job descriptions have been established and all constraints that will inhibit objective achievement have been recognised. The original concept decreed that MBO would largely be participative—managers having the opportunity, if not the right, to debate and, perhaps, reject them. Motivation to achieve objectives, it is thought, has always stemmed from participation. Added to this there must be a salary–reward structure geared to the achievement of objectives—i.e. the system of appraisal must be based on MBO.

JOB DESCRIPTIONS. Any attempt to introduce MBO will nearly always unearth unclear and ambiguous job descriptions. Job descriptions of a type may exist, but inevitably they will have to be rewritten. Responsibilities will be blurred; special company arrangements may have been made that will impinge on resource control, bringing numerous constraints that will inhibit objective establishment.

One of the first activities in applying MBO, therefore, will be to appraise job descriptions so that appropriate objectives can be established at each managerial level. It will be necessary to indicate the degree of responsibility for:

1   Decision making—plans and company development, specific functions and operations
2   Certain personnel—their functions and operations
3   Equipment—machinery, buildings, stocks or money
4   Any other responsibilities, either in full or shared—if it is not possible to avoid sharing

The constraints imposed on decision making and the limitations implicit in carrying out the functions and operations must be stated clearly and taken into account when objectives are established.

SETTING OBJECTIVES.   There are two major problems in establishing objectives:

1   At what management level should the responsibility for specific objectives be established?
2   What kind of objectives need to be set?

The role of the chief executive will largely determine what policy decisions are or are not given to line management. Policy, in this instance, is defined as those decisions that vitally affect corporate profit making operations—particularly those that change the path the company is taking. These decisions will include the role and scope of the company, the products or services it sells, the organisation's capital structure, various important trade-offs concerning immediate profit *v* growth, etc.

All these decisions have a long-term impact on the company and are strategic and not tactical. They can be reversed but only in the long term. Other decisions that should be taken out of the hands of local line management are those that cover more than one department or function, factory or operating unit, for example: those affecting promotion and salary levels, decisions affecting morale and personnel motivation, items of a confidential nature, major items of capital expenditure, etc.

What objectives need to be set? Every area in the company should be given some objectives. Managers, departments, functions should all be judged on the contribution each makes to company profit. Often objectives in consequence will need to be extremely detailed.

A danger might exist that there will be a superfluity of objectives. Too many could be as bad as too few. It is important, therefore, that only the most important or key results are initially established.

KEY RESULTS. A key result is one that will have a decisive impact on the ability of the organisation to meet its major corporate objectives. A key result for a line manager is one that will have a decisive impact on the achievement of the objectives agreed for him. These definitions indicate that:

1 The organisation knows what profit it requires and what key factors must be considered in attempting to achieve it. These key factors relate to costs, turnover and performance achievements of various kinds for the products or service the organisation provides
2 The factors stated in 1 above must be quantified
3 The major factors must be capable of being broken down into local line management objectives, while still retaining the importance of being key results. A hierarchy of key results is therefore established

Once key results have been established it follows that:

1 They should receive priority in the use of management time and organisational resources
2 Though they relate to jobs and not job holders they should be used to judge job performance by the holders. Equally, training needs should be based on the success or otherwise of achieving the key results
3 Appropriate control systems should be prepared so that appraisal can be carried out

APPRAISAL REVIEW. An appraisal of management performance is extremely important in MBO. For example:

1 What has the line manager achieved?
2 How far has he failed to achieve his objectives?
3 What reasons for his failure can be given?
4 Are these reasons under the control of the manager?
5 What can be done to correct out of line performance?
a In the short term?
b In the long term?
c For the reasons quoted?
6 List the personal factors that have inhibited the manager from achieving his objectives
7 On the basis of current performance does the manager deserve:
a Promotion
b Demotion
c Training in depth—quote subjects
d Merit increase of some kind
8 Has the manager's performance been discussed with him?
9 If so what was his general attitude towards his performance appraisal?

This minor checklist indicates the kind of performance appraisal usually carried out. There is an obvious link between performance standards training, and the elimination of all factors which inhibit the improvement of performance standards.

39:3   Successful areas of application and examples

MBO has been successfully applied in many companies. Smith's Industries was one pioneer. Mullard Valve Company (now a subsidiary of Philips) was not far behind. GKN Spear and Jackson Sheffield, The Scottish Gas Board and British Leyland are among some of the other users.

John Humble, Director of Urwick Orr and Partners, has been one of the main protagonists of the method in Britain and has written numerous articles and books on the subject.

39:4   Problems in the use of the technique and conditions for success

MBO, like any other behavioural technique, will raise the problem of compatability between corporate and individual objectives. What is needed at corporate level may not necessarily be what a line manager will readily accept. All the indications given by current behavioural science theory point towards giving managers greater job enrichment, if necessary at the expense of the discipline of MBO. But is it possible to have management by participation?

This factor alone could be a potent reason why MBO will not be accepted with any enthusiasm.

Setting performance standards will be a strain for managers who have never had their performance measured before. For many the situation could be completely alien.

Improving managerial performance will not be easily achieved. Something that has eluded many organisations for a long time will not be gained by introducing a new technique. Changes in company style and attitudes, better leadership, substantial pretraining may all be necessary before MBO starts to have any effect at all.

A rigid approach to the establishment of objectives and the setting of key results, may take away any entrepreneurial activity a manager may with success have indulged in.

MBO could establish a rigid uniformity in the jobs which are held. Job descriptions and appropriate objectives may dictate a determination to succeed by one individual at the expense of other line managers' activities. Without some give and take in the proceedings, life could get very difficult.

Too rigorous an analysis may have a diametrically opposed effect to that intended. Morale could suffer dramatically if performance appraisal is not absolutely fair and in line with what is acceptable psychologically.

Setting objectives—even though they may have been discussed—that are beyond the competence of managers to achieve will also have a serious effect on morale and the whole method of MBO will quickly get into total disrepute.

The potential dangers of introducing MBO are therefore very real. It is extremely important that the needs of the company and management are reconciled from the outset. If they are not, MBO will fail as it has in many organisations. Fundamentally, however, there could be too great an emphasis on objectives and not enough on the means of achieving them. If MBO is regarded as part of a profit planning method, this problem need not arise.

As with profit planning the conditions for success are really simple: commitment by the chief executive, management involvement, training to meet objectives, unambiguous aims and strategies.

39:5   Conclusion

The technique of MBO makes explicit what many organisations have never done or have done badly.

It sounds and is simple. Perhaps the protagonists have tried to make it appear too easy to apply, so giving an aura of "there's nothing to it." This does not help others to understand the idea.

My main criticism of MBO is that it has tended to be considered as synonymous with profit planning. This is highly dangerous. Profit planning is a complex methodology of which MBO is only a part. Advocates of MBO should be wary of this failing on their part.

39:6   Further reading

1   J W Humble, *Management by Objectives in Action*, McGraw Hill, 1970
2   W J Redden, *Effective MBO*, Management Publications, 1969
3   J W Humble, *Improving Management Performance*, Management Publications, 1969
4   *Management by Objectives and Target Setting*, Industrial Society, 1969
5   G S Odiorne, *Management by Objectives*, Pitman, 1969
6   Charles H Granger, "The Hierarchy of Objectives," *Harvard Business Review*, May–June 1964
7   Dale D MacConkey, *How to Manage by Results*, AMA, 1965
8   Peter Drucker, *Managing for Results—Economic Tasks and Risk-taking Decisions*, Heinemann, 1964
9   Edward C Schleh, *Management by Results: the Dynamics of Profitable Management*, McGraw Hill, 1961
10   D E Olsson, *Management by Objectives*, Pacific, 1967

Value analysis

40:1 Introduction

Value analysis has suffered in its application as a cost reduction method by being considered a sweeping-up technique. Though first introduced into the USA (in the GE Co) in the 1950s, it has not gained great acceptance in the UK. Other more resplendent methods of reducing costs have been preferred.

Yet in its logic it is similar to budget validation and all the other techniques that use a challenge method to attack costs. Consequently it should appeal to all those who wish to see a logical relationship between money spent and profit earned.

40:2 Description

Value analysis is a questioning technique which helps to ensure that product costs are directly related to the value that is obtained.

Normally, products only are analysed from this value view-point but there seems no reason why any cost situation cannot be challenged in the same way.

A "test for value check" is usually used by a specially selected team, to probe product costs.

40:3 Successful areas of application and examples

The essential factor in carrying out a value analysis assignment is to devise and appropriately use tests for value. These tests are demanding statements that should be used to challenge cost situations.

Many such tests have been devised and an appropriate list is given below, for use in critically analysing a bought-in product to see if its cost can be reduced:

1   Do we really need the item at all?
a   What intrinsic value has it to us in achieving profit?
b   What would be the worst possible event if the item was discontinued?
2*a*   Why is an item of this value required?
b   Is it possible in some way to provide an item of less value that will provide the same or nearly the same (still acceptable) function?
3   What parts in the item can be substituted for standard parts that will be cheaper to make and process?
4*a*   Is anyone else making the item or providing the function more cheaply than we are?
b   Why is this so?
c   Why do we continue to provide such items if we can obtain them elsewhere more cheaply?
5   Are there any parts of the item that are expendable, so that the item will cost less but provide the same service?
6   Have we ever considered:
a   Cheaper materials—e.g. plastic not steel
b   Cheaper labour—standard machine settings etc
7*a*   Has a proper relationship between money spent and profit obtained been established?
b   In profit terms, is the item essential?

Such lists can be extended so that any company operation can be challenged, starting from the effectiveness and efficiency of the canteen to the use of generating equipment to provide power. Value engineering is nearly as popular as value analysis.

Value analysis began by analysing products, particularly in the car industry. It has now been extended to all activities undertaken in a company.

Any company in the United States that wishes to tender for a government contract over £30 000 must prove that they are carrying out value analysis.

Many companies in Britain (particularly engineering companies) have used value analysis and value engineering. Large savings have been claimed.

40:4 Problems in the use of the technique and conditions for success

The use of senior management's time ought to be strictly controlled. Setting up a value analysis committee or team to carry out various investigations might produce a very inferior rate of return on effort expended. Investigations should be chosen with care. It should be known that the result of the investigation could produce major savings.

Accountants, therefore, ought to be members of a value analysis team and costs and profit performance need to be continually before the eyes of the value analysis committee.

A committee might comprise: an accountant, an engineer, a production man, the purchasing manager and someone from the sales force who has knowledge of customer requirements. The essential element in the team is creative thinking about costs, cost reduction and whether the results of the challenge are acceptable. It may be necessary to provide leg-work personnel for the team in the guise of junior managers in the departments where products or activities are being investigated.

An immediate problem will arise concerning the status of the committee. Should it be executive and allowed to impose its findings? The majority of companies that have used value analysis have given their committees executive status, though there must be obvious constraints on how far they can impose their ruling against the wishes of senior managers. (It depends, of course, on the committee's ability to make their decisions totally logical, so that they will be accepted.) This situation will be made easier if a program of work has been laid down, so that everyone knows what is being investigated. An even happier solution might be to ask all senior members of the company to suggest items to undergo value analysis treatment.

In any case a fairly rigorous sieve process should be in operation to eliminate items that will yield little or no reward without too much analytical time being spent on them.

Some relationship should be established between effort expended and results achieved. Appropriate controls need to be established to ensure that the value analysis committee is not another way of wasting managerial time.

40:5   Conclusion

Value analysis is a comparatively simple technique which can be applied to a variety of circumstances. It uses a challenge methodology that can only serve to improve company style and philosophy for the better.

40:6   Further reading

1   Lawrence D Miles, *Techniques of Value Analysis and Engineering*, McGraw Hill, 1961
2   R E Fountain, *The Importance of Value Analysis*, AMA, 1956
3   W D Falcon (editor) *Value Analysis*, AMA 1965

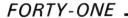

FORTY-ONE

Brainstorming

41:1 Introduction

Brainstorming is a technique with very loose rules of operation, but this brief outline suggests that a formalised approach will provide a greater probability of finding a solution to the problems discussed.

41:2 Description

Brainstorming is a technique for the motivation of free, if not original, thinking, so that problems can be quickly solved and a fund of ideas built up. Its beauty lies in its simplicity.

A group of personnel interested in a particular problem are drawn together and asked to throw out ideas. Two officers are elected. One is a chairman who very gently directs the meeting towards its appropriate objectives. The other is a secretary who will record every idea that comes from the meeting despite the fact that some may be far-fetched, even ludicrous.

The main function of the group meeting will be to throw up ideas, the more the better. Personnel should be encouraged to "free-wheel"—to feel completely free to say anything. All customs, conventions and company ideology should be ignored.

Each idea should be recorded in detail and presented to the appropriate technical and administrative staff in the organisation. The team member making the suggestion should be asked to discuss his proposal with such technical staff who should be prepared to help foster the idea by making drawings, appropriate technical comment, etc.

The next meeting should have a full report on all ideas made at the previous session with the results firmly stated.

Team members must not be upset if their ideas are taken up and processed further by technical staff of various kinds. The brainstorming committee should be set up with this in mind right from the start.

41:3   Successful areas of application and examples

The areas where brainstorming is applicable are numerous. Some are given below:

1   In problem solving generally—for example, in making the inductive leap between the method study analysis of record, examine, etc, and the stages of develop and implement
2   In designing checklists to carry out any of a multiplicity of company activities
3   In considering new strategies for the company to adopt in tackling competition—in the marketing, distribution and production areas, etc
4   In considering new products for the company
5   In searching for R & D activities
6   In assessment of training requirements

41:4   Problems in the use of the technique and conditions for success

If morale is low or if anything hinders the easy flow of ideas and discussion generally, introducing a brainstorming session will have little or no effect. It will not correct psychological and behavioural problems which may be deep-rooted in the organisation.

No one should ridicule any idea that is suggested. People laughed at Galileo. Anyone who is hooted down is unlikely to make any further positive contribution.

Members must be free to express themselves. It is unlikely, therefore, that personnel of considerable difference in status should be collected together. Members should be selected on the basis that they will not be inhibited in any way from expressing their opinions and giving ideas.

Each brainstorming session should be limited to one subject. Two or more subjects will disperse effective thought and a disparate result will occur.

41:5   Conclusion

It is often difficult to gather together personnel with flair, imagination and intuition. Brainstorming is one way in which ideas that might otherwise be lost can be taken up and channelled so as to provide the ability for the company to take them up.

41:6   Further reading

1   P I Slee Smith, *Think Tanks and Problem Solving*, Business Books.
2   "New Ways to Find New Ideas," *Time,* February 1957
3   Charles Clark, *Brainstorming,* Doubleday, 1958
4   H Sasson, "A Think-Tank Approach to Business Planning, *Management by Objectives,* July 1971

FORTY-TWO

Project evaluation and control

42:1 Introduction

Perhaps the most crucial factor in guaranteeing the future profitability of a company lies in the decisions concerning how capital expenditure is agreed and controlled. The quality of managerial decisions associated with new investment is vital in achieving high future growth and performance.

Once such decisions appeared to be deceptively simple. A project had to pay for itself within X years otherwise it was rejected. This approach is still utilised in many successful companies. Yet increased sophistication in management decision making generally has had its effect on project evaluation and control. Discounted cash flow and sensitivity techniques have been formulated to carry out a more rigorous evaluation of how money is to be spent on new investment. Even so (as will be discussed later) these techniques have serious weaknesses.

42:2 Description

A capital expenditure decision is a commitment of resources in the hope that the gain achieved will be commensurate with:

1   The risk involved
2   The borrowing rate of money
3   The taxation involved
4   The objectives of the company in terms of:
a   Growth
b   Profitability

c   Diversification

d   Market share—etc

5   The opportunities that the company has in other investment areas—i.e. other opportunities that may have to be foregone. These will largely be trade-offs that face the company decision makers

6   To improve the company's competitive position and ensure its long-term survival—e.g. by decreasing company vulnerability to technological change, substitution of all kinds and obsolescence generally. Improving company competence in some field may be a potent reason for the investment. Computers could perhaps be seen in this light

It is possible that a too restricted view of capital expenditure decisions will be taken—for example, the discounted cash flow technique has reached an extremely wide usage. Yet applied narrowly this technique sets out only to evaluate the difference between cash in and outflows in a mathematical way and it is quite possible for all the underlying data requirements—impact on market share, cost reduction, etc—to be ignored. Even with the use of sensitivity analysis, DCF may still be pursued as a series of mathematical equations.

Capital expenditure ought to be a concomittant of a rigorous application of profit planning and corporate strategy. Only when company vulnerability and competence have been assessed and future objectives calculated, is it likely that a coherent strategy for capital expenditure will be formed. Future cash flow needs to be assessed. The various trade-offs that are necessary in choosing between alternative investment decisions have to be set out.

Without such a framework for making investment decisions the time-horizon for capital expenditure will be much too short. *Ad hoc* decision making will predominate. The less valuable of competing opportunities will often be chosen.

It is essential, therefore, that any capital expenditure procedure must be viewed in the long term. A method that reviews each capital investment decision individually has obvious weaknesses. Yet this is what the application of DCF as a technique tends to suggest should happen.

Once agreed and implemented, each decision must be strictly controlled. There is, of course, the view that investment decisions are part of planning methodology and as such they need little post auditing as their control is implicit in making the original decision. There is basic truth in this assertion except profit planning usually has a budgetary control and standard costing mechanism built into the total system. Capital expenditure needs to have an equally detailed control mechanism. Annual, or perhaps six monthly, assessments of actual as opposed to theoretical cash flows are required. Where there is a substantial difference (say, above 10 per cent), detailed explanations of the causes for such variations should be demanded.   .

The results from such control mechanisms ought to be utilised in assessing new capital expenditure proposals. For example, any senior manager who is persistently overoptimistic about his projects should be penalised by having his future capital expenditure requirements more strictly reviewed, and also the required return increased to allow for any inbuilt optimism.

42:3 Successful areas of application and examples

One of the first methods of project evaluation was the "payback system." If a project paid for itself within X years, it was acceptable. While this worked very well when a short time span was used (say, three years) it became progressively less so, the longer the investment period.

For example, if seven years were the payback period utilised, the money gained in the seventh year would be considered to have equal value with that achieved in the first year of the project's life. Obviously this is not true. Money gained in the first years could be reinvested and a further return gained.

Another failing of the payback system was that it was very difficult to calculate objectively the value of one project when compared with another.

The important element introduced by the discounted cash flow method was that less value was placed on cash inflow the more distant in time it was to be achieved. It did this by discounting the cash flow—i.e. an appropriate weighting in terms of their comparative value was given to each year. For example, if a project was required to produce a 9 per cent return after tax over ten years, the first year's return is at unity, but each subsequent year is weighted less and less until the tenth is multiplied by a figure of 0.422.

The project is discounted at a fixed target percentage return (9 per cent) in order to determine a "present value." The original capital sum can be deducted from the present value so producing a net present value (NPV). The NPV indicates (after X years) how valuable to the company the project will be and is therefore a useful method of comparing alternatives. The DCF can also be used either as a means of assessing the NPV of a project after X years at a given percentage return or alternatively discovering the true rate of return after discounting has taken place.

It is more usual to have a target or cut-off rate (usually based on current borrowing rates) than to rely on a "resulting rate."

DCF forms will usually contain most of the column headings listed below:

1   The year, starting with the year that any cash flow (in or out) commences
2   A description of the item. (It may be categorised so that a particular discount rate is applicable. For example, machinery may have a much higher discount rate than buildings—i.e. the latter having a much longer payback period
3   The anticipated life of the asset
4   If a target rate is used, the yearly discounting rates

Subsequent columns may be divided between cash outflow and inflow and a valuation or NPV. Under cash outflow will be:

1   The project's capital value and how it is to be paid for:
a   By equal payments
b   By one payment
c   Rent
d   Lease

2   Discounting rates and the valuation will also be shown
3   Cash inflow columns should show:
a   Investment grants
b   Net profit or cost savings before depreciation
c   Savings from tax allowances—from which corporation tax will have to be deducted; the result must be discounted
d   Proceeds of the sale of the assets at the end of the payback period

Various tables have been published which aid the calculation of net present values. [For example, A L Kingshott, *Investment Appraisal*, Ford Business Library; R B Jones, *DCF Tables of Present Value*, Technical Press.]

PROJECT EVALUATION MODEL MAKING. The characteristics of the capital investment decision—the need for alternatives to be specified and evaluated, the testing of projects against a desired return, the use of sensitivity analysis in considering various values of data to be used—all make a reasonable basis for model making. Indeed ICL have a capital evaluation model—PROSPER—which carries out an evaluation of making various investment decisions.

The system of screening and evaluating competing projects will only be as good as the profit planning and corporate strategy techniques that the company employs. These will:

1   Establish the company environment
2   Suggest desired returns on investment from new projects
3   Give all the constraints that will inhibit investment—cash flow from current investment etc
4   List the likely projects which the company should pursue, including their cost and various methods of funding them

The model, therefore, evaluates the projects it has been given against the ROI criteria; at the same time it takes account of all the constraints that profit planning and corporate strategy techniques suggest. The data given to the model will need to be reviewed carefully and normally sensitivity analysis (a technique that uses various possible outcomes from the data given in order to identify key results and possible areas where a forecast could go astray) will also be used.

The result will be a ranking of the projects in terms of their potential value in achieving corporate objectives as well as a straight screening process. A potential cash flow forecast over the lives of the projects will also be made.

Where numerous projects have to be reviewed and sufficient data is available from corporate strategy and profit planning, financial modelling of the type briefly outlined is strongly recommended.

CONTROL MECHANISMS. A suitable control mechanism should provide the following major factors:

1   Appropriate objectives for personnel involved
2   Budgets of cost performance

3   Appropriate timescales for evaluation–review purposes
4   Method for collecting actual data so that a comparison with standard is possible
5   A reporting mechanism that shows the actual result for each objective or budgeted cost
6   The ability for personnel whose objectives have not been achieved to comment on their performance and suggest their corrective action

Targets should be provided for the personnel who submitted the original request for capital which matches the rate of return required. The audit-control system should provide senior management with sufficient data to ensure that a project is proceeding satisfactorily or if not that suitable corrective action is taking place. If such corrective action is not possible, then a suitable report on the changed circumstances must be made. Control should be an educational process, through which it will be possible to make better investment decisions in the future.

42:4   Problems in the use of the technique and conditions for success

No technique, least of all DCF, will have any value if data supplied to it is not accurate. DCF is an extremely valuable financial tool, but someone (perhaps personnel other than accountants) needs to evaluate the data that accompanies the request for capital expenditure. It is extremely easy to provide figures that give an appropriate return. It is often difficult to refute their accuracy, but some challenge should be made to them.

An investment decision demands data that only a sophisticated market research and management information system generally will be capable of supplying.

Objectives should be known; market research in depth carried out; technological research completed; financial analysis undertaken—only then should an investment decision be considered.

Undoubtedly one investment decision should not be treated in isolation. Each demand for company money ought to be viewed as a request for the use of scarce company resources. As such, capital investment decisions are competitive.

Only if profit planning is well developed will the appropriate data be available for an evaluation of competing projects. Consider, for example, the following information which is the least that will be needed.

1   Objectives—profit, turnover, market share, competitive ability, long-term survival, cost of production, now and in the future, etc
2   Company resources and vulnerability.   Competence to install new plant, buildings, factories, etc
3   Selling prices.   What future selling prices are possible? Competition, environment, technical change, must all be taken into account

4   The investment. Is it the best buy—technically, from a maintenance point of view, from a cost situation? How is the investment to be funded?

5   Residual value of the investment

6   Performance. What performance is required from the investment? What work measurement, market research, other measurement activities have been carried out?

7   The risks involved. How have these been assessed?

Only consideration of company strategies for long-term survival will truly answer a request for some of the data outlined.

The use of target rates of return implies that a company has unlimited funds available for capital expenditure. The target return is often used as a sieve through which projects have to pass. If they do, it is assumed that unlimited finance is available at that price. In practice this cannot be so. There is a limit to a company's borrowing capacity or ability to generate cash flow for investment purposes. There should therefore, be a limit to capital investments depending upon their number, value and current borrowing rates. The target rate should logically be changed constantly or it should be abandoned altogether in favour of an annual capital project plan. The formalising of strategies provides the only environment where such an annual appraisal can effectively be carried out.

The use of target returns over five to seven years operates against the basis on which DCF was designed. For example, two projects could have the same resulting total of discounted cash flows over seven years. Consequently the projects would appear to have the same attraction. But it is impossible to be indifferent to the rate of cash flows. The evaluation method should discriminate between early and late cash flows and the rate of cash flows should be discounted so that projects where variable cash flows occur can be compared.

DCF or any other investment evaluation technique should always take account of the risks involved in the project. Discrimination between high- and low-risk decisions is essential. A universal application of a standard required rate of return, no matter what the project, what part of the company it is required for or how well or badly it is likely to be managed, will inevitably be wrong.

High risk is usually associated with new fields of activity, insufficient research data, superior competition, inferior company competence and an uncertain technological base. Likely high risk projects can easily be recognised, therefore, and a suitably high return on investment should be demanded.

42:5   Conclusion

Too often investment decisions are based on mythology, hunch, bias and the strength of one powerful manager. How many times is it remarked that "forecasts are impossible in this situation."

Control of capital expenditure must result as much from appropriate attitudes of mind as from data and the application of an appropriate methodology.

The aim of any investment appraisal system should be to make all management take a responsible and well-considered view of a situation where emotion has often ruled.

42:6 Further reading

1   L E Rockley, *Capital Investment Decisions*, Business Books, 1968
2   E C Townsend, *Investment and Uncertainty*, Oliver & Boyd, 1969
3   A L Kingshott, *Investment Appraisal*, Ford Business Library, 1965
4   A J Merritt and A Sykes, *The Finance and Analysis of Capital Projects*, Longman, 1965
5   A J Merrett and A Sykes, *Capital Budgeting and Company Finance*, Longman
6   R M Adelson "Discounted Cash Flow—a Critical Examination," *Journal of Business Finance*, Summer 1970
7   A R Megarry, "The DCF Method of Capital Expenditure Appraisal," *Cost and Management* (Canada), September/October 1969
8   A M Alfred and J B Evans, *Appraisal of Investment Projects by Discounted Cash Flow*, Chapman Hall, 1965

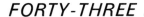

FORTY-THREE

Risk and sensitivity analysis

43:1 Introduction

All decisions have some element of risk, some more than others. Uncertainty is the key factor, no matter how trivial the decision or how minor the decision's timescale.

The past is often a poor guide to what might happen in the future. Environments change, decision conditions rarely remain static. Each decision will be affected by some undetermined future factor. This is a situation that somehow has to be discounted. Risk and sensitivity analysis have been designed to help with this problem.

43:2 Description

Risk and sensitivity analysis are mathematical techniques that help to evaluate the probabilities and risks associated with decision making.

Decision rules are important in determining what a decision should be, but the inclusion of risk and sensitivity analysis will help to produce a decision that may be not only more accurate, but one where the possible failures have been discounted. Risk and sensitivity analysis could be considered to be an intrinsic part of decision making.

As part of the decision making process it is important that a decision should be broken down into its component parts, each part being reviewed in depth. A decision can then be made for each component part, after which the components can be built back into the whole.

In this way, recognising the key results or most important parts of the decision is facilitated and at the same time an assessment of the probable outcome of the decision components and the total decision is made easier.

This activity forms the base from which the application of risk and sensitivity analysis can be progressed.

43:3   Successful areas of application and examples

The outcome of a decision will always be probabilistic to some degree; nothing can be completely determined beforehand. However, there are decisions that entail little or no risk while others have immense risk. Predicting the weather accurately has a high risk; making a journey to a local shopping centre on foot, a low risk, if one only considers the possibility of being killed while crossing the road. There is a high risk of spending money, however.

It is possible, therefore, to assess the probable outcome of a situation statistically. Past experience or the amount of data collected help to determine the risk involved.

For example, an investment decision could be either a low or a high risk activity depending upon the degree and accuracy of market research carried out, the general competence of the personnel involved, their success at making investment decisions in the past, the environment in which the company operates, the resources available, the technological climate when viewed against the investment being made, the product life cycle situation, etc.

Where few, if any, of these criteria are soundly established, the decision is bound to be a high-risk one, no matter how good the investment appraisal appears to be. The danger in such appraisal techniques as discounted cash flow is that due analysis of the probable risk is not attempted. The acceptance of financial and other data, the discounting of future cash flows and the arrival at a high net present value is very easy, too easy in most instances.

An assessment of the decision's parameters will help in deciding the probable outcome and the risk involved. Inadequate data, a poor record of previous success in decision making should mean a low probability of success, but how low?

M J Moroney, in that excellent Penguin publication *Facts From Figures* (a book that has probably taught more people about statistics than any other), gives the whole of his Chapter 2 to the laws of chance. Unfortunately business life is considerably more complicated than determining the chances of whether a tossed penny will come down heads or tails.

Even Mr Moroney's "empirical probability of an event" where probability equals *total number of occurrences of the event* divided by *total number of trials* is not very relevant.

It assumes that the decision's parameters—environment, competence etc— always remain the same. This may well be so in deciding the probability of pulling a ball of a desired colour from a bag containing a number of different coloured balls, but not in real life.

It is possible to ask knowledgeable managers of the likely outcome of a decision and assess a probability of the outcome from their answers. For example, if ten people were asked to give, in their-opinion, the most likely return on investment before tax on a particular investment, their answers might be as follows:

ROI	NUMBER THAT GUESSED
17%	1
16%	2
15%	3
14%	2
13%	1
12%	1

Such answers could be shown as a frequency distribution as shown: Figure 43.1. What can be assumed from such a frequency curve?

1　The probability of the ROI being between 12 and 17 per cent is 100 per cent
2　The probability of the ROI being between 14 and 16 per cent can be found by measuring the area of the graphical outline between vertical lines when drawn from the two forecast points to the forecast ROI axis (approximately 60 per cent)

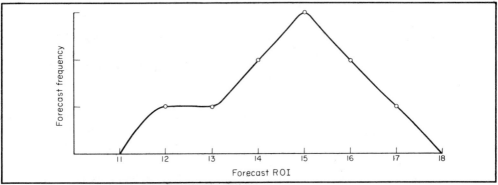

Figure 43.1 FREQUENCY DISTRIBUTION GRAPH

In such an experiment it is important that the assumptions implicit in the estimates can be calculated independently and also that the results can be verified experimentally. Because of the considerable calculations usually needed to carry out such mathematical verification, a short-cut method using random samples taken from the distribution can be utilised. For this a random number generator is required to select forecasts from the distribution ranges and usually (especially where a computer is being used) a Monte Carlo random number selecting technique is used (sometimes dice are used for the purpose).

SENSITIVITY ANALYSIS. As its name suggests sensitivity analysis is concerned with evaluating the various facts or pieces of data on which a decision is based or on which a decision might founder. Sensitivity analysis tests such facts or data, by assuming probable fluctuations in them and tests the assumption on the result. An extremely simple sensitivity table is shown below:

ITEM	PESSIMISTIC	OPTIMISTIC	LIKELY
Cost of investment	£6.2M	£5.6M	£5M
Sales revenue per year	£3.4M	£4.6M	£4.0M
Market share	18%	24%	21%
Manufacturing costs	£1.5M	£1.2M	£1.3M
Admin costs	£0.3M	£0.2M	£0.25.
Plant capacity	60 tons a week	65 tons a week	62 tons a week
Return on investment before tax	23%	30%	24%

The permutations possible between such figures even in a table of such simplicity are considerable.

When a piece of new investment is required or a new product launched, up to a 100 pieces of data may have to be analysed. Often a pessimistic, optimistic and likely table (as in the example) is produced. The analysis should show the variation between items in the three possible outcomes. This should indicate which item is the most important in achieving an optimum result. Company resources can then be channelled towards ensuring that the item or items concerned are achieved as planned.

The table should also indicate which items are important to the result of the project and which are outside the control of the project commanders. The possible effect of such out-of-control items must be known in order to assess the total probability of success. If many important items are out-of-control, then the whole project may have to be abandoned.

Equally, the important items thrown up by sensitivity analysis need to be evaluated against the competence of the individuals that are involved with them. This will help to establish the probability of success.

The control of the project, therefore, should be established according to the relative importance of each data item suggested by sensitivity analysis. The results should show what might be the best course of action and also the decision that the company may have least cause to regret, even if the most pessimistic forecasts actually come true.

43:4   Problems in the use of the technique and conditions for success

Like cost benefit analysis, probability and sensitivity analysis have an aura of scientific accuracy which on investigation does not exist. Probability theory, in particular, relies upon what, in most circumstances, will be the subjective judgement of the same people that may have made poor decisions in the past. This inevitably may nullify the whole technique.

In practice, however, it tends not to. The basis for decision making may be insecure. Probability analysis will often bring this to light. Like decision theory itself, probability analysis helps to bring logic into what might otherwise be a completely emotional situation.

Sensitivity analysis, on the whole, has been more neglected than probability analysis. However, applied with discrimination it has a major role to play in decision making, particularly decisions concerned with capital investment. It should have an integral part to play in investment decision evaluation with the discounted cash flow technique.

Both probability and sensitivity analysis, therefore, are aids to decision making. Like decision theory, they can concentrate the mind logically but they are still no substitute for good data collection and evaluation and skill and experience in the field.

43:5 Conclusion

Probability and sensitivity analysis are both items that need to be used and the results judged. With decision theory, research needs to be carried out upon their value and how this can be improved.

An old cliché on management stated that a manager needed only to get 51 per cent of his decisions right to be successful. What might have been true a generation ago no longer applies. More and more, decisions have to be right all the time, especially major capital investment decisions. Decision theory, probability and sensitivity analysis, if appropriately used, will help to increase the rate of making successful investment decisions, in particular, and major decisions of all kinds.

43:6 Further reading

1   T R Dyckman and others, *Management Decision and Uncertainty*, Macmillan 1968

2   D J Aigner, *Principles of Statistical Decision Making*, Collier Macmillan, 1968

3   D E Farrar, *The Investment Decision under Uncertainty*, Prentice Hall, 1962

4   R B Maffei, "Simulation, Sensitivity and Management Decision Rules," *Business*, July 1958

5   W C House "The Usefulness of Sensitivity Analysis in Capital Investment Decisions," *Management Accounting*, February 1966

6   D B Hertz, "Risk Analysis in Capital Investment," *Harvard Business Review*, January/February 1964

7   W T Morris, *The Analysis of Management Decisions*, Irwin 1964

8   T Lucey, *Investment Appraisal—Evaluating Risk and Uncertainty*, Gee & Co, 1970

Work simplification

44:1 Introduction

Work simplification has many attributes similar to those of method study. While the latter technique is usually applied by professionals, work simplification, like cost reduction planning, should be part of a line manager's life. Of all techniques this is the one that can truly be said to be a do-it-yourself kit. In its application, line managers and supervisors should play the prime role.

44:2 Description

Work simplification is a method of simplifying work and reducing costs by recording and analysing one or a series of operations, and then, by applying a questioning technique and a certain amount of common sense, evolving simpler methods.

The first operation, as with methods study, is to find out what is going on. To do this two records are necessary:

1   What is going on at present
2   How long this now takes to perform

Daily log sheets, filled in by the personnel taking part in the exercise, will solve both of these problems. Each participant should be asked to complete a form with the headings listed below. The form is an "activity log sheet," dated and headed with the name of department and section that is undergoing the simplification.

Next follows the man's name and job title. The man then records the work performed under the following headings:

1   Job duty—e.g. order translation, material allocation, filing etc
2   The category of the job. These are:
a   Repetitive jobs. Entering an item on a stock record card etc
b   Conditional. These are activities that will occur when certain conditions apply—re-ordering a product once a re-order point has been reached etc
c   Contingent. The proportion of repetitive and conditional jobs that give rise to complications—looking for a missing record card etc
d   General queries which arise from carrying out the job duty
e   Special jobs which occur at regular intervals
f   Supervisory or advice giving activities
3   Number of items processed
4   Time taken in minutes
5   Interruptions—telephone calls, general discussions etc

The sheets are usually completed daily and handed to supervisors, who, from their knowledge of the job duly being performed, can check that the form has been completed with the accuracy and detail that are possible.

Once these sheets have been completed, there is a variety of collation, compilation and general analysis that has to be performed. In a clerical operation it might work like this:

1   The easiest and perhaps most effective record of what is happening is a document flow chart. Copies of all documents used are collected, specimen entries made and then the documents are set out to form a wall chart showing how the system operates. This is often a very instructive operation, especially when everyone concerned can view it at a glance
2   The methods study process of charting all operations with symbols should not be ignored, as this too will show weaknesses in the system
3   Various consolidations of job activity will be needed. Function analysis should be tried, for example. This should collect together all operations of the same type—filing, recording, etc—and should lead to suggestions that such operations might be done at the same time, so leading to cost reduction

Work distribution charts are also useful in this field. These show—under various functional headings such as order translation, material allocation, filing, etc—the number of man hours each individual spends on them. This activity highlights duplication and shows which activities can be combined or eliminated. It also pinpoints where highly paid individuals are doing simple, routine jobs.

Movement diagrams are also extremely useful in indicating excess movement and activities carried out in obviously wrong locations. Journey times should be calculated and total non-productive time assessed. Lessening movement is an important element in reducing the complexities of activities.

All this analysis should lead to the consolidation of the following information:

1   What work is done?
a   By definition
b   By category
c   By time
d   By person
2   Where is it done?
a   Location
b   Time
c   Travel distance between activities
3   What activities are productive? Time spent on these
4   What activities are non-productive? Time also spent on these
5   The following should be highlighted:
a   Duplication of effort
b   Effort not commensurate with reward
c   The purpose of documents
d   Indications where work can be simplified

This latter part should be helped by the use of a checklist that the line manager might complete. The following checklist has been designed for the investigation of clerical systems:

GENERAL CHECKLIST

1   Is the organisation correct? Use organisational theory and general precepts for this challenge
2   Is the work load equalised between personnel of the same grade?
3   Is it obvious that every same-grade operation is necessary?
4   What idle time has been found?
5   Are too many clerks doing the same job?
6   Can work be reorganised so that senior personnel do only work for which their seniority fits them?
7   Is more than one record, checking operation or analysis being carried out for the same transactions?
8   Can work-flow be improved by cutting down transfer and movement time?
9   What duplication of effort is obvious?
10   Can handwriting take the place of typewriting?
11   Does each operative fully understand what he is doing?
12   Can peak periods be overcome in some way?
13   Is all equipment useful, in good repair and appropriate to the function it is designed to carry out?

14   Could more equipment be used with benefit?
15   Are operatives well trained?
16   Is interchangeability practised frequently?
17   Can standard forms (especially letters) be used more, so that clerical effort
      can be reduced?

There are five key words in carrying out work simplification analysis: elimination,
combination, reduction, rearrangement and simplification.

Elimination is obviously the most important. If something can be eliminated
then the long search for improvement in an operation is not required. Elimination
should be attempted before simplification or any other of the key challenge
activities.

1   Is the operation necessary?
2   Why is it carried out?
3   What benefit accrues from it?
4   Is it a duplication?
5   Can any of the associated contingency operations or general interruptions
     be eliminated?
6   What does each part of the operation contribute?
7   How many of the filing movements, inspections, etc, can be eliminated?
8   Can any forms be eliminated?

Combination often results from the answers to the questions which begin
where? when? who? Functional analysis often suggests where operations can be
combined.

1   Can any of the operations be combined?
2   Who should do the job?
3   Where is the best place for the total function to be carried out?
4   When should the operation be performed?
5   Are the right people now carrying out the function?

Reduction should be taken into account, when looking at the size of reports or
of documents generally. Reductions in time are important and these should be
looked for diligently.

1*a*   Can any part of the system be shortened or speeded up?
  b   If so, how?
2   Why are so many copies of documents produced?
3   Can these be reduced?
4   Can the size of documents be reduced?
5   Can filing and recording be reduced by using copies of documents stored
     away in order?

Rearrangement. Improvements in a system can also stem from the questions which begin where? when? who?

1 What rearrangement can be carried out in function, location and job duties so as to improve document flow?
2 When should work be done?
3 Where should work be done—in what location?
4 Who should do what work?
5 What is the best sequence of operations?
6 Can work be rescheduled so that bottlenecks are avoided?
7 Can work be issued so that each clerk has a regular work pattern and output to achieve?
8 When is the best time to carry out the operations?
9 Can an operation be simplified by moving it out of its current sequence?

Simplification. When all operations have been carried out, operations can often be simplified, so simplification should be used as a final challenge to current methods of operating practice.

1 What appears to be complex in the activity being performed?
2 Is it possible to eliminate any non-routine work?
3*a* Is it possible to simplify any operations?
 b How?
4*a* Do operatives find difficult any part of the jobs they perform?
 b Why?
5 What parts of the system are obviously wasteful in manpower and other resources?
6*a* Is too much time spent in discussions and interruptions which could be eliminated?
 b If so, how can the job be simplified to enable such elimination to take place?

44:3 Successful areas of application and examples

The technique has been most widely used in administrative/clerical activities, though there is no reason why any operational part of an organisation should not undergo the disciplined recording and analysis of work simplification.

A useful example of the technique in operation was in a sales order processing system. It operated as shown below.

OFFICE	FUNCTION	STAFF	TIME
1 Sales order processing	1 Order receipt, translation and recording	2	Day 1
2 Accounts office	2 Credit control check	1	Day 1

3 Sales order processing	3 Order typed and sets run off	2	Day 2
4 Production planning and control	4 Delivery promises inserted (stock records searched)	1	Day 3
5 Sales order processing	5 Order set completed and issued. Acknowledgement sent to customer	1	Day 4
6 Production planning and control	6 Stock records again searched to confirm if ex stock or to be made by production. Works order set made out	1	Day 5
7 Transport office	7 Transport order set made out. Vehicles ordered for dispatch	2 1	Day 7 (if ex stock)
8 Planning department	8 Mark off production planning records when delivery made	1	Day 8
9 Sales order processing office	9 Mark off office records, send copy of order to A/C's dept	1	Day 9
10 Accounts department	10 Make out invoice	1	Day 10

Set out like this, the system shows immediate defects, but to the local personnel, each function was necessary and the delay in dispatch (even from stock) seemed reasonable in the circumstances.

A project team of local line management supported by MS personnel was set up and the system recorded. Document flow charts, procedure charts, movement diagrams and a time analysis schedule similar to the one above was made.

Some functional analysis was also carried out. The result of the application of work simplification techniques in this case was as follows.

One combined office for sales order processing, production planning and control (including stock control) and transport/distribution was established. The system was amended to:

		TIME
1	Order receipt and translation—record made	Day 1
2	Delivery promise and stock check	Day 1
3	Order set completed including works and transport documentation	Day 1
4	Credit control check carried out (1 order copy to accounts)	Day 1
5	Transport arranged	Day 1
6	Dispatch of goods	Day 2
7	Invoice sent to customer	Day 2

Benefits

1   Reduction in dispatch time from 10 to 2 days
2   Reduction in paper work, filing and record keeping
3   Reduction of staff involved by 45 per cent

The application was in practice more complicated than that outlined, but in principle this makes no difference to how the technique was employed.

44:4   Problems in the use of the technique and conditions for success

Too much emphasis on the technique and not enough on the behavioural problems it raises will certainly not help a successful application. It is a technique that needs the co-operation of staff at all levels and if, in consequence, personnel are made redundant or asked to take less interesting and perhaps less rewarding jobs, then it is not likely that co-operation will be forthcoming.

If work simplification has any element of the suggestion scheme idea in it, then some of the savings that will be made should be passed on to the personnel, at desk or shop-floor level, who have co-operated in the assignment.

If suggestion schemes have been tried and no suggestions made, it is unlikely that work simplification will have great success. It needs high morale and good co-operation from staff.

It has been proved, however, that where straightforward professionally applied method study has failed to produce expected savings, work simplification carried out in the same area has done so. In work simplification, the professional management services team should remain strictly in the background. They should do some of the charting, give advice when requested, perhaps even help with the analysis, but their role should be passive, if possible a hidden one.

Communication in its widest sense is important. Lectures about the technique should be given. Discussions with the local trade unions and worker's representatives should be carried out. Questions of redundancy, retraining, new job opportunities should all be explored and agreed, before the application begins.

Participation is the key to success. Anything that aids this process should be welcomed. Brainstorming sessions on potential improvements might be tried. More detailed checklists than the ones given in this chapter might be evolved.

The way work simplification has been sold to participants is by suggesting that:

1   There will be no redundancies
2   Some benefits of the exercise will accrue to those taking part in it
3   More meaningful work will result from the exercise—i.e. the rearrangements which will follow from the analysis should result in everyone doing a worth-while job, with nobody repeating what someone has done already or carrying out some activity which has little or no value

This latter point has greater attractions for most people than the cynics in management might think.

					Date
Name H Rogan			Section / department Production planning and control		
Activity	Job category	Number of documents processed	Time taken	Interruptions	
1 Program detailing	1	1	4hr	Discussion with works personnel 1½hr	
2 Filing	2	54	½hr		
3 Control meeting	1	-	½hr		

This sheet should be completed daily and given to supervisor

Figure 44.1 ACTIVITY LOG SHEET

44:5 Conclusion

The benefits from a work simplification exercise should not only be in monetary and efficiency gains. If appropriately applied, and staff are totally involved as they should be, then a legacy of friendliness, mutual co-operation, team work and improved human relationships should also follow.

However, if work simplification has been applied badly and staff ignored, or the gains ultimately made are abrogated entirely by management, then the result could be the reverse. Morale will worsen, enmity, not co-operation, will predominate; short-term savings will be made; long-term benefits will be negligible.

Section Sales order processing		Week ending 1/7/73			Names						
	Total	HAMMOND D	HANKIN G	FORSYTH E	ADAMS A	DEAR D	GAWTHROP P	SMITH S	COOPER E	WARREN S	DIXON V
Order translation	18	6	6	6	6	0	0	0	0	0	0
Credit checking	18	0	0	0	0	6	4	2	2	2	2
Order pricing and coding	63	10	10	10	6	6	7	7	7	0	0
Customer contact	138	24	24	24	24	12	10	6	8	4	2
Total	380	38	38	38	38	38	38	38	38	38	38

Figure 44.2 WORK DISTRIBUTION SHEET

44:6   Further reading

1   Robert N Lehrer, *Work Simplification—Creative Thinking about Work Problems*, Prentice Hall, 1957
2   Herbert F Goodwin, "Work Simplification: an Effective Program of Improvement," *Advanced Management*, Volume 22 January 1957
3   W L Wallace, *Work Simplification*, Systems and Procedures Association
4   C O Reynolds, *Work Simplification for Everyone*, Pyramid, 1954
5   Oliver Standingford, *Simplifying Office Work*, Pitman, 1964

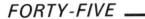

FORTY-FIVE

Motion study

45:1   Introduction

Work study, the early pioneers in the subject stated, was a combination of methods study and work measurement. A large element in the methods study section was motion study. Some practitioners have used methods and motion study as synonymous terms. This chapter suggests that motion study is only a part (and sometimes not a very important part) of methods study.

It is unlikely that a motion study exercise will ever be conducted in isolation from all the other elements that make up work study.

45:2   Description

The Gilbreths first defined motion study as "the science of eliminating wastefulness resulting from using unnecessary, ill-directed and inefficient motions." The aim of motion study is to find and perpetuate the scheme of least wasteful methods of labour.

The principles of motion economy were also established by the Gilbreths and the following list is a summary of their findings:

1   The hands of operatives should begin and end their activity at the same time and should also work simultaneously
2   Hands, if possible, should not be idle at any time during the work cycle, or, if this is impossible, only one hand should be idle
3   The method of operation should have as few motions as possible
4   Hands should not work if other body members can perform the task—so long as the hands have other work to do

5   The tools, jigs, fixtures, work to be performed, etc, should be so located that hands have to travel the minimum distance. At the same time, the work activity, and especially the work place should be so organised that smooth, uninterrupted movement is possible. Repetitive rhythm should be the aim, with sympathetic motion

6   Only natural movements, as far as possible, should be made. Excessive strain or effort whether of arm or eye should be avoided

7   Motions of the arms should be in opposite and symmetrical directions instead of in the same direction and should be made simultaneously

8   Hand motion should normally be confined to the lowest satisfactory classification—i.e. in ascending order:

a   Finger motions

b   Finger and wrist motions

c   Finger, wrist and forearm motions

d   Finger, wrist forearm and upper arm motions

9   Whenever possible, momentum should be used to assist the worker in the task being performed

10 The need for "eye fixations" should be the minimum—none if possible

11 The worker should not, if possible, use the trunk of the body to perform operations

12 Drop deliveries should be used where possible

13 The height of the work place should be flexible; allowing changes in operator and jobs being performed, also for sitting and standing positions

14 Tools used most frequently should be positioned closest to the operator. Pre-positioning of all tools is important

15 The skills in the job should be reduced to the minimum

16 Mechanical devices should be used to eliminate any "hold" situations

17 All tools should be so designed that maximum hand contact is possible

18 All tools, work areas, etc, should be so positioned that only normal working areas for arms and hands are utilised

19 Chairs of appropriate height and type to permit good posture should be used

20 Handles, foot pedals, tools, etc, should be designed to permit the fewest number of muscle groupings to be used for activating them

The normal working area for a person of approximately 1.75m (5ft 9in) high and with an arm length of 61cm (24in) is as follows.

The area for the lower arm is an arc approximately 35cm (14in) from the body for each arm. The outer limit arc will be approximately 66cm (26in) forward from the body. The total work area will be 1.2m × 35cm (47 × 14in) for the inner arc and 1.75m × 66cm (69 × 26in) for the outer arc.

45:3   Successful areas of application and examples

The application of motion study follows the normal method study pattern:

1   A job is chosen and objectives laid down
2   The job is analysed and the basic motions identified
3   The motions are recorded
4   Search is made for better or more economical motion patterns, following an examination of the recorded motions
5   The better motions are developed
6   Implementation takes place

OBJECTIVES.   It is very easy to utilise motion study and save a fractional part of an operative's time. If the time saved can be utilised for further productive work, all is well. Often the worker is on a production line and dependent on others for work input. Saving cycle time in this situation may be valueless.

RECORDING
Therbligs.   A special method of recording motion movements was developed by the Gilbreths. This utilised a series of symbols (see Figure 45.1) which recorded each motion.

These symbols are called *therbligs* (Gilbreth spelt backwards—except for the *th*) and the normal recording media are therblig charts. These provide a symbolic and systematic analysis of the work being performed, mainly being used for two-handed analysis.

Micromotion is a technique that uses a camera to record movements that are difficult to distinguish by visual observation alone. The film is critically examined and a simultaneous or simo-chart is drawn. Therbligs are used for this purpose.

Symbol	Name
	Search
	Find
	Select
	Grasp
	Hold
	Transport load
	Position
	Assemble
	Use
	Disassemble
	Inspect
	Pre-position
	Release load
	Transport empty
	Rest for overcoming fatigue
	Unavoidable delay
	Avoidable delay
	Plan

Figure 45.1 LIST OF THERBLIGS

Memomotion also uses a ciné-camera to record motion cycles. Detail, however, is less than in micromotion. The camera is slowed from approximately sixteen frames a second to as little as one frame a second. The technique is used for analysing longer work cycles and especially activities where teams of up to four operatives are engaged.

Chronocyclograph. This is a technique that was also developed by the Gilbreths, where a light is attached to the middle finger of each operator's hand. A relay is built into the light circuit which flashes the light on and off. A still camera is then used to record both the motion of the operator's hands and to some extent the speed. In the cyclograph technique, the lights are left on continuously and instead of dots of light being recorded, a photograph of continuous white light is taken.

FINDING A BETTER MOTION PATTERN. The conversion of the principles of motion economy into a checklist should help to formulate optimum patterns. Improved motion economy is often achieved by resiting equipment work boxes, jigs, tools, feed trays, etc.

Once operatives have been taught to use both hands simultaneously, they often arrive at optimum motion economy unaided.

VALUE IN USE. The obvious value of motion study lies in the application of the methods–time–measurement of work measurement. In this system it is imperative that motion patterns are recognised so that appropriate job times can be assessed.

45:4   Problems in the use of the technique and conditions for success

As with most techniques where the minutes detail is recorded and analysed, motion study can be used too readily. The application of the work simplification principles—elimination, simplification, reduction, combination or rearrangement—could perhaps save more operator time than most motion studies. There are times and occasions when motion study should be used; there are others when it would be wrong not to use methods study or work simplification in preference.

Training is one of the most important elements in ensuring that the results of motion study are achieved. Operatives tend to have "natural" ways of performing activities. Sometimes these are good and conform to the best motion patterns, but often they do not. Training over a fairly long period may be necessary.

Motion study, depending as it does on finite analysis of an operative's activities, impinges even more than work measurement and methods on the consciousness of the operator. Very careful preconsultation is required if operative dishumour is to be avoided.

The job to be studied must be chosen very carefully. It must have an independent existence of its own, if at all possible. Many like jobs should be in existence, otherwise the effort expended may not produce commensurate economies.

The jobs studied should have a fairly long future in front of them or, once again, the effort may not bring suitable economies.

The use of therbligs does not record the difficulties of the motions being attempted. These have to be guessed at. Neither too is the effort or speed required recorded. Mental effort (mental dexterity) is also excluded. Motion study recording, therefore, has serious limitations.

45:5 Conclusion

The benefits that will accrue from a careful application of motion study are:

1   Increased production
2   Lower operative fatigue
3   Increased machine and equipment utilisation
4   Greater control over production flow

45:6 Further reading

1   Ralph M Barnes, *Motion Study and Time Study*, Wiley 1949
2   C S Thompson, "Chronophotography—Cameras and Pitfalls," *Work Study*, August 1968
3   M E Mundel, *Motion and Time Study—Principles and Practice*, Prentice Hall
4   Anne G Shaw, *The Purpose and Practice of Motion Study*, Columbine Press
5   W R Sprieght and C E Myers (editors), *The Writings of the Gilbreths*, Irwin

FORTY-SIX

Standardisation and variety reduction

46:1 Introduction

The urge to expand the product range, to proliferate systems of all kinds, to buy different kinds of equipment, to multiply bonus payment rates, the desire to have more and more variety and less and less standardisation, seems overwhelming in many organisations. Yet, standardisation and variety reduction does yield positive and, in some cases, huge rewards. That it is not more rigorously pursued is possibly due to a lack of disciplined analysis of the company's activities from a variety reduction viewpoint.

46:2 Description

Standardisation and variety reduction is a disciplined analysis of all company activities to ensure that they are limited to the degree or form that will yield an appropriate profit.

Normally standardisation and variety reduction is applied to the product range and this forms the basis for the example given on page 416, but there is no reason why any other of the company's activities sh uld not be similarly constrained. For example, there seems no reason why:

1   Procedures and methods
2   Forms and stationery
3   Duties
4   Office equipment

5   Job rates
6   Buildings and building layouts
7   Hours of work
8   Organisation

—should not all undergo the same rigorous standardisation analysis as the product range. The advantages of standardisation are many, these are the main ones:

1   Longer machine runs are possible (following the exercise). This should reduce setting-up time and generally improve the possibility of producing at lower unit product costs
2   Learning and other routines will be minimised, so that there should be higher productivity and better quality products
3   The use of more labour-saving equipment—machines, jigs, tools and handling equipment—will be possible
4   A smaller range of tools, jigs, spare parts, components, raw materials will be needed. There should, in consequence, be considerable savings in paperwork and general administration, leading to cost reduction in most indirect personnel
5   As the product range will be reduced, marketing effort (advertising especially) should be concentrated on fewer products. Hence it should be considerably more effective
6   All administrative activities—stock control, order processing, production planning and control, credit control, data processing—should benefit, with corresponding savings being made
7   There should be fewer errors in dispatch and order processing with improved customer good-will. Customer service generally should improve
8   There should be a greater possibility for interchanging staff at all levels and decreasing the probability of product, machine and skill obsolescence

46:3   Successful areas of application and examples

Product elimination is not easy. Each product or product group usually has its protagonists—managers who have grown up with it, launched it, nursed it, gained promotion from it, fought for it against competition, suffered for it. It is not something that anyone associated with it will give up easily. Products decline in importance. Some never were important, but for others, technical and competitive obsolescence creeps up. A long and distinguished product life only makes the inevitable end all the more sure.

It is important to recognise the product profit life cycle and where on it products happen to be. This will often indicate whether standardisation and variety reduction is possible. Normally however, data should be provided as follows and should form the initial measurement in considering variety reduction. For each product or product group obtain:

1   Turnover
2   Profit
3   Average profit margin
4   Unit cost
5   Marginal cost
6   Variable cost
7   Price
8   Sales compared with total product range, sales and total sales

Such data will help to rank each product and product group by profitability. A comparison should be made quarterly between current results and those of past quarters. Any deterioration should be highlighted. The lower tenth of the product range should be listed and an appropriate analysis carried out.

A committee or project team should be established to carry out this analysis and report on how savings will be made if standardisation and variety reduction are implemented. The project team should comprise: management services, production engineering, research and development, marketing and accounting or costing personnel. They should first determine (for the items under suspicion) the following:

1   Does the data produced suggest a weakness of the product range?
2   Why is this?
3   Has total market volume declined?
4   Have all profit margins declined?
5   Is it possible to increase sales of the suspect items?
6   How and what would it cost?
7   Could technical, price, quantity, service or other adjustments aid greater sales? If so, by how much?
8   How much managerial time and effort is spent in promoting the suspect items?

The answers to these questions will help to determine whether there is any value in continuing to make the suspect items. If these items are dropped, the problem of whether customers will still continue to buy the rest of the range is a highly emotive one that can be answered only by market research. Such research will be necessary anyway and the question should be included in any that is carried out.

The savings that would ensue if standardisation and variety reduction were implemented need to be calculated. These would include:

1   Plant layout and machinery. A new layout may be necessary. Obsolete equipment could be sold
2   Handling equipment—containers, pallets, racks, bins, conveyors etc
3   Stocks of new materials
4   Clerical work and paperwork of all kinds

5   Machine tool redesign. Production method amendment
6   Component range reduction
7   Reduction in labour utilisation of all kinds

The mixed discipline team suggested earlier is ideal for carrying out such an investigation. To help further in the choice of product for elimination, it would be useful to ascertain the following:

8   The cost of order processing
9   The general make up of orders
10   Which customers take the full range
11   Of these customers, what is their average order value and number of orders per year?
12   Do a predominance of small customers take only low profit margin items? (Giving a customer a category according to the sales value of their orders would help)
13   If nil or low profit makers are taken out of the product range, what extra marketing effort could be made (price, quality, service, advertising, etc) to ensure that the remaining products achieve the same turnover?

Adequate and complete costing information will be required at all stages of the investigation. A before and after series of manufacturing and administrative costs is highly desirable.

Once a decision has been taken to carry out standardisation and variety reduction, a strategy for the activity must be made:

1   How will the new product range be sold?
2   How will important customers be retained?
3   What retraining of the field force will be necessary?
4   What catalogue reprinting, etc, will be required?
5   How will all the savings postulated at the end of the analysis be achieved?
6   What personnel will be made redundant?
7   How is the problem to be handled?
8   When will the savings be achieved?
9   What extra resources will be needed?
10   What new equipment, etc, is required?

Action plans—listing the timetable activities, those that will be responsible for carrying them out and savings that will accrue—will be necessary in considerable detail.

46:4   Problems in the use of the techniques and conditions for success

The psychological problems of attempting to carry out product standardisation or rationalisation of any activity in an organisation are considerable. The benefits of a standardisation program are not always easy to calculate and personnel with long vested interests in the products or activities being standardised will bitterly resent changes. A tough "sale" of standardisation will often be required.

Customers, too, will often resent a shortening of the product range being sold. This resentment will often be compounded if the company's salesmen believe that they must match competitors line by line and item by item. This has been proved many times to be a fallacy.

In a highly competitive market, it is possible that a customer will take his trade elsewhere if he is not sold precisely what he wants. But there are few who can resist the temptation of lower prices, better service and higher quality which should result from a policy of standardisation.

Standardisation may encourage lethargy in new product design. Many an R & D department has quietly slept once a standardised product range has been introduced. This is a psychological trap into which many development engineers and scientists may fall, after the benefits of standardisation and all its ramifications have been worked out and achieved. A reluctance to change from a standardised range of products may be even greater than the reluctance to change originally, if considerable benefits have since ensued.

If obsolescence hits a particular product or part of the product range of the new standardised items, it will be more difficult to concentrate on other products or parts of the product range. A standardised range makes it more vulnerable to technological change.

It is obvious that a knife wielded too quickly and brutally will cut away muscle as well as fat. Data must be obtained that will ensure that only non-viable products or activities are eliminated.

46:5   Conclusion

The failure to eliminate marginal products, through standardisation and variety reduction activities, often shows a dangerous psychological condition on the part of the company's management.

Often there is a real danger that management is scared to face up to the problem that product elimination is vital for corporate survival. Instead, individual prejudice, past experience and a failure to adapt to changing circumstances lead to a situation where too much time and other resources are put into selling a product range that is largely obsolete and in most part not contributing to profit.

Because of this inability to see the "key result" and push resources into activities and products that will pay most dividends, the company may well degenerate into a death spiral which, eventually, only bitter surgery may arrest.

46:6   Further reading

1   C P Dufresne, "Forms Standardisation and Control," *The Office* (USA) March 1971
2   N Martin, *Variety Reduction*, British Standards Institute and Institute of Production Engineers 1961
3   B H Walley, "Standardisation," *Time and Motion Study*, 1963

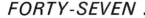

FORTY-SEVEN

Fatigue study

47:1 Introduction

Fatigue study has usually been discussed within the broad context of method and work study. It is one of the major factors in job study in the broadest sense.

Its links with other techniques range from attitude surveys and morale generally to ergonomics and work measurement.

In work measurement, fatigue is usually expressed in the relaxation allowances that are built into many or all work incentive schemes. This implies that fatigue can be measured accurately—a doubtful suggestion.

47:2 Description

Fatigue study is the analysis of the causes of fatigue with the objective of ameliorating such causes and/or making allowances for them in work measurement and payment schemes.

Can fatigue be measured? For many decades work study personnel have made fatigue estimations and had an allowance built into their incentive calculations for fatigue.

A rest allowances table is normally used by work study practitioners, through which, it is hoped, fatigue-inducing situations can be measured. Normally three major factors are considered:

1   Working conditions
2   Physical effort
3   Mental effort

Under working conditions, an attempt to quantify the effect of the following is made:

1   Heat
2   Noise
3   Dust
4   Fumes
5   Light
6   Ventilation
7   Humidity
8   Danger
9   Wetness
10 Need to wear protective clothing

Physical effort is usually divided as follows:

1   Force applied by operatives to carry out the job
2   Postures needed
3   Type and number of motions required perhaps per job cycle
4   Eye strain
5   Manual dexterity required—where this is not included in the motion pattern analysis

Mental effort is broken down into:

1   Monotony of the job
2   Mental dexterity needed
3   Concentration required
4   Short cycle operation fatigue

As in job evaluation, each factor is awarded a points weighting. This can be given by work study personnel, by the factory manager, or by a team formed by these two and trade union representatives or officials.

The weighting will indicate the relative importance of each factor. A marking system must then be used to determine the total score of the fatigue-inducing elements.

How the score is to be made may be difficult to determine. Are absolute values to be used? Is job ranking an appropriate method? Is no more than a vague comparison between jobs desired?

The difficulty of measuring absolutely is stressed. For example, what criteria are to be used? What objective standards can be introduced into the analysis? It would appear that such a method of evaluation is useful only if it can bring equity between jobs.

Measuring fatigue and what are the most important fatigue-inducing factors will very often be highly subjective, especially when psychological factors are also involved. Experience is needed, particularly of shop-floor psychology and how it relates to fatigue study generally. Production personnel, therefore, are often in a strong position to help to determine fatigue situations and the allowances which should be made for them.

47:3 Successful areas of application and examples

The amelioration of fatigue is the most important element in fatigue study. Once fatigue-producing factors have been determined and by objective criteria measured, corrective action is required.

WORKING ENVIRONMENT.   A study of the working environment is essential. Humidity control has been recognised as a paramount need for some time. Similarly, dust and noise suppression have been studied. Dust is often associated with lung illness and its suppression is important.

Only in recent years have the deleterious effects of noise been recognised. Now it is considered to be one of the worst polluters of the environment (social as well as working) and noise suppression activities are being followed vigorously. Some machine activities, such as press shops or forges scarcely respond to noise elimination techniques, but many machine activities do. Light and ventilation are two aspects that have been improved, particularly in offices and administration buildings generally. As far as offices are concerned colour has been proved to be an important factor. It has an influence on productivity and there are several generally accepted axioms as regards colours which should or should not be used in offices. Dark colours absorb light and so increase the amount of illumination required. Large areas of dark colour tend to overwhelm and depress people. Conversely light warm colours are stimulating, especially when used with high quality illumination.

PHYSICAL EFFORT.   Physical effort can be lessened by elimination of the job altogether and where fatigue is excessive this is obviously one consideration that should be borne in mind. If this rather drastic move is not available, there are several other alternatives which might be taken:

1   Fit the man to the job. This can be done by utilising ergonomics or motion study
2   Improve the job by eliminating some of the job contents. Method study will help to do this as well as capital investment
3   Fit the right man to the job. Job grading, rating and job study generally will help to do this. Extra fatigue will often ensue where an employee is either over- or underextended

MENTAL EFFORT.   Correct motivation of an employee will help to decrease fatigue. The psychologists and behavioural science personnel propound job enrichment theories which they suggest will help to improve motivation and lessen fatigue. Some psychologists go further than this and state that a uniform approach to employee routines, such as tea breaks and rest periods is of little value. It is stated that there is an optimum period of intense physical or mental activity for most people. This tends to vary from person to person, so that non-standard rest periods and rest allowances should be the rule rather than the exception.

It is difficult to divorce morale from fatigue. All the factors that lead to poor morale will also motivate fatigue, or at least lack of effort. Once again controlled experiments will help to show the effects that poor morale has on output rates and fatigue generally.

It is curious perhaps that good organisation has been proved to help reduce fatigue. For example, a steady workflow, work periods free from alarms or difficulties, availability of tools and equipment when required, will all help to establish conditions for steady uninterrupted work activity where a reasonable pace can be set and continued at length.

47:4   Problems in the use of the technique and conditions for success

Fatigue and morale and psychological conditions are inextricably bound together. In one organisation where fatigue-inducing conditions predominate—heat, fumes, dust, etc—output is high, morale is good, fatigue apparently small. In another organisation where environmental conditions are superior, output is low, morale poor, fatigue apparently very high.

By itself the study of fatigue-producing environments and their improvement may produce only marginal improvements in fatigue situations.

Little has been done in calculating fatigue in the office. If greater control over clerical work output is required (and the trend towards the greater use of clerical work measurement indicates that this is so) fatigue-inducing situations and fatigue allowances in offices need to be analysed.

Office managers can either adapt factory orientated fatigue allowances or consider the possibility of carrying out controlled experiments of their own. For example, the work output of a clerical working group in one environment can be compared with a clerical work group carrying out exactly the same tasks but in another environment.

The main problem of carrying out such experiments lies in obtaining two comparable clerical working groups. There will also be the psychological factors to discount. Nevertheless, controlled experiments of the type suggested should prove effective in judging different working environments.

The problems of closed- or open-plan offices as suitable environments for clerical/administrative activities has been debated at length. [See Axel Boje, *Open-Plan Offices*, Business Books, 1971.] It would be interesting to study fatigue-inducing situations in clerical activities from this viewpoint.

47:5 Conclusion

The benefits that should accrue from fatigue study include:

1 Increased output
2 Lower unit cost
3 Improved morale
4 Lower absenteeism
5 Improved quality
6 Improved safety record

47:6 Further reading

1 "Fatigue Study," *Work Study*, February 1971
2 P J Carter, "Manual Lifting and Carrying," *Work Study and Management Services*, June 1969
3 A Parker, "What About the Workers?" *Business Systems and Equipment*, September 1968
4 K F H Murrell, "Gone to Tea," *Personnel Management*, July 1969
5 N Aquilano, "Why Industrial Engineers Can't Measure Fatigue," *Industrial Engineering*, (USA), March 1970
6 A L Minter, "The Estimation of Energy Expenditure," *Work Study and Management Services*, July 1970
7 G Comman, "Fatigue Allowances," *Industrial Engineering* (USA), April 1970

Cost benefit analysis

_____

48:1   Introduction

Where there is no profit motive as in local or national government organisations there is often a fundamental difficulty in assessing the value of capital projects, indeed in spending money at all. How is it possible to judge the value that will be gained on money spent?

Similar problems are faced even in profit-motivated organisations. What quantifiable benefits will accrue from improving the canteen facilities or making a sports ground? Is it possible to quantify the benefits which are gained?

Cost benefit analysis (CBA) has been developed in order that such expenditure can be compared with the result it achieves.

48:2   Description

Cost benefit analysis is a technique that sets out to compare investment inputs with expected results. It helps to make investment decisions where the possible results cannot easily be calculated.

In an investment situation where the discounted cash flow technique can be used, costs of all kinds—cash flow, profit, return on investment (net present value)—can be calculated. In CBA, social benefit, opportunity cost (the benefits forgone by making a particular choice) and excess social benefit over cost are factors which are substituted. CBA has been accorded a series of different titles. Systems analysis, cost effectiveness, operations analysis, cost-utility analysis, planning programming and budgeting systems have all been used as synonyms for the original.

The methodology of cost benefit analysis is as follows.

A specific statement of objectives is made—sometimes on uncertain occasions or where problems are ill defined, objectives may indeed not be so completely explicit. If wrong or misleading objectives are stated a wrong solution can quickly be advanced. For example, if a new road junction is being proposed, what objectives have been defined? These may be a reduction in the number of road casualties at the junction or perhaps of road deaths. Perhaps a speed up in the traffic flow is required. If so what extra traffic speed is anticipated? Each objective might determine a different strategy and so a different investment program.

Alternatives to achieve the objectives are stipulated. These could represent different strategies, policies and tactics. Each alternative also suggests how a resource allocation should be made—men, money, machines, raw material, plant capacity, etc. "Resources" can be divided into basic investment criteria, but also into a skills audit and utilisation.

In attempting to reduce road accidents, the alternatives that might be posed are:

1   Education for vehicle drivers and pedestrians
2   Expansion of road traffic police
3   Better existing roads
4   New road systems
5   Separation of pedestrians from road traffic
6   Vehicle-free shopping precincts
7   Slum clearance allied with urban motorways
8   Bigger fines for motoring offences etc

The potential effectiveness of the alternatives is then assessed. Each alternative or if necessary, two or more combined alternatives ought to be analysed to ascertain their potential effect. Appropriate measurements need to be applied, though these can be quite complicated.

An urban motorway to reduce accidents may also clear away some slums and so, in the long run, improve housing standards. It may also depreciate property values and provide environmental nuisance of a high order, adding noise and fume pollution. The measurement of effect can be complicated. Often a single measurement is inappropriate. Ratios often have to be used. Weighted single answers might also be necessary.

How is improved morale to be measured for example? In an industrial context labour turnover, absenteeism, lateness, attitudes to good housekeeping, quality, work output, will all have to be considered.

Cost estimates are made. Normally money will be used, but this grows more complex if opportunity costing is used. Only a certain amount of money is available for any activity. How quickly should it be spent? Skills of various kinds are limited. Can a job be done now, in two months' time or next year? Can it be spread over several years (i.e. can the rate of expenditure be changed though the total remains the same)?

Costs have to be evaluated. Are they all relevant? Are they relevant to the current project or can they be spread elsewhere?

Decision criteria have to be formulated. What degree of effectiveness is required? Are all the traffic accidents to be eliminated and if so what will the cost be? Or is only 10 per cent reduction considered feasible? If so, how much must be spent to achieve such a reduction?

Is the cost involved fixed and the effectiveness of its use to be minimised? Or must a degree of effectiveness be achieved with a minimum of cost?

Normally a trade-off or scale of cost benefit alternatives are made. For example, if twice the cost will quadruple the benefit then this should be a desirable alternative. Or conversely, half the cost may result in only 25 per cent reduction in benefit.

It is very easy to adopt invalid criteria. What happens to traffic accidents, for example, if an edict is issued to maximise effectiveness but minimise cost? The two are obviously incompatible.

Creation of cost benefit equations are then necessary. Once objectives, alternatives, effectiveness of alternatives, cost estimates and decision criteria have been formulated, cost benefit equations have to be made.

The necessary analysis and weighting of factors must be built into the various equations. The aim of each equation will be to establish in a quantified way the cost benefit of each alternative. The results of the trade-offs should be known.

One important aspect of operation of the equations should be to determine the marginal value of extra cost. Would 10 per cent extra cost on roads reduce road accidents by more than that amount?

Calculus is often used to solve the equations but mathematical programming is the more usual technique.

48:3   Successful areas of application and examples

The technique first gained wide publicity when it was used in the Department of Defense in the USA. The then Secretary of Defense, Robert McNamara, brought in many new staff from the Rand Corporation, where the formal approach had been developed. The first major areas of application, therefore, were in defence projects.

In Britain, however, local and national government applications predominate:

1   Traffic/road schemes
2   Housing sites
3   Amenities of all kinds—playgrounds, recreation centres, community halls etc
4   Hospitals and all medical care
5   Police force
6   Public health
7   Libraries

Nationally the greatest cost benefit application could be in defence spending.

In commerce and industry there are also many areas where cost benefit should be applied:

1　In welfare decisions of all kinds and provision of:
a　Recreation grounds
b　Canteen facilities
c　Health facilities
　　—where improved morale should result
2　In social and national activities:
a　Anti-pollution measures
b　Safety
c　Taking part in trade affairs, national organisations etc
3　Any activity or area which has a predominance of unmeasurables. A new or improved office block might come into this category.

48:4　Problems in the use of the technique and conditions for success

Cost benefit analysis is widely believed to be a science-based technique with precise and unequivocal cost benefit equations. It is hardly this. At best it is a logical but often a non-quantifiable way of assessing the likely benefits of a course of action—usually an investment decision. Such decisions can still be extremely subjective even when cost benefit analysis has been used.

As a corollary of the above paragraph, the wide ranging problems that are tackled by cost benefit analysis leave considerable decision making freedom to the analyst. Judgement of a high order is required at each stage in the construction and solution of the equations. These ultimately are no better than the skill of the analyst who designs them.

Information in most cost benefit analysis is rarely adequate. A wrong cost or benefit diagnosis and inevitably a wrong alternative will be chosen. Occasions where non-quantifiable factors have been missed out of the equations will also produce an erroneous choice of alternatives.

The benefits that accrue from a piece of social investment may prove advantageous to one section of the community only. The cost benefit analyst must, therefore, also determine whether the outcome of the decision will produce inequalities in areas other than the one gaining benefit.

If industrial and commercial organisations are to be pressured to consider more and more non-profit-making activities, such as employee welfare or anti-pollution operations, it is likely that the need for some form of cost benefit analysis will grow.

Out of such a need should grow as definitive an activity as that of providing data, carrying out the calculation and controlling the result of a DCF based investment decision. Whether the accountant or a cost benefit analyst should do this is debatable.

Data collection ought to be a continuous activity. In the same way that information flows for such subjects as standard costing and budgetary control, data flows need to be organised for cost benefit analysis.

The application of regression analysis (see Chapter 19) should be an essential part of the technique.

A whole variety of constraints impinge on the decision—political, social, geographical, economic. All these have to be taken into account. If the decision is a political one, then cost benefit should still be used, even if the results are a foregone conclusion. The discipline of applying the technique and the results might help to rescue some good from what otherwise might be a disastrous decision.

Further benefits, if these can be quantified monetarily, should be discounted in a similar way to that used in the DCF technique of investment appraisal.

A most likely estimate, an optimistic and a pessimistic view of the outcome of the decision should be made.

48:5   Conclusion

In normal decisions concerning capital investment (for example, where the DCF technique would normally be used) sensitivity analysis and probability theory are often applied as well. Cost benefit analysis has rarely, if ever, attempted to accommodate this refinement. Consequently the results from using the technique have often not been as good as even the use of the limited data and subjective appraisal could make them.

Even so, cost benefit analysis has gained wide application in local and national government activities. It is likely to undergo further modification and sophistication to make it more effective.

The implications of using the technique are widespread, not least for accountants. The need for much better cost estimating and forecasting is paramount if cost benefit analysis is to be truly worth while.

The situation most important to avoid is the use of subjective cost benefit analysis merely to reinforce prejudice or a political decision which has already been made.

48:6   Further reading

1   E J Mishan, *Cost-Benefit Analysis*, George Allen & Unwin, 1973
2   E J Mishan, Elements of Cost-Benefit Analysis, George Allen & Unwin, 1972
3   E J Mishan, "The ABC of Cost Benefit," *Lloyds Bank Review*, July 1971
4   J Morley English (editor), *Cost Effectiveness, the Economic Evaluation of Engineered Systems*, Wiley, 1968   -
5   Roland N McKean, *Efficiency in Government through Systems Analysis*, Wiley

6   G H Peters, *Cost Benefit Analysis and Public Expenditure*, Eaton paper
     number 8, Institute of Economic Affairs, 1966
7   *Cost Benefit Analysis in local Government*, The Institute of Municipal
     Treasures and Accountants, 1969
8   K Seiler, *Introduction to Systems Cost-Effectiveness*, Wiley 1968
9   E A French, "Cost Benefit Analysis—an Examplification," *Local Govern-
     ment Finance*, August 1971
10   A Gilchrist, "Cost Effectiveness," *Aslib Proceedings*, September 1971
11   R H R Armstrong, "The Use of Cost Benefit in Decision Making," *Local
     Government Finance*, October 1970
12   B G King, "Cost Effectiveness Analysis: Implications for Accountants,"
     The Journal of Accountancy (USA), March 1970

Other techniques

The foregoing chapters describe in some detail the major techniques which management services personnel and others who wish to improve company performance need to understand and apply when necessary. It is, of course, possible to utilise common sense in reducing costs or improving productivity, but in many organisations the scope for this approach is limited. The application of a technique, even when it is not applied expertly, will usually produce better results than common sense alone.

Regrettably, techniques seem to have proliferated throughout the 1960s until even technique orientated management services personnel start to wonder whether they will soon be obsolete. Equally regrettably, many of the new techniques have proved to have little or nothing to offer against those which have gone before.

This final chapter briefly describes some of the techniques that have so far proved to have had little practical impact on a company's profitability. This is not to say that they will not grow in importance in the future.

Also included are some of the less demanding techniques on which organisation and methods personnel first cut their teeth in the late 1950s. These are usually well recorded and there seems no need to repeat well-documented activities.

49:1 Office layout and environment

The subject is one that all O & M men used to know by heart. There are basic principles that anyone wishing to design a new office ought to know. For example:

1   Space—minimum space allocations are required for:
a   Desks
b   Filing cabinets
c   Aisle widths
     Standard space requirements for these have been established and should be followed
2   The office environment needs to be studied under the following headings:
a   Lighting
b   Heating
c   Noise
d   Ventilation
e   Good housekeeping—accident and fire prevention etc
f   General facilities—washing, drinking water, lavatories etc
3   Office equipment—should be studied under the following headings:
a   Desks
b   Filing cabinets
c   Chairs etc
4   Methods of resolving office layout and communication problems should be known. Some of the more important of these are:
a   List main departments and functions. Indicate their interdependence—this will help to determine internal office arrangements
b   List all work and equipment specifications—these will help to determine space requirements
c   "Quiet offices" should always be at the back of buildings away from traffic noise
d   Work activities demanding most light should be on the south side of the building except drawing offices which should face north
e   String diagrams of work flow and people's movement records will help to determine layouts which provide least movement. Templates on squared paper will also help
f   Structural condition of buildings will largely determine their use.
g   As far as possible all service departments should be placed near major users
h   Facilities (washing, WCs, etc) should be placed centrally
5   The benefits of improving office layout should include:
a   Better utilisation of existing floor area so avoiding new building
b   Improved:
i   Communications
ii   Morale of administrative staff
iii   Work flow
iv   Work output
c   Decreased fatigue

The advantages of open and closed offices have been debated at length. Such debates should be read and their conclusions studied (see section 49:8). The Offices Shops and Railway Premises Act 1963, published by HMSO, sets out standards which most offices should exceed. The British Lighting Council, HMSO, and The Electrical Development Association all have booklets describing the various environmental factors in office design.

49:2   Forms design

This, too, was one of the major techniques taught to early O & M personnel. It has often been carried to absurd limits. Companies have been bleeding to death for the want of good management control systems while the personnel that could install such systems have been calmly and deliberately redesigning job application forms. Why should the destruction of ten forms and their replacement by one have a significant impact on profitability? Early O & M courses are largely to blame for such an attitude gaining strong ground.

Systems study rather than forms control should be the key result area of O & M personnel. Even so the principles of good forms design should be known:

1   Employ standard paper sizes at all times
2   The title should be bold enough to proclaim the purpose at a glance
3   Gripper edge should be left for printing purposes
4   Room for a signature should be made
5   Instructions for filling in the form should be made at the top of the form
6   Boxes for information should be utilised as far as possible
7   As much preprinting as possible should be done
8   Spacing is important. Distance between lines should be standard for typewriting—if this is to be used
9   Ruling—thick and thin to denote form boundaries
10   Completion should be sequential—top to bottom, left to right
11   EDP needs should be included
12   Information flow should be natural
13   Data required should be yes/no, a number or a tick or cross as far as possible
14   Method of document copying should help suggest form outline and type of paper it is printed upon

49:3   Document reproduction and office equipment

The techniques of document reproduction do not seem to have the importance of former years. Systems were largely designed around one or the other of the document reproduction methods: dyeline, reflex, autopositive, transfer, infra red, electrostatic, spirit and offset litho.

What none of the originators of the tables showing the comparative advantages and disadvantages of the various kinds of document reproduction knew was that in large part, convenience would eventually outweigh cost. The sales promotion of Rank-Xerox has won predominance for the electrostatic type of document reproduction, despite its cost. Yet the electrostatic method is still not systems orientated and largely dyeline and spirit duplication hold sway.

Office equipment is not really a technique but knowledge of such equipment is essential if full cost reduction in administrative areas is to be achieved. The various equipment guides that are now published (as well as the catalogues of suppliers) give useful headings under which details of office equipment can be collected. The following main headings might be used:

1 Data processing equipment
a Accounting and invoicing machines
b Manual accounting methods
c Desk-top mini-computers
d Computers and computer peripherals
e Computer software
2 Correspondence equipment
a Dictation equipment
b Typewriters
c Mailing equipment
3 Recording equipment
a Plans, charts and visual aids
b Filing and indexing
4 Office furniture
a Desks
b Chairs
c Tables
d Bookcases
5 Other equipment

Details of document reproduction techniques and advantages and disadvantages of various forms of office equipment are given in *Manual of Office Administration*. The *Business Equipment Digest* contains details of office equipment.

49:4   Operations research techniques

The major OR techniques discussed in Chapter 20 are model making and simulation, forecasting and optimisation through programming. It is my contention that it is with these techniques that OR will continue to play a significant role. Largely the techniques are fairly well defined, indeed some have now reached the state of maturity where even line managers consider that they themselves can apply them safely.

Regrettably it is in the nature of things that more and more esoteric OR techniques are being developed. That such developments provide a happy sanctuary for university personnel far from the front line of industrial and commercial experience is granted. That they can be applied with tremendous benefit in the harsh world of real life is doubtful. Academics will only bring themselves and their techniques into disrepute if they persist in trying to apply half-considered ideas in areas of practice of which they know little.

The following techniques do not all warrant the term "esoteric" but all should be applied with care. Any line manager faced with an OR specialist keen to apply such techniques should be more cynical than usual about OR applications.

QUEUEING THEORY.　　This deals with the problems of congestion and the theory is often referred to as the theory of congestion or theory of waiting lines. The mathematics involved is usually complicated and simulation is often the only way in which to find a practical solution.

A typical example of a queue is a shop with only one assistant. At various times of the day one or more customers may be waiting for service. Would an extra assistant increase service so much that improved profitability would be gained? The length of a queue will depend upon:

1　　　Input—the way in which customers arrive—quantity and speed
2　　　The queue—the way in which customers wait for service
3　　　The service—how the queue will be serviced

By analysing and altering these factors the cost of service and the service time itself can be optimised. For example, customers can arrive singly or in batches, constantly, intermittently or randomly. The queue can be one line, or several. Queue discipline can dictate that customers are served by priority, by first in first out, or randomly. The service mechanism dictates whether there are one or more service point, whether service speed can or can not be amended, whether service availability can or cannot be altered.

Queues and queueing theory are applicable in a variety of situations apart from shops. For example:

CUSTOMER	QUEUE	SERVICE
Ship	Waiting to be unloaded	Unloading
Inventory	Warehouse	Issues
Telephone	Waiting a call	Connection to desired number
Machine	Useful life	Replacement
Product waiting manufacture	Waiting at a machine	Machine operation

This latter activity has most relevance to industrialists. The problem of eradicating queues in a factory is dependent upon the number of production or line units available, plus the service facilities such as internal transport, cranes, hoists, storage and space. Queueing theory should help determine what the optimum level of service facilities should be.

Production lines, therefore, can be designed to give a least cost/best service level. At least this is the theory. In practice, comparatively few applications of queueing theory have been successful. The reasons are not difficult to find:

1　　　The mathematics are quite complicated
2　　　The relationship between customers, queues and service is often much more complex than is capable of being handled by the theory

3   If a too simplistic view is taken, the result is usually so obvious that the use
     of the theory is superfluous

Will the theory be used more in the future? As yet there are no signs that there is
an increasing acceptance rate, though the influx of business school graduates to
industry may bring about a greater acceptability.

REPLACEMENT THEORY.   This theory has achieved quite wide use, especially in the area of vehicle replacement. The problems of replacing such items are
similar to that of changing a new production machine, except that a commercial
vehicle has a use and reliability rate more discernible than, say, a production unit
of some kind.

At various stages of a vehicle's life, its efficiency, use rate, depreciation rate and
maintenance cost will vary. At the same time a better type of vehicle may have
become available, which may give a better pay load at lower cost.

The service life of such assets as vehicles is beset by its own inherent decline in
efficiency over the years; also it will be affected by technical obsolescence. Owners
of such assets, therefore, can choose between investing more capital in new equipment, so that they have the most advanced pieces, or they can minimise their
capital payments by maintaining their current assets, but denying themselves
technical superiority.

Replacement theory sets out to optimise the situation between capital and
technical superiority/obsolescence.

THEORY OF GAMES.   This technique is intrinsic with model making. It has
been used—not very satisfactorily so far—to represent the activities of one company and the reactions that it will provoke in another. For example, where company strategies are opposed, as in advertising or pricing, games theory is likely
to help in reaching probable ripostes which competitors might make, so enabling
the company to prepare in advance to counter competitors' moves.

In real life, basic knowledge about competitors is often sparse or non-existent.
However, competitors' past decisions are known and these can be projected and
some probability attached to them. In this way the probable outcome of a real-
life business game can be deduced. However, application of games theory so far
suggests that the results will not be very practical. Companies that do not even
have good management information systems are unlikely to want to use games
theory. Even so, some help in the difficult decisions concerned with competitive
strategy is always desirable. Setting up a game and thinking about probabilities
will help in this respect.

CONCLUSION.   Other even more esoteric techniques, which come under the
broad heading of operations research, are available—for example, dynamic
evaluation, markov chain analysis, and evolutionary operation.

Dynamic evaluation uses the learning curve to help to measure performance
improvement. It is a statistical analysis technique and helps to measure the rate
of change to date and the likely rate of change in the future.

Markov chain analysis has been developed to help to solve queueing theory problems.

Evolutionary operation (EVOP) is a dynamic method of running process plants that, through continuous feedback of control data, will help to achieve optimum performance.

Any technique to be of use has to be:

1   Practical—it has to be capable of being applied in a real-life situation and must achieve calculable benefits
2   Within limits understandable in layman's terms—for example by a reasonably intelligent line manager

Regrettably it must be admitted that OR does not always meet these criteria.

Sophistication for sophistication's sake will only bring ridicule to the subject. The techniques mentioned have to be viewed in this light.

49:5   Technological forecasting

Technological forecasting owes little to the statistical techniques of demand forecasting. Statistics are used, but only as a means of suggesting, through various techniques, what the future might be.

These techniques are still in a formative stage and, as with modelling and many of the OR techniques, there is no final indication that TF has a great and fundamental value for management. It would be wrong, however, to ignore it.

Technological forecasting is a methodology through which, it is hoped, an idea of what the technological future might be is gained. It is not one technique but a series, any of which can be used to suit prevailing circumstance. Two approaches are normally made: speculative and normative. The speculative approach encompasses the trend in events, largely using extrapolation to arrive at a future point. The normative approach takes a specific objective some time in the future and then plots how this point might be reached.

The delphi technique is one of the most used of those which make up TF. In the delphi situation a panel of informed personnel is established (perhaps forty strong) but they never meet each other. A series of questions are then asked and a time limit is imposed for the answers. Questions may be asked three times over, based on the general opinion expressed by the panel. What should emerge are answers that have been given at leisure after considerable thought.

Time series. Various time series techniques have been used in TF. Among the more important are:

1   Correlation analysis—based on the assumption that the demand for one product has a directly relateable effect on the other
2   Input–output analysis carries correlation analysis further. It was first considered by Leontieff over thirty years ago. The analysis starts with the design

of a matrix which quantifies input and output in particular industries. Once the amounts have been quantified, an input–output coefficient can be calculated by relating the amount of input needed to produce x value of output. By tracing the interrelationship of industrial and social consumption a better indication can be made of the impact which changes in output will have

Conditional demand analysis. This analysis considers under what conditions and time new techniques might take over from existing ones. The new technology may already be in existence but the potential may still not be fully exploited.

Opportunity identification. Market research often results in suggestions being made that a technology with a limited use currently could be used for a different range of products—plastics instead of steel; metal cans instead of glass bottles, etc. Cost performance is often the key factor.

Technological limit analysis. Technologies tend to decline before their performance limit is reached. They also rise and decline in a reasonably smooth progression. It is possible, therefore, to forecast the comparative decline of a technology and the moment when a new technology will take over from it. Envelope curves projected on a graph have been utilised for this purpose.

Diffusion analysis has been used to predict how quickly a new technology once devised will spread.

Morphological research is particularly useful in identifying goals. It employs "total thinking" or exploration. A systematic investigation of all parameters of a "future" is the basic aim.

Scenario writing is a term given to the logical train of thought which moves from a current situation to future areas of likely research.

These techniques suggest some of the features of technological forecasting. The cynic may be forgiven a smile, but anything that concentrates logically on the likely technological future is important and should be worth pursuing, unless it is made a fetish.

49:6 Cybernetics

Cybernetics is the study of the operation of control and communications systems. It is a technique that deals with both biological systems and man-made machinery. A car is a system in the same way that the human body can also be so designated.

As with much operations research, cybernetics is largely concerned with input and output of systems which are mostly highly complex and, in the case of output, probabilistic—that is, where it is not known precisely what the output from a given input will be.

The cyberneticians talk glibly of a "black box" approach to systems. They have an input which is known and an output which is measurable, but the working of the system itself is totally obscure. By putting in less or more input and continuing to measure output it is possible to deduce how the black box operates.

The effect of the measurement of output and its effect on input establishes a feedback system or a servo-mechanism which, more or less, has created control even though it is a "black box."

The cybernetic system can be considered to be an information handling machine. In an organisation, for example, there are a multiplicity of inputs with a multitude of outputs. The system which produces them is highly complex. Handling a group of such organisations and analysing all inputs and outputs and hoping to establish servo-mechanisms, is the area where cybernetics is thought to help. Additional vocabulary used with the technique is:

1   Isomorphism—a characteristic that helps to interchange systems
2   Homomorphisms—a characteristic that helps the partial change of system
3   Ultra-stability—a characteristic that helps systems to accept change and restore stability
4   Homeostat—a device for holding variables within desired limits
5   Entropy—the tendency of a system to reach stability

Where cybernetics hopes to help the line manager is difficult to suggest. The areas where cybernetics is apparently useful is in automation situations where the human brain is being replaced by machine automation. Highly complex problems that are difficult to define and systems that are "black boxes" are all cybernetics situations.

For anyone for whom profit planning methodology glows dimly somewhere on a distant horizon, cybernetics is totally irrelevant. It may one day have profound effects on government and on industry. It may revolutionise thinking about systems generally, but not just yet. Management sciences personnel and line managers can sleep easily in their beds.

49:7   Ergonomics

This technique, like cybernetics, has been available for some time but has failed to make a major impact on industry. Ergonomics is the study of the mental and physical capacities of people in relation to the demands made upon them by their work, and the equipment they utilise to carry out their work. As part of this process it is aimed that a job or machine will be made to fit a worker. The basis of this is to produce working conditions that will minimise fatigue and maximise efficiency. General environmental conditions which affect efficiency, such as noise, heat, humidity, etc, are included.

Despite the fact that ergonomics is assumed to be totally scientific and that most of the work associated with the technique—on anthropometrics, for example—is done in laboratories, it has considerable relevance to the shop-floor and office. The layman has been practising ergonomics for years. Desk and chair heights in offices, machine controls on a production line have all been amended to suit workers' body measurements. This has largely been done through method study not ergonomics.

Even so the technique has been followed and some good results have been achieved. The design of complex control panels such as those in aircraft, is an obvious area where ergonomics helps. The design of car seats has improved, but they still show the limits of using "standard men" for design purposes. Ergonomics is really an amalgam of factors:

1   Anthropology—the study of the human body and the calculation of standard body measurements
2   Method study—improvement of the work positon, work flow, layout etc
3   Engineering and machine design study
4   Environmental and fatigue study—the physiological and psychological factors that induce fatigue

Ergonomists to be successful, therefore, will have to co-operate with method study personnel, engineers and medical practitioners. In practical use ergonomics has been applied in the design of:

1   Machines—production and service
2   Control panels
3   Office furniture
4   Products
5   Seating of all kinds—e.g. in cars
6   Machine tools

The employment of ergonomics has helped to:

1   Improve output rates
2   Lessen fatigue
3   Improve working conditions generally
4   Reduce accidents

Whether it is necessary to utilise the full paraphernalia of ergonomics instead of the less-esoteric techniques is debatable. Is it another case where simple and well-tried techniques have been doctored to provide a science-based technique for university staff? This is certainly possible.

It would be wrong, however, to dismiss ergonomics and then fail to apply even the simple techniques on which it is largely based. To design a machine, for example, and not to take account of anthropometric considerations is ludicrous. Equally it would be wrong of work study men to ignore the working environment and limitations of the human body when carrying out method study.

49:8   Further reading

1   B H Walley, *Manual of Office Administration*, Business Books, 1968
2   Axel Boje, *Open Plan Offices*, Business Books, 1971
3   *Better Offices*, Institute of Directors, 1960

4   B Roblichand, Selecting, Planning and Managing Office Space, McGraw Hill, 1963

5   H R Verry, *Document Copying and Reproduction Process*, Fountain, 1960

6   *Reproduction Encyclopaedia*, Reproduction Review Staff Wogill, 1965

7   *Guide to Photocopying in the Office*, Institute of Office Management, 1961

9   J D Williams, *The Complete Strategist*, McGraw Hill, 1966

10 Weisselberg and Cowley, *The Executive Strategist*, Orbit, 1969

11 D R Cox and W L Smith, *Queues*, Methuen, 1961

12 Churchwood, Ackoff and Arnoff, *An Introduction to OR*, John Wiley, 1957

13 P M Morse, *Queues, Inventories and Maintenance*, John Wiley, 1959

14 Neumann and Morgenstern, *Theory of Games and Economic Behaviour*, Princeton University Press, 1961

15 Francis T Koen, *The Newest Problem-Solving Tool*, Dynamic Evaluation Factory, 1959

16 E J Cormick, *Human Engineering*, McGraw Hill

17 E Grandjean, *Fitting the Task to the Man*, Taylor and Francis, 1969

18 W T Singleton, *The Industrial Use of Ergonomics*, DSIR, 1964

19 F H George, *Cybernetics in Management*, Pan, 1969

20 J Rose, *Survey of Cybernetics*, Iliffe, 1970

21 J F Young, *Cybernetics*, Ilffe, 1969

22 R Marien, *Forms Control*, Prentice Hall 1958

23 F M Knox, *Design and Control of Business Forms*, McGraw Hill, 1960

24 *The Design of Forms in Government Departments*, O & M Division of the Treasury, 1962

25 V Earl, "Technological Forecasting," *The Economist*, 1969

26 "Technological Forecasting at WIRA," *Radius*, November 1970

27 F Zwicky, *Morphology of Propulsive Power*, Monographs of Morphological Research, number 1, 1962

28 Wills and others, *Technological Forecasting*, Penguin Books, 1972

29 E Juntsch, "Forecasting the Future," *Science Journal*, volume 3, number 10 October 1967

30 N K Gill, "Technological Forecasting," *Research*, April 1971

Profit improvement programs

Profit improvement programs have been designed to improve management performance and, it is hoped, to influence long-term attitudes towards profitability. It should be warmly recommended. Many major companies have carried out such programs—Shell, Dunlop, Albright and Wilson—though usually with the help of consultants such as McKinsey. [See "How to Improve Profits" in *Management Today*, May 1969, which describes how the technique has been used in Albright and Wilson Ltd.]

It is interesting to consider why such programs should be necessary if an active MS department is in existence. First, they supplement and perhaps improve upon the calibre of the existing MS team. Second, managers will probably respect and communicate with other managers and gain improvements, while MS personnel arouse suspicion if not antagonism. Third, it is suggested that PIP teams make a major short-term impact on profit, while MS personnel make less impact, but one which continues over a longer period.

A major benefit appears to be in exposing line personnel to profit improvement situations where they might bring originality to areas where they have never worked. Total amateurism may not be significant when three or four people are operating as a team.

A team is established in order to carry out the required assignment—in some organisations, the term "task force" is used. The assignment is usually directed towards achieving major savings in the shortest possible time and some element of stress is built into the situation. The team is composed of line managers and staff personnel. MS personnel are not excluded though not necessarily included. The emphasis is largely on behavioural rather than technique aspects.

Usually the team has three or four members and they are seconded to work full time for as long as the assignment lasts—usually six to twelve weeks.

The practice of recruiting amateur team leaders on a short-term basis has been the rule rather than the exception. Without considerable indoctrination (longer in fact than the three days usually given) there could be a weakness in analytical thinking. The basic difference between MS and line staff is largely in this field. Line managers have usually not been trained in or exposed to non-routine problem solving.

The team is loosely structured without any formal constraints. This does not appear to have any serious deleterious effect, though harmony is often missing. If a demanding series of objectives has been established (a necessity) disharmony could actually help to achieve them. A fairly common objective is a profit improvement ten times (at least) the combined annual salaries of the team members.

Only managers of the highest calibre are chosen to become members of a PIP team—senior accountants, trained engineers, successful line managers; these are people that work well under considerable pressure and will be motivated to achieve the results required. Pressure, it is hoped, will create a sense of anxiety.

Strong emphasis is made on implementation and achievement of results. PIP reports usually give one or two pages of analysis, as many as possible of recommendations and a full account of how the recommendations can be implemented. Implementation is stressed as this will eradicate frivolous suggestions.

One of the team is usually seconded to aid implementation (it is hoped that local line management will largely carry out the implementation) and this activity may go on even though the original PIP team has been disbanded.

Once implementation has been successfully completed, various controls are introduced that will ensure that the success in reducing costs and improving profits is maintained.

Broadly, the steps in the investigation are those that are usual for a method assignment: select, record, examine, develop, install and maintain.

Various recording and analysis sheets have been developed (task force analysis) and ought to be used. However, the general method study forms would serve equally well.

Index